**Reference
Does Not Circulate**

EVANSTON PUBLIC LIBRARY

3 1192 01215 6590

R 809.93358 Holocau v. 1
Holocaust literature /

D1679179

Holocaust Literature

MAGILL'S CHOICE

HOLOCAUST LITERATURE

Volume 1

The Accident - Letters and Papers from Prison

Edited by
John K. Roth
Claremont McKenna College

EVANSTON PUBLIC LIBRARY
1703 ORRINGTON AVENUE
EVANSTON, ILLINOIS 60201

SALEM PRESS, INC.
Pasadena, California   Hackensack, New Jersey

Cover photo: © iStockphoto.com/Jason Walton

Copyright © 2008, by Salem Press, Inc.

All rights in this book are reserved. No part of this work may be used or reproduced in any manner whatsoever or transmitted in any form or by any means, electronic or mechanical, including photocopy, recording, or any information storage and retrieval system, without written permission from the copyright owner except in the case of brief quotations embodied in critical articles and reviews or in the copying of images deemed to be freely licensed or in the public domain. For information address the publisher, Salem Press, Inc., P.O. Box 50062, Pasadena, California 91115.

The paper used in these volumes conforms to the American National Standard for Permanence of Paper for Printed Library Materials, Z39.48-1992 (R1997).

Essays originally appeared in *Magill's Literary Annual* (1990-2007), *Masterplots*, Revised Second Edition (1996), *Masterplots II: American Fiction Series*, Revised Edition (2000), *Masterplots II: British and Commonwealth Fiction Series* (1987), *Masterplots II: Christian Literature* (2008), *Masterplots II: Drama Series*, Revised Edition (2004), *Masterplots II: Juvenile and Young Adult Biography Series* (1993), *Masterplots II: Juvenile and Young Adult Fiction Series* (1991), *Masterplots II: Juvenile and Young Adult Literature Series Supplement* (1997), *Masterplots II: Nonfiction Series* (1989), *Masterplots II: Poetry Series*, Revised Edition (2002), *Masterplots II: Short Story Series*, Revised Edition (2004), *Masterplots II: Women's Literature Series* (1995), *Masterplots II: World Fiction Series* (1987), and *World Philosophers and Their Works* (2000). New material has been added.

Library of Congress Cataloging-in-Publication Data

Holocaust literature / edited by John K. Roth.
   v. cm.
   Includes bibliographical references and index.
   ISBN 978-1-58765-375-9 (set : alk. paper) — ISBN 978-1-58765-376-6 (vol. 1 : alk. paper) — ISBN 978-1-58765-377-3 (vol. 2 : alk. paper) 1. Holocaust, Jewish (1939-1945), in literature. I. Roth, John K.

PN56.H55H655 2008
809'.93358405318—dc22

2007051349

PRINTED IN CANADA

Contents

Publisher's Note vii
Editor's Introduction xi
Contributors xix
Nazi Concentration Camps xxi
Holocaust Chronology xxiii
Complete List of Contents xxxix

The Accident—*Elie Wiesel* 1
After Auschwitz—*Richard L. Rubenstein* 6
Albert Speer—*Gitta Sereny* 12
All Rivers Run to the Sea—*Elie Wiesel* 18
And the Sea Is Never Full—*Elie Wiesel* 24
"The Angel of History"—*Carolyn Forché* 30
Anya—*Susan Fromberg Schaeffer* 35
At the Mind's Limits—*Jean Améry* 40
Auschwitz and After—*Charlotte Delbo* 44
Austerlitz—*W. G. Sebald* 48

"Babii Yar"—*Yevgeny Yevtushenko* 53
Badenheim 1939—*Aharon Appelfeld* 57

Constantine's Sword—*James Carroll* 65

"Daddy"—*Sylvia Plath* 71
Daniel's Story—*Carol Matas* 76
"Death Fugue"—*Paul Celan* 80
The Deputy—*Rolf Hochhuth* 85
The Destruction of the European Jews—*Raul Hilberg* 92
The Diary of a Young Girl—*Anne Frank* 96
The Double Bond—*Carole Angier* 100
The Drowned and the Saved—*Primo Levi* 105

Eichmann in Jerusalem—*Hannah Arendt* 111
"Elegy for N. N."—*Czesław Miłosz* 118
Enemies—*Isaac Bashevis Singer* 123
Europe Central—*William T. Vollmann* 129
Explaining Hitler—*Ron Rosenbaum* 135

Holocaust Literature

The Fall of France—*Julian Jackson* 141
Fateless—*Imre Kertész* 147
The Fifth Son—*Elie Wiesel* 152
Friedrich—*Hans Peter Richter* 157

The Gates of the Forest—*Elie Wiesel* 161
Ghetto—*Joshua Sobol* 166
God's Presence in History—*Emil L. Fackenheim* 170
Gone to Soldiers—*Marge Piercy* 176

The Hiding Place—*Corrie ten Boom with
 John and Elizabeth Sherrill* 182
The History of Love—*Nicole Krauss* 187
History on Trial—*Deborah E. Lipstadt* 192
Hitler—*Ian Kershaw* 197
The Hitler of History—*John Lukacs* 204
Hitler's Willing Executioners—*Daniel Jonah Goldhagen* 210
The Holocaust in American Life—*Peter Novick* 216
Holocaust Politics—*John K. Roth* 223
Holocaust Testimonies—*Lawrence L. Langer* 227
House of Dolls—*Ka-tzetnik 135633* 234

I Will Bear Witness—*Victor Klemperer* 238
In Kindling Flame—*Linda Atkinson* 244
"In the Blue Distance"—*Nelly Sachs* 249
Incident at Vichy—*Arthur Miller* 254
An Interrupted Life—*Etty Hillesum* 259
Into That Darkness—*Gitta Sereny* 264

Jews—*Arthur Hertzberg and Aron Hirt-Manheimer* 268
The Journey Back—*Johanna Reiss* 274
"Journey Through the Night"—*Jakov Lind* 278

The Last of the Just—*André Schwarz-Bart* 282
Lest Innocent Blood Be Shed—*Philip P. Hallie* 286
Letters and Papers from Prison—*Dietrich Bonhoeffer* 291

Publisher's Note

The personal accounts are horrific beyond belief. Survivor David Bergman, a boy at the time of his first deportation to Auschwitz from Czechoslovakia, recalled how he was "crammed in an open cattle car with 150 living skeletons headed for another concentration camp":

> One by one they fell down and were trampled. After half died, it was possible to sit on the dead. Someone fell on me—he was dying. I hadn't had any food or water in four days. With all my remaining strength I pushed the body off and fell on top of him. He tried to push me away, but we were both too weak. In a final effort, he bit my leg and then died.

Survivor Alice Lok Cahana, from Hungary, recalled arriving at the Bergen-Belsen concentration camp:

> Nothing ever in literature could compare to anything that Bergen-Belsen was. When we arrived, the dead were not carried away any more, you stepped over them, you fell over them if you couldn't walk. There were agonizing . . . people begging for water. . . . Day and night. You couldn't escape the crying, you couldn't have escaped the praying, you couldn't escape the [cries of] "Mercy," it was a chant, the chant of the dead. It was hell.

And of course, as Leo Schneiderman remembered, there were those who did not survive:

> It was late at night that we arrived at Auschwitz. When we came in, the minute the gates opened up, we heard screams, barking of dogs, blows from . . . those Kapos, those officials working for them, over the head. And then we got out of the train. And everything went so fast: left, right, right, left. Men separated from women. Children torn from the arms of mothers. The elderly chased like cattle. The sick, the disabled were handled like packs of garbage. They were thrown in a side together with broken suitcases, with boxes. My mother ran over to me and grabbed me by the shoulders, and she told me "Leibele, I'm not going to see you no more. Take care of your brother."

Between the rise of Nazi Germany in 1933 and the end of World War II in 1945, six million Jews—and hundreds of thousands of Roma Gypsies, disabled persons, homosexuals, Jehovah's Witnesses, communists, and others who did not fit the Nazi regime's plan for a "master Aryan race"—perished in a state-sponsored program of persecution and murder. Their civil rights, their human rights, and ultimately their lives were progressively, and legally, relegated to nonhuman status. Now known as the Holocaust, this systematic destruction of "degenerates" lasted so long, reached so far, and destroyed so many that its horrors are hard for some to accept, both then and now. The world looked away while the evil spread. Even today, some self-described "revisionists" deny that the Holocaust ever took place.

State documents, however, remain; they list, in nauseating, bureaucratic detail, the statistics of death. Those who managed to survive have recorded their experiences on videotape and in oral histories maintained by the United States Holocaust Memorial Museum and other archives. And those who personally witnessed the hell of the Holocaust have generated a rich and thought-provoking body of memoirs, analyses, social criticism, novels, plays, and poetry to mark an event that threatened not only humankind but also humanity—the humanity of both the persecuted and the persecutors.

Holocaust Literature offers literature reviews of more than 100 core works about the Holocaust. In these two volumes, editor John K. Roth, Edward J. Sexton Professor of Philosophy and Director of the Center for the Study of the Holocaust, Genocide, and Human Rights at Claremont McKenna College, has succeeded in identifying the most important works on the Holocaust by both first- and second-generation survivors as well as by philosophers, novelists, poets, and playwrights reflecting on the Holocaust today.

Teachers and students will find the key works here, from Anne Frank's *Diary of a Young Girl* to Hannah Arendt's *Eichmann in Jerusalem*, Primo Levi's *Survival in Auschwitz*, Elie Wiesel's *Night*, and Simon Wiesenthal's *The Sunflower*. Core works of nonfiction—histories, biographies, memoirs, diaries, survivor testimonies, reflections on religion, philosophy, ethics—form two-thirds of the list, joined by literary fiction, poetry, and drama: classics such as Aharon Appelfeld's *Badenheim 1939*, William Styron's *Sophie's Choice*, and Yehuda Amichai's *Open Closed Open*. Also represented are more recent works, such as Joshua Sobol's play *Ghetto* (1984), Władysław Szpilman's *The Pianist* (1999), Ian Kershaw's two-volume biography *Hitler* (completed in 2000), Deborah E. Lipstadt's *History on Trial* (2005), William T. Vollmann's *Europe Central* (2005), and Heather Pringle's *The Master Plan: Himmler's Scholars and the Holocaust* (2006). The resulting set of essays introduces the literature of one of the defining events of our time, essential reading for all serious students of history, literature, social psychology, ethics, and philosophy.

Each volume includes a list of the major European concentration camps and a time line of Holocaust events. At the end of volume 2, three appendixes point readers toward additional Holocaust literature and resources: a secondary "General Bibliography" of works about the Holocaust, a list of more than 200 additional works in "More Holocaust Literature," and a list of Web sites devoted to the Holocaust and/or Holocaust literature. Three finding aids round out the second volume: a Genre Index (works by genre and subgenre), a Title Index (complete list of contents), and an Author Index (works by author).

As the last survivors of the Holocaust grow into old age and pass on, the rich literary legacy of their experiences will remain to remind the world not only of the atrocities perpetrated by the Nazi state but also of the banality and efficiency of the evil that gives rise to such inhuman acts. They also leave us with the mandate to deny complacency in the face of modern genocide: in the Balkans, in Chechnya, in Rwanda, in Darfur, in terrorism driven by a variety of extremist ideologies. The literature of the Holocaust reminds us never to forget—what happened in Hitler's Germany, and also what can happen, is happening, now.

Editor's Introduction
When Only Words Remain

If my life ends—what will become of my diary? (Chaim Kaplan, August 4, 1942)

Driven by twenty-first century threats of climate change and global warming, Alan Weisman published his profoundly thought-provoking book called *The World Without Us* (2007). Based on extensive scientific, anthropological, and historical research, Weisman's work invites readers to consider what would happen to Planet Earth if human life disappeared completely. Over time, Weisman asks, how would the natural world change? As centuries and millennia pass, what traces of human existence, if any, would remain?

Humanity, Weisman emphasizes, has arrived in the cosmos recently, at least if one considers how long the galaxies and earlier life-forms existed before anything resembling human life evolved. The emergence of that life made history. Consciousness of past, present, and future grew and expanded. Eventually, human memory led to the recording of experience in storytelling, art, writing, and then through contemporary forms of communication such as radio, film, television, and the Internet. People became linked together ever more closely. In time's eons, however, these developments are but brief episodes. Long after human beings have come and probably gone, the universe will continue.

Anyone who reads *The World Without Us* becomes newly aware that, in the cosmic scheme of things, one's life and the existence of one's people, nation, culture, or religion may turn out to be insignificant. Weisman's purpose, however, is not to argue that humanity's existence lacks importance and meaning. On the contrary, while urging us to gain perspective about our finite place in reality, he wants people to feel deeply that our humanity is distinctive and precious, that what we think and do makes a huge difference not only in history but also because human activity has awesome implications for our world's environment and even for the vast universe that is Earth's home and ours as well.

Weisman wants his readers to understand that humanity has done great harm in and to the world. There may well be ways, he suggests, in which the world would be better off without human beings who consume, even ravage and destroy, its natural splendor. His predominant points, however, are that nature has immense recuperative power and that too much of irretrievable value would be lost if the world were really to exist without us. What is needed, he urges, is a renewed sense of respect, reverence, and responsibility for the gift of life and the wondrous universe in which it moves and has its being.

The World Without Us does not concentrate on the Holocaust, the subject of the entries in this two-volume set, *Magill's Choice: Holocaust Literature*. Nevertheless, there are links between these two works; the implications that they have for each other are noteworthy. First, Weisman's thought experiment leads to reflection on the significance of history and on the importance of particular events within it. A part of his analysis indicates that human consciousness may eventually disappear from reality. If that happened, history would be null and void; arguably, it would be as if no particular event had happened, because historical awareness, and in that sense history itself, depends on memory. Historical documents would decay, artifacts would erode, places would eventually disappear virtually without a trace. If anything human did remain—Weisman thinks plastics of various kinds are among the human artifacts that have the best prospect of lasting longest—the chances of detecting their meaning would probably be slim or none. By this cosmic standard, no human event, including the Holocaust, looms very large.

At the same time, if people are to heed Weisman's urgently needed call for a renewed sense of respect, reverence, and responsibility for the gift of life, then the Holocaust and memory of it loom very large indeed. A key reason for that assertion is that Adolf Hitler, his German followers, and their allies engaged in much more than a thought experiment when they launched their genocide against the Jewish people and other so-called inferior groups. From 1933 to 1945, they acted on their anti-Semitic and racist creed with an arrogant tenacity. That creed entailed that it would be better for their world, indeed for the world as a whole, if entire human groups were consigned to oblivion. What followed was a systematic, bureaucratic, unrelenting, state-sponsored process of destruction that, under the cover of World War II, annihilated two-thirds of Europe's approximately nine million Jews and millions of other defenseless children, women, and men as well.

Nazi Germany's genocidal project was not entirely successful, but as the essays in this book make clear, its aims came too close for comfort. If there is not to be a world without us, then we ignore the Holocaust at our peril because disrespect for the particularity and diversity of human existence harbors selfishness, insensitivity, and hubris, which, in turn, can spark devastating violence, none of which makes humanity fit for survival.

As the pages in this book reveal, the Holocaust has much to teach us. One thing that can be learned from that event and this book is that many Jews—the murdered ones as well as those who survived—wrote about

Editor's Introduction

what happened to them and their families. As those diaries and memoirs describe an unremitting catastrophe, they frequently include observations about the seasons of the year, the weather, the sky, and other features of the natural world. *Night*, Elie Wiesel's famous Holocaust memoir, is a case in point. Narrating how the Holocaust engulfed his family and community, dispatching them to enslavement and murder in Auschwitz, that text repeatedly notes small but significant seasonal details as time went from the spring of 1944 to the spring of 1945. A collection of Wiesel's comments illustrates that their combination can be poetic, even as such words form a jarring context in which genocide is embedded:

> Spring 1944. . . . The trees were in bloom.
> The eight days of Passover. The weather was sublime.
> Some two weeks before Shavuot. A sunny spring day . . .
> All this under a magnificent blue sky.
> A summer sun.
> The lucky ones found themselves near a window; they could watch the blooming countryside flit by.
> The night had passed completely. The morning star shone in the sky.
> It was a beautiful day in May. The fragrances of spring were in the air. The sun was setting.
> "All of creation bears witness to the Greatness of God."
> Winter had arrived.
> An icy wind was blowing violently.
> Snow was falling heavily.

Taken by themselves in this listing, removed as the individual descriptions are from the context in which they appear within Wiesel's *Night*, these references to the natural environment are entirely ordinary. In fact, however, they are an extraordinary contrast and backdrop to the events that make *Night* as ominous as it is unforgettable. One more brief passage from Wiesel's testimony makes this point in a particularly powerful way: "Never shall I forget," writes Wiesel, "the small faces of the children whose bodies I saw transformed into smoke under a silent sky." That sentence is part of a tipping point in *Night*, for upon Wiesel's entry to Birkenau, the part of Auschwitz that was both the arrival point for his deportation transport and the main killing center in the vast Auschwitz camp complex, he was forever changed as he saw children, alive and dead, thrown into flaming pits and consumed. "Never shall I forget," he repeats seven times. "Never shall I forget those things, even were I condemned to live as long as God Himself. Never."

Night's descriptions of nature anticipate, foreshadow, or help to recall what Wiesel cannot forget and what human beings should remember as a warning if there is not to be a world without us. There are at least three dimensions to these relationships.

First, at times the beauty of nature contrasts markedly with the brutality that human beings inflict. That brutality includes cattle-car deportations to human-created places of human-created degradation, filth, starvation, disease, death-dealing labor, violence, murder, and graves unmarked, often massive but also nonexistent because corpses were turned into smoke and ash, traversing and permeating in ways unseen but real nonetheless the earth's atmosphere and the air people have breathed. Second, in *Night*'s descriptions, nature sometimes appears to be conspiratorial in compounding the suffering that the Jews experienced at the hands of their German captors. Particularly the extreme heat of summer or the icy cold of winter diminished life chances for those who had no protection against the weather's extremes. Even more pronounced, a third implication in *Night* is that nature was indifferent to the Jewish plight during the Holocaust. The sun rose and set, twilight gave way to night and then to morning, the stars shone and the moon beamed, the seasons passed, the earth stayed in its orbit while devastation raged and seemed to make no difference in nature's order. Yet, it is possible that a fourth dimension exists in these relationships as well, for we may miss much of what can be learned from the Holocaust if we overlook how that event did and should affect the natural environment that is our home.

Specifically, while ours may be a world where contemporary concerns (global warming, for instance, or the ongoing war against terrorists) loom so large that attention to the Holocaust sometimes seems beside the point, it remains the case that we ought not to ignore the Holocaust, let alone forget it. If we remember well, Holocaust-related memories will impel us to bear witness for the living and the dead in ways that protest against and resist the forces that lay waste to human well-being. In addition, this protest and resistance will be less than fully responsible if we do not recognize and respond effectively to the fact that caring for our natural environment is crucial. If we fail to remember the Holocaust, we lose a resource that can help to ensure that there will not be a world without us.

Such concerns and hopes include other Holocaust-related connections. Consider, for example, that a teacher of Hebrew named Chaim Kaplan kept a journal in the Warsaw ghetto. Dated August 4, 1942, the final line in its last entry asks a question: "If my life ends—what will become of my diary?" Kaplan sensed that there was nothing hypothetical about the first part of his uncertainty. No "if" existed; it was only a matter of "when." And "when" was soon. By the end of that month, Kaplan had been murdered in the gas chambers at Treblinka, a Nazi killing center northeast of Warsaw. About 800,000 Jews were gassed to death there.

The only open part of Kaplan's question was "what will become of my diary?" That issue was not on Kaplan's mind alone. Diaries—thousands of them, Anne Frank's among the best known—were kept by men, women, and children wherever the Nazi scourge targeted Jews. It is likely that some version of Kaplan's question was asked by most of those writers.

A picture, it is often said, is worth a thousand words. Yet neither the haunting silence of melodies that have disappeared nor the speechless power of line and color or of a photograph can substitute for words. Especially during the Holocaust, words were the most available resource for recording what had to be remembered. Whether spoken or written, they could give the dying a lasting voice. Focusing on the written testimony, we cannot know how many eyewitness accounts have been lost forever. Those that survived make one wonder how they did. Smuggled, buried, occasionally just left behind—some of these scrolls of agony resurfaced, many of them from people who did not survive the Holocaust. These include the testimonies of Janusz Korczak, who accompanied the children of his orphanage to their deaths at Treblinka, and Emmanuel Ringelblum, who coordinated *Oneg Shabbat*, the historical archive in the Warsaw ghetto, as well as the tragic witness borne in writings buried by Jews in the *Sonderkommando*, who had to burn the bodies of their fellow Jews before their own lives were consumed in the flames of Auschwitz. Linked with their company are survivors such as Primo Levi and Jean Améry, Charlotte Delbo and Ruth Klüger, to mention only a few, who have groped for words to write memoirs that tell as directly as possible what happened, disappeared, and remained.

In addition, there are other writers—some of them survivors, others who were not in the Holocaust, still others who were and did not survive—who have enlisted the characters of fiction, the cadences of verse, the analyses of historical research, the insights of philosophical and religious reflection to respond to the catastrophe that engulfed European Jewry and other populations targeted by Nazi Germany and its collaborators. Such work constitutes what can be called Holocaust literature. That category includes books and essays—historical, philosophical, and religious—as well as diaries and autobiographical accounts of eyewitnesses, in addition to those works of poetry and prose fiction that are substantively governed by the Jewish plight under Hitler. As the entries in this book illustrate, Holocaust literature at its best underscores especially well the major implications and lingering questions that are fundamental for anyone who studies the Holocaust with the respect and concern that its history deserves.

Just as Holocaust literature includes diverse genres, its authors represent varied nationalities and traditions, and they write in different languages as well. Many, though by no means all, are Jewish, but even that shared identity promotes a broad stylistic spectrum. Permeating the diversity, however, are issues that these writers and their interpreters, including the authors of the essays found here, confront in common. They invite their readers to wrestle with them too. Despite their literary gifts, nearly all of these authors feel a profound ambivalence, one that is shared by the best Holocaust historians as well as by the most able poets, novelists, philosophers, and theologians who write about this event and its aftereffects: It is impossible to write adequately about the Holocaust; yet that task must be attempted. They regard themselves as less than fully equipped to do such work; yet they are compelled to try. The corresponding tension for a sensitive reader—at least for one who was not "there"—is between an effort to understand and an awareness that, at least to some extent, the Holocaust eludes representation, let alone full comprehension.

These dilemmas have multiple dimensions. The Holocaust, for example, outstrips imagination. It is one thing to be creative when the possibilities open to imagination exceed what has become real. It is quite another to find that reality has already given birth to persons, places, and events that defy imagining. "Normal men," observed a survivor named David Rousset, "do not know that everything is possible."

Perhaps history, including Weisman's book *The World Without Us*, prepares post-Holocaust minds to be more accepting of the idea that "everything is possible." Nonetheless, how is one to comprehend that the Nazi way included "idealism" that did not merely permit torture and murder but commanded that they occur day and night? So a problem remains: Can poetry or prose—in essay or fictional forms—help one to know what really happened, in its concreteness and detail, and to cope with its impact? There are no metaphors or adequate analogies for the Holocaust. Nor, arguably, can Auschwitz appropriately be a metaphor or an analogy for anything else. If those realizations inform the ambivalence of those who write poetry or reflective and analytical prose about the Holocaust, still they must feel that their expressions are at least potentially capable of communicating something urgent that can be said in no other way. But that conviction makes their task no easier, and when a reader works to grasp what the best of the Holocaust writers say, he or she will sense how the Holocaust makes those writers struggle with words. How can words tell the truth, describe what must be portrayed, convey and yet control emotion so that clear insights will emerge? Every sensitive and imaginative author faces such questions, but they become unusually demanding when one en-

Editor's Introduction

gages the Holocaust. Now words and art forms must be used against themselves, because they are unable to say all that is required, and yet no other resources can substitute for them.

When writers emphasize the impossibility of communicating the realities of the Holocaust via words, they are sometimes accused of mystifying that event. They either make the Holocaust so exceptional that it loses contact with the rest of human history, the argument goes, or they obscure and becloud it in rhetoric that invests the Holocaust with a mythical or mystical aura that opposes lucid, rational analysis. Critical opinion may reach varied verdicts on those charges where different authors and works are concerned, but the works explored in these pages do not pull the Holocaust out of worldly reality. On the contrary, they are rooted both in the enormity of human loss brought about by the Holocaust and in the need to retrieve whatever can be left of a human future after Auschwitz has exposed the illusory quality of so many cherished assumptions.

When only words remain, the Holocaust-related themes they emphasize—including survival, honesty, bearing witness, and protest—help to reveal what can and ought to be communicated about the Holocaust and its reverberations. Doing so, such reflection reminds us of much that needs to be remembered if we are to care well for a world that, we should hope, will not be without us.

—*John K. Roth*

Contributors

Michael Adams
City University of New York Graduate Center

JoAnn Balingit
University of Delaware

Carl L. Bankston III
Tulane University

Cynthia A. Bily
Adrian College

Margaret Boe Birns
New York University

Nicholas Birns
The New School

Peter Brier
California State University, Los Angeles

Diane Brotemarkle
Aims Community College

Jeffrey L. Buller
Florida Atlantic University

Barbara Carol Calderoni
Emerson College

Edmund J. Campion
University of Tennessee at Knoxville

John J. Carney
University of New Hampshire

Diane L. Chapman
William Carey College

Jane Claes
Carrollton, Texas

Bowman L. Clarke
University of Georgia

Richard Hauer Costa
Texas A&M University

Frank Day
Clemson University

Thomas L. Erskine
Salisbury University

Thomas R. Feller
Nashville, Tennessee

Ann D. Garbett
Avarett University

Erlis Glass-Wickersham
Rosemont College

Donald Gochberg
Michigan State University

Jay L. Halio
University of Delaware

Karen Harris
University of New Orleans

Maverick Marvin Harris
East Texas Baptist University

Rosemary Horowitz
Appalachian State University

Edelma Huntley
Appalachian State University

Steven G. Kellman
University of Texas at San Antonio

Howard A. Kerner
Polk Community College

Rita M. Kissen
University of Southern Maine

Jordan Leondopoulos
St. John's University

Bernadette Flynn Low
Community College of Baltimore County

Joanne McCarthy
Tacoma, Washington

Kevin McNeilly
University of British Columbia

Paul Madden
Hardin-Simmons University

Marsha Kass Marks
Alabama A&M University

Patricia Masserman
Microsoft Learning

Mira N. Mataric
Emporia State University

Charles E. May
California State University, Long Beach

Michael R. Meyers
Pfeiffer University

Vasa D. Mihailovich
University of North Carolina at Chapel Hill

Gordon R. Mork
Purdue University

John H. Morrow, Jr.
University of Georgia

Daniel P. Murphy
Hanover College

Robert J. Paradowski
Rochester Institute of Technology

Jay Paul
Christopher Newport University

David Powell
Western New Mexico University

Tessa Li Powell
University of North Texas

Cliff Prewencki
Delmar, New York

Maureen Puffer-Rothenberg
Valdosta State University

Edna B. Quinn
Salisbury University

Kevin B. Reid
Henderson Community College

Rosemary M. Canfield Reisman
Charleston Southern University

Joan A. Robertson
U.S. Air Force Academy

Bernard Rodgers
Bard College at Simon's Rock

Joel M. Roitman
Eastern Kentucky University

Carl Rollyson
Baruch College, City University of New York

Joseph Rosenblum
University of North Carolina at Greensboro

Sidney Rosenfeld
Oberlin College

John K. Roth
Claremont McKenna College

Victor Anthony Rudowski
Clemson University

Margaret T. Sacco
Miami University of Ohio

June H. Schlessinger
University of North Texas

R. Baird Shuman
University of Illinois, Urbana-Champaign

Laura Shumar
Purdue University

Charles L. P. Silet
Iowa State University

Julius J. Simon
University of Texas at El Paso

Marjorie Smelstor
Truman Medical Centers

Katherine Snipes
Spokane, Washington

Leon Stein
Roosevelt University

William L. Urban
Monmouth College

Michelle Van Tine
Columbus, Ohio

Sue Brannan Walker
University of South Alabama

Cynthia Wong
Western Illinois University

Laura M. Zaidman
University of South Carolina at Sumter

Nazi Concentration Camps

This partial list of Nazi concentration camps shows the location and the estimated number of deaths that occurred at each.

Camp	Location	Estimated Deaths
Amersfoort	Amersfoort, Netherlands	1,000
Auschwitz-Birkenau	Oświęcim, Poland	1,100,000
Bełżec	Bełżec, Poland	435,000 to 600,000
Bergen-Belsen	Near Celle, Germany	35,000
Buchenwald	Near Weimar, Germany	56,000
Chełmno	Chełmno, Poland	152,000 to 320,000
Dachau	Dachau, Germany	28,000 to 32,000
Flossenbürg	Near Nuremberg, Germany	30,000
Gross-Rosen	Gross-Rosen, Germany (now in Poland)	40,000
Janówska	L'viv, Poland (now in Ukraine)	At least 40,000
Jasenovac	Jasenovac, Croatia	700,000
Koldichevo	Baranovichi, Belarus	20,000
Majdanek	Lublin, Poland	360,000
Mauthausen	Mauthausen, Austria	119,000
Mittelbau/Dora	Near Nordhausen, Germany	20,000
Natzweiler-Struthof	Natzweiler, France	At least 17,000
Neuengamme	Near Hamburg, Germany	At least 50,000
Płaszów	Kraków, Poland	At least 9,000
Ravensbrück	Near Berlin, Germany	90,000
Risiera di San Sabba	Near Trieste, Italy	5,000
Sachsenhausen	Near Berlin, Germany	At least 30,000
Sobibór	Sobibór, Poland	167,000 to 250,000
Soldau	Działdowo, Poland	13,000
Stutthof	Sztutowo, Poland	At least 60,000
Theresienstadt	Terezín, Czechoslovakia	33,000
Treblinka	Treblinka, Poland	870,000 to 925,000
Warsaw	Warsaw, Poland	200,000

Holocaust Chronology

1933

Jan. 30	Adolf Hitler is appointed chancellor of Germany by German president Paul von Hindenburg.
Feb. 3	Hitler presents his *Lebensraum* program, in which he argues that Germany needs more "living room" and should find it in the East.
Feb. 27	The Reichstag (German parliament) building is set on fire.
Mar. 20	The first concentration camp is established at Dachau, near Munich, Germany. The camp opens in June.
Mar. 23	The Enabling Act is adopted, giving Hitler the legislative authority to assume dictatorial powers.
Apr. 1	The Sturm Abteilung (SA), the paramilitary organization of the Nazi Party, begins a boycott of all Jewish businesses, physicians, and attorneys. Jews in Germany are barred from attending universities.
Apr. 7	A law is adopted that prevents Jews from holding civil service jobs, except for veterans who fought on the front lines in World War I. This is the first of about four hundred anti-Semitic laws that will be enacted in Nazi Germany.
Apr. 11	Laws defining "Aryans" and "non-Aryans" are adopted. "Non-Aryans" include anyone descended from non-Aryans, especially from Jewish parents or grandparents.
Apr. 26	The Gestapo, the Nazi secret police organization, is established.
May 10	After Nazis declare that books containing material that is "subversive" to German thought and the German people shall be destroyed, a massive book-burning campaign begins. Many of the books burned are those written by Jews as well as by opponents of the Nazis.
July 14	Opposition political parties are banned, allowing the Nazis to be the only political party in Germany. Laws are adopted whose primary purpose is to revoke naturalization and cancel German citizenship for Jews from Bulgaria, Hungary, Poland, Romania, Croatia, and other eastern territories.
July 20	The Nazi Party and the Vatican sign a concordat.
July 21	In Nuremberg, Germany, the SA arrests hundreds of Jews and parades them through the streets for hours.

Sept. 22	The Reich Chamber of Culture Law is created to control literature, the press, radio, theater, music, and art, with these efforts to be directed by the Ministry of Propaganda under Joseph Goebbels.
Oct. 4	The Editor Law is adopted, regulating the role of newspaper and magazine editors and restricting Jews from working as editors.
Oct. 14	Germany quits the League of Nations, releasing the country from the international controls over rearmament that had been accepted by the Weimar Republic.
Oct. 23	Martin Buber and fifty-one other Jewish educators are fired from their university jobs.
Oct. 24	A law against "habitual and dangerous criminals" is adopted to justify the confinement of the homeless, alcoholics, and the unemployed in concentration camps.
Dec. 18	A law is adopted barring Jews from working as journalists and in associated professions.

1934

Jan. 24	Jews are banned from the German Labor Front, the Nazi Party's organization of trade unions.
Jan. 26	Germany and Poland sign a ten-year nonaggression pact.
May 17	Jews are prohibited from obtaining health insurance.
June 29-30	The Nazis murder Hitler's rivals in the SA, including SA head Ernst Röhm. This purge is kept secret until July 13, when Hitler publicly announces what he calls "the Night of the Long Knives."
July 20	The Schutzstaffel (SS), the Nazi Party's military and security organization, which had been controlled by the police, becomes an independent organization. Heinrich Himmler is appointed chief of the SS.
Aug. 2	President Hindenburg dies, and the positions of chancellor and president are combined, with Hitler assuming both offices. Hitler also becomes commander in chief of the armed forces.
Oct. 1	Hitler defies the Treaty of Versailles by expanding the German army and navy and creating an air force.
Oct. 7	Jehovah's Witnesses in Germany declare their political neutrality and vow to defy Nazi restrictions on the practice of their religion.

1935

Mar. 16	Germany begins military conscription.

Apr. 1	Jehovah's Witnesses are banned in Germany because members of the group will not declare allegiance to the Third Reich.
May 21	A defense law is adopted that requires Aryan heritage as a prerequisite of German military duty.
June 28	The German criminal code is revised to criminalize all acts of male homosexuality.
Sept. 15	In a special session, the German parliament adopts the Nuremberg Laws, which comprise the Law for the Protection of German Blood and Honor and the Reich Citizenship Law. The Law for the Protection of German Blood and Honor prohibits marriage and sexual relations outside of marriage between Jews and Germans. The Reich Citizenship Law deprives Jews of German citizenship.
Nov. 14	In the first decree issued under the Reich Citizenship Law, Jews are barred from voting and holding public office, and all Jews are fired from their civil service jobs, including World War I frontline veterans. In the first decree issued under the Law for the Protection of German Blood and Honor, Jews are prohibited from marrying non-Jews, Jews are prohibited from working in all but a few professions, and Jewish children are prohibited from using the same playgrounds and locker rooms as non-Jewish children.

1936

Mar. 7	German troops occupy the Rhineland.
July 12	Construction begins at the Sachsenhausen concentration camp, located near Berlin.
Aug. 1	The Olympic Games open in Berlin. During the two weeks of the games, anti-Semitic posters are temporarily taken down and the Nazis downplay their militarism and anti-Semitic agenda.

1937

July 16	The Buchenwald concentration camp opens near Weimar, Germany.
Autumn	The Nazis begin systematically to take over Jewish property. Jews also are forced to sell their businesses, usually at prices far below their value.

1938

Mar. 13	Germany annexes Austria and begins to persecute Austrian Jews.
Apr. 22	Jews are required to declare all property worth more than 5,000 reichsmarks ($1,190).
June 9	The synagogue in Munich, Germany, is destroyed.

June 14	Jews are required to register and identify all of their industrial enterprises. Lists of wealthy Jews are created at treasury offices and police districts.
June 15	About 1,500 Jews who were previously convicted of crimes, including traffic violations, are arrested and scheduled to be sent to concentration camps.
July 21	Jews begin to receive identity cards. All Jews are required to have these cards by November, 1939.
July 28	Medical certification is canceled for all Jewish physicians, effective September 30. After that date, Jewish physicians can work only as nurses for Jewish patients.
Aug. 10	The synagogue in Nuremberg, Germany, is destroyed.
Aug. 17	All Jews are mandated to add either "Israel" or "Sara" to their names, effective November, 1939.
Sept. 12	Jews are prohibited from attending public cultural events.
Sept. 27	The licenses of all Jewish lawyers are canceled, effective November 30.
Sept. 29	The Munich Agreement is adopted, in which Britain and France accept Germany's plan to annex the Sudetenland, a part of Czechoslovakia.
Oct. 1	German troops enter the Sudetenland.
Oct. 5	A passport decree is issued requiring the confiscation of all passports held by Jews. Passport reissuance is made more complicated, and all passports newly issued to Jews must be stamped "J" to identify the holders as Jews.
Oct. 15	German troops occupy the Sudetenland.
Oct. 28	Between 15,000 and 17,000 Jews of Polish origin are expelled to Zbąszyń on the Polish border.
Nov. 9-10	Kristallnacht, a Nazi-organized pogrom against Jews in Germany, results in the murder of at least 91 Jews, the destruction of 191 synagogues, and the looting of 7,500 shops. More than 26,000 Jewish men are arrested and scheduled to be sent to the Dachau, Buchenwald, and Sachsenhausen concentration camps.
Nov. 12	The Nazis issue decrees mandating Jews to pay for all damages caused during Kristallnacht. German Jews also are required to make "atonement payments" of one billion marks, are eliminated from involvement in the German economy and are prohibited from attending movies, concerts, and other cultural performances.
Nov. 15	Jewish children are expelled from German schools.

Holocaust Chronology

Nov. 25	About fifty male concentration camp prisoners are transferred to Ravensbrück, near Berlin. The prisoners will build the Ravensbrück concentration camp, which will be the primary camp for women prisoners in Germany.

1939

Jan. 17	A decree mandates the expiration of permits for Jewish dentists, pharmacists, and veterinarians.
Feb. 21	Jews are required to give up all of their gold and silver.
Mar. 14	Slovakia declares itself an independent state to be protected by Germany.
Mar. 15	Germany occupies Czechoslovakia, creating the Protectorate of Bohemia-Moravia and introducing the anti-Semitic decrees that are already in force in Germany.
Apr. 18	Anti-Semitic laws are passed in Slovakia.
Apr. 27-28	Germany rescinds its nonaggression pact with Poland and its 1935 Naval Agreement with Britain.
Apr. 30	Laws are adopted that regulate rental agreements with Jews and cancel eviction protection for Jews. Legal preparations are made to move Jewish families into "Jewish houses."
May 15	The SS transfers almost 900 women prisoners from the Lichtenburg concentration camp to Ravensbrück.
June 29	About 440 Romani (Gypsy) women and their children arrive in Ravensbrück from Austria. By 1945, about 5,000 Romani women will pass through this camp.
July 4	Jews are barred from holding government jobs in Germany.
Aug. 23	Germany and the Soviet Union sign a nonaggression pact.
Aug. 31	The British fleet mobilizes, and civilian evacuation begins in London.
Sept. 1	World War II begins after Germany invades Poland. The Nazis start to conduct numerous pogroms in Poland.
Sept. 3	Britain, France, Australia, and New Zealand declare war on Germany.
Sept. 10	Canada declares war on Germany.
Sept. 17	The Soviet Union invades Poland.
Sept. 21	Reinhard Heydrich, second in command of the SS, orders the creation of Jewish ghettos and *Judenräte* in occupied Poland. The *Judenräte*, or Jewish Councils, were charged with maintaining order in the ghettos.
Sept. 23	Radios are confiscated from Jews.

Sept. 27	Warsaw surrenders to Germany.
Sept. 29	The Germans and the Soviets divide Poland. More than 2 million Jews live in the German area, and 1.3 million live in the Soviet-controlled territory.
Oct.	The Nazis begin to implement a program of euthanasia, targeting sick and disabled Germans.
Oct. 6	Poland surrenders to Germany.
Oct. 7	Jews are resettled in the Lublin district of Poland.
Oct. 8	The first Jewish ghetto is established in Piotrków, Poland.
Oct. 12	The first group of Jews from Austria and the Protectorate of Bohemia-Moravia is deported to Poland.
Oct. 18	Jews in Włocławek, Poland, are required to display the Star of David on their clothing.
Oct. 26	Jews in German-occupied Poland begin to be used for forced labor.
Nov. 12	Forced deportation begins for Polish Jews from West Prussia, Poznań, Gdańsk, and Łódź.
Nov. 23	Jews throughout German-occupied Poland are required to display the Star of David on their clothing.

1940

Jan. 25	Oświęcim (in German, Auschwitz), Poland, is selected as the location of a new concentration camp.
Jan. 28	Wartime rationing of goods begins in Britain.
Feb. 10-13	Deportation begins for Jews from the Pomerania area of Poland to Lublin, Poland.
Apr. 9	Germany invades Denmark and Norway.
Apr. 20	The high command of the German armed forces issues a secret order that all persons of "mixed blood" and men who are married to Jewish women are to be discharged from the military.
Apr. 30	The first guarded Jewish ghetto is established in Łódź, Poland.
May 1	Norway surrenders to Germany.
May 10	Germany invades the Netherlands, Belgium, and France.
May 15	The Netherlands capitulates to Germany.
May 20	The Auschwitz concentration and extermination camp is established.
May 26	Evacuation of all Allied troops from Dunkirk begins.
May 28	Belgium capitulates to Germany.

Holocaust Chronology

June 3	Evacuation of Dunkirk ends.
June 10	German troops defeat Denmark and Norway. Italy declares war on Britain and France.
June 14	The Nazis occupy Paris.
June 18	Hitler presents a plan to Italian dictator Benito Mussolini to transfer Madagascar from France to Germany and resettle all European Jews in the new Mandate of Madagascar.
June 22	The French army surrenders and Marshal Philippe Pétain signs an armistice with Germany.
June 30	All Jews living in Łódź, Poland, are required to live in the ghetto, which is sealed off.
July 10	The Battle of Britain begins.
July 23	The Soviet Union captures Latvia, Estonia, and Lithuania.
Aug. 8	Romania adopts anti-Semitic laws.
Aug. 17	Hitler declares a blockade of the British Isles.
Sept. 7	Germany begins a military blitz against England.
Sept. 16	The United States adopts a military conscription bill.
Oct. 3	The new Vichy government of France adopts the Statut des Juifs (Anti-Jewish Laws).
Oct. 7	German troops enter Romania.
Oct. 22	Jews are deported from Alsace-Lorraine, Saarland, and Baden to southern France and, in 1942, to Auschwitz. Jewish businesses in the Netherlands are required to be registered.
Oct. 28	Jews in Belgium are required to register their property.
Nov. 15	The Warsaw ghetto is sealed off.
Dec. 29-30	Germany launches a massive air raid on London.
1941	
Jan. 22-23	The Nazis begin to massacre Jews in Romania.
Feb.-Apr.	About 72,000 Jews are sent to the Warsaw ghetto.
Feb. 22-23	About 400 Jewish hostages are deported from Amsterdam to the Mauthausen concentration camp in Austria.
Mar. 1	Construction begins on the Auschwitz II-Birkenau concentration and extermination camp.
Mar. 2	German troops occupy Bulgaria.
Mar. 11	U.S. president Franklin D. Roosevelt signs the Lend Lease Act, which allows the United States to send war supplies to Britain, the Soviet Union, and other Allied nations.

Apr. 6	Germany invades Yugoslavia and Greece.
Apr. 24	The Lublin ghetto is sealed off.
May 14	About 3,600 Parisian Jews are arrested. Romania adopts laws requiring Jews to perform forced labor.
June	The Vichy government revokes the civil rights of French Jews in North Africa and issues numerous restrictions against them.
June-July	Mass shootings of Jews begins in the Ponary Forest, near Vilna, Lithuania. By 1944, 70,000 to 100,000 people are murdered there.
June-Aug.	Numerous pogroms are conducted in German-occupied areas of the Soviet Union.
June 6	About 300 male prisoners from Dachau arrive at Ravensbrück, where the SS holds them in a separate camp for men. These men are forced to build factories in the area.
June 22	Germany attacks the Soviet Union.
June 27	The *Einsatzgruppen* (Nazi mobile extermination squads) and local residents murder some 2,000 Jews in Luts'k, Ukraine.
June 28	The Romanian Iron Guard, an anti-Semitic paramilitary group, murders 1,500 Jews in Iasi.
June 30	Germany occupies L'viv, Poland (now in Ukraine), and 4,000 Jews are murdered by July 3.
July	The Majdanek concentration and extermination camp is established in Lublin, Poland.
July 1	The *Einsatzgruppen* begin operating in Bessarabia, Soviet Union, where 150,000 Jews are shot by August 31.
July 8	Jews in the Baltic countries are required to display the Star of David on their clothing.
July 20	A Jewish ghetto is established in Minsk, Belarus.
July 24	A Jewish ghetto is established in Chişinău, Moldavia (now Moldova), where 10,000 Jews are killed.
Aug.	Jewish ghettos are established in Bialystok and L'viv, Poland.
Aug. 5-8	About 10,000 Jews are killed in Pinsk, Belarus.
Aug. 15	The Jewish ghetto in Kaunas, Lithuania, is sealed off.
Aug. 20	The Nazis begin the siege of Leningrad.
Sept.	Janówska, an extermination camp, opens near L'viv, Poland.
Sept. 1	Police order all Jews in Germany age six and older to display a yellow Star of David on their clothing at all times, effective September 19.

Holocaust Chronology

Sept. 3	The experimental gassing of prisoners at Auschwitz with Zyklon B begins.
Sept. 6	A ghetto is established in Vilna, Lithuania, with a population of 40,000 Jews.
Sept. 15	About 150,000 Jews are sent to Trans-Dniestria, Moldavia (now Moldova), where 90,000 die.
Sept. 19	The Zhitomir ghetto in the Ukraine is liquidated, resulting in the murder of 10,000 Jews.
Sept. 28-29	The mass murder of Jews at Babi Yar near Kiev, Ukraine, results in the deaths of 33,751. In 1961, Soviet poet Yevgeny Yevtushenko publishes "Babiy Yar" ("Babii Yar," 1965) a poem that relates anti-Semitism in the Soviet Union to the atrocities committed there.
Oct.-Nov.	The *Einsatzgruppen* begin the mass murder of Jews throughout the southern Soviet Union.
Oct. 3	German Jews are required to perform forced labor.
Oct. 4	Thousands of Jews are murdered at Fort IX in Kaunas, Lithuania.
Oct. 8	The Vitsyebsk ghetto in Belarus is liquidated and more than 16,000 Jews are killed.
Oct. 10	A Jewish ghetto is established in Theresienstadt, Czechoslovakia.
Oct. 11	A Jewish ghetto is established in Czernowitz, Romania.
Oct. 12-13	About 11,000 Jews are massacred at Dnipropetrovs'k, Ukraine.
Oct. 14	The Nazis order the deportation of all Jews from Germany as defined by the country's 1933 borders.
Oct. 16	German Jews begin to be deported to the ghettos in Łódź, Poland; Riga, Latvia; and Minsk, Belarus.
Oct. 23	About 34,000 Jews are massacred in Odessa, Ukraine.
Oct. 28	About 34,000 Jews are massacred in Kiev, Ukraine.
Nov. 1	Construction begins on an extermination camp at Bełżec, Poland.
Nov. 6	About 15,000 Jews are massacred in Kaunas, Lithuania.
Nov. 24	A "model" concentration camp is created at Theresienstadt, Czechoslovakia.
Nov. 26	The Auschwitz II (Auschwitz-Birkenau) concentration-extermination camp is established.
Nov. 30	About 30,000 Jews from Riga, Latvia, are shot in the Rumbuli Forest.

Dec. 1	A unit of the *Einsatzgruppen* in Lithuania reports that it has murdered 136,441 Jews during 1941.
Dec. 7	The Japanese bomb Pearl Harbor.
Dec. 8	The Chełmno extermination camp opens in Poland, where 360,000 Jews will be murdered by April, 1943.
Dec. 8	The United States and Great Britain declare war on Japan.
Dec. 11	Germany and Italy declare war on the United States.
Dec. 21	More than 40,000 Jews are shot at the Bogdanovka concentration camp in Romania.
Dec. 22	Of the 57,000 Jews who once lived in Vilna, Lithuania, about 33,500 have been murdered.
Dec. 30	About 10,000 Jews are killed in Simferopol', Ukraine.
1942	
Jan. 14	The Nazis start to expel Jews from the Netherlands.
Jan. 15	Prisoners from Łódź, Poland, are sent to the extermination camp at Chełmno.
Jan. 20	Nazi officials hold the Wannsee Conference, where they finalize their plans for the "final solution"—the deportation and extermination of European Jews.
Jan. 26	The first American armed forces arrive in Britain.
Jan. 31	A unit of the *Einsatzgruppen* reports it has murdered 229,052 Jews in the Baltic states.
End of Jan.	The Nazis begin deporting Jews to the Theresienstadt concentration camp.
Feb.-Mar.	About 14,000 Jews are murdered in Kharkiv, Ukraine.
Feb. 24	More than 30,000 Jews from Łódź, Poland, are sent to the Chełmno extermination camp.
Mar. 1	The first Jews are murdered at the Sobibór extermination camp in Poland, where 250,000 Jews will be killed by October, 1943.
Mar. 6	The Nazis hold their first conference on sterilization, where they define the use of sterilization for persons of "mixed blood."
Mid-Mar.	Germany begins Aktion Reinhard, an operation that aims to murder Jews in the interior of occupied Poland within the time line of the "final solution."
Mar. 16-17	The Bełżec extermination camp begins operations. Some 600,000 Polish Jews from Lublin, the Lublin district, and Galicia will be murdered there.

Holocaust Chronology

Mar. 21	The Jews in the ghetto in Lublin, Poland, are resettled, with 26,000 sent to extermination camps at Bełżec, Majdanek, and other locations.
Mar. 23-24	The SS transfers 1,000 German Jewish and Romani (Gypsy) women from Ravensbrück to Auschwitz-Birkenau in Poland, where a women's camp is created.
Mar. 26	About 60,000 Jews from Slovakia are sent to the extermination camps at Auschwitz and Majdanek.
Mar. 28	The first Jews from Paris are transported to Auschwitz.
Apr.	Jews are prohibited from using public transportation, except for forced laborers who must travel to workplaces more than seven kilometers from their homes.
Apr. 30	A Jewish ghetto is established in Pinsk, Belarus.
Early May	The first mass murders are conducted in the Sobibór extermination camp.
May 4	Prisoners at Auschwitz-Birkenau who are considered weak, sick, or "unfit" are the first people to be murdered there.
June 1	Jews in France and Holland begin wearing the Star of David. An extermination camp opens in Treblinka, Poland, where gassing of prisoners begins on July 23; about 700,000 Jews will be murdered there by August, 1943.
June 2	The Nazis begin deporting German Jews to the Theresienstadt concentration camp.
June 12	Anne Frank, a Jewish girl living in the Netherlands, celebrates her thirteenth birthday and receives as a gift a diary, in which she immediately begins to write.
June 22	The first prisoners from the Drancy assembly camp in France arrive at Auschwitz.
June 30	Jewish schools in Germany are closed.
July 1	Jews are massacred in Minsk, Lida, and Slonim, Belarus.
July 2	Jews from Berlin are sent to the Theresienstadt concentration camp.
July 4	The mass gassing of prisoners begins at Auschwitz.
July 6	Anne Frank and her family leave their home and go into hiding in an empty section of a warehouse building in Amsterdam.
July 15	The first Jews from the Netherlands are transported to Auschwitz.

July 22	The *Umsiedlung*, or mass deportation of Jews from the Warsaw ghetto to Bełżec and Treblinka extermination camps, begins. By September 13, about 300,000 Jews will be sent to Treblinka, where 265,000 will be murdered.
July 23	The gassing of prisoners begins at Treblinka.
Aug.-Sept.	Jews are deported from Zagreb, Croatia, to Auschwitz.
Aug. 4	The Nazis begin deporting Belgian Jews to Auschwitz.
Aug. 10-22	About 40,000 Jews from the ghetto in L'viv, Poland, are sent to extermination camps.
Aug. 14	The Nazis arrest 7,000 Jews in unoccupied France.
Aug. 17	The first all-American air attack is launched in Europe.
Oct. 4	The Nazis decree that all Jews who are imprisoned in concentration camps will be sent to Auschwitz.
Oct. 28	The first group of prisoners from the Theresienstadt concentration camp is sent to Auschwitz.
Oct. 29	About 16,000 Jews are executed in Pinsk, Belarus.
Nov. 1	The first group of Jews from Bialystok, Poland, is deported to Auschwitz.
Nov. 25	The deportation of Jews from Norway to Auschwitz begins.
Dec. 10	The first group of German Jews arrives at Auschwitz.
1943	
Jan. 18	The Jews in the Warsaw ghetto stage their first act of armed resistance to deportation.
Jan. 29	The Germans order that all Gypsies be arrested and placed in concentration camps.
Feb. 2	The Germans surrender at Stalingrad—the first significant defeat for Hitler's armed forces.
Feb. 15	About 10,000 Jews are killed in the ghetto in Bialystok, Poland, before the rest are sent to the extermination camp at Treblinka.
Feb. 25	The first group of Jews from Salonika, Greece, is transported to Auschwitz.
Feb. 26	The first group of Gypsies arrives at Auschwitz.
Feb. 27	Jewish armament workers from Berlin are sent to Auschwitz.
Mar.	Dutch Jews are transported to Sobibór, while Jews from Prague, Vienna, Luxembourg, and Macedonia are sent to Treblinka.

Holocaust Chronology

Mar. 13	The Jewish ghetto in Kraków, Poland, is liquidated and its residents are deported to the Płaszów concentration camp. Oskar Schindler, a member of the Nazi Party and owner of an enamel factory near Kraków, is moved by these events and is determined to transfer his Jewish employees out of the area so they can avoid a similar fate. He obtains permission from the camp commandant to open a branch of his factory outside the Płaszów camp, and this action saves 900 Jewish workers from being imprisoned at Płaszów.
Apr. 19	The Warsaw Ghetto Uprising begins on the eve of Passover. Ghetto residents continue their resistance as German troops surround the area.
Apr. 23	Marek Lichtenbaum, the *Judenrat* chairman in the Warsaw ghetto, and his deputies are murdered by the Nazis.
May 8	The Nazis liquidate Mila 18, the bunker that serves as headquarters for Jewish resistance fighters in the Warsaw ghetto.
May 10	Many of the Warsaw ghetto resistance fighters escape through the sewers, arriving in the non-Jewish area of the city.
May 16	German officials proclaim that the Warsaw ghetto is free of Jews and set fire to a Warsaw synagogue.
May 19	The Nazis declare that Berlin is *Judenfrei* (free of all Jews).
June 11	Himmler orders that all Polish ghettos be liquidated. On June 21, this order is expanded to include ghettos in the Soviet Union.
June 21-27	About 20,000 people are killed during the liquidation of the L'viv ghetto.
July 9-10	The Allies land in Sicily, Italy.
Aug. 2	Prisoners revolt at the Treblinka extermination camp and the Krikov labor camp in Poland.
Aug. 16-23	The Bialystok ghetto is destroyed following a revolt there.
Sept. 3	A group of Belgian Jews is arrested and scheduled to be deported to Auschwitz.
Sept. 11	The Nazis begin to raid Jews in Nice, France.
Sept. 11-14	The Jewish ghettos in Minsk and Lida, Belarus, are liquidated.
Sept. 23	The Vilna ghetto is liquidated.
Oct. 2	The Nazis order the expulsion of Jews from Denmark. However, rescue operations by the Danish underground enable 7,000 Jews to be evacuated to Sweden, and the Nazis capture only 475 Danish Jews.
Oct. 13	Italy declares war on Germany.

Oct. 14	Prisoners in the Sobibór extermination camp stage a revolt.
Oct. 18	The first Jews from Rome are sent to Auschwitz.
Oct. 21	The Minsk ghetto is liquidated.
Nov. 3	The Riga ghetto is liquidated. About 17,000 Jews who remain in the Majdanek extermination camp are killed.

1944

Jan. 22	The Allies land at Anzio, Italy.
Feb. 11	Primo Levi and other Italian Jews interned at a camp near Modena, Italy, are transported to Auschwitz in twelve cramped cattle cars. Levi spends eleven months at Auschwitz before the extermination camp is liberated, and he later writes a memoir of his experiences in the camp.
Feb. 24	The Gestapo raids a house in Haarlem, Netherlands, where Casper ten Boom and his daughters, Corrie and Betsie, have been hiding Jews and members of the Dutch underground. The three are arrested. Corrie and Betsie eventually are taken to Ravensbrück, where Betsie dies. Corrie survives and in 1971 publishes *The Hiding Place*, a book about her experiences.
Mar. 19	Germany invades Hungary.
Apr. 14	The first Jews from Athens are sent to Auschwitz.
Apr. 16	The Hungarian government orders that all Jews must be registered and confiscates their property.
May 15-July 8	About 438,000 Hungarian Jews are sent to Auschwitz.
June 6	D day, the start of the Allied invasion of Normandy.
July	Raoul Wallenberg, a Swedish diplomat, arrives in Budapest and starts issuing documents aimed at saving Hungarian Jews.
July 7	The Hungarian government stops the deportation of Jews.
July 8	The ghetto in Kaunas, Lithuania, is liquidated.
July 13	Jewish resistance fighters help liberate Vilna, Lithuania, where only 2,500 of the city's 57,000 Jews survive.
July 23	Soviet troops liberate the Majdanek death camp. The Red Cross visits Theresienstadt.
Late summer	Oskar Schindler receives permission from the German army and the SS to move his Jewish workers and other endangered Jews from Płaszów to Brünnlitz in the Sudetenland. There, he and more than 1,000 of his employees establish a bogus munitions factory in order to protect the Jewish employees until the end of World War II. Schindler's efforts to save Jews are later recounted in Thomas Keneally's novel *Schindler's List* (1982).

Holocaust Chronology

Aug. 4	Anne Frank and her family are discovered and arrested by the Gestapo in Amsterdam.
Aug. 6	About 27,000 Jews from camps east of the Vistula River are deported to Germany.
Aug. 7	Nazis begin to liquidate the Łódź ghetto, deporting 74,000 Jews to Auschwitz.
Aug. 25	Paris is liberated from the Nazis.
Sept.	All Jews in Dutch camps are transported to Germany. Additional prisoners are deported from Theresienstadt to Auschwitz. The final group of prisoners is transported from France to Auschwitz.
Sept. 4	The Allies liberate Antwerp, Belgium, where fewer than 5,000 Jews survive.
Sept. 11	British troops enter the Netherlands.
Sept. 14	American troops arrive at the German border.
Sept. 23	Jews in the concentration camp in Kluga, Estonia, are murdered.
Oct. 31	About 14,000 Jews from Slovakia are sent to Auschwitz.
Nov. 2	The gassings at Auschwitz are terminated.
Nov. 18	About 38,000 Jews from Budapest are sent to Buchenwald, Ravensbrück, and other camps.
Nov. 26	In an effort to hide evidence of the extermination camps, Himmler orders the destruction of the crematorium at Auschwitz-Birkenau.
Dec. 16-27	The Battle of the Bulge is fought in the Ardennes.
1945	
Jan. 16	Soviet troops liberate 800 Jews at Częstochowa and 870 in Łódź.
Jan. 17	Soviet troops liberate Warsaw, where few Jews remain.
Jan. 17	About 80,000 Jews in Budapest are liberated.
Jan. 17	Auschwitz is evacuated and the prisoners begin their "death march."
Jan. 27	Soviet troops liberate Auschwitz.
Feb. 13-14	Dresden, Germany, is destroyed in a firestorm after massive Allied bombing attacks.
Apr. 6-10	About 15,000 Jews are evacuated from Buchenwald.
Apr. 12	American troops liberate Buchenwald.
Apr. 15	British troops liberate the Bergen-Belsen concentration camp.
Apr. 23-May 4	The Sachsenhausen concentration camp is evacuated. The SS conducts its last massacre of Jews.

Apr. 27	The final prisoners are evacuated from Ravensbrück, where the SS forces about 15,000 prisoners on a death march.
Apr. 29	American troops liberate Dachau.
Apr. 30	Hitler commits suicide.
May 2	Representatives of the International Red Cross take over Theresienstadt.
May 5	The Mathausen concentration camp is liberated.
May 7-9	Germany unconditionally surrenders, ending the war in Europe.
May 8	V-E (Victory in Europe) Day.
May 23	Himmler is captured and commits suicide.
Nov. 20	The Nuremberg war crime trials begin.

Complete List of Contents

Volume 1

Contents. v
Publisher's Note vii
Editor's Introduction xi
Contributors xix
Nazi Concentration Camps xxi
Holocaust Chronology xxiii

The Accident—*Elie Wiesel* 1
After Auschwitz—*Richard L. Rubenstein* 6
Albert Speer—*Gitta Sereny* 12
All Rivers Run to the Sea—*Elie Wiesel* 18
And the Sea Is Never Full—*Elie Wiesel* 24
"The Angel of History"—*Carolyn Forché* 30
Anya—*Susan Fromberg Schaeffer* 35
At the Mind's Limits—*Jean Améry* 40
Auschwitz and After—*Charlotte Delbo* 44
Austerlitz—*W. G. Sebald* 48

"Babii Yar"—*Yevgeny Yevtushenko* 53
Badenheim 1939—*Aharon Appelfeld* 57

Constantine's Sword—*James Carroll* 65

"Daddy"—*Sylvia Plath* 71
Daniel's Story—*Carol Matas* 76
"Death Fugue"—*Paul Celan* 80
The Deputy—*Rolf Hochhuth* 85
The Destruction of the European Jews—*Raul Hilberg* 92
The Diary of a Young Girl—*Anne Frank* 96
The Double Bond—*Carole Angier* 100
The Drowned and the Saved—*Primo Levi* 105

Eichmann in Jerusalem—*Hannah Arendt* 111
"Elegy for N. N."—*Czesław Miłosz* 118
Enemies—*Isaac Bashevis Singer* 123

Holocaust Literature

Europe Central—*William T. Vollmann* 129
Explaining Hitler—*Ron Rosenbaum* 135

The Fall of France—*Julian Jackson* 141
Fateless—*Imre Kertész* 147
The Fifth Son—*Elie Wiesel* 152
Friedrich—*Hans Peter Richter* 157

The Gates of the Forest—*Elie Wiesel* 161
Ghetto—*Joshua Sobol* 166
God's Presence in History—*Emil L. Fackenheim* 170
Gone to Soldiers—*Marge Piercy* 176

The Hiding Place—*Corrie ten Boom with
    John and Elizabeth Sherrill* 182
The History of Love—*Nicole Krauss* 187
History on Trial—*Deborah E. Lipstadt* 192
Hitler—*Ian Kershaw* 197
The Hitler of History—*John Lukacs* 204
Hitler's Willing Executioners—*Daniel Jonah Goldhagen* 210
The Holocaust in American Life—*Peter Novick* 216
Holocaust Politics—*John K. Roth* 223
Holocaust Testimonies—*Lawrence L. Langer* 227
House of Dolls—*Ka-tzetnik 135633* 234

I Will Bear Witness—*Victor Klemperer* 238
In Kindling Flame—*Linda Atkinson* 244
"In the Blue Distance"—*Nelly Sachs* 249
Incident at Vichy—*Arthur Miller* 254
An Interrupted Life—*Etty Hillesum* 259
Into That Darkness—*Gitta Sereny* 264

Jews—*Arthur Hertzberg and Aron Hirt-Manheimer* 268
The Journey Back—*Johanna Reiss* 274
"Journey Through the Night"—*Jakov Lind* 278

The Last of the Just—*André Schwarz-Bart* 282
Lest Innocent Blood Be Shed—*Philip P. Hallie* 286
Letters and Papers from Prison—*Dietrich Bonhoeffer* 291

Volume 2

Contents xlvii
Nazi Concentration Camps xlix
Holocaust Chronology. li
Complete List of Contents. lxvii

Life with a Star—*Jiří Weil* 295

Man's Search for Meaning—*Viktor Emil Frankl* 300
The Master Plan—*Heather Pringle* 306
Masters of Death—*Richard Rhodes* 311
Maus—*Art Spiegelman*. 317

The Nazi Doctors—*Robert Jay Lifton* 322
Nazi Germany and the Jews—*Saul Friedländer* 326
Nazi Terror—*Eric A. Johnson* 332
Never to Forget—*Milton Meltzer*. 338
Night—*Elie Wiesel* 342
Nightfather—*Carl Friedman*. 346
Number the Stars—*Lois Lowry* 350

O the Chimneys—*Nelly Sachs* 355
On the Natural History of Destruction—*W. G. Sebald* 360
Open Closed Open—*Yehuda Amichai* 366
Ordinary Men—*Christopher R. Browning* 372
The Origins of Totalitarianism—*Hannah Arendt* 376
Our Golda—*David A. Adler*. 383

Paul Celan—*John Felstiner* 388
The Pawnbroker—*Edward Lewis Wallant* 393
The Periodic Table—*Primo Levi* 399
Perpetrators, Victims, Bystanders—*Raul Hilberg* 405
The Pianist—*Władysław Szpilman* 411
Playing for Time—*Fania Fénelon* 415
The Portage to San Cristóbal of A. H.—*George Steiner* 419
Preaching Eugenics—*Christine Rosen* 425
"A Problem from Hell"—*Samantha Power*. 430

Rethinking the Holocaust—*Yehuda Bauer* 436
Return to Auschwitz—*Kitty Hart* 442

Reunion—*Fred Uhlman* 446
The Rise and Fall of Adolf Hitler—*William L. Shirer* 450

Schindler's List—*Thomas Keneally* 455
A Scrap of Time, and Other Stories—*Ida Fink* 459
The Second World War—*Martin Gilbert* 463
The Shawl—*Cynthia Ozick* 468
Shoah—*Claude Lanzmann* 474
Sophie's Choice—*William Styron* 478
The State of Israel vs. Adolf Eichmann—*Hanna Yablonka* 483
Still Alive—*Ruth Klüger* 489
The Sunflower—*Simon Wiesenthal* 493
Survival in Auschwitz—*Primo Levi* 498

The Terezín Requiem—*Josef Bor* 503
The Texture of Memory—*James E. Young* 508
"This Way for the Gas, Ladies and Gentlemen"
  —*Tadeusz Borowski* 512
Time's Arrow—*Martin Amis* 516
Touch Wood—*Renée Roth-Hano* 521
Tzili—*Aharon Appelfeld* 525

The Upstairs Room—*Johanna Reiss* 533

The Wall—*John Hersey* 538
War Against the Weak—*Edwin Black* 545
Why Did the Heavens Not Darken?—*Arno J. Mayer* 551
The Wilkomirski Affair—*Stefan Maechler* 558
A World at Arms—*Gerhard L. Weinberg* 563

More Holocaust Literature 571
General Bibliography 581
Web Sites 594

Genre Index 605
Title Index 612
Author Index 615

THE ACCIDENT

AUTHOR: Elie Wiesel (1928-   )
FIRST PUBLISHED: *Le Jour*, 1961 (English translation, 1962)
GENRE: Novella
SUBGENRE: Psychological realism

Wiesel draws on his own experience as a Holocaust survivor in telling the story of Eliezer, a young man who, some years after World War II, struggles to live with ever-present memories of the horrors of the Nazi concentration camps. For Eliezer, the tragedies of the past make impossible any hopes for the present or the future.

PRINCIPAL CHARACTERS:
  Eliezer, the narrator, a journalist
  Kathleen, Eliezer's sweetheart
  Eliezer's grandmother, a victim of the Holocaust but still present in Eliezer's memory
  Dr. Paul Russel, the young resident who cares for Eliezer in the hospital
  Sarah, a prostitute who as a twelve-year-old girl was sexually abused by the Nazis
  Gyula, a painter of Hungarian origin

OVERVIEW

The Accident, a novella of little more than one hundred pages, is a psychological, philosophical, and spiritual journey. The narrator of the story, Eliezer, is a young journalist who has been spiritually immobilized by the Holocaust, in which he lost his family and of which he is a survivor. The narrative opens as Eliezer and Kathleen, his sweetheart, who loves him profoundly but to whom he is unable to make a commitment, are going to see the film version of *The Brothers Karamazov* in New York City. Hot, tired, bored, and lifeless, Eliezer lags behind Kathleen in crossing a street and is struck and dragged several yards by a taxicab. Suffering severe injuries, he is taken to a hospital, where, after three days, he undergoes surgery. The young doctor who attends him, Paul Russel, takes a special interest in him, showing a curiosity that makes Eliezer suspect that the doctor knows something about him. The reader discovers that Eliezer was subconsciously a willing victim of his nearly fatal accident.

Dr. Russel's mention of Kathleen causes Eliezer to recall meeting her for the first time in Paris, some five or six years earlier. At that time, as now, he had come to the end of his hope and strength because of the oppressive memories of his experiences during the Holocaust. For years he has suffered from what is called "survivor guilt," just as, when a young boy, he felt guilty for being happier than a less fortunate orphan boy. Throughout the narrative, as it moves back and forth between present and past, Eliezer returns to thoughts of his grandmother and the rest of his family, all of whom were executed by the Nazis. He thinks of himself as being dead with them and the other six million people destroyed by the Holocaust. Kathleen attempts to alleviate his guilt and suffering by suffering herself; still, she is never able to penetrate the wall that Eliezer has put up around himself.

During his recovery from the accident, Eliezer wonders whether Kathleen knows the cause underlying it and that he allowed himself to be hurt because he did not care enough to get out of the way. Dr. Russel, who has just felt the joy of saving a young boy's life, asks Eliezer one day why his patient does not care about living. Eliezer evades the doctor's angry questioning, but the reader is apprised of the answer: Those who have survived the Holocaust are no longer normal human beings; a spring has snapped inside them from the shock, and the results must appear sooner or later. Eliezer does not want the doctor to understand and thus lose his equilibrium. By abstractions and grandiloquence and evasions akin to lying, Eliezer persuades the doctor to believe that he does love life, proving it by his love for Kathleen.

Eliezer's relationship with Kathleen provides one of the main transitional devices in the narrative. For example, Kathleen asks him who Sarah is, since Eliezer, she says, had spoken her name during a coma. Sarah, he tells her, was his mother's name. It was also, however, as a flashback reveals, the name of a prostitute whom Eliezer had met in Paris long before he came to know Kathleen. That Sarah was twelve years old when she was sent to a special barracks for the pleasure of the Nazi officers at a concentration camp. Eliezer considers Sarah to be a saint, like his mother. Kathleen's slight resemblance to his mother turns Eliezer's thoughts back to the time of Kathleen's emotional struggle when they became lovers again after a separation of five years. The past—and all that it meant to Eliezer—stood between them; thus, Kathleen extracted a promise from him that he would allow her to help him in his fight against memories of the train station from which his mother and father and little sister were taken to their deaths.

The last chapter of the book introduces Gyula, a painter, originally from

Hungary, who ignores Eliezer's attempts to explain his suffering and the reason behind the accident. Gyula pleads for him to forget the tragic past and make a commitment to life. He then paints a portrait of his friend in which the eyes are those of a man who had seen God commit the unforgivable crime of senseless killing. Enraged because Eliezer is intent on perpetuating the past rather than returning to the present, Gyula sets fire to the canvas and leaves, forgetting—as Eliezer says in ending his narrative—to take along the ashes.

Consonant with the story in which they appear, the characters in Elie Wiesel's novella are shadowy and disembodied, either alive in the midst of death or dead in the midst of life, depending on their purpose in the narrative. The characters can be no other way, as the narrator sees life only with the eyes of death. His grandmother has long been dead, but she is more of a presence in the work than the physically living Kathleen or any of the other characters.

Gyula and Dr. Russel are an evanescent opposition to the nihilism of Eliezer. They pass quickly through the novella without being fully developed. Wiesel wanted nothing more from them, artistically, than their appearance as voices in support of life and love. Kathleen is like them, ineffectual in spite of her love and energy. No character can counter the gloominess of Eliezer, while characters such as Sarah and his grandmother act as constant reminders of death.

Though Wiesel's characters are grounded in his own Holocaust experience, the story springs more from his imagination than from his life. There are many influences working on his imagination: culture, history, stories, myths, and the Bible. For example, from Jewish culture Wiesel draws the Hebrew name of God (El) in the naming of Eliezer; other characters—Sarah, Shmuel, and Sarah the prostitute—also have biblical origins.

Self-annihilation by surrendering to death is a central theme of *The Accident*. Some years after surviving the death camps, in which he lost his family, Eliezer can no longer continue struggling to live. Even his love for Kathleen is insufficient to give meaning to his existence. It is easy, therefore, for the reader to accept that Eliezer passively intended to take his life when he stepped in front of the taxicab that seriously injured him. Suicide among survivors of the Holocaust is a phenomenon that Wiesel explicitly addresses in a preface written for the 1985 edition of *The Accident*. Referring to the hundreds of Jewish children in Poland who quietly surrendered to death after World War II, he suggests that they "were abruptly forced to realize to what extent they were depleted. And vanquished. And stigmatized. And alone." Eliezer's state of mind, affected by the same tragedy, is similar to that of those children.

The primary message of *The Accident* is that one who has experienced the Holocaust and survived it is almost certainly doomed to live it obsessively over and over again, to feel self-hatred as a consequence of survivor guilt, to resent those who are not outraged by the individuals responsible for the Holocaust, and to cry out against God for apparently acquiescing to the horror.

Life and love, the other central themes of the novella, are set in contrast to the themes of death and hatred and suffering. Eliezer is urged again and again to return to life, just as he is urged to put the past behind him and to accept love and give it. The effort to achieve forgetfulness is too much for him, however, and the last line of *The Accident* ("He [Gyula] had forgotten to take along the ashes") reveals the finality with which Eliezer has chosen death over life. Neither love nor life can erase the ever-present memory of the Holocaust. The tragedies of the past make impossible any hopes for the present or the future for him.

The Accident was Elie Wiesel's third book and should be read in sequence following its predecessors. His first book, a memoir recounting his experience of the Holocaust, had a complex publishing history. Originally written in Yiddish, and running to some nine hundred pages in manuscript, it first appeared in its present form in French translation, radically condensed, as *La Nuit* (1958; *Night*, 1960). Wiesel himself has said that "*Night* is not a novel, it's an autobiography. It's a memoir. It's testimony." Nevertheless, it has frequently been classified as fiction. *Night* was followed by the novellas *L'Aube* (1960; *Dawn*, 1961) and *The Accident*. Unfortunately, the English title chosen for the latter obscures the thematic progression of the three books: *Le Jour*, the original French title of *The Accident*, means "day." Metaphorically, the French title suggests the survivor's full confrontation with the ongoing reality of life after the "night" of the Holocaust; the sequence of "night," "dawn," and "day" traces an ongoing struggle, not a neatly resolved movement from despair to hope.

As the winner of the Nobel Peace Prize in 1986, Wiesel has enhanced an already considerable worldwide literary reputation. He has long been recognized as one of the foremost interpreters of the Jewish experience and, inseparable from that experience, the Holocaust. Eliezer, the protagonist of *The Accident*, the victim, the survivor, may be seen as a living counterpart of any one of the six million who did not survive the death camps. With other writers who cover the Holocaust—such as André Schwarz-Bart, Primo Levi, Nelly Sachs, Paul Celan, Ernst Weichert, Vladka Meed, Pierre Gascar, and Tadeusz Borowski—Wiesel has helped create a literature intended to ensure that victims, living or dead, of any kind of inhumanity will never be forgotten.

Sources for Further Study

Brown, Robert McAfee. *Elie Wiesel: Messenger to All Humanity*. Notre Dame, Ind.: University of Notre Dame Press, 1983.

Fine, Ellen S. *Legacy of "Night": The Literary Universe of Elie Wiesel*. Albany: State University of New York Press, 1982.

Freedman, Samuel G. "Bearing Witness." *The New York Times*, October 23, 1983, p. A32.

Kolbert, Jack. *The Worlds of Elie Wiesel: An Overview of His Career and His Major Themes*. Selinsgrove, Pa.: Susquehanna University Press, 2001.

Rosen, Alan, ed. *Celebrating Elie Wiesel: Stories, Essays, Reflections*. Notre Dame, Ind.: University of Notre Dame Press, 1998.

Rosenfeld, Alvin H., and Irving Greenberg, eds. *Confronting the Holocaust: The Impact of Elie Wiesel*. Bloomington: Indiana University Press, 1978.

Wiesel, Elie, and Richard D. Heffner. *Conversations with Elie Wiesel*. Edited by Thomas J. Vinciguerra. New York: Schocken Books, 2001.

—David Powell

After Auschwitz
History, Theology, and Contemporary Judaism

AUTHOR: Richard L. Rubenstein (1924-)
FIRST PUBLISHED: *After Auschwitz: Radical Theology and Contemporary Judaism*, 1966 (revised and enlarged as *After Auschwitz: History, Theology, and Contemporary Judaism*, 1992)
GENRE: Nonfiction
SUBGENRES: Philosophy; ethics; religion and spirituality

In this work, Rubenstein, one of the first Jewish thinkers to explore deeply the ethical and religious implications of the Holocaust, questions the credibility of claims about God's presence in history and also addresses the topics of overpopulation, modernization, bureaucracy, and the persistent threat of genocide in the modern world.

Overview

Calling their regime the Third Reich, Adolf Hitler and his Nazi Party ruled Germany from 1933 to 1945. The Holocaust, Nazi Germany's planned total destruction of the European Jews and the actual murder of nearly six million of them, took place during those years. More than a million Jews were gassed at Auschwitz. The catastrophe that befell his people, the Jews, during the Holocaust led Richard L. Rubenstein to write *After Auschwitz*. The first edition, published in 1966, assured Rubenstein's significance in Jewish theology. Revised and expanded in 1992, this book remains required reading for anyone interested in post-Holocaust philosophy and religion.

Significantly, the Holocaust did not occur until the mid-twentieth century, although conditions necessary, but not sufficient, to produce it were forming centuries before. *After Auschwitz* helps to show how Christian anti-Judaism and its demonization of Jews were decisive antecedents of the Holocaust. It also discusses the importance of the post-Holocaust emergence of the State of Israel, but the book is best known for its emphasis on a collision between faith in the God of history—some Christian beliefs about such a God have produced Christian anti-Judaism—and the disastrous reality of the Holocaust.

The 1992 version of *After Auschwitz* is more a new book than a second edition of an old one. Nine of the original version's fifteen chapters were eliminated; those that remain were substantially rewritten. Ten new chapters that had been published elsewhere were also added to the revised edition, which is the source for all of the quotations in this article.

In the 1992 edition of *After Auschwitz*, Rubenstein describes a meeting with Swami Muktananda of Ganeshpuri, a deeply religious man. "You mustn't believe in your own religion," the swami advised him, "I don't believe in mine. Religions are like the fences that hold young saplings erect. Without the fence the sapling could fall over. When it takes firm root and becomes a tree, the fence is no longer needed. However, most people never lose their need for the fence."

Rubenstein found the swami's advice helpful because he received it at a time when he was feeling very pessimistic about humanity, a mood that included what he acknowledged as an intolerance toward people in his own Jewish tradition who apparently declined to face difficulties about the relationship between a God of history and the Holocaust. Rubenstein heard the swami saying something that spoke to him in ways that are reflected in the opening paragraph of *After Auschwitz*'s second edition. The first version, Rubenstein explained, contained a "spirit of opposition and revolt, which was an almost inevitable consequence of my initial, essentially uncharted attempt to come to terms theologically with the greatest single trauma in all of Jewish history." Governing the second edition, he went on to say, was a "spirit of synthesis and reconciliation." Rubenstein stated that he had kept his fundamental insights but had done so in the second edition "with a greater degree of empathy for those who have reaffirmed traditional Jewish faith in the face of the Holocaust." Rubenstein discerned that Swami Muktananda had urged him not to give up his fundamental insights but to use them to look deeper and to see beyond their limited meanings.

Even before he received the swami's advice, Rubenstein showed that he had already been practicing some aspects of it in the first edition of *After Auschwitz*. This book challenged some of the most fundamental beliefs held by Jews and Christians. Specifically, Rubenstein argued, the Holocaust calls into question the existence of a redeeming God, one who is active in history and who will bring the upheavals of human existence to a fulfilling end. In the late 1960's, *After Auschwitz* provoked considerable controversy. One result was that Rubenstein found himself linked with three American Protestant thinkers—Thomas Altizer, William Hamilton, and Paul van Buren—and all four were identified as key players in what came to be known as the "death of God" movement.

At the time, the three American Protestants hailed the "death of God" with considerable enthusiasm. Optimistic about the human prospect, they celebrated the liberation that men and women could experience when they moved beyond an outmoded theological past to see that the whole world was no longer in God's hands but solely in the hands of the people. Rubenstein's outlook differed in important ways. He was not alone among those thinkers in denying that he was an atheist who literally believed "God is dead," but Rubenstein made clearer than most his view that "the ultimate relevance of theology is anthropological," a perspective reflected in his long-standing use of psychoanalytic insights in his discussion of religion. What Rubenstein meant was that whenever people speak about God, they are talking about what they believe about God, which is not the same as talking about God directly. Therefore, it can make sense to say, as Rubenstein did in *After Auschwitz*, that "we live in the time of the death of God," but, as Rubenstein explained further, we cannot say whether "the death of God" is more than an event within human culture.

Rubenstein's emphasis on the anthropological dimensions of theological discourse did not mean that he was indifferent about the nature of ultimate reality. One place, for example, where he parted company with the Christian "death of God" theologians involved his impression that they "'willed' the death of the theistic God" with very little regret. In contrast, Rubenstein found himself unwillingly forced to conclude that the idea of a God of history lacked credibility after Auschwitz and felt saddened by that outcome. He recognized that history had shattered—at least for him—a system of religious meaning that had sustained people, especially Jews and Christians, for millennia. The destruction of such meaning was no cause for celebration. On the contrary, it suggested to Rubenstein the melancholy prospect that human existence is ultimately absurd and meaningless.

That conclusion, however, was not to be Rubenstein's last word on the subject. Seeking an alternative that could work for him and for others who might share his outlook about the God of history, Rubenstein went on to write movingly and positively about his vision of "God after the death of God," as the final chapter of the revised version of *After Auschwitz* is titled. Instead of "faith in the radically transcendent Creator God of biblical religion, who bestows a covenant on Israel for His own utterly inscrutable reasons," Rubenstein affirmed that "an understanding of God which gives priority to the indwelling immanence of the Divine may be more credible in our era."

Drawing on both Eastern and Western mystical traditions, including strands from his Jewish heritage, Rubenstein amplified the idea of divine immanence by speaking of God as the Holy Nothingness. Submitting that "omnipotent Nothingness is Lord of all creation," he used that concept to refer to "the ground, content, and final destiny of all things," adding that "God as the 'Nothing' . . . is not a thing" but "no-thing." Beyond distinctions between the masculine and the feminine or human understandings of good and evil, Rubenstein's Holy Nothingness is not the "absence of being, but a superfluity of being . . . a *plenum* so rich that all existence derives therefrom." The best metaphor for this concept, he suggested, is that "God is the ocean and we the waves. Each wave has its moment when it is identifiable as a somewhat separate entity. Nevertheless, no wave is entirely distinct from the ocean, which is its substantial ground."

This perspective's advantages, Rubenstein argued, include "a judgment on the overly individualistic conception of the self which has predominated in the Western world." Emphasizing the interdependence of all things, Rubenstein insisted that "the world of the death of the biblical God need not be a place of gloom or despair. One need not live forever for life to be worth living. Creation, however impermanent, is full of promise." Granted, if omnipotent Nothingness is Lord of all creation, we can ask but never really answer the question "Why is there something rather than nothing?" Far from reducing the horror of "ethnic cleansing" and the Holocaust, that outcome may make human life more tragic than ever. However, it does remove the theological "problem of evil" that intrudes when such devastations are interpreted as part of a world created and sustained by a powerful biblical God of history whose providential purposes are supposedly governed by goodness, justice, and love.

The concerns that drove Rubenstein to reject the traditional God of history, however, were never directed by unsatisfactory attempts to solve a dilemma whose dissonance had been reduced to the abstract question, "If there is radical evil in the world, how can God be omnipotent and completely good?" His issue was far more concrete, particular, and historical. After Auschwitz, how could sense be made of a Jewish tradition of covenant and election, a perspective in which Jews interpreted themselves to be specially chosen by God, bound to God in a covenant that entailed God's blessing for faithfulness and God's judgment against infidelity? Common to that tradition's self-understanding was the belief that "radical communal misfortune," as Rubenstein called it, was a sign either that God found the Chosen People wanting and dispensed punishment accordingly, or that God called on the innocent to suffer sacrificially for the guilty, or that an indispensable prelude for the messianic climax of Jewish history was under way, or some combination of such outlooks. In any case, the Holocaust, an event in which Nazi Germany was hell-bent on destroying Jewish life root and branch, made Rubenstein collide head-on with the biblical tradition of covenant and election, which seemed to him to lead consistently to a positive answer to the question "Did God use Adolf Hitler and the Nazis as his agents to inflict terrible sufferings and death upon six million Jews, including more than one million children?" Such an answer Rubenstein could not accept. He wrote *After Auschwitz* instead.

Rubenstein had to decide whether to affirm the logical implication that he found belief in the God of history to entail, namely, that God was ultimately responsible for Auschwitz. Finding that affirmation obscene, he looked elsewhere to make sense of his Jewish identity. Rubenstein's developing religious perspective led him to reject a providential God and to emphasize instead a sense of the sacred in which "creation and destruction are part of an indivisible process. Each wave in the ocean of God's Nothingness has its moment, but it must inevitably give way to other waves." Nevertheless, Rubenstein affirmed, we have considerable freedom to direct the journey we take during our limited time on earth. That journey can be joyful and good.

After Auschwitz was a crucial departure point for Rubenstein's distinctive journey. Decades later he returned to that work and saw that "no person writing about the religious significance of contemporary history can rest content with what he or she has written at a particular moment in time. As history is an ongoing process, so too is theological writing concerning history." As the second edition of *After Auschwitz* made clear, however, Rubenstein consistently followed his conviction that theology's basic relevance is anthropological—what it tells us about humankind. Thus, the accent of his work fell increasingly on history, politics, economics, and sociology—always with reference to religious thought and practice but with emphasis on the conditions that produce human conflict and the safeguards that must be shored up to limit that conflict's destructiveness.

Important though they are, none of Rubenstein's other books is likely to eclipse the significance of *After Auschwitz*. Particularly in the United States, its sustained impact has rightly been considerable in Jewish circles and on many Christian audiences as well. Rubenstein's reflections were among the first to probe the significance of Auschwitz for post-Holocaust religious life. Few, if any, have better stood the test of time.

Sources for Further Study

Braiterman, Zachary. *(God) After Auschwitz: Tradition and Change in Post-Holocaust Thought*. Princeton, N.J.: Princeton University Press, 1998.

Cohn-Sherbok, Dan. *Holocaust Theology*. London: Lamp Press, 1989.

Haynes, Stephen R., and John K. Roth, eds. *The Death of God Movement and the Holocaust: Radical Theology Encounters the Shoah*. Westport, Conn.: Greenwood Press, 1999.

Katz, Stephen T. *Post-Holocaust Dialogues: Critical Studies in Modern Jewish Thought*. New York: New York University Press, 1983.

Roth, John K., ed. *Ethics After the Holocaust: Perspectives, Critiques, and Responses*. St. Paul, Minn.: Paragon House, 1999.

Rubenstein, Betty Rogers, and Michael Berenbaum, eds. *What Kind of God? Essays in Honor of Richard L. Rubenstein*. Lanham, Md.: University Press of America, 1995.

Sontag, Frederick, and John K. Roth. "The Death of God in American Theology." In *The American Religious Experience: The Roots, Trends, and Future of American Theology*. New York: Harper & Row, 1972.

Zvielli, Alexander. "Routine Murder." *Jerusalem Post*, November 6, 1992, p. 26.

—*John K. Roth*

Albert Speer
His Battle with Truth

Author: Gitta Sereny (1921-   )
First published: 1995
Genre: Nonfiction
Subgenre: Biography

Sereny's biography of Albert Speer is concerned primarily with the years 1933-1946 and focuses on the factors in Speer's character that prevented him from admitting to the world that he had known about the systematic murder of Jews before 1946.

Principal personages:
Albert Speer (1905-1981), an architect who was the German minister of armaments from 1942 to the fall of the Third Reich and was a close confidant of Adolf Hitler
Adolf Hitler (1889-1945), the chancellor of Germany, 1933-1945
Margarete Speer, Albert's wife
Annemarie Kempf, Speer's secretary
Rudolf Wolters, an architect who was Speer's friend and chronicler
Karl Hanke, the state secretary in the German ministry of propaganda and later gauleiter of Lower Silesia who greatly aided Speer's rise in the Nazi hierarchy
Joseph Goebbels (1897-1945), the German minister of propaganda, 1933-1945
Hermann Göring (1893-1946), the German interior minister and minister of aviation, 1933-1945, and Hitler's designated successor
Rudolf Hess (1894-1987), the deputy leader of the Nazi Party
Heinrich Himmler (1900-1945), the commander of the Schutzstaffel (SS) and Gestapo
Martin Bormann (1900-1945), Hitler's secretary and a great rival of Speer

Overview

Hungarian-born journalist and free-lance writer Gitta Sereny based this gossipy and critical biography of Albert Speer primarily on extensive interviews with Speer himself, his wife, and a host of individuals who knew him at some time during his life. She also made use of Speer's own writings, the memoirs and diaries of many people who had an influence on his life, and on extensive research in the archives of several countries. In a number of instances, the author uncritically accepts dubious assertions by the people she interviewed. Professional historians will be dismayed by her failure to provide exact citations for the sources of the many quotations she includes.

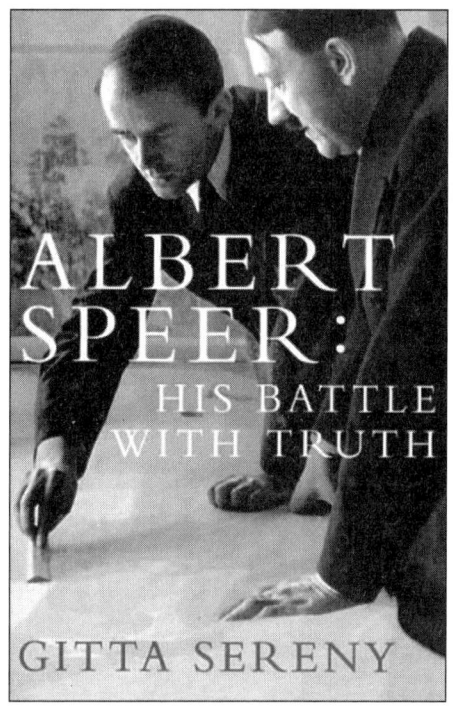

Albert Speer emerges from Sereny's pages as a complex, clever, charming man of considerable genius with a hopelessly flawed character that he never managed to overcome. According to Sereny, Speer's flawed character prevented him from ever admitting to the world that he knew about the assembly-line murder of Jews before the revelations at the Nuremberg Trials, even though he must have known about the "final solution" no later than 1943. Despite the knowledge that Sereny insists he had, Speer continued to serve Hitler's regime until the end. His genius in organizing the German armaments industries prolonged the war by at least a year and resulted in hundreds of thousands if not millions of deaths, according to the author.

Sereny's biography devotes few pages to Speer's early life. Born into an upper-middle-class family in Heidelberg in 1905, Speer enjoyed all the advantages wealth could provide. The author briefly recounts Speer's childhood, portraying it as unhappy despite his affluent upbringing. The unhappiness stemmed from Speer's conviction that he was not well loved by his parents, and from the bullying he endured from his brothers. Sereny suggests that his lonely and loveless childhood contributed to the lack of compassion and ruthless ambition she sees as his most defining adult characteristics.

Speer's marriage and family life also receive only cursory coverage in Sereny's biography. According to Sereny, Speer's parents never approved of his wife Margarete, whom they considered of a lower station. The author suggests that Speer married in part as an act of rebellion. Despite the five children she bore him, Sereny portrays Margarete as having had little influence on Speer's career. According to the author, Speer was incapable of showing real affection to his children, most of whom became estranged from him, or for his wife. Sereny's Speer was much too intent on aggrandizing himself to devote any appreciable time to his family, either before or after his confinement in Spandau prison. Sereny writes that only shortly before his death did Speer form a close human relationship—with a much younger woman.

Sereny writes little about Speer's university years during which he trained as an architect, first at Karlsruhe, then at the Munich Institute of Technology, and finally as a graduate student in Berlin studying with the famous architect Heinrich Tessenow. The author portrays Speer as being cushioned by his father's wealth from the hardships suffered by most students during the economic depression. Oddly, Sereny's compassionless Speer shared both his food and his living quarters freely with other students who were in need. In 1931, Speer attended a speech delivered by Adolf Hitler and became a member of the National Socialist German Workers' Party (NSDAP, or Nazis). According to the author, Speer joined the party not out of ideological conviction but because of his ambition and his fascination with Hitler. Speer's life changed forever.

Most of Sereny's biography focuses on the next period of Speer's life: his actions as a member of the Nazi Party and as an important functionary in Hitler's government. She also explores at great length Speer's strange relationship with Hitler, whom she surprisingly portrays in many cases as a likable and relatively benign (if tyrannical) father-figure. Throughout her account of the fifteen years Speer served the Nazis, Sereny constantly explores Speer's attitudes about the Jews, his reactions to the Nazis' treatment of them, and his knowledge of their ultimate fate.

Sereny portrays the relationship between Speer and Hitler as one of subconscious and unfilled sexual love. Driven by his desire to please Hitler and his lust for power, Speer became oblivious to the crimes of the Nazi regime and to the suffering of the millions of workers under his authority. As the overseer of Germany's war industries, Speer sacrificed the welfare of German and foreign workers in a spectacularly successful attempt to increase the production of weapons of war. Sereny writes that Speer must have been aware of the brutal treatment, inhuman working conditions, and insufficient food and medical treatment that many of the millions of (often involuntary) foreign workers later related at war crimes trials. Sereny insists that he must also have known about the attempted extermination of the Jews, not only because of his high position in the government but also because of his intimate knowledge of the German economy. Sereny argues that the diversion of trains to take the Jews of Europe to the extermination camps in Poland and the huge quantities of material diverted to the camps could not have escaped Speer's notice. Nevertheless, Speer did little to alleviate the plight of the workers and failed to protest or intervene on behalf of the Jews. Sereny identifies these two omissions as Speer's greatest crimes, both of which stemmed from his love for Hitler and his lust for power.

The most effective and informative sections of Sereny's book deal with the personalities of the Nazi leaders and the power struggles and political infighting between them. The author shows that Speer himself became a master of political intrigue and as amoral as his rivals in his efforts to accumulate power and please his master. The leading figures of the Third Reich (and the women in their lives) emerge from Sereny's pages as having been without political or moral convictions and completely dominated by the personality of Hitler. Although all of the surviving leaders denied any knowledge of the fate of the Jews of Europe during World War II at the subsequent war crimes trials, Sereny expends many pages attempting to prove that all of them not only knew what was going on but also were willing participants.

Sereny provides only a brief account of Speer's attempts during the last year of the war to prevent the implementation of the "scorched earth" policy ordered by Hitler to slow his enemies' advance. She also largely dismisses Speer's supposed plan to assassinate Hitler as having never been serious. The author gives the impression that Speer's defiance of Hitler's orders only began after he realized that the war was lost and were part of a clever plan by Speer to save his own life once Germany's enemies triumphed and began meting out punishment. Sereny develops this same theme through her account of the trial of the "major war criminals" before the International Military Tribunal at Nuremberg in 1946.

During the trial, Speer alone of the twenty-two defendants accepted responsibility for the crimes of the Nazi regime, while denying any knowledge of specific atrocities. In his later writings, Speer attributed his admission of guilt to a belated realization that Hitler was a criminal, that the German government had perpetrated criminal actions, and that as a member of that government he himself was guilty. Sereny strongly suggests that Speer admitted responsibility for German crimes not because of conscience or, as he himself wrote later, to divert guilt from the German people. Instead, his admission was part of a desperate strategy he adopted to escape the gallows. Her evidence for this thesis was Speer's refusal—

throughout the rest of his life—to admit personal knowledge before 1946 of any specific crime or atrocity committed by the Nazi government. The author implies that Speer succeeded in tricking the tribunal into giving him a sentence (twenty years' imprisonment) much too lenient considering his involvement in Nazi criminality.

Sereny's book contains little concerning Speer's years of incarceration at Spandau prison in Berlin. She bases her account of that lengthy period of Speer's life largely on the letters he wrote to his family and others, the first draft of his 1970 best-selling book *Inside the Third Reich*, and interviews with two clergymen who attempted to help Speer overcome what he admitted were shortcomings in his own character. Sereny apparently believes that Speer's constant denunciations of Hitler and his supposed quest to become "good" were part of Speer's carefully conceived plan to rehabilitate his reputation once his prison term ended in 1966.

Sereny scatters comments about Speer's personality and life after Spandau throughout her biography, drawing from her many interviews with him. Some sections of the book are almost stream-of-consciousness excerpts from the interviews with Speer and others that confusingly deal with many different segments of Speer's life. Sereny describes him during the post-Spandau years as a charming and brilliant man who sought public attention to proclaim at the same time his guilt and his innocence. Friendly but withdrawn, he stubbornly refused to acknowledge that he knew about the fate of the Jews before Nuremberg. Sereny feels that such an acknowledgment would have done much to still the clamor from a growing element in world society that insists that there was no official or systematic attempt to exterminate the Jews by the German government during World War II. Sereny denounces these "revisionist" historians in her book. She points out that Speer was disgusted by what he termed this attempt to perpetrate a new "war guilt lie" to mislead yet another generation.

Sereny's biography convincingly portrays Speer as a complex, cold, calculating, brilliant man whose desire for power and psychological domination by Hitler blinded him to the brutality of the regime he served. Her accounts of Speer's relationships with the leading personalities of the Third Reich provide perceptive insights into the nature of the Nazi regime. She also persuades that Speer admitted responsibility for Nazi actions at Nuremberg and later not out of conviction or true remorse but in order to save his life and rehabilitate his reputation. She ultimately fails, however, to prove her major contention: that Speer had personal knowledge before Nuremberg of the murder of European Jews. The documentary and testimonial evidence she presents seem to show that Speer, too overwhelmed with the burdens of his responsibilities to read the many clues concerning the fate of the Jews, remained ignorant of the true situation until confronted with the evidence at Nuremberg.

Sources for Further Study

Fest, Joachim. *Albert Speer: Conversations with Hitler's Architect*. Translated by Patrick Camiller. Malden, Mass.: Polity Press, 2007.

Hudson, Christopher. "Exposed at Last: Speer, the Architect of Lies." *Evening Standard*, May 13, 2005, p. 16.

Koonz, Claudia. "Blind by Choice." *The New York Times Book Review*, October 8, 1995, p. 711.

Lehman-Haupt, Christopher. "A Psychological Portrait of a Witness to Hitler." *The New York Times*, October 9, 1995, p. C18.

Myers, Kevin. "Speer Knew: It Was All in the Papers." *Sunday Telegraph*, May 22, 2005, p. 20.

Weintraub, Stanley. "Bookshelf: Hitler's Architect and the Pleasure of Power." *The Wall Street Journal*, September 25, 1995, p. A17.

Wheatcroft, Geoffrey. "Hidden Truths About the Mary Bell Author: Gitta Sereny's Subjects Range from Nazi War Criminals to Mary Bell, but in Many Ways Her Own Life Story Is Just as Fascinating—and Morally Ambivalent." *Daily Mail*, May 1, 1995, p. 11.

—Paul Madden

All Rivers Run to the Sea
Memoirs

AUTHOR: Elie Wiesel (1928-   )
FIRST PUBLISHED: *Tous les fleuves vont à la mer*, 1994 (English translation, 1995)
GENRE: Nonfiction
SUBGENRE: Memoir

Haunted by the Holocaust but determined to bear witness for the dead and the living, Wiesel remembers the persons and places, the traditions and tragedies, and the dreams, hopes, and questions that have governed his life and thought.

PRINCIPAL PERSONAGES:
Elie Wiesel (b. 1928), a Jewish writer and survivor of the Holocaust
Sarah Wiesel, Elie's mother
Shlomo Wiesel, Elie's father
Hilda,
Bea, and
Tsiporah, Elie's sisters
Rabbi Israel, Elie's parents' rabbi

OVERVIEW

Autobiographies pour out names and faces. Memoirs are detailed by encounters large and small. While conforming to those conventions, this book is unconventional. It is distinctive not only because Elie Wiesel recalls extraordinary encounters and remembers striking names and faces but also because it shows how his remarkable moral and spiritual outlook emerged from the twentieth century's greatest darkness.

Intertwined, three fundamental facts pulse at the heart of Wiesel's story. He is a Jew, a writer, and a survivor of the Holocaust, which was the systematic, state-sponsored persecution and murder of nearly six million Jews by Nazi Germany and its collaborators. Wiesel weaves the particularity of his life into the fabric of twentieth century history, which has been ripped by unprecedented mass murder and torn by immeasurable human suffering.

One day when he was eight years old, Wiesel accompanied his mother, Sarah, when she went to see her rabbi. After speaking to her in the boy's presence, Rabbi Israel spent time with him alone. What was he learning about Judaism? the old man wanted to know. After the young Wiesel responded, Rabbi Israel spoke to his mother again—this time privately.

When Sarah Wiesel emerged from that encounter, she was sobbing. Try as he might, Elie Wiesel never persuaded her to say why. Twenty-five years later, and almost by chance, he learned the reason for his mother's tears. Anshel Feig, a relative in whom Wiesel's mother had confided on that day, told him that Elie's mother had heard the old rabbi say, "Sarah, know that your son will become a *gadol b'Israel*, a great man in Israel, but neither you nor I will live to see the day. That's why I'm telling you now."

Wiesel tells this story early in his memoirs. It reveals much about him and sets the autobiography's tone. For Wiesel, stories are important because they raise questions. Wiesel's questions, in turn, lead not so much to answers as to other stories. Typically, autobiographies settle issues; memoirs put matters to rest. Wiesel, however, has a different plan for this book as well as for its projected second volume. His storytelling invites readers to share his questions, but the questions his stories provoke do not produce indifference and despair. Instead they lead to more stories and further questions that encourage protest against those conditions.

Wiesel's life makes him wonder—sometimes in anger, frequently in awe, often in sadness, but always in ways that intensify memory so that bitterness can be avoided, hatred resisted, truth defended, and justice served. The stories within Wiesel's story can affect his readers in the same way.

Rabbi Israel was right about Elie Wiesel. The shy, religious Jewish boy grew up to become an acclaimed author, a charismatic speaker, and a dedicated humanitarian. In 1986, he received the Nobel Peace Prize, one of the world's highest honors. In his particularity as a Jew—it includes dedicated compassion for Jews who suffered under Soviet rule and passionate loyalty to Israel—as well as in his universality as a human being, Wiesel qualifies as "a great man."

Rabbi Israel was also right about Sarah Wiesel. Neither she nor Rabbi Israel, nor Wiesel's beloved father, Shlomo, lived to see Elie's major accomplishments. Wiesel insists that none of his success is worth the violence unleashed, the losses incurred, and the innocence demolished in a lifetime measured not simply by past, present, and future, but through time broken before, during, and after Auschwitz. He would be the first to say that it would have been better if his cherished little sister, Tsiporah, had lived and all of his many books had gone unwritten, for in that case the Holocaust might not have happened. Wiesel's honors weigh heavily on him. They are inseparable from a question that will not go away: How can I justify my survival when my family and my world were destroyed?

Wiesel did not expect to survive the Holocaust. Ever since, he has wondered how and why he did. At the same time, his Jewish tradition and his own experience underscore that events never happen purely by accident. And yet—Wiesel's two favorite words—especially where the Holocaust is concerned, the fact that events are linked by more than chance does not mean that everything can be explained or understood, at least not completely. Only by testifying about what happened in the Holocaust, only by bearing witness as truthfully and persistently as possible about what was lost, does Wiesel find that his survival makes sense. The sense that it makes, however, can never be enough to remove the scarring question marks that the Holocaust has burned forever into humanity's history and God's creation.

Wiesel's memoirs are not triumphal vindications. They are drenched in sadness and melancholy. Yet sadness and melancholy, and the despair to which they might yield, are not their last words. Out of them Wiesel forges something much more affirmative. Optimism, faith, hope—those words are too facile to contain his outlook. Defiance, resistance, protest—those terms come closer, but even they have to be supplemented by an emphasis on friendship, dialogue, reaching out to others, helping people in need, working to make people free, and striving to mend the world.

This book's greatest contribution is ethical and spiritual. It shows how Wiesel found ways to transform his suffering into sharing, his pain into caring. These transformations do not mean that Wiesel forgives any more than he forgets. The Holocaust was too immense, too devastating, to be redeemed by forgiveness that God or anyone else can give. Because the world has been shattered so severely, Wiesel believes that the moral imperative is to do all that one can to repair it. Otherwise, hatred and death win victories they never deserve.

In 1964, Elie Wiesel revisited his hometown. For more than one reason, his return to Sighet, that place in Eastern Europe where Sarah Wiesel and Rabbi Israel had their fateful conversation, was anything but easy. After his liberation from Buchenwald in April of 1945, Wiesel had gone to France, where he eventually became a reporter for an Israeli newspaper. Years later, his journalistic work took him to New York, where he became an American citizen.

Sighet was far away. The distance, however, did not involve mileage alone. Once a part of Romania, then annexed by Hungary, and once more under Romanian control, Sighet stood behind the Iron Curtain in the 1960's. Cold War politics made the journey difficult and dangerous. Nevertheless, Wiesel was determined to go back to Sighet, "the town beyond the wall," as one of his best novels calls it.

Memory drew him there, even though Wiesel already knew what his visit would confirm: Sighet no longer existed—at least not as it was when he was born there in 1928, or as he had known the place until he left it at the age of fifteen in 1944. More than time had passed. People had come and gone, but that fact only began to tell Sighet's story. Those things happen everywhere, but the way they happened in Sighet, the particularity and enormity of what happened there and in thousands of places like it, made Sighet's disappearance so devastating that the world itself could never again be what it was before. Sighet vanished in the Holocaust's night and fog. Only traces remained of what once had been. Sighet's streets looked familiar to Wiesel in 1964, although one called the Street of Jews contained apartments that seemed as modest as they now were empty. His boyhood eyes must have been unaware of the poverty that many of Sighet's Jews experienced.

The motion picture house still existed. The family house still stood. It had not been sold but taken; strangers occupied it. Wiesel found that Jewish cemetery. He lit candles at his grandfather's grave. Elsewhere, Sighet was filled with living people, but Wiesel's hometown was gone. As the Germans liked to say twenty years before, Sighet had become *judenrein*. Along with hundreds of thousands of Hungarian Jews, the largest remaining community of European Jews that had not yet been decimated by the Nazis, the Jews of Sighet were deported to Auschwitz in the spring of 1944.

Wiesel and his two older sisters, Hilda and Bea, survived the Holocaust, but most of Sighet's Jews, including his father, mother, and little sister did not. Few of the survivors went back to Sighet after the Nazis surrendered in May, 1945. Poignantly, Wiesel reflects on all that was lost as he describes his visit to one of the few synagogues that was still open two decades later. Stacked inside were hundreds of books—Wiesel calls them "holy books"—that had been taken from abandoned Jewish homes and stored there. He discovered some that had belonged to him. Tucked inside one were "some yellowed, withered sheets of paper in a book of Bible commentaries." Wiesel recognized the handwriting they contained. It was his. Summing up his sadness, his memoirs observe that the finding of those pages is "a commentary on the commentaries I had written at the age of thirteen or fourteen." This story, the existence of yellow, withered sheets of paper, a boy's reflections on the Bible—all are part of a world that disappeared. Wiesel seeks to make it live again through memory, testimony, and writing. The episodes he records make questions explode: Why did the Allies refuse to bomb the railways to Auschwitz? Why did Wiesel's family not accept the help of their housekeeper, Maria? One of the very few Christians in Sighet who offered assistance to Sighet's Jews, she might have hidden the family successfully. Why was the world so indifferent to Jewish suffering? Why was God?

Wiesel's narrative does not follow a strictly chronological form. His story does not fit the usual style of beginning-middle-end. The memories of his life circle around one another too much for that. From time to time, Wiesel breaks this commentary on himself even further by reflecting on his dreams. In one of them, the Wiesel family has gathered for a holiday celebration. Elie is asked to sing, but he cannot remember the traditional songs. He is asked for a story, but the stories have been forgotten, too. "Grandfather," Wiesel calls out in his dream, "help me, help me find my memory!" Astonished, Wiesel's grandfather looks back at him. "You're not a child anymore," he says. "You're almost as old as I am."

Elie Wiesel has lived for a long time. He has experienced and remembered more than most people, but he wrote profoundly about forgetting. If we stop remembering, he warns, we stop being. Wiesel is older now than most of his extended family who perished in the Holocaust. Taking his memoir's title from the biblical book of Ecclesiastes, which speaks of how generations come and go and of how the eye is not satisfied with seeing, nor the ear filled with hearing, Wiesel sounds a characteristically mystical note as he considers how all rivers run to the sea.

Beginning in obscurity, streams of experience and memory rush forth. As they grow and merge, life's currents become a flood that eventually pours into the ocean's awesome depth. Like Elie Wiesel's memoirs, the sea does not yield all of its secrets. Instead its storms rage, its waves crash, its tides ebb and flow, and there are moments of beauty, calm, and silence, too. Through it all, the sea endures, which is not an answer but an invitation to more stories and to their questions about how and why.

Sources for Further Study

Berenbaum, Michael. *Elie Wiesel: God, the Holocaust, and the Children of Israel*. West Orange, N.J.: Behrman House, 1994.

Berger, Alan L. *Crisis and Covenant: The Holocaust in American Jewish Fiction*. Albany: State University of New York Press, 1985.

Brown, Robert McAfee. *Elie Wiesel: Messenger to All Humanity*. Notre Dame, Ind.: University of Notre Dame Press, 1983.

Cargas, Harry James. *Conversations with Elie Wiesel*. South Bend, Ind.: Justice Books, 1992.

Ezrahi, Sidra DeKoven. *By Words Alone: The Holocaust in Literature*. Chicago: University of Chicago Press, 1980.

Gornick, Vivian. "The Rhetoric of Witness." *The Nation* 261, no. 22 (December 25, 1995): 839.

Horowitz, Sara. *Voicing the Void: Muteness and Memory in Holocaust Fiction*. Albany: State University of New York Press, 1997.

Kakutani, Michiko. "Remembering as a Duty of Those Who Survived." *The New York Times*, December 5, 1995, p. A19.

Kolbert, Jack. *The Worlds of Elie Wiesel: An Overview of His Career and His Major Themes*. Selinsgrove, Pa.: Susquehanna University Press, 2001.

Langer, Lawrence L. *The Holocaust and the Literary Imagination*. New Haven, Conn.: Yale University Press, 1975.

Patterson, David. *The Shriek of Silence: A Phenomenology of the Holocaust Novel*. Lexington: University Press of Kentucky, 1992.

Phillips, Melanie. "Bearing Witness: Holocaust Survivor Elie Wiesel Explains the Importance of Memory to Melanie Phillips." *The Observer*, June 9, 1996, p. 16.

Rittner, Carol, ed. *Elie Wiesel: Between Memory and Hope*. New York: New York University Press, 1990.

Rosen, Alan, ed. *Celebrating Elie Wiesel: Stories, Essays, Reflections*. Notre Dame, Ind.: University of Notre Dame Press, 1998.

Roth, John K. *A Consuming Fire: Encounters with Elie Wiesel and the Holocaust*. Atlanta, Ga.: John Knox Press, 1979.

Stern, Ellen N. *Elie Wiesel: Witness for Life*. New York: Ktav, 1982.

Wiesel, Elie, and Richard D. Heffner. *Conversations with Elie Wiesel*. Edited by Thomas J. Vinciguerra. New York: Schocken Books, 2001.

Zesmer, David M. "Not Quite an Icon: The Complex Private Self of Holocaust Survivor Elie Wiesel." *Chicago Tribune*, December 31, 1995, p. 1.

—*John K. Roth*

And the Sea Is Never Full
Memoirs, 1969-

AUTHOR: Elie Wiesel (1928-   )
FIRST PUBLISHED: *Et la mer n'est pas remplie*, 1996 (English translation, 1999)
GENRE: Nonfiction
SUBGENRE: Memoir

In his second volume of memoirs, Wiesel explores the paths that took him through the Nazi concentration camp at Auschwitz to international recognition as a humanitarian, influential writer, and post-Holocaust interpreter of Jewish tradition.

PRINCIPAL PERSONAGES:
Elie Wiesel (b. 1928), a Jewish writer and survivor of the Holocaust
Marion Erster Rose, Elie's wife
Elisha Wiesel, Elie and Marion's son
Sarah Wiesel, Elie's mother
Shlomo Wiesel, Elie's father
Hilda,
Bea, and
Tsiporah, Elie's sisters

OVERVIEW

"All rivers run to the sea," says Ecclesiastes, "and the sea is never full." Elie Wiesel took the title of his first volume of memoirs from that biblical verse's initial phrase. *Tous les fleuves vont à la mer* (1994; *All Rivers Run to the Sea*, 1995) ended where its sequel begins, with his marriage to Marion Erster Rose in Jerusalem on April 2, 1969. On June 6, 1972, their son Elisha was born. Both events, life-changing and joyful ones for Wiesel, figure prominently in his second volume, which also takes its title from Ecclesiastes. That title theme—the sea is never full—identifies the rhythm that governs this autobiography: Wiesel's memoirs contain amazing success stories, but each is linked to twentieth century darkness, to a labyrinth of heartbreaking memories that breed unanswerable questions. Exploring those tensions in compelling ways, Wiesel's memoirs provide moral guidance at the dawn of a new century.

Wiesel's life brims with accomplishment: more than thirty widely read books, distinguished professorships, literary awards, and honorary degrees, the confidence of political leaders, the Nobel Peace Prize. His parents, Shlomo and Sarah, had the more modest dream that he would become a *rosh yeshiva*, the leader of a Jewish school where the Talmud is studied. Assaulted by Nazi Germany's fanatical anti-Semitism, the world of Eastern European Jewry that spawned their hope no longer exists. Nevertheless, Wiesel fulfilled a version of his parents' longing; few persons have done more to encourage the post-Holocaust study of Jewish texts and traditions. At the time of his birth in 1928, however, it could scarcely have been imagined that events would take him from his humble origins in Sighet, Romania, to the international acclaim that he achieved seventy years later. Yet—that theme is among Wiesel's favorites—the sea is never full, for the events that took Wiesel to fame include what he calls "the Event"—the Holocaust, Nazi Germany's attempt to annihilate the Jewish people.

Hasidism, Wiesel's best-loved Jewish tradition, emphasizes the celebration of life's goodness. It also recognizes what Wiesel understands profoundly; namely, that life's preciousness must be acclaimed in spite of the forces of hate, injustice, indifference, and violence that push humanity to the brink of hopelessness and despair. So the sea is never full. However much Wiesel has done, whatever his successes may be, he cannot forget that his status in the high-powered worlds of New York and Washington, Paris and Moscow, Oslo and Jerusalem, is not so far removed from the boyhood home that he shared with his older sisters, Bea and Hilda (they, too, survived the Holocaust), or from Auschwitz, where the Germans murdered his mother and his little sister Tsiporah, or from Buchenwald, where American troops liberated Wiesel but not before his father perished there.

Wiesel works to sustain memory. "I am afraid of forgetting," he writes, and thus a single photograph hangs above his writing desk. "It shows my parents' home in Sighet," he explains. "When I look up, that is what I see. And it seems to be telling me: 'Do not forget where you came from.'" In one of the book's most moving episodes, Wiesel describes a journey in July, 1995. He takes his son Elisha and his nephew Steve Jackson to see where their grandparents had lived in Sighet and then guides them on the memory path to Auschwitz. Grief and joy, loss and promise mix and mingle. "Ours is the tree of an old Jewish family whose roots touch those of Rashi and King David," Wiesel recalls. "And look: Its branches refuse to wither." That refusal comes in spite of what memory recalls. Wiesel brings Elisha and Steve to Birkenau, the killing center at Auschwitz. It was in Birkenau, 1944, that Wiesel discovered what he calls "evil that saps all joy." Nevertheless, he testifies, the sapping, let alone the elimination, of joy must not have the last word.

Above all, "death is never a solution," a point that Wiesel registers as he contemplates the apparent suicide of Primo Levi, another Holocaust survivor who became a brilliant writer. Although Wiesel says that he understands Levi's ending, Wiesel's memoir seems to rule out suicide as an option for him. Instead, his life stays charged with energy that shows little sign of waning. True, he travels less enthusiastically. Yes, he guards his writing time more jealously. Although time is not on his side, he still envisions books to write; he alludes to works in progress, a study of his teachers and a novel about judges. He speaks of doors still to be opened, secrets yet to be discovered, questions that have not been fully pursued, among them why he remained so reluctant to talk with his sisters about their Holocaust experiences or to speak more explicitly, more often, about the Event itself.

These unfinished and perhaps unending quests often revolve around Wiesel's father, whose presence surrounds the book. Frequently, that presence emerges in italicized meditations—often they involve dreams—in which Wiesel's father appears to him. The two hold silent conversations that raise more questions than they answer. The questions usually intensify Wiesel's uneasiness about whether he is living up to his own imperative: "For the dead *and* the living, we must bear witness."

His prose typically spare and lean, Wiesel favors a minimalist style that permits the silence created by what is not said to provoke thought that goes beyond the written or spoken word. *And the Sea Is Never Full* contains no observation more understated than the one expressed in a simple sentence that says: "I have lived a few lives." One of them involves the United States Holocaust Memorial Museum in Washington, D.C. That remarkable institution—it receives millions of visitors annually—bears Wiesel's imprint in more ways than one. Not only are the words of his imperative, quoted above, inscribed on the museum's walls, but also from 1979 to 1986 he oversaw the planning that led to the museum's opening on April 19, 1993, the fiftieth anniversary of the Warsaw Ghetto Uprising.

Wiesel recalls the museum's birth pangs. They ranged from factional disputes and personal rivalries to crucial debates about "the specificity or universality of the Holocaust." Wiesel's position on that point has been unwavering: Far from being "just another event," the Holocaust is unique, "the ultimate event, the ultimate mystery." It is "a Jewish tragedy with universal implications" that are best examined through a focus on the Event's Jewish particularity. Wiesel did not win all the battles he fought during the museum's creation, but without him, it would not exist. His feelings about this success include ambivalence. The museum, he thinks, tries "to illustrate too much." He preferred "a more sober, more humble edifice, one that would suggest the unspoken, the silence, the secret," and thereby leave visitors saying: "Now I know how little I know." Nevertheless, he acknowledges that the museum is "undeniably impressive." It plays, he affirms, "a pedagogical role of the first order."

While Wiesel led the museum planning, his public impact emerged in two other notable ways. On April 19, 1985, he went to the White House to receive the rarely awarded Congressional Gold Medal. After Ronald Reagan bestowed it on him, Wiesel appealed to the president: He must not go to the German military cemetery at Bitburg, where the dead include members of the Schutzstaffel (SS), the elite who carried out Nazi Germany's so-called final solution to the "Jewish question." For some time, controversy had swirled about Reagan's acceptance of Chancellor Helmut Kohl's invitation to visit Germany on the fortieth anniversary of the end of World War II in Europe. At the award ceremony, Wiesel said to Reagan, Bitburg "is not your place, Mr. President. Your place is with the victims of the SS." Probably Wiesel's retrospective judgment is an exaggeration—he thinks that his White House speech "touched a thousand times more people than I had with all my previous writings and speeches"—but even though it was unsuccessful, his plea to Reagan (it was shared with the White House in advance) became not only a media event but also a moral moment that made Wiesel more visible than ever.

Less than two years later, Wiesel's stature as a defender of justice and human rights—his untiring support for oppressed Jews in the Soviet Union is only one example—was magnified by the Nobel Peace Prize, which he received in Oslo, Norway, on December 9, 1986. Wiesel recalls listening to Egil Aarvik, the chair of the Nobel Committee. As he wondered silently whether Aarvik could really be speaking about him, Wiesel saw himself again in his parents' house. His son at his side, Wiesel accepted the prize, but before he could deliver his response, he saw his father and relived, for a moment, his death in Buchenwald. His father's last moments had included cries to which Wiesel could not respond because he would have been beaten to death. Wiesel's memoirs make clear that his protests against injustice and indifference, his passion to be with those who suffer, his emphasis on friendship are all intensified by the memory of those cries, which "tore me apart" then and "tear me apart still."

Early in this book, Wiesel remarks that "the introvert will yield to the extrovert." The forecast proves correct as Wiesel writes at length about his encounters with influential figures around the globe. The list is as long as it is illustrious: Mikhail Gorbachev and Henry Kissinger, Jimmy Carter and Bill Clinton, as well as Israeli leaders such as Golda Meir, Yitzhak Rabin, and Shimon Peres. Just as Israel and particularly Jerusalem hold a special place in Wiesel's heart, which leads the media to keep waving "the Israel-Arab problem" and questions about Palestinians at him, France and especially Paris are also dear to him. France was his post-Holocaust haven. He writes in French. Parisian publishers get the first options on his books. For years, moreover, the French president François Mitterrand was among Wiesel's best friends. Their friendship, however, did not last, for it eventually became apparent that Mitterrand had ties to the Vichy regime, which collaborated with the Nazi occupation of France and expedited the deportation of French Jews to Auschwitz. The full extent of that story broke in 1994 with revelations of Mitterrand's support of René Bousquet, the French chief of police who had organized the deportations of French Jewry. As Wiesel recalls Mitterrand's death on January 9, 1996, he takes no joy in his passing or in the demise of their friendship. Both leave haunting questions summed up by "why?" That most human of questions is one that Wiesel asks again and again. He seeks to understand where it leads, especially when "why?" interrogates the God with whom he argues and against whom he protests in the tension of his post-Holocaust Jewish faith.

Another encounter with a French friend raises additional questions for Wiesel, among them, "What can I say to a converted Jew?" The converted Jew in question is not inconsequential. He is Cardinal Jean-Marie Lustiger, the archbishop of Paris. Not least because the cardinal's mother died at Auschwitz, Wiesel wonders about Lustiger's Christian identity, for Wiesel cannot forget that the Holocaust took place in Christian Europe. Although it pains Wiesel that Lustiger calls himself a "fulfilled Jew," they engage in sustained dialogue—a word and practice that Wiesel values—and their friendship grows. Lustiger's Christianity remains robust, but he stops calling himself a "fulfilled Jew," and his commitment to Jewish causes and to Israel deepens. Wiesel finds Lustiger's presence disturbing, and not only because of his conversion. Lustiger, he says, is "an ally of all those who militate against fanaticism and injustice wherever they are found." Against tough odds, both men create disturbances that make the world more humane. Built on persisting and yet respected differences, their friendship endures.

Upon finishing this book, its readers understand that they have spent time with an exceptional storyteller. Whether the narratives are about contemporary political leaders, Wiesel's beloved Hasidic teachers such as Rebbe Nahman of Bratzlav, or the biblical figures he brings to life in books and lectures, Wiesel's stories always highlight ethics. It is fitting, therefore, that these memoirs include a story about Adam, the Bible's human father of us all, who provoked God to ask "*Ayekha*, where are you?" when Adam fled after eating the forbidden fruit. As Wiesel tells the story, God knew Adam's whereabouts, but the story's moral insight depends on the Hebrew word *Ayekha*, which means: "Where do you stand in this world? What is your place in history? What have you done with your life?" These are questions that Wiesel asks himself and his readers as well. His ways of doing so in *And the Sea Is Never Full* make this book significant, as humanity begins a century more full of promise and also of greater potential for destruction than any other.

Sources for Further Study

Carroll, James. "Witness." *The New York Times Book Review*, February 2, 2000, p. 10.

Jacoby, Jeff. "Memoirs of a Man with One Foot Still in Auschwitz." *Boston Globe*, April 3, 2000, p. A15.

Kolbert, Jack. *The Worlds of Elie Wiesel: An Overview of His Career and His Major Themes*. Selinsgrove, Pa.: Susquehanna University Press, 2001.

Rosen, Alan, ed. *Celebrating Elie Wiesel: Stories, Essays, Reflections*. Notre Dame, Ind.: University of Notre Dame Press, 1998.

Rosenfeld, Albert H. "A Commitment to Memory." *New Leader* 82, no. 15 (December 13-27, 1999): 24.

Tugend, Tom. "The Burden of Memory." *Jerusalem Post*, December 10, 1999, p. 12B.

Wiesel, Elie, and Richard D. Heffner. *Conversations with Elie Wiesel*. Edited by Thomas J. Vinciguerra. New York: Schocken Books, 2001.

—*John K. Roth*

"The Angel of History"

AUTHOR: Carolyn Forché (1950-   )
FIRST PUBLISHED: 1988 (revised and collected in *The Angel of History*, 1994)
GENRE: Poetry
SUBGENRES: Meditation; war poetry

The mental and emotional work of comprehending shapes Forché's poem, which recounts the horrors of war and the Holocaust-related experiences of a European Jew through disconnected fragments as well as repeated phrases that create powerful rhythms.

Overview

Many of the eighteen sections of Carolyn Forché's poem "The Angel of History" recount recollections of World War II, particularly horrors of persecution, dislocation, and loss. The memories belong primarily to a war victim named Ellie, a deported Jew whom the speaker befriended and has known for a number of years. Ellie is the poem's magnetic center, attracting a variety of associations, some of which are clarified in notes. While the poem does not proceed chronologically, images and repeated phrases link the sections, some analytical, others narrative.

Indeed, the mental and emotional work of comprehending shapes the poem. The first section portrays the shock of knowledge on the speaker, and the next three sections elaborate. When children are destroyed in concentration camps, windows seem blank, games become ominous, sleep is impossible, and "the silence of God is God." The speaker's descent into the poem takes the form of disconnected fragments, but images of sea, light, vigilance, sleeplessness, fire, and memory create a matrix of emotion.

The next seven sections develop Ellie's experience—the loss of sons, her husband's death from cholera, her affliction with Saint Anthony's fire, the memory of her wedding dress, prompted by news of a plane crash. The events range from the war to her confinement much later in a French sanatorium. Her suffering and hatred of France have made her bitterly defiant. Homeless, sure that no country is safe, she believes that God is "insane," and she wants "to leave *life*." The speaker devotes herself to caring for Ellie, missing events of her own son's childhood. She laments that Ellie's predicament "is worse than memory, the open country of death."

Whereas many poems move toward resolution, the last seven sections of "The Angel of History" emphasize disturbance. The speaker is haunted by an undefinable presence ("as if someone not alive were watching"). An unidentified voice in section 12 recounts a nightmare of nonexistence in the process referring to sites of atrocities in El Salvador. The process of empathizing, recounted in the thirteenth section, affects the speaker to the extent that it seems "as if it were possible to go on living for someone else." The next two sections depict her disorientation. A letter from Ellie describes changes over eight years, but in the speaker's memory, Ellie does not change: "Here you live in an atelier."

The sixteenth section opens with a bitter definition—"Surely all art is the result of one's having been in danger, of having gone through an experience all the way to the end"—and recounts the terrifying evacuation of Beirut, Lebanon, where the women first meet and the speaker first tried to comfort Ellie. The repeated phrase "And it went on" suggests not only the rigors of the evacuation but also their lasting impact on the speaker. Just as her recollection of Ellie seems more vital than the more recent events Ellie describes in her letter, the speaker's mind has associated (her word is "confuse") Ellie and the entirety of wartime horror. Logic and language both falter, as difficulties in translation illustrate. Initially a polite inquiry, Ellie's "Est-ce que je vous dérange?" ("Am I disturbing you?") sounds here and in the final section like a bell tolling and assumes ironic resonance. The final section serves as a musical coda, reiterating emptiness and irreparability. The poem ends not with any final pronouncement but with the voice of Ellie, or perhaps a nameless victim, inquiring of the reader what the speaker has said.

One understands that the poem, while cohesive, cannot resolve. The horrors that Ellie (and countless others) endured radically alter the world and the way one speaks of it. Like writers who endured the horrors of Nazism—Nobel laureate Elie Wiesel, critic George Steiner, and poet Paul Celan, to name a few—the speaker becomes a witness even as she questions the adequacy of language to carry out her task.

"The Angel of History" looks unconventional. Its lines are sentences—one or more. Never enjambed, they cross the page like prose. Often the sections have divisions, but they have more to do with content than with stanza structure. On the other hand, "The Angel of History" *sounds* like a poem. The lines are lyrical and emotional, the limpid images a consistent synthesis of the beautiful and the ruined. Repeated phrases (repetends) create powerful rhythms and a sense of recurring dream.

That the subject is distant, even exotic, contributes to the mystique. That the poem is not continuous or linear may also contribute, at least at first. Forché is employing montage—the technique of combining disparate elements into a unified whole. In Forché's hands, montage means composing without violating essential qualities of the vision she describes in her notes on the poem as "polyphonic, broken, haunted, and in ruins, with no possibility of restoration." Individual images may not be surreal, but the world about which Forché writes and her discontinuous presentation of it may seem to be. Montage thus permits the reader to share in comprehending and feeling.

Few American poets of the past hundred years have dedicated themselves to witnessing great human rights catastrophes. From Forché's early interest in people's vibrancy and suffering has grown a poetry that applies a persuasive lyricism to some of the worst horrors of the age. In portraying what she observes (and what she feels while observing), Forché imparts immediacy and emotional intensity to vignettes of political significance. After observing the grisly prelude to El Salvador's civil war in the 1970's, she vowed, "I will live/ and living cry out until my voice is gone/ to its hollow of earth." The power and desperation of this declaration must be understood against the background of two realizations that Forché made at that time. First, language lacked the means to describe horrors she was seeing; in fact, the shock might well render one speechless. Second, among the societies and nations of the world, Americans were anomalous—protected yet confined in relative calm "like netted fish." Witnessing events in various parts of the world severed Forché from the complacency of her country and from the hope of comfort and rest.

Carolyn Forché. (Courtesy, Blue Flower Arts)

The travel—geographical and spiritual—that led to "The Angel of History" might be seen as fulfilling the legacy of Anna, the Slovak grandmother Forché mentions throughout her poetry, who had firsthand experience of World War II and became, in "What It Cost," the first other voice to speak an entire Forché poem. Forché's program, explicit by the end of the 1970's, has included intensive study of languages, translations of poets such as Salvadoran Claribel Alegría, and the production of the 1993 anthology *Against Forgetting: Twentieth-Century Poetry of Witness*. Thirteen years separate the publication of her second and third books of poems, a period that she calls "the muffling and silence of a decade." When the "wound" of her accumulated experiences opened, "The Angel of History" took her beyond the limits of the "first-person, free-verse, lyric-narrative of my earlier years."

Another valuable context for appreciating the poem is its epigraph, the German Jewish Marxist philosopher and critic Walter Benjamin's description of the angel of history's helplessness amid ruin. To the angel, history is "one single catastrophe which keeps piling wreckage." He would like to "make whole what has been smashed," but he is propelled "irresistibly . . . into the future." The storm blows from Paradise, indicating both the origin of the angel and the standard against which he views history. Moreover, the storm, carrying him backward, blows so hard that the angel cannot close his wings. That such a figure, longing to repair the infinite ruins, cannot free himself from the catastrophe suggests the immensity against which Forché's characters struggle.

When the modernist poet T. S. Eliot wrote of the horrors and disillusionment of World War I in his famous poem *The Waste Land* (1922), he chose urban European settings and pitted imagery of illness and dissipation against the vulnerable beauty of the month of April. Seven decades later, when Carolyn Forché wrote of the horrors of World War II in "The Angel of History," April was the time when "the tubercular man offers his cigarette and the snow falls, patiently, across the spring flowers." Eliot composed, from fragments of the world's cultures, allusions to traditions that he and many of his contemporaries believed had been destroyed by World War I. Forché, too, composes from fragments, but "The Angel of History" consists of individuals' memories. Her main character has survived the horrors of persecution, grief, dislocation, and continuing trauma, while the speaker herself has lived through the evacuation of Beirut.

The speaker's carrying and giving birth to her boy emphasize one of the great causes of Ellie's suffering—the loss of two sons. Forché also makes gestation and birth her metaphor for the immense importance of "The Angel of History" and the other poems published with it, referring to it as "a work which has desired its own bodying forth." In the language of the poem's opening, the speaker's time of "intimacy and sleep" has given way to a "vigilance" of the irreparable damages that the rest of the poem—as well as the book it initiates—reveals.

SOURCES FOR FURTHER STUDY

Bergen, Dan. "Muses of History: 'The Angel of History' by Carolyn Forché." *The Nation* 259, no. 13 (October 24, 1994): 464.

Cohen, Leslie. "Resisting Catastrophe." *Jerusalem Post*, May 1, 1997, p. 5.

Gregory, Eileen. "Poetry and Survival: H. D. and Carolyn Forché." In *H. D. and Poets After*, edited by Donna Krolik Hollenberg. Iowa City: University of Iowa Press, 2000.

Owens, Rochelle. Review of "The Angel of History," by Carolyn Forché. *World Literature Today* 68, no. 4 (Fall, 1994): 816.

Ratiner, Steven. "Carolyn Forché: The Poetry of Witness." In *Giving Their Word: Conversations with Contemporary Poets*, edited by Steven Ratiner. Amherst: University of Massachusetts Press, 2002.

—*Jay Paul*

Anya

Author: Susan Fromberg Schaeffer (1941-   )
First published: 1974
Genre: Novel
Subgenres: Historical fiction; young adult literature

This novel relates the story of Anya Savikin, a happy young Jewish woman who is studying to become a doctor until the Nazis invade Poland. After the invasion, Anya's world is destroyed, and she must struggle to survive.

Principal characters:
   Anya Savikin, a beautiful, studious young woman who is one of the first women and one of the first Jews to study medicine at her university
   Boris Savikin, Anya's vegetarian and atheist father, a businessman who prefers scholarly activities
   Rebecca Savikin, Anya's mother, a strong woman who is proud that her daughter is studying medicine
   Verushka Savikin, Anya's younger sister, who is a gifted pianist and more of a romantic than Anya
   Stajoe Lavinsky, Anya's first husband and the father of Ninushka
   Ninushka Lavinsky, Anya's daughter
   Rutkauskus Vishinskaya, a Catholic Lithuanian who gives Ninushka a home during the war
   Onucia Vishinskaya, Rutkauskus's wife, who Ninushka, for a while, thinks is her mother
   Max Meyers, Anya's second husband, an Auschwitz survivor
   Erdmann, a Jew disguised as a German soldier, who helps Anya escape from a concentration camp to find her daughter

Overview

The horror of World War II and Nazi persecution changes Anya Savikin's life and causes her to contemplate God's existence and why she survived when so many did not. Until the war, Anya lives an idyllic, family-oriented life in Vilno, Poland, with her Jewish parents, sister, and two brothers. Her family observes some Jewish traditions, more because of a love for the custom than because of strong religious beliefs.

To her parents' delight, Anya becomes a medical student. A telephone call in which her father warns her that some students are attacking and disfiguring the faces of Jewish girls makes Anya ponder about God: She decides it was fate and not an accident that allowed her father to hear about the incident and call to save her. She begins to believe in a supernatural power, although not necessarily the God about whom she has been taught. While in medical school, Anya marries Stajoe Lavinsky, a Polish Jew and engineer. They move to Warsaw, where Anya plans to continue school but never does. She has one miscarriage and then bears a daughter, Ninushka.

When the Germans invade Warsaw, Anya, Stajoe, and the baby leave for Vilno, but the situation is no better there. From her parents' house, Anya watches as her father is taken from the street and put in a truck to be sent to a concentration camp. She remembers that her father always said that justice does not exist in the world. Eventually, the Germans take the rest of the family to a concentration camp. Soon Anya is numbed by the murdering of her family: her sister, brothers, husband, and earlier her father. Only mothers and daughters are left: Rebecca, Anya, and Ninushka. Later Anya learns that young children are to be killed, so she manages to have her daughter taken from the camp and left on church steps. She finds out that a childless, Catholic Lithuanian couple, Rutkauskus and Onucia Vishinskaya, have her daughter and call her Luisa Vishinskaya.

Shortly after giving up Ninushka, Anya and her mother are forced from the concentration camp and separated. Recognizing that her mother is in the line of those too old or disabled to work and therefore most likely to be killed, Anya tries to join her but is stopped by a soldier. Rebecca shouts to remind Anya that she must live for her daughter, Ninushka. Anya is sent to another camp but escapes and makes contact with the man who has Ninushka. He takes her to her daughter, but Ninushka, young when taken from Anya, does not recognize her mother. After the Lithuanian Gestapo search for Jews in the Vishinskayas' house, Anya decides she must leave without Ninushka. Anya, again thinking of all the times she has escaped and survived, decides that a supernatural power that wants her to live must exist. She apologizes to her dead father, who was an atheist.

When the Soviets arrive to liberate the Poles from the Germans, Anya tries to make contact with the Vishinskayas to reclaim her daughter. She learns, however, that the Vishinskayas were shot for hiding Jews and that Ninushka is in an orphanage somewhere. When Anya finds Ninushka, she discovers that her daughter still does not know who she is. Eventually, however, Ninushka accepts that Anya is her mother, but Anya is aware that Ninushka is very different from what she might have been if the Jewish Anya had reared her without war instead of the Catholic Vishinskayas during the war. After learning that her husband's family was also killed, Anya decides to leave Europe and move to the United States. She and Ninushka settle in New York City, where Anya marries Max Meyers, a Jewish Auschwitz survivor.

Four important themes in *Anya* are the senselessness and horror of bigotry and war, the confirmation of the existence of a supernatural power, the special relationship between mothers and daughters, and women's need for work outside the family. The brutality of war is shown not only by the book's numerous details of atrocities committed by the Nazis against the Jews but also by changes in Anya's psyche: The trusting, optimistic young Anya becomes a suspicious, pessimistic older woman. Ultimately the changes in Anya convey that the survivors of war are victims as much as the dead; the war is never over for Anya, for she constantly relives the past.

Yet, ironically, this nightmare is what makes her believe in God. Anya thinks that her own survival is a miracle that only a supernatural power could have performed. Still, the war raises questions Anya cannot answer; she longs to find a purpose, a reason, for the war but cannot. The war also illuminates the importance of constancy and nurturance in the relationship between mother and daughter. Anya's relationship with her mother is compared with Ninushka's relationship with Anya. The former relationship, which was nurtured and bloomed before the war, is a warm and trusting one, but the latter, disrupted and distorted by war, is, at times, explosive and distant. Even so, Ninushka was Anya's motive for surviving, and, even after the war, Ninushka is the one Anya loves most.

Although family and child are most important to Anya, she also has a strong need for meaningful work. The necessity of work for women and the questioning of the female traditional role are highlighted by Anya's two marriages. The first marriage occurs when Anya is young and before the war; the girlish Anya unwittingly gives up the role of doctor for the roles of wife and mother. After the war and one marriage, Anya makes it clear to her prospective second husband that she is going back to school and must work. Her second husband, moreover, serving as a foil to her first husband, is supportive of Anya's desire for a career, and, therefore, Anya's second marriage is, in a sense, more successful than her first. The war, however, ruins Anya's chances to be a doctor, for courses taken in Europe cannot transfer to American schools. When Anya then chooses to be a nurse, she cannot, for she associates the pain she sees in the sick with the afflictions she saw during the war. The effect of the war on Anya is all-consuming.

Anya is poet and novelist Susan Fromberg Schaeffer's second novel. Schaeffer's novels often focus on women who are undergoing crises. Her first novel, *Falling* (1973), is about Elizabeth Kamen, a Jewish woman who attempts suicide; therapy reveals Kamen's traumatic childhood and unstable family relationships. Elizabeth, then, like Anya, must relive her past and try to make some sense of it.

Agnes Dempster, the heroine of Schaeffer's fifth novel, *The Madness of a Seduced Woman* (1983), is committed to an asylum after being convicted for murder and being found insane. The book reveals that, like Anya and Elizabeth, the protagonist Agnes is a complex person whose life has been a disturbing one and consequently has a severe psychological effect on the heroine. While *Anya* is historical fiction, it is also, like *The Madness of a Seduced Woman* and *Falling*, psychologically realistic.

Critics have noted that, unlike many novelists who have written about the Holocaust, Schaeffer, in *Anya*, does not rely on allegory and mythology. Instead, with its numerous details about the concentration camps and ghettos and with Anya's inability to find any meaning in suffering, the book abounds in realism. The critic Alan Mintz, moreover, believes that the lack of Jewish symbols makes Schaeffer's work more appealing to non-Jews as it seems more about universal suffering. The critic William Novak, however, believes that Schaeffer joins other Jewish American writers, such as Cynthia Ozick and Arthur Cohen, in a move away from literature dealing with identity and assimilation problems to literature that shows a greater consciousness about being Jewish.

For young adult readers, *Anya*, having a universal appeal while being about the Holocaust, is important because it vividly portrays the nightmare of the Nazi persecution of the Jews and makes readers more aware of the evils of bigotry. In addition, *Anya* is important because it personalizes history: Unlike textbooks filled with facts, the novel brings history to life by showing the effect of a specific period of time on an individual. Yet *Anya* also deals with significant contemporary issues that young adults must face, such as career and marriage, which allows young readers to empathize and identify with the protagonist.

SOURCES FOR FURTHER STUDY

Aarons, Victoria. "Responding to an Old Story: Susan Fromberg Schaeffer, Leslea Newman, and Francine Prose." In *Daughters of Valor: Contempo-*

rary Jewish American Women Writers, edited by Jay L. Halio and Ben Siegel. Newark: University of Delaware Press, 1997.

Bloom, Harold, ed. *Caribbean Women Writers*. Philadelphia: Chelsea House, 1997.

Kremer, S. Lillian. *Women's Holocaust Writing: Memory and Imagination*. Lincoln: University of Nebraska Press, 1999.

Pearlman, Mickey, and Katherine Usher Henderson. *Inter/View: Talks with America's Writing Women*. Lexington: University Press of Kentucky, 1990.

Sicher, Efraim, ed. *Holocaust Novelists*. Vol. 299 in *Dictionary of Literary Biography*. Detroit: Gale Research, 2004.

—Michelle Van Tine

At the Mind's Limits
Contemplations by a Survivor on Auschwitz and Its Realities

AUTHOR: Jean Améry (Hans Mayer; 1912-1978)
FIRST PUBLISHED: *Jenseits von Schuld und Sühne: Bewältigungsversuche eines Überwältigen*, 1966 (English translation, 1980)
GENRE: Nonfiction
SUBGENRES: Essays; autobiography; history

In five essays, Améry presents reflections on his experiences as a Jewish refugee, as a prisoner in the Nazi concentration camp at Auschwitz, and as a survivor of genocide. Améry discusses his ethical and historical views on being an intellectual in a concentration camp, on the meaning of torture, on the collective guilt of the Germans for the Holocaust, and on the "necessity" of being a Jew.

Overview

Jean Améry was the name taken by Hans Mayer, a writer who was born in Vienna, Austria, to a Jewish father and a Catholic mother. His father died in World War I, when Améry was a small child. He was raised as a Catholic by his mother, aware of his Jewish ancestry and in contact with his Jewish paternal grandparents but with little exposure to Jewish religion or traditions. Against his mother's wishes, Améry married a young Jewish woman.

In 1935, Germany passed the Nuremberg Laws, a set of legal restrictions on Jews. As Améry later recounted, in *At the Mind's Limits: Contemplations by a Survivor on Auschwitz and Its Realities* and elsewhere, reading the Nuremberg Laws convinced him that he had been defined as a Jew and that the laws were a death sentence on Jews, to be carried out at some undetermined time in the future. Three years later came the Anschluss (Germany's annexation of Austria). The German troops who entered Austria were enthusiastically welcomed by the Austrians, and the two countries were joined together into a single Reich, or empire.

Améry and his bride fled Austria for Belgium, but with the outbreak of war between Belgium and Greater Germany, the Belgians classified Améry as a German enemy alien and deported him to France. The French

The entrance to the Auschwitz concentration camp. (Tulio Bertorini)

interned him in a camp, but he escaped and returned to Belgium, where he became involved with the Belgian Resistance after that country was occupied by the Germans. The Germans arrested him while he was handing out propaganda, and he was tortured and then imprisoned at Auschwitz for the rest of the war. These events form the subject matter of the five essays that make up *At the Mind's Limits*. In the book, Améry reflects on the questions of his own identity, the human experience in extremity, his homelessness, and the guilt of the Germans.

The first essay, from which the book takes its title, treats the case of the intellectual in Auschwitz. Améry defines an intellectual as someone who lives in the realm of the spirit, who is dedicated to the humanistic arts of the mind. Remaining close to his autobiographical base, he puts himself forward as the representative of the intellectual. For such an individual, there is no place in a concentration camp; the intellectual must be a total outsider in a place that utterly rejects the values of the spirit. In Auschwitz, those prisoners who had some manual skills were relatively advantaged. In contrast, those who had been members of the "higher professions" became the lowest within the camp order. Lacking colleagues with whom to share their thoughts, intellectuals received no satisfaction or consolation from their aesthetic views or their stores of ideas. Auschwitz, for Améry, really was the utmost limit of the mind, in which thought could offer no connection to other people, no assurance in the face of death, and no wisdom.

Améry's second essay, titled "Torture," is a contemplation of the torture he underwent after his arrest and of the meaning of torture both for those who experience it and for those who administer it. Améry describes his own place of torture, at Fort Breendonk in Belgium, and recounts the events that led up to his arrest and then his agonies. In discussing his torturers, the author rejects a sexual motivation but maintains that they indulged in a "sadism" of a broader sense, a satisfaction derived from the assertion of complete control by one human being over another. Améry confesses that the reason he did not give up the information his torturers wanted, the names of other Resistance members, was only that he did not know the true names of his colleagues. This leads him to consider the true nature of moral courage and who may be said to possess it and under what circumstances.

The third essay in *At the Mind's Limits* is titled "How Much Home Does a Person Need?" Here, Améry examines the nature of homeland and homelessness, especially for Jews during and following the Holocaust. Améry contrasts the position of the Jews from the German lands or lands occupied by Germany with that of anti-Nazi German exiles. The latter could feel homesickness. The former, the Jews, might feel homesickness, but it was of an entirely different order because they had been utterly deprived of their homes and rendered completely rootless. Austria had become a foreign land to Améry as soon as it was annexed by Germany. He suggests that for conquerors, the sense of home can be replaced by an imperial consciousness, and he indicates that this had already happened for great-power states such as the United States and the Soviet Union. Some critics have suggested that Améry's emphasis on the nation as "home" and "fatherland" echoes some of the sentiments in the enemy Nazi perspective. Ultimately, Améry is unable to say how much home a person needs and can only end with the observation that it is not good to be homeless.

Améry's third essay, titled "Resentments," is perhaps the most controversial in the book. Here he addresses the issue of German national collective guilt for the Holocaust. Améry's own resentments against Germany were strong. He had changed his own ethnically German name to a French one in order to distance himself from things German. He observes that international attitudes toward Germany had changed from the last years of World War II to the time at which he was writing, in the 1960's. The view that the German nation should bear moral responsibility for the atrocities carried out by its soldiers and in its name had largely disappeared, replaced by a general acceptance or forgiveness and a rejection of the concept of collective guilt. Améry argues that even if every individual German did not support the program of genocide, enough accepted or actively participated in the program that the nation as a whole should be considered to bear moral responsibility. Moreover, if young Germans, born after the war, wanted to consider themselves heirs to the highest achievements of German thought, literature, and music, they also had to accept the Holocaust as part of their heritage. The victims of the war's atrocities had the burden and the frustration of reminding a forgetful world of the misdeeds of the perpetrators while still suffering from those misdeeds and seeing the German nation return to general worldwide acceptance and prosperity.

Améry's essay "On the Necessity and Impossibility of Being a Jew" evokes some of the sense of being placeless. Here, the issue is one of identity. In many senses, Améry was not a Jew. As he remarks in this essay, he was brought up attending Catholic Mass and celebrating Christmas, the father he knew only from a photograph was a soldier in the Austrian army, and he had little knowledge of Jewish culture or tradition. Even if he were to move to Israel and learn to speak Hebrew, he could not really become a Jew because he could not leave the earlier life that had shaped him. At the same time, the experience of Auschwitz had removed from him every identity but that of a Jew, and this would remain with him forever.

In *At the Mind's Limits*, Améry brings together discussion of personal, historical, and ethical aspects of the Holocaust. The essays make painful reading because they present dilemmas that cannot be finally resolved and confront readers with bitterness and pain that will not disappear. With these essays, Améry encourages readers to face the tragedy of the Holocaust rather than try to explain it away.

SOURCES FOR FURTHER STUDY

Brudholm, Thomas. "A Confiscated Past: Jean Améry on Home and Exile." *Hedgehog Review* 7, no. 3 (September 22, 2005): 7-19.

_____. *Resentment's Virtue: Jean Améry and the Refusal to Forgive*. Philadelphia: Temple University Press, 2008.

Goodheart, Eugene. "The Passion of Reason: Reflections on Primo Levi and Jean Améry." *Dissent* 41 (1994): 518-527.

Niven, Bill, ed. *Germans as Victims: Remembering the Past in Contemporary Germany*. New York: Palgrave Macmillan, 2006.

—*Carl L. Bankston III*

AUSCHWITZ AND AFTER

AUTHOR: Charlotte Delbo (1913-1985)
FIRST PUBLISHED: *Auschwitz et après*, 1970-1971 (English translation, 1995): *Aucun de nous ne reviendra*. 1965 (*None of Us Will Return*, 1968); *Une Connaissance inutile*, 1970 (*Useless Knowledge*, 1995); *Mesure de nos jours*, 1971 (*The Measure of Our Days*, 1995)
GENRE: Nonfiction
SUBGENRES: Memoir; poetry

In these three volumes, Delbo, who was a member of the only group of non-Jewish Frenchwomen sent to the Nazi concentration camps, recounts her struggles during her imprisonment and after her release.

PRINCIPAL PERSONAGES:
    Charlotte Delbo (1913-1985), a member of the French Resistance who was imprisoned in Auschwitz
    Georges Dudach, Delbo's husband
    Viva,
    Lulu Thenevin,
    Jeannette "Carmen" Serre,
    Madeleine "Mado" Doiret, and
    Germaine, companions of Delbo in Auschwitz

OVERVIEW

    Charlotte Delbo, an essayist, poet, and playwright who is well regarded in her native France, was until 1995 largely unknown in the United States. Her greatest work is her trilogy about her imprisonment in the Nazi concentration camp at Auschwitz. Although Delbo completed a manuscript shortly after her return to France after World War II, she was unsure of the importance and the authenticity of her own work, and she did not publish the first volume, *Aucun de nous ne reviendra*, until 1965. In 1970 and 1971 she published the second and third volumes, *Une Connaissance inutile* and *Mesure de nos jours*. An English translation of *Aucun de nous ne reviendra* by John Githens, titled *None of Us Will Return*, was published in 1968, but it attracted little notice at the time. It was not until 1995 that Rosette C.

Lamont's masterful translation of the entire trilogy, published with the collective title *Auschwitz and After*, introduced a large group of American readers to Delbo's work. Lamont's translations of the three volumes—titled *None of Us Will Return, Useless Knowledge,* and *The Measure of Our Days*, respectively—have been examined by critics and read widely by college students in the twenty-first century, more than half a century after the experiences Delbo describes.

None of Us Will Return opens with several poems under the heading "Arrivals, Departures." Their central images are the trains and the train stations that prisoners passed through on their way to the Nazi concentration camps. The first and longest poem includes a narrative of hundreds of people arriving at the camps, the men being separated from the women and children, and then the children being separated from their mothers. All are made to remove their clothes as part of their processing, and the shame of mothers forced to strip in front of their children is an idea to which Delbo returns again and again.

This first set of poems introduces important characteristics of Delbo's approach to her material. The language and imagery are stark and unblinking, moving in close to focus on one person or one dialogue and back again to show large groups of people. Rather than an extended narrative, the book is a collection of short prose scenes and poems in roughly chronological order, generally told in present tense and in the first person. Rarely does Delbo argue a position or take on philosophical or sociological questions, or even describe how she feels about what she is telling; rather, she presents vivid scenes so that the reader will see what happened without intellectual filters. Delbo's gaze is unrelenting, whether she is describing in minute detail the movement of one foot in a pile of dead and nearly dead bodies or the mesmerizing glimpse of a single tulip growing at an abandoned house near a work site.

None of Us Will Return is made up of thirty-three titled pieces as well as several short, untitled poems. The titles of the individual pieces are brief, and often, as in the cases of "Evening" and "Morning," they seem to reveal little. Others, including "Alice's Leg" and "The Tulip," are more evocative. Several of the titles, including "The Men," "Roll Call," "Farewell," and "Thirst," are repeated in this and the second volume, creating a resonance and a feeling of circling back and looking again that is the centerpiece of Delbo's structure. *None of Us Will Return* also introduces some of the women who were imprisoned with Delbo: tough-minded Lulu, who helps Delbo avoid inattentive mistakes; Viva, who nurses Delbo through a fever; and Alice, who dies of exhaustion.

Delbo herself was not Jewish, but she and her husband, Georges Dudach, were active in the French Resistance, writing, printing, and distributing anti-Nazi materials. When France was invaded by the Germans in 1940, Delbo was working in Argentina, but she chose to return to France to work against the Nazis. In 1942, she and her husband were arrested and sent to separate camps. *Useless Knowledge*, the second volume of the trilogy, opens with "The Men," a prose piece and a poem about being allowed to say good-bye to her husband shortly before he was shot. Months later, Delbo and 228 other women of the Resistance were sent to Auschwitz and held together in a compound separate from the Jewish women imprisoned at the camp; of these, only 49 survived. *Useless Knowledge* moves more loosely through time than does the first volume, as Delbo remembers small details of life in France before the occupation and moves ahead of her story to tell the fate of a comrade or further ahead to reflect on her own writing process years later.

Although its descriptions of hardships and despair are vivid, *Useless Knowledge* is in some ways the most hopeful of the three volumes. One prose piece, "The Stream," recounts a delicious few minutes when the women were uncharacteristically allowed to wash themselves quickly in a stream during a lunch break. There is an account of a Christmas celebration the women managed to put together by sharing and smuggling food and even creating costumes for a play. Later in the volume, Delbo, her friends Lulu and Carmen, and others are transferred to another camp, Ravensbrück, where they are put to work growing experimental crops. This work is a bit less brutal than the work at Auschwitz. Finally, at the end of the volume, word reaches the women that they will be released, and they are eventually freed. The final piece in *Useless Knowledge* is a poem titled "Prayer to the Living to Forgive Them for Being Alive."

The third volume of the trilogy, *The Measure of Our Days*, deals with material that has been examined perhaps less frequently by writers about the Holocaust: the difficulties that survivors faced after they were released from the camps. Delbo describes months of lethargy, of confusion and frustration when faced with what had before been simple choices, such as what to buy at the market. Delbo is paralyzed at first, but over a period of years she finds her way back to the world while maintaining tentative relationships with some of the women who were imprisoned with her. When one of them, Germaine, becomes ill and then dies, Delbo and others re-establish contact.

The Measure of Our Days contains longer prose pieces than those that make up the earlier volumes, many of them titled with the names of other women Delbo knew in the camps, spoken in their voices and presenting a variety of ways these women dealt with their trauma. Newly released

Gilberte is unable to make simple arrangements at a hotel until a stranger intercedes. Mado mourns that she should not have survived; she speaks the words most often quoted from the book: "I'm not alive. I died in Auschwitz but no one knows it." Marie-Louise seems to be living in a blissful state of denial with her husband, insisting to everyone that she is happy. Delbo does not comment on or interpret these women's narratives; she simply allows each woman to present her own story. *The Measure of Our Days* ends with Germaine's funeral and Delbo's reflections on reality, starting over, and hope.

With the three volumes of *Auschwitz and After*, Delbo created an intensely personal account of one non-Jewish woman's experiences in the Nazi concentration camps. Delbo was a writer before she was a prisoner, and this may have contributed to the effectiveness of the trilogy. Her language and imagery are powerful, her structure is inventive and controlled, and her focus is on lived experience rather than on ideology or politics.

Sources for Further Study

Baer, Elizabeth Roberts, and Myrna Goldenberg. *Experience and Expression: Women, the Nazis, and the Holocaust*. Detroit: Wayne State University Press, 2003.

Delbo, Charlotte. *Convoy to Auschwitz: Women of the French Resistance*. Boston: Northeastern University Press, 1997.

Geddes, Jennifer L. "Banal Evil and Useless Knowledge: Hannah Arendt and Charlotte Delbo on Evil After the Holocaust." *Hypatia* 18, no. 1 (Winter, 2003): 104-115.

Lamont, Rosette C. "The Triple Courage of Charlotte Delbo: A Place Without a Name." *Massachusetts Review* 41, no. 4 (Winter, 2000-2001): 483-497.

Langer, Lawrence L. "Charlotte Delbo and an Age of Ashes." In *The Age of Atrocity: Death in Modern Literature*. Boston: Beacon, 1978.

Sheldon, Sayre P., ed. *Her War Story: Twentieth-Century Women Write About War*. Carbondale: Southern Illinois University Press, 1999.

—*Cynthia A. Bily*

Austerlitz

Author: W. G. Sebald (1944-2001)
First published: *Austerlitz*, 2001, in Germany (English translation, 2001)
Genre: Novel
Subgenre: Psychological fiction

Jacques Austerlitz, evacuated as a child to Wales by his doomed Czech Jewish parents when the Nazis invaded Prague, relates to an unidentified narrator the haunting stories of his "false" English life and his journeys—physical and psychic—to the "far side of time," where he must keep appointments with his history's unburied dead.

Principal characters:
  The narrator, unnamed but presumably a doppelgänger for Austerlitz
  Jacques Austerlitz, an architectural historian whose evocative conversations with the narrator convey a determination to relive his parents' fate
  Emyr and *Gwendolyn Elias*, a dour Calvinist preacher and his troubled wife, who raise the six-year-old wartime emigré as Dafydd in a remote Welsh village
  Penrith-Smith, a kind headmaster who informs the boy of his double identity
  Andre Hilary, a history teacher whose description of the battle of Austerlitz awakens the boy to the strangeness of his new name
  Maximilian and *Agáta Aychenwald*, Jacques's biological parents
  Vera Rysanova, Agáta's former maid, who recalls the family history

Overview

The death of W. G. Sebald in an auto accident in December, 2001, brought an abrupt end to a challenging literary career. It was easy to classify Sebald's *The Emigrants* (1996), his first novel for American readers, as an example of Holocaust literature. The last of the book's four stories presented a famous painter, Max Ferber, a German Jew sent out of Nazi Germany as a child to safety in England. *The Rings of Saturn* (1998) and *Vertigo* (1999) resist so easy a label. *Saturn*'s dark intimations included not just

Jews but all of Western life and achievement. *Vertigo* introduced Sebald's favorite motif, the man without a habitation, the "foreigner" whose mind, Susan Sontag suggests, is in mourning and, because it can never accept the past as buried, is itself posthumous.

With *Austerlitz*, although Sebald again orchestrated slowly but surely toward the Holocaust, it would be a mistake to pigeonhole so exceptional a novel under so confining a rubric. To be sure, Austerlitz, like Ferber, has been uprooted as a boy to England from Central Europe—in this case not Kissingen, Germany, but Prague, Czechoslavia. However, in this novel, the word "Jewish" does not even appear until page 172—nearly two-thirds into the book. It would appear that the author wished to avoid the label, that he wanted this novel, unanchored by events alone, to join a distinguished lineage. To do so, Sebald, like every serious fiction writer, set up a system of narrative decoding that he believed could best illuminate even the darkest mindscape.

In *Austerlitz*, Sebald deepens his examination of the dispossessed by focusing solely on one member of his haunted company. He anatomizes Austerlitz's inner life but does so with the narrative assistance of a secret sharer, an inside outsider, a doppelgänger who, distanced in time from him for as long as twenty years, can yet provide a continuity Austerlitz as sole speaker would lack. The narrator and Austerlitz encounter each other

W. G. *Sebald*. (© Jerry Bauer/ Courtesy, New Directions)

for the first time in an Antwerp railway station in the late 1960's and periodically reconnect in chance meetings in similarly transient travel zones over the next thirty years. Finally, in 1996, Austerlitz begins to relate his life story.

Although superficially *Austerlitz* is closer to a conventional narrative structure than Sebald's previous novels, this conventionality is an illusion. For instance, readers, unless endlessly vigilant, may encounter difficulties in remembering Austerlitz's unnamed spokesperson at all. Translator Anthea Bell apparently saw no alternative but to insert "said Austerlitz" scores of times, but never after quotation marks, to remind readers they are getting Austerlitz's story secondhand. In fact, there are no quotation marks and only eleven paragraph breaks in the book's 298 pages. Sebald relies for sequence on special devices of his own, of which his noncommittal narrator is only one.

In the words of the animated sign outside the magic theater in Hermann Hesse's *Der Steppenwolf* (1927; *Steppenwolf*, 1929), this novel is "not for everyone." What Princeton Germanist Theodore Ziolkowski wrote of the title character in the Hesse novel can be applied to Austerlitz. As a storyteller, he is eidetic; that is, he is a commentator capable of producing subjective images out of what the deceptively passive narrator might seem to take as vast stockpiles of facts on military fortifications, rail stations, or the secret lives of moths.

While Austerlitz appears to be only a traveler with his inevitable rucksack, his alter ego is really filtering—and elevating—mundane déjà vu to some higher level of consciousness. What keeps Sebald's writing evocative, even in translation, are the pictures framed in Austerlitz's mind's eye—never more vividly than during a visit to London's Royal Observatory when Austerlitz explains why he has never owned a clock of any kind:

> I have always resisted the power of time . . . keeping myself apart from so-called current events in the hope . . . that I can turn back and go behind [time], and there I shall find everything as it once was . . . in which case none of what history tells us would be true, past events have not yet occured but are waiting to do so at the moment we think of them . . .

If humans are indeed formed forever by what happens long before puberty, is Jacques Austerlitz, intellectually advanced, ruled by the damnation of not knowing his earliest past and obsessed, like Proust's Marcel, by the compulsion to rescue it from oblivion?

As if to reinforce an inner journey about whose source and destination he remains puzzled—almost diffident—Austerlitz documents every visitation in the real world with photos and all sorts of graphics that are amazingly reproduced on the very pages where they are relevant. There are eighty-five of these—far too many—and their efficacy is mixed. Without them, Sebald would have had a book of less than two hundred pages. With them, that quality that Sontag praised collectively in *Vertigo* as "an exquisite index of the pastness of the past" can become in *Austerlitz* a distraction. Album photos from the Prague years are the best, including the book's cover illustration of Jacques, at five, lavishly costumed as the Rose Queen's page. It is easy to infer that this is Sebald.

In fact, it is in recounting his childhood that Austerlitz finally engages the reader's interest. Austerlitz was brought up as the son of a Calvinist pastor named Emyr Elias and his wife Gwendolyn. His is not the displaced child's life so classically portrayed in W. Somerset Maugham's *Of Human Bondage* (1915). Its poignancy is muted by its being as-told-to. Yet the scene at boarding school where he learns his real name resonates. Even a year later, told that Napoleon won a great victory at a town named Austerlitz and more recently that dancer Fred Astaire was born Frederick Austerlitz, he still deplores his name's alien sound.

Although frequently referring to his English years as "false," Austerlitz settles there as an architectural historian. Britain stands as a buffer against a past he resists. Many of his reunions with his alter ego take place at London's Great Eastern Hotel, perhaps talismanic of the direction he will finally take to solve the mystery of his identity.

At last, Austerlitz finds himself—in both senses of the word—in Prague, where he locates an old woman, Vera Rysanova, who once worked as a maid for his real mother, Agáta, who was an actress. Agáta did not make it out of Czechoslovakia; first she was interred in the camp of Terezín, then transferred, presumably, to Auschwitz and died. Vera produces the photo of the costumed Jacques, age five, which triggers the memory of a dream in which he returned to the family apartment whose burned-out remains he now photographs:

> I know that my parents will be back from their holiday, and there is something important which I must give them. I am not aware that they have been dead for years. I simply think they must be very old, around ninety or a hundred ... But when at last they come through the door they are in their midthirties at the most.

Austerlitz is moved to another disclaimer about time: "It does not seem to me that we understand the laws governing the return of the past.... [W]e who are still alive are unreal in the eyes of the dead."

From Prague he goes to Paris, the last-known whereabouts of his businessman father, Maximilian Aychenwald, and then to the suburb of Drancy, where doomed internees were placed on trains for the death camps. He leaves his interlocutor in Paris and changes trains, appropriately, at the Gare d'Austerlitz. He must now go to the foothills of the Pyrenees, to a village called Gurs where in 1942 there was a camp, his father's last-known stop.

In "A Mind in Mourning," the first comprehensive essay in English on W. G. Sebald's three translated novels, written nearly two years before the publication of *Austerlitz*, Susan Sontag stresses the primacy of the journey. In Sebald, she emphasizes, "it is the return to a place of unfinished business, to retrace a memory, to repeat (or complete) an experience; to offer oneself up . . . to the final, most devastating revelations." The reader welcomes late starters like Sebald, who published his first book at forty-six. Only Joseph Conrad, who wrote his first novel in his fortieth year, comes to mind as being, like Sebald, one who traveled widely in seldom-charted realms and out of whose memory an eidetic universe reveals itself on the printed page.

Sources for Further Study

Klebes, Martin. *Wittgenstein's Novels*. New York: Routledge, 2006.

Kunkel, Benjamin. "The Emigrant." *The Nation* 274, no. 12 (April 1, 2002): 42.

Long, J. J., and Anne Whitehead, eds. *W. G. Sebald: A Critical Companion*. Seattle: University of Washington Press, 2004.

McCulloh, Mark R. *Understanding W. G. Sebald*. Columbia: University of South Carolina Press, 2003.

Stavan, Ivan. "W. G. Sebald, 57, German Writer Who Placed Shoah at Center of His Work." *Forward* 105, no. 31 (December 12, 2001): 1.

"W. G. Sebald." *The Times* (London), December 17, 2001, p. 17.

—*Richard Hauer Costa*

"Babii Yar"

AUTHOR: Yevgeny Yevtushenko (1933-   )
FIRST PUBLISHED: "Babiy Yar," 1961 (English translation collected in *The Poetry of Yevgeny Yevtushenko, 1953 to 1965*, 1965)
GENRE: Poetry
SUBGENRES: Dramatic monologue; lyric poetry

In this simple poem, Yevtushenko uses metaphor to establish his thesis of the existence of anti-Semitism in the Soviet Union, despite official disclaimers, and to protest against that anti-Semitism by using the powerful symbol of Babii Yar, the Ukrainian site of a Nazi massacre of thousands of Jews.

OVERVIEW

"Babii Yar" is a poem in free verse consisting of ninety-two lines. The title, roughly translated as "Women's Cliff," refers to a ravine near Kiev where thousands of Jews were massacred during the Nazi occupation of the Ukraine in the Soviet Union. The name of the place in itself has no symbolic connotation in the poem, even though Babii Yar (also known as Babi Yar, Baby Yar, or Babiy Yar) has become one of the most recognizable symbols of the Nazi crimes perpetrated against the Jews. The Holocaust is not the main focus of the poem. The very first line, "No monument stands over Babii Yar," reveals Yevgeny Yevtushenko's main concern. The original crime was bad enough, he seems to say, but it has been compounded by a lack of visible recognition and respect for its victims.

The poet immediately identifies with the Jewish people. He goes back to ancient Egypt and the agony of crucifixion, then leaps across the centuries to Alfred Dreyfus, who was the subject of a celebrated case of prejudice and persecution in nineteenth century France. The poet then turns to a boy in Byelostok, a town in Byelorussia (now Belarus) near the Polish border that had a large Jewish population that has been decimated—first in the pogroms in czarist Russia, then during the Holocaust. Finally, the poet identifies with the feelings of fear and the needs for love and kindness expressed by the young Holocaust victim Anne Frank in her *Het Achterhuis* (1947; *The Diary of a Young Girl*, 1952).

In the final verses, the poet identifies with the victims buried in Babii

Yar; this is his most powerful declaration of solidarity. As the trees stand as judges and "all things scream silently," he sees himself transformed into one massive, soundless scream, thus becoming the voice of each old man, each child who was murdered and buried there. He vows never to forget the tragic fate of these innocent victims, which brings him to his last point. He believes that there is no monument at Babii Yar because of the forgetfulness of the non-Jewish survivors and, more ominously, because of the anti-Semitism that existed before the advent of the Nazis and remains latent in the Russian people. This is illustrated by the shout of the pogrom bullies: "Beat the Yids, Save Russia!" By invoking the name of the "Internationale," the battle cry of the Russian revolution, the poet declares that he will fight against the anti-Semites until the last of them is defeated. He is not concerned that the anti-Semites hate him as a Jew even though there is no Jewish blood in his veins. On the contrary, it is because of their hatred that he sees himself as a true Russian, since the Russians are "international to the core."

Yevgeny Yevtushenko. (Jean-Claude Bouis)

"Babii Yar" is a simple, unambiguous, declarative poem, told in the first person and replete with straightforward rhetorical statements such as "O my Russian people!" "I am behind bars," "I am afraid," "I know the goodness of my land," "And I love." Such direct, terse statements fit a particular style of verse making that was popularized in Russia by Vladimir Mayakovsky and in the United States by William Carlos Williams. Such verses often consist of only one or two words lined in a cascading fashion. They are used primarily for emphasis, but they also add a dramatic flair, which Yevgeny Yevtushenko, a gifted actor and skillful reader of poetry, inherited from Mayakovsky, who was also a powerful declamator.

The main device Yevtushenko uses in this poem is metaphor. In a series of identification metaphors already mentioned, he not only drives his points home but also makes his references in an interesting way. When he says that he is an old Jew plodding through ancient Egypt, he immediately establishes a link between a history-laden people and himself as a present-day observer of history. When he sees himself crucified, he subtly reminds the reader or listener of the common origin of Christ and the Jewish people. A very brief mention of Alfred Dreyfus (only six words) is sufficient to evoke the terrible injustice done to him and all Jews. The metaphor of a young boy in Byelostok being kicked while lying in the blood that is spilling over the floors brings into stark relief the bestial cruelty of crimes among whose victims are the innocent young.

The poet reserves the most powerful metaphor for Anne Frank, to whom he devotes one-fourth of the poem. During his "conversations" with her, Anne's innocence and tenderness evoke the noblest feelings in him. Even the love he professes for her is ethereal, just as she is "transparent as a branch in April." By emphasizing the innocence of a young girl on a threshold of life, the poet underscores the depth of the injustice perpetrated against her and all young people like her. The images employed here tend to highlight the interplay of innocence and injustice. In addition to the visual image of a branch in April, the poet uses auditory images such as the steps of the police Anne hears and the smashing down of the door; to soothe Anne's fears, he tells her they are the booming sounds of spring and the ice breaking, respectively. The love that his encounter with her brings forth is unreal, desperate, and painfully tender, used to raise hope in a hopeless situation and to confirm the existence of humaneness in an inhumane world. Yevtushenko is at his best in creating metaphors and images that flesh out and animate his references.

It is clear that "Babii Yar" is a poem with a thesis. The thesis is that anti-Semitism exists in the Soviet Union, the official disclaimers notwithstanding. Yevtushenko protests against it by using perhaps the most suitable symbol—Babii Yar. The fact that the atrocities were committed by the hated enemy, the Nazis, amplifies the unforgivability of anti-Semitic attitudes, let alone actions. The fact that this anti-Semitism is camouflaged makes the original crime even more heinous.

Throughout his career, Yevtushenko has been known as a fiery dissident. He has used many of his poems to express his dissatisfaction with, and disapproval of, things that have happened in his country (next to "Babii Yar," "The Heirs of Stalin" is perhaps the best example). His protests have met with varying degrees of success, and his animosity toward the system has had its ebb and flow, but he has never been reluctant to speak his mind. In "Babii Yar," as a member of a post-Holocaust generation of Soviet citizens, Yevtushenko makes a strong statement on behalf of his peers.

"Babii Yar" is, however, more than a political statement about a problem in the Soviet Union. It is a declaration of solidarity with the oppressed, no matter who they may be, no matter where and when the oppression may be practiced. This solidarity with all humankind gives the poem a universal appeal, raising it above local politics and ideology. That is why the poet identifies with ancient figures as well as modern ones such as Dreyfus, Anne Frank, and the boy from Byelostok. It is evident, therefore, that Yevtushenko is warning not only the Soviet authorities and his compatriots but also the entire world against the pernicious effects of anti-Semitism and, in fact, of all injustice. While it is true that he has written other poems to this end, "Babii Yar" can be considered Yevtushenko's main protest against injustice, and a plea for a better world.

The ultimate merits of this poem lie in its aesthetics, however, and in the poet's ability to dress his basically nonliterary aim in a formidable artistic garb that transcends all mundane concerns. The best proof of the effect of the poem is its use by Dmitri Shostakovich in the opening movement of his Thirteenth Symphony.

SOURCES FOR FURTHER STUDY

Elliott, Philip. "Poet Yevtushenko Takes on Russian Establishment." *Evansville Courier and Press*, February 12, 2006, p. D1.

Hammond, Margo. "The Dangerous Poet of Love." *St. Petersburg Times*, March 12, 2006, p. 7.

Kinzer, Stephe. "A Russian Poet Steeped in America." *The New York Times*, December 11, 2002, p. E1.

Penhollow, Steve. "Noted Poet Yevgeny Yevtushenko Bucked Russian Leadership—and Won." *Ft. Wayne Journal Gazette*, March 2, 2002, p. 10W.

Radin, Charles A. "Passion, Daring Stir Russian Poet." *Boston Globe*, November 24, 2000, p. A1.

—Vasa D. Mihailovich

Badenheim 1939

Author: Aharon Appelfeld (1932-   )
First published: *Badenheim, 'ir nofesh*, 1975 (English translation, 1980)
Genre: Novel
Subgenre: Historical fiction

Set in an Austrian resort town shortly after the Anschluss, Appelfeld's novel reports the steps taken by the "Sanitation Department" to gain control of the town and abridge the freedoms of its inhabitants while revealing how specific people react to each succeeding deprivation.

Principal characters:
   Dr. Pappenheim, the "impresario" and director of the summer festival in Badenheim
   Martin, the pharmacist
   Trude, Martin's wife, considered "disturbed" because of her visions of the impending Holocaust
   Frau Zauberblit, a guest who has escaped from a nearby sanatorium
   Leon Samitzky, a Polish musician who reflects attitudes toward Eastern Europeans relative to the impending Holocaust
   Professor Fussholdt, a vacationer at the resort and a famous historian
   Mitzi Fussholdt, Professor Fussholdt's young, vain wife
   Dr. Schutz, a mathematician who lives off his mother's money
   Karl, a divorced vacationer who terrorizes people
   Lotte, Karl's girlfriend
   Princess Milbaum, an elegant woman who believes others are conspiring against her
   Nahum Slotzker, a boy singer from Poland who grows fat at the resort
   Professor Mandelbaum, a violinist
   Salo, a traveling salesman
   Peter, the pastry shop owner
   Dr. Langmann, an angry Jew who hates Jews
   The rabbi, who is old and sick
   Sally and
   Gertie, middle-aged prostitutes

Overview

Badenheim 1939 displays a sequence of both realistic and symbolic events beginning in the early spring of 1939 in the Austrian resort town of Badenheim and ending with the deportation of the Jews in late fall of the same year. A third-person narrator, in detached and understated style, reports the steps taken by the Sanitation Department to gain control of the town and abridge the freedoms of its inhabitants while revealing how specific people react to each succeeding deprivation.

The novel opens in 1939, amid swirls of unidentified rumors, as a foreboding, uneasy spring returns to Badenheim with the sound of country church bells ringing, two Sanitation Department inspectors examining a flow of sewage, and Trude delirious with a haunting fear that is also beginning to infect her husband. Shortly after the arrival of Dr. Pappenheim, the director of the summer festival, the perennial vacationers arrive and the town is abuzz with activity as the city people, anxious to relieve themselves of worry and the memories of an unusually strange past winter, stream toward the forest.

With the arrival of the feisty musicians, the vacationers wildly vent their emotions on liquor and pastries, and an inspector from the Sanitation Department appears at the pharmacy, asking peculiar details about the business and taking measurements with a yardstick. As time passes, Trude worries even more about her daughter, Helena, who married a non-Jewish military officer against her parents' wishes and, in Trude's visions, is being held captive on her husband's estate, where she is beaten every evening when he returns from the barracks. Concurrently, the Sanitation Department expands its power to conduct independent investigations as it spreads all over town, taking measurements, putting up fences, planting flags, unloading rolls of barbed wire, and preparing cement pillars. The large south gate to Badenheim is closed, and a small, unused gate is opened for pedestrians. The guests, interpreting these activities as attempts to make the summer festival the best one ever, pursue gluttonous merriment even though Dr. Pappenheim's "artists" are breaking their promises to appear at the festival. With a memory of the past summer, when the musicians surprised even themselves and annoyed the regular guests by sliding into playing Jewish melodies, a new theme is introduced.

Badenheimers become estranged, suspicious, and mistrustful of one another as the Sanitation Department completes its investigations and in the middle of May posts a "modest" sign requiring all Jewish citizens to register with the Sanitation Department. Who is and is not Jewish becomes a matter of heated debate, with some denying Jewishness because of either personal conviction or conversion and others readily proclaiming their Jewishness. Foremost for all is the belief that they are Austrian first and Jewish second and that their national allegiance supersedes all others. Badenheimers are discomforted, and several begin remembering their past while some of them blame the Department's intrusion on the Ostjuden, the Eastern European Polish Jews, many of whom have not abandoned their Jewish heritage to assimilate into the Austrian culture.

As brief glimpses into the background of some of the guests are revealed and alliances and schisms among people are developing, the Sanitation Department posts pictures and descriptions of Poland and invitations to leave Austria and go to Poland. Twin-brother readers foreshadow the future by performing their specialty, readings of the death poetry of Rainer Maria Rilke, and the Sanitation Department denies everyone except the milkman and the fruit truck driver entrance to or exit from the town. More deprivations follow as forest walks, picnics, and excursions are terminated as well as swimming in the pool, because the water supply is closed. Meanwhile, the non-Jews are leaving Badenheim.

The lives of other guests and their feelings about being Jewish are revealed as people are forced into closer contact with one another, and the "alien orange shadow" and "leaden sun" symbolize the town atmosphere. Vegetation grows unchecked as people learn that they are prisoners in the town with no postal service and that all Jews, even Jews who renounced Judaism or whose parents had converted to Christianity, will be forced to "transfer" to Poland. With only a few exceptions, people accept the edict, and many try to find the positive in the transfer. Food supplies begin to dwindle as the town fills with strangers—people dragged in from all over Austria because they were born in Badenheim. Even the feeble town rabbi, long ago relegated to an isolated old-age home, is brought into town. Derangement and chaos erupt as people seeking drugs loot the pharmacy and the musicians steal the hotel's dinnerware in preparation for their forced "transfer" to Poland. Finally, Helena comes home without her non-Jewish husband. ("A goy will always be a goy. And your goy too is a goy. I'm not sorry," says Trude.)

Even the four dogs, pets of the headwaiter, try to escape by jumping the fence; driven back, all but one is shot. Ultimately, blame is placed on Dr. Pappenheim as "the arch Ostjude and source of all our troubles," because he invented the festival and "filled the town with morbid artists and decadent vacationers."

At last, the time for deportation arrives: "How easy the transition was—they hardly felt it." In fact, the policeman who escorts the Badenheimers to the train station has a very easy task because people, glad to be free of their confinement, are in fine spirits as they discuss the advantages of Poland. As if he were responsible for the "transition" as part of the happy festival arrangements, Dr. Pappenheim is overcome with tears of joy. As they are "all sucked in as easily as grains of wheat poured into a funnel" into the four filthy freight cars that come to take them away, the narrative ends with the impresario's observation: "If the coaches are so dirty it must mean that we have not far to go."

Rather than being rounded, the characters of *Badenheim 1939* are archetypes of people and conflicts repeated throughout the Holocaust. Unnamed and defying rational explanation, the Holocaust is the most powerful force in this novel. Revealed as a symbolic orange shadow enveloping Badenheim and gnawing at the geraniums, as a leaden sky blotting out the sun of the once-beautiful resort town, and as a general, undirected fear, its reality is confirmed only by its effects. Like William Blake, who cannot comprehend "The Tyger" although he sees it, the Badenheimers neither comprehend the actions of the Sanitation Department nor foresee the consequences of those actions. The power of evil is clearly felt, however, as it directs an increasingly and overwhelmingly destructive course.

The Sanitation Department, efficiency and thoroughness personified, is the agent of the Holocaust. As the orange shadow symbolizes the Holocaust, the Sanitation Department is both literally and symbolically the organizer and collaborator of the Holocaust—the Nazis and others who, in not defying them, become their agents. The Badenheimers never rise up against the Sanitation Department, a faceless, large, well-equipped omnipotent agency, because they cannot even imagine the Department's ultimate purpose. Instead of directing their anger about the increasing deprivations and humiliations toward the Sanitation Department, the Badenheimers make the grave error of assuming an unseen rationality and instead look to themselves for the cause of their problems.

Aharon Appelfeld. (© Jerry Bauer)

Except for Trude, whose initial visionary perceptions of the truth and resultant fears are considered hallucinations and signs of disease, the characters remain blind to their mortal danger. Trude, like the other characters, however, is a loosely drawn type—one who sees the Holocaust coming but who is considered mad even to fear its portents. Still, when their daughter Helena returns home as Trude has predicted all along, "Martin knew that everything that Trude said was true."

Dr. Pappenheim, the impresario who has arranged for the town's summer entertainment for thirty years, was considered the most important person in Badenheim because summer was devoted solely to the pursuit of pleasure. With the confinement of Jews to the town and their imminent deportation, however, people blame the impresario and begin to treat him with hostility, which he does not recognize in his futile and continuing efforts to make the summer festival a success. Dr. Pappenheim's greatest pleasures appear to be making people happy and seeing the regulars return to Badenheim each summer. Ignoring each succeeding Sanitation Department imposition and perpetually rationalizing his way to optimism, Dr. Pappenheim tries to dispel the mounting anxiety about the Sanitation Department's increasing restrictions. He succeeds so well that a holiday atmosphere prevails as the Jews board the deportation trains to the sound of his optimistic prediction about the train ride.

Among other residents of Badenheim in 1939 is the musician Samitzky, who is the prototypical Ostjude whom the others hold responsible for their rejection by the Austrian world. Unpretentious, simple, and open, he is proud of his Polish roots, loves the Yiddish language, and becomes the lover of Frau Zauberblit, another prototype and an escapee from a nearby tuberculosis sanatorium whose non-Jewish husband has divorced her and whose daughter had brought her papers to sign renouncing all claims of motherhood. Thoroughly depressed and seeing no escape, Samitzky chooses to spend each day in a drunken stupor.

The Jews' perceptions of and reactions to specific government actions leading to the Holocaust are the focus of this novel. Badenheim and its inhabitants symbolize the Jews' tenure in Austria—outsiders enjoying a deceptively gay vacation in a death row that masquerades as a festival. The Sanitation Department, the organization and its agents who want to cleanse the city of its "waste" in the most expeditious manner, prepares for the Jews' deportation to the "Poland" of death. As the Jews' freedoms are increasingly abridged until they are prisoners, the naïve victims accept what the Department does with minor grumblings, some despair, and, in some cases, great anger at one another for causing the problems. Excepting only a few people who consider themselves non-Jews but whom the Department nevertheless considers Jews, no one confronts the Department or even tries to leave, despite the ominous warnings. Situational irony, confirmed by an analysis of the historical period, highlights these opposites. Because the Jews were condemned as targets for the Sanitation Department, the deportation was tolerated by many rational "non-Jews." Yet the Jews' willingness to cooperate fully and be model citizens in a country they loved but that did not love them enabled the Department to deport them without encountering fierce attempts to ensure self-preservation. Similarly ironic, Trude, the only Badenheimer able to sense the impending catastrophe, is considered insane because of her fears; those who accept the unfolding plot by ignoring what they see or through frenzied drinking and gluttony are considered sane.

Dramatic irony, painful because the events are historical while also highly symbolic, pervades almost every line of the deceptively simple prose. Instead of perceiving the deportation to Poland as the next step toward death, the guests and Jewish townspeople, despite the forced return of all former Badenheimers to the town and many deaths among them, greet the filthy trains of death with joyful anticipation, seeing them as the vehicles of escape from their imprisonment.

Euphemistic symbolism names events and interprets actions with simultaneously figurative and literal images. The orange shadow that "gnaws at the geraniums" ominously predicts illness, death, and crematorium fires. As the vacationers compliment the thoroughness and efficiency of the Sanitation Department, they reflect both a historically documented pride in "their" country and the dramatically ironic efficiency of the technology and psychology used to exterminate them.

Because Badenheim is representative of Europe, each event symbolizes its larger European counterpart. Included are the initial acceptance of deprivations, the internal conflicts among Jews that hindered their leaving earlier, the carefree holiday illusions of security that clouded a clear image of reality, and finally, the misplaced optimism of a possible new "Golden Age," in which Jews would be fully enfranchised citizens, an idea that lulled them into believing that the evil would disappear with the orange shadow, leaden sky, and the cutting of the "creeping vines" that sealed the doors.

Other images that enhance the action include the forest, symbolizing freedom; the new blue fish placed into the tank, which are deceptively fun-loving during the day but strew the tank with corpses at night; and finally the clichéd reversal—instead of people being treated like dogs, dogs are treated like people and are killed.

Matching the simple naïveté of the unsuspecting but fearful Badenheimers is the deceptively simple writing style. Short, simple sentences predominate, but the reader must attend to every word, lest important ideas be lost. Subtleties shade and enhance nuances of meaning and reveal symbolic imagery requiring thought, and each subsequent reading opens new avenues for consideration.

Badenheim 1939, Aharon Appelfeld's first work published in English translation, introduced his writing to American readers. Although he had produced, in Hebrew, volumes of poetry, more than three hundred stories, and more than twenty volumes of fiction and essays, and although he emerged as a major Israeli author in the 1960's, he was largely unknown outside Israel until the publication of *Badenheim 1939* in English translation. Almost immediately, the novel was recognized as a new form of Holocaust literature, and each succeeding novel has enhanced the author's reputation.

The novel also established a set of images and techniques that Appelfeld used in his subsequent novels, the most unusual being his treatment of the Holocaust, whereby he evokes its atrocities without direct allusion to the historical events that led to them, taking his readers "through the chill of enveloping horror without ever wallowing in the horror itself," as Stephen Lewis has put it.

Also introduced in *Badenheim 1939* are images found throughout Appelfeld's work—travel, trains, forests, abandoned children, lost mothers, ugly fathers, intermarriage, and the negative prewar Jewish image. All are woven into an allegorical but realistic world that intensifies the reader's vision of the inception of the Holocaust.

Sources for Further Study

Appelfeld, Aharon. *The Story of a Life: A Memoir*. Translated by Aloma Halter. New York: Schocken Books, 2004.

Bernstein, Michael André. *Foregone Conclusions: Against Apocalyptic History*. Berkeley: University of California Press, 1994.

Brown, Michael, and Sara R. Horowitz, eds. *Encounter with Aharon Appelfeld*. Oakville, Ont.: Mosaic Press, 2003.

Budick, Emily Miller. *Aharon Appelfeld's Fiction: Acknowledging the Holocaust*. Bloomington: Indiana University Press, 2005.

Coffin, Edna Amir. "Appelfeld's Exceptional Universe: Harmony out of Chaos." *Hebrew Studies* 24 (1983): 85-98.

Langer, Lawrence L. "Aharon Appelfeld and the Uses of Language and Silence." In *Remembering for the Future*, edited by Yehuda Bauer et al. 3 vols. Elmsford, N.Y.: Pergamon Press, 1989.

Ramraz-Ra'ukh, Gilah. *Aharon Appelfeld: The Holocaust and Beyond*. Bloomington: Indiana University Press, 1994.

Roth, Philip. "A Conversation with Philip Roth." In *Beyond Despair*, by Aharon Appelfeld, translated by Jeffrey M. Green. New York: Fromm International, 1994.

Schwartz, Yigal. *Aharon Appelfeld: From Individual Lament to Tribal Eternity*. Translated by Jeffrey M. Green. Hanover, N.H.: University Press of New England for Brandeis University.

Wisse, Ruth R. "Aharon Appelfeld, Survivor." *Commentary* 76, no. 2 (August, 1983): 73-76.

—*June H. Schlessinger*

Constantine's Sword
The Church and the Jews — A History

Author: James Carroll (1943-   )
First published: 2001
Genre: Nonfiction
Subgenres: History; religion and spirituality

Carroll presents a lengthy account of Christians' attitudes toward Jews. His highly personal approach reveals his own piety and the anguish he has suffered over the Holocaust and the questions it has raised about Christian responsibilities.

Principal personages:
   Saint Paul (c. 10 C.E.-c. 64 C.E.), the brilliant thinker whose spiritual struggle illuminates the New Testament
   Constantine the Great (c. 272-285 C.E.-337 C.E.), first Christian emperor of Rome
   Saint Augustine (354 C.E.-430 C.E.), one of the most important Christian theologians
   Pius XII (1876-1958), controversial Roman Catholic pope during the years of Adolf Hitler's regime

Overview

James Carroll constructs his long story of the Christian attitude toward Jews in eight parts, and the first, "The Cross at Auschwitz," begins with the indignation many Jews expressed when, in 1984, a group of Carmelite nuns established a convent outside the gate at Auschwitz and prayed for the souls of the almost two million who died there and at Birkenau. As part of their efforts, the nuns planted in a nearby field the wooden cross from the papal altar in Kraków. Perhaps 250,000 non-Jewish Poles died in the two camps, but Jews protested Christian prayers for the 1.5 million Jews murdered there with banners bearing slogans such as "Do Not Christianize Auschwitz and Shoah!" In 1994, Pope John Paul II prevailed on the nuns to move their convent a few hundred yards away, and in return Jewish leaders allowed the cross to stand temporarily. The dispute intensified until 1998, when Catholic fanatics planted explosives on the site along with more than one hundred small crosses. Finally, in 1999, the Polish government had the small crosses removed but left the large cross at Auschwitz permanently. Carroll concludes of the controversy, "The cross here was simply wrong." He explains: "When suffering is seen to serve a universal plan of salvation, its particular character as tragic and evil is always diminished. The meaningless can be made to shimmer with an eschatological hope, and at Auschwitz this can seem like blasphemy." His reasoning resembles that of Jews who reject the term "holocaust," which means "burnt offering," with the repugnant implication that the genocide was an offering to God. The Hebrew word *Shoah*, or "catastrophe," avoids the suggestion of a "redemptive, sacrificial theology of salvation."

Carroll's revisionary reading of the history of supersessionism—the replacement of the Jews as God's chosen people by the "Jesus movement"—increases the responsibility of the Romans and lessens the role of the Pharisees. The Romans' destruction of the Temple convinced Christians that God was on their side, and the result was "the Judaism of the Jesus movement, which evolved into the Church, and the Judaism of the Pharisees, which evolved into rabbinic Judaism." The received reading of the relationship between Jesus and the Pharisees derives from second-generation non-Jewish followers and has poisoned relations between Jews and Christians ever since. Tying Jesus' fate to the assault on the money changers has made the name "Pharisee" a pejorative, whereas in Carroll's reading "almost nothing said by Christians about these particular Jews is true." Paul, who had been a Pharisee himself, tried to avert the breach developing between Christians and Pharisees, especially in his "hymn of love" to the Corinthians, but became a victim of it, the "martyr of Shalom" (or harmony), as Carroll describes him.

In 285, the emperor Diocletian divided the Roman Empire in half, taking the eastern part for himself and naming the general Maximian his counterpart in the west. In 306, Constantine assumed the Western Empire; and in 312, after experiencing a vision of a cross in the sky, he defeated the rebel Maxentius and converted his army—and eventually the empire—to Christianity. Constantine transformed the cross into his sword—that is, a long spear with a bar across it—putting the cross at the center of Christianity and thereby emphasizing death and violence rather than the hope of the Resurrection. This shift in focus hurt the Jews, who were blamed for the crucifixion, and the cult of St. Helena (Constantine's mother), with its legends of the True Cross and the Seamless Robe, encouraged Saint Ambrose (339-397) to stress Jewish guilt.

Saint Augustine (354-430) took a more humane position than Ambrose, but his mercy derived from his understanding of Jews as witnesses to Old

Testament prophecies. Carroll explains the irony: "Those first, grief-struck followers of Jesus had created a narrative of his Passion and death in part out of reports of what had happened, but more out of the consoling Scriptures of their Jewish religion. All too soon, that creation narration had come to be understood as 'history remembered' instead of 'prophecy historicized.'" Carroll calls the years 306 to 429 the Age of Constantine, unified by the Council of Nicaea in 325. It was a period in which the joining of Christianity to the Roman Empire was disastrous for Jews, with Christians making Jerusalem "the spiritual navel of the world." The result was a crisis: "How could the Gospel base its validity on its being the fulfillment of Jewish prophecy, yet be repudiated by the holders of title to the prophecy?"

Persecution of Jews intensified in 1096, when the Church defined violence as a sacred act, enabling the First Crusade and its butchery of Jews in the Rhineland. Saint Anselm (1033-1109) taught that God became man and suffered on the cross in expiation of humanity's sins, a teaching that inevitably stressed Jewish guilt. He was unsuccessfully rebutted in 1130 by Peter Abelard, who argued that Christ's life was meant as a guide to humans, not a sacrifice to a monstrous Father. So-called blood libels began in the twelfth century, with claims of ritual murders of children by Jews; in 1215, Pope Innocent III convened the Fourth Lateran Council, which decreed no salvation outside the Church; and in 1231, Pope Gregory IX's *Excommunicamus* authorized the Dominican and Franciscan Inquisition trials. These events reached a culmination in 1242, when thousands of copies of the Talmud were publicly burned in Paris.

Carroll's section on "The Inquisition: Enter Racism" tells the story of how attempts to convert Jews to Christianity ultimately led from anti-Judaism, or hatred of Jews as Christ killers, to anti-Semitism, a hatred based not on religion but on race. When Christians won Iberia back from the Muslims in 1212, the region's three million people included several hundred thousand Jews who had been living peacefully with Muslims and Christians in a relationship known as *convivencia*, or "coexistence." King James I of Aragon, apparently unsettled by Jews' aggressive teaching of the Kabbala, ruled in 1242 that all Jews in his kingdom must listen to conversionist sermons preached by Dominicans and Franciscans. The failure of this policy was followed by the plague that hit Europe between 1348 and 1351, killing over twenty million people. Its terror spawned rumors of wells being poisoned by Jews and led to terrible pogroms beginning in the Rhineland. Riots in Seville, Valencia, and Barcelona killed hundreds of Jews in 1391. Fear led many Jews to convert, and by 1425 as many as 200,000 of these *conversos* were living in Spain. At mid-century, Jews were being defined not by religion but by blood, and by the end of the century, the *conversos* were being scapegoated as much as the unconverted Jews. The blood purity regulations, called by one scholar "the ancestor of the Nazi Nuremberg laws," continued into the twentieth century. In its early stages, the Inquisition did its work only halfheartedly, but with the appointment of Fray Tomás de Torquemada (1420-1498) as the first grand inquisitor, torture and execution of *conversos* in Spain became common under the auspices of the Crown. Rome even established, in 1552, its private Inquisition, which led to the burning of dozens of Jews under Gian Pietro Caraffa. When Caraffa became Pope Paul IV, his 1555 bull *Cum Nimis Absurdum* confined Rome's Jews in a foul ghetto for three centuries. Of sixteenth century Spain, Carroll observes, "If the beginning of what we think of as modern anti-Semitism can be located anywhere, it is here."

Carroll is alert to the role played by secular philosophers in his story. He admires the "pluralistic ideal"of Benedict Spinoza (1632-1677), but it is Voltaire's "false promise of emancipation" that gets most of Carroll's attention. Voltaire (1694-1778) had no use for Christianity, but he developed an anti-Semitism based on his reading of the hatred of Jews in pagan antiquity. Carroll is contemptuous of those modern Christians who "claim exoneration on the basis of Voltaire's paean to paganism," and he rejects Hannah Arendt's thesis that the Enlightenment represented a break between Christian anti-Judaism and Nazi anti-Semitism. Carroll, in fact, scorns "the self-satisfied illusion of an Enlightenment that regarded its age—Reason!—as superior to the point of being discontinuous with what went before."

Carroll pays special attention to Martin Luther (1483-1546) and to Karl Marx (1818-1883). He follows historian Richard Marius in explaining Luther's *On the Jews and Their Lies* (1543) as a product of his terrible fear of death and the threat to Gospel consolation represented by Jews. Carroll notes that on November 10, 1938, Luther's 455th birthday, the Lutheran bishop of Thuringia, Martin Sasse, "exulted" that "the synagogues are burning in Germany." The occasion was Kristallnacht (the "night of broken glass"). Marx's "Jewish self-hatred" (Edmund Silberner's phrase) burst out in "On the Jewish Question" (1843), in which Marx ranted at Jews for their "huckstering," and Carroll concludes that "in the European imagination ... and in the socialist imagination, thanks in no small part to Marx, the figure of the Jew and the capitalist would be identical. The Jewish 'financier,' as the target of revolutionary hatred, would dominate the age." After the suppression of the Paris Commune in 1871, Marx wrote a defense of the movement that led to his demonization by conservatives as "that

Jew." Carroll is blunt in his judgment that Nazism and the Church both identified the Jew as "financier and communist."

Carroll's survey of Christian-Jewish relations in the nineteenth century includes a critical account of Pius IX's attack on "Modernism," accusing the Church of preparing for the "fascist/Nazi campaign of Jewish degradation." Carroll also lays out how persecution of the innocent Alfred Dreyfus, a Jewish officer in the French army, was prolonged bitterly by the vicious attacks on him in *La Croix*, the most popular Catholic publication in France. Carroll traces the rise of anti-Semitism (a word coined in 1879 by Wilhelm Marr, a German journalist) to its usefulness as a "source of connection between Catholic clergy and people buffeted by modernity." The so-called Kulturkampf in Germany began in 1871 under Otto von Bismarck, enforcing many restrictions on the activities of Catholics, but it withered under Catholic resistance after the formation of the Catholic Center Party in 1870.

The twentieth century brought changes. In 1919, the Center Party won six million votes, and its growth weakened the Jews' position in Germany because Catholics saw no need to ally themselves with a group so vulnerable. The Center press, in fact, although a "moderating influence" in the 1920's, exploited the anti-Semitism of its readers; soon after Hitler was elected in 1933, Cardinal Eugenio Pacelli proved eager to sign a treaty with the Nazis. Carroll quotes the historian John Cornwell: "When Hitler became Pacelli's partner in negotiations, the concordat thus became the supreme act of two authoritarians, while the supposed beneficiaries were correspondingly weakened, undermined, and neutralized." Carroll attributes much of Hitler's success to "the connivance of the Roman Catholic Church" in his transition period. Pacelli became Pope Pius XII, but Carroll—obviously no admirer—dismisses charges that he was a coward and a Hitler sycophant yet holds him responsible for the deportation to Auschwitz of the Jews from the Roman ghetto. Carroll's final explanation for Pius XII's callous indifference to the Jews' fate was that he knew he had the support of the Catholic masses, a support he needed to solidify papal power.

Carroll has written a history that will stimulate controversy for some time, but to the common reader it will be informative and often shocking. How many know, for instance, that while the Nazi Franz von Papen was sentenced at Nuremberg to eight years in prison, in 1959 he was made a papal private chamberlain by the Vatican? Whatever weaknesses scholars may find, *Constantine's Sword* deserves high praise.

SOURCES FOR FURTHER STUDY

Carroll, James. *An American Requiem: God, My Father, and the War That Came Between Us*. Boston: Houghton Mifflin, 1996.

Karabell, Zachary. "A Writer and Former Priest Sees Anti-Semitism as the Rock on Which His Church Is Built." *Chicago Tribune*, February 4, 2001, p. 1.

Morris, Charles R. "The Worst Thing About My Church." *The Atlantic Monthly* 287, no. 1 (January, 2001): 80.

Olsen, Diane, ed. *The Book That Changed My Life: Interviews with National Book Award Winners and Finalists*. New York: Modern Library, 2002.

Rourke, Mary. "A Faithful Catholic Indicts His Own Religion: Former Priest James Carroll Lights a Fire with His Examination of the Catholic Church's History of Behaviour Toward Jews." *Los Angeles Times*, January 21, 2001, p. E1.

Sullivan, Andrew. "Christianity's Original Sin." *The New York Times Book Review*, January 14, 2001, p. 5.

—*Frank Day*

"Daddy"

Author: Sylvia Plath (1932-1963)
First published: 1965, in *Ariel*
Genre: Poetry
Subgenres: Dramatic monologue; confessional poetry

Plath's poem employs images of Nazis and fascism in addressing the author's unhealthy attachment to and anger toward her father. It may be said that "Daddy" is about individual freedom and two of its principal prerequisites: self-knowledge and courage.

Overview

Written on October 12, 1962, four months before her suicide, Sylvia Plath's "Daddy" is a "confessional" poem of eighty lines divided into sixteen five-line stanzas. The persona, a daughter speaking in the first person, seeks to resolve the manifold conflicts with her father and paternal authority that have dogged her life. Her readiness for the task is unambiguously evident in the first stanza's opening lines: "You do not do, You do not do/ Anymore."

"Daddy," begins the second stanza, "I have had to kill you." The deceased, titanic patriarch, first represented as "Marble-heavy, a bag full of God," has his godliness immediately modified when he is referred to as a "Ghastly statue," with that phrase's related intimations of corpses and ghosts. The death of her father, an awesome figure with "one gray toe/ Big as a Frisco seal" and "A head in the freakish Atlantic," had not daunted the speaker's hopes of reunion; as she puts it in the third stanza, "I used to pray to recover you./ Ach du." Her belief in the power of prayer is, however, a thing of the past, no longer tenable.

The father's European roots—he is imaged as a Nazi in the fourth stanza—prove elusive to the speaker, a relatively unimportant handicap, given the significant affliction she discovers in the fifth stanza: "I never could talk to you./ The tongue stuck in my jaw." A less circumscribed and more dire speechlessness emerges in the sixth stanza.

In the seventh stanza, the Holocaust is introduced, and the speaker recovers her powers of speech in the context—if not as a result—of having pointedly established herself as a Jew. A couple of overworked Nazi emblems are demythologized in stanza 8: "The snows of Tyrol, the clear beer of Vienna/ Are not very pure or true," while she identifies herself with Gypsies, another group much hated by the Nazis. In stanza 9, she brazenly mocks fascist discourse as "gobbledygoo," and does much the same to her father's Nazi image: "And your neat mustache/ And your Aryan eye, bright blue./ Panzer-man, panzer-man, O You—." When, in stanza 10, one reads "Not God but a swastika/ So black no sky could squeak through," one is confronted with a profoundly potent evil capable of overwhelming the heavens.

The penultimate patriarchal image appears in stanza 11: father as teacher-cum-devil. Although, she recalls, "You stand at the blackboard, daddy,/ In the picture I have of you," the innocuous snapshot of a pedagogue does not distract her from perceiving the father's demoniac nature. The hauntingly sadistic image, in the twelfth stanza, of the father who, before dying, "Bit my pretty red heart in two," is juxtaposed with her vain pursuit of him ten years hence, in an attempted suicide. Failing at that, she tries, in stanzas 13 and 14, a more effective, somewhat less self-destructive tactic: "I made a model of you/ A man in black with a Meinkampf look/ And a love of the rack and the screw," and marries the surrogate.

Predatory and erotic, the ruinous, eerie image of the father as vampire in stanza 15 anticipates the speaker's ritualistic solution. "There's a stake in your fat black heart/ And the villagers never liked you," begins the poem's sixteenth and final stanza. The speaker's decisive, triumphant patricide permits her to say, "Daddy, daddy, you bastard, I'm through," and, for the first time, call her life her own.

Given the emotionally damaged speaker's mercurial discourse and her father's protean nature, Plath's characterizations of the two and their interrelations—particularly the series of continually modulating images of the father—are among the most psychologically sound, aesthetically impeccable, and effective formal accomplishments in "Daddy."

There is a significant conceptual corollary to the poem's frequent nursery-rhyme rhythms when, in the first stanza, the speaker echoes, with wit and irony, the nursery rhyme about the "old woman who lived in a shoe . . . [who] didn't know what to do." This character, however, is a woman who knows exactly what to do in order to end her thirty-year habitation in her old man's shoe and to exorcize the related intimidation, control, passivity, and entrapment: She must commit a symbolic patricide.

For all the speaker's strident declamations, however, there is nothing to obscure the fact that hers is an ambivalent discourse. Savior and tormentor, the object of nostalgic affection and vituperation—these are the conflicting dualisms that form her troubled attachment to the first man in her life (and to his reincarnation, her husband), dualisms that have set the terms of her persecution and imprisonment. Although she "used to pray to recover [her father]," her present goal, transformed by experience, no longer aimed at *re*covering, is to *un*cover—to lay bare the inventory of her heart's wounds, which shaped and dogged the future, all father-inflicted during childhood. The resulting narrative, awash with untrammeled emotion, produces an intricately wrought compound image of the father.

Sylvia Plath. (Eric Stahlbert, Sophia Smith Collection, Smith College)

The permutations that produce the compound image of the father follow a devolving trajectory. In broad terms, the father, first imaged as a god of titanic proportions (stanza 2), is transformed in short order into a sadistic devil (stanza 11) before being finally described as a vampire (stanza 15). Introduced as a worshiped and scorned god-cadaver-statue, the paternal image is modulated and degenerated into the image of a viciously racist, sadistically misogynistic Nazi. When, with bitter irony, the speaker says, "Every woman adores a Fascist," the statement is cast as an affront to feminist sensibilities, so typical is it of male presumptions about what "every woman" wants. The feminist theme continues into the succeeding image of the father as teacher-devil, as traditional gender roles would typically represent, as complementary images, male tutors and untutored females. The semantically dense imagery and characterization that occur here are typical of Plath's poetry.

In the poem's final degenerative permutation, the speaker integrates her father and husband into a single ghastly image of a vampire, a parasitic male who has been drinking her lifeblood. The father's precipitous fall from deity to evil incarnate, conveyed in the serial pattern of paternal imagery, sets up the poem's denouement: a ritual killing of evil, the one necessary prerequisite for the speaker to regain a life worthy of the name.

In the course of discussing Sylvia Plath's poetry, Joyce Carol Oates has contended that the poet did not like other people because she doubted "that they existed in the way that she did, as pulsating, breathing, suffering individuals." The ostensible subject of "Daddy" is the speaker's somewhat belated acknowledgment of her unhealthy attachment to and anger toward her father and her eagerness to explode the Oedipal prisonhouse in which she has been captive so that she might have a life that is truly her own. Accordingly, it could be said that "Daddy" is about individual freedom and two of its principal prerequisites: self-knowledge and courage.

Like all good poetry, "Daddy" raises many questions. In the case of "Daddy," among the most compelling of these questions is, What is the speaker's understanding of the predicament from which she seeks to escape? Certainly, the sincerity of her testimony is as apparent as her anguish and rage. She speaks as if she were the victim of an error that her current insights empower her to rectify. Herein lies a major source of the poem's pathos: Plath's speaker fails to detect the resemblance between her situation and that of the Greek hero for whom Sigmund Freud named her presumed psychopathology, Oedipus. She suffers from the intractable consequences of fate.

The speaker's account also implies a subscription to a bizarre mutation of the doctrine of Original Sin, the central postulate of which is that all errors are the result of unconscious guilt. This moral drama entails two shaky assumptions: that the world is just and that, despite all contrary evidence, people who suffer have only themselves to blame. As Dorothy Van Ghent, however, once pointedly asked about tragic heroes, "Is one guilty for circumstances?" One must deal tactfully if not compassionately with human fictions—while under one's breath lamenting their folly—and Plath's speaker surely deserves such consideration. Unfortunately, redefining herself and reclaiming her life by assuming full responsibility for her dilemma offer the same prospects for complete success as railing at the world for not being just. Perhaps Plath understood the speaker's inadequate sense of her situation sufficiently for suicide to emerge in her life as the more decisive, if unhappy, alternative.

Sources for Further Study

Alexander, Paul. *Rough Magic: A Biography of Sylvia Plath*. New York: Da Capo Press, 1999.
Bassnett, Susan. *Sylvia Plath: An Introduction to the Poetry*. New York: Palgrave Macmillan, 2005.
Gill, Joe, ed. *The Cambridge Companion to Sylvia Plath*. New York: Cambridge University Press, 2006.

Hungerford, Amy. *The Holocaust of Texts: Genocide, Literature, and Personification*. Chicago: University of Chicago Press, 2003.
Kendall, Tim. *Sylvia Plath: A Critical Study*. London: Faber, 2001.
Kirk, Connie Ann. *Sylvia Plath: A Biography*. Westport, Conn.: Greenwood Press, 2004.
Rowland, Anthony. *Holocaust Poetry: Awkward Poetics in the Work of Sylvia Plath, Geoffrey Hill, Tony Harrison, and Ted Hughes*. Edinburgh: Edinburgh University Press, 2005.
Swiontkowski, Gale. *Imagining Incest: Sexton, Plath, Rich, and Olds on Life with Daddy*. Selinsgrove, Pa.: Susquehanna University Press, 2003.
Wagner-Martin, Linda. *Sylvia Plath: A Literary Life*. 2d ed. New York: Palgrave Macmillan, 2003.

—Jordan Leondopoulos

Daniel's Story

AUTHOR: Carol Matas (1949-   )
FIRST PUBLISHED: 1993
GENRE: Novel
SUBGENRES: Historical fiction; young adult literature

This novel tells the story of a German Jewish adolescent's four-year struggle to survive as he and his family are shunted from Frankfurt to the Jewish ghetto in Łódź, Poland, then to the Auschwitz and Buchenwald concentration camps.

PRINCIPAL CHARACTERS:
    Daniel, a fourteen-year-old German Jewish boy, the novel's narrator
    Erika, Daniel's younger sister
    Joseph, Daniel's father
    Ruth, Daniel's mother
    Oma "Grandma" Miriam, Daniel's paternal grandmother
    Leah, Daniel's aunt
    Peter, Daniel's uncle
    Rosa, Daniel's Polish girlfriend
    Karl, a non-Jewish Buchenwald internee

OVERVIEW

In 1987, Carol Matas published *Lisa's War*, a novel for young adults that recounts the experiences of a young Jewish girl living under the Nazi regime between the early 1930's and 1945. This novel attracted considerable attention for its success in relating for young people the horrors that the Nazis perpetrated in their attempt to eradicate European Jews. Some six million Jews were killed by the German Nazi regime between 1938 and 1945, more than one million of them children.

When directors of the United States Holocaust Memorial Museum in Washington, D.C., decided to mount an exhibition to detail the ordeals that many children suffered during the Holocaust, they titled the exhibition *Daniel's Story: Remembrances of the Children*. They invited Carol Matas to write an accompanying novel that would focus on Jewish youth under Nazism, as she had in *Lisa's War*. The museum directors wanted the novel they commissioned to relate to the photographs displayed in the Holocaust exhibition, and this caveat provided the framework for *Daniel's Story*. Matas met this requirement by creating Daniel, a German Jewish protagonist, to narrate the story. An adolescent interested in photography, Daniel is fourteen when the story begins and eighteen when it ends.

Some reviewers have criticized Matas's device of having Daniel refer often to the photographs that he carries with him or, after they have been confiscated, that he envisions in his imagination. The criticism is perhaps valid, but Matas had to make Daniel's photography central to the story as requested by those who commissioned it. Actually, Matas uses the prescribed framework to good advantage, making Daniel's photography an effective way for him to describe many of the pertinent scenes throughout the book. As the story develops, Daniel expresses his hope that what he is recording on film will eventually stand as testimony to what happened to innocent people during the Holocaust. Daniel has a strong sense of history, and he realizes that the details of the Nazi horrors must be documented and remembered if the world is to prevent the recurrence of such events.

In several parts of *Daniel's Story*, Matas refers to the slavery of Jews in ancient Egypt, establishing the long history of anti-Semitism that predated the common era. Pogroms, the organized annihilation of Jews, have long pervaded Jewish existence. Throughout *Daniel's Story*, Matas reveals the techniques the Nazis used to make the annihilation of the Jews seem acceptable, even desirable, to most of those who permitted the Holocaust to happen. She describes the Nazis' depiction of Jews as insects or rodents, distasteful organisms to be eradicated without qualms about their extermination.

Daniel's Story devotes several passages to scenes in which the Jews held in custody are killing the lice that infest their barracks, vermin that can spread diseases such as typhus. Matas creates a parallel that reinforces the notion that extermination is acceptable, but, ironically, the incarcerated Jews are to the lice what the Nazis are to the Jews in their custody. By dehumanizing their captives, the Germans were able to rationalize the "ethnic cleansing" that was the Holocaust.

Daniel's family has lived in Germany for as long as any of his relatives can remember. Daniel's father's family can trace its German roots back more than six hundred years, his mother's more than a thousand. His father, Joseph, owned a flourishing hardware store, but when the Nazis took command, the word "JEW" was painted on the windows of the store and Schutzstaffel (SS) guards stood outside the establishment forbidding customers to enter. In time, the hardware store was confiscated, taken over by a German who then employed Joseph to work for him in order to keep Joseph's faithful clientele as customers. To justify the confiscation, the Nazis paid Joseph a pittance for his valuable business.

Daniel's family still lived in Frankfurt in their residence, although they bore many indignities. Daniel, a student in a public school, was humiliated by his teacher for being a Jew. In front of Daniel's classmates, the teacher, declaring that true Aryans have specific head measurements, measured Daniel's head and said, "You see! Inferior species. Head too small, no room for brains, a close relative to the vermin in our gutters." Daniel soon left the public school and entered a Jewish school.

Daniel's favorite uncle, Peter, discharged from his teaching job in the public schools because of his ethnicity, was arrested and imprisoned because some years earlier he had received two citations for illegal parking. During his first year in prison he wrote to his family frequently. His release seemed imminent, but then his letters ceased. A year later, a box arrived containing his ashes. Peter's wife, Leah, and their four children moved in with Daniel's family. Leah gave Peter's camera to Daniel, who used it to record what was happening as Nazism made inroads on human rights.

Daniel's paternal grandmother, Oma Miriam, feeble and confined to a nursing home, made Daniel a Hitler Youth uniform, which he kept hidden and occasionally wore to gain access to places closed to Jews. There he took pictures to document the effects that the rise of Nazism was having on German society. Oma Miriam, realizing that the life she had known was disintegrating, hoarded her sleeping pills until one night she swallowed them all and fell into a sleep from which she did not awaken.

Daniel's family was soon ordered to report to the railway station for redeployment. They ended up in Łódź, Poland, where they lived in the crowded Jewish ghetto for two years doing forced labor. While there, Daniel met and fell in love with a girl named Rosa. The family members, including Leah and her children, were still together, although they were forced to live under unbearable circumstances. Finally, however, people in the ghetto were to be deported if they were unfit for work. Two of Leah's daughters were to be sent away—as it turned out, they were to be sent to Auschwitz, where they would certainly be killed. When Leah, who was to remain in Łódź, tried to rescue her daughters, the SS guards killed all three of them. Throughout the novel, the wrenching disintegration of families forms a major part of the story.

Eventually, Daniel and his father are shipped out of the ghetto, first to Auschwitz, then to Buchenwald. There they see Erika, Daniel's younger sister, still alive but so frail that she can barely stand. Daniel is assigned to work with Karl, a political prisoner who has been at Buchenwald since 1939, a punishment for his being a Communist. Karl, a photographer, leads a clandestine resistance movement within Buchenwald and soon enlists Daniel. The Russian troops are approaching from one direction, the Americans from another. The nightmare of World War II will end soon.

Karl has hidden weapons that he now distributes to members of the resistance, including Daniel, who is forced to use his to shoot two SS guards, one of whom dies. Daniel wants vengeance, and he refuses to help the other guard he has shot, but Joseph tells him to tie a cloth around the dying man's wound. Daniel's father reminds him that if the Nazis have made him like them, they have succeeded.

Soon, American troops arrive, and Daniel and Joseph are liberated. Erika is also set free, but prolonged starvation has so weakened her that she dies. At her deathbed is Rosa, the Polish girl with whom Daniel fell in love in Łódź and with whom he is reunited when he returns there. The book ends on a note of hope. Daniel and Rosa will undoubtedly marry and create a new generation. They talk of joining the Jewish community in Palestine.

SOURCES FOR FURTHER STUDY

Bradburn, Mark. Review of *Daniel's Story*, by Carol Matas. *Wilson Library Bulletin* 68 (December, 1993): 118-119.

Kaminow, Susan. Review of *Daniel's Story*, by Carol Matas. *School Library Journal* 39, no. 5 (May, 1993): 107.

Matas, Carol. *Lisa's War*. New York: Charles Scribner's Sons, 1987.

Smith, William J. Review of *Daniel's Story*, by Carol Matas. *Book Report* 12, no. 2 (September/October, 1993): 45.

Sullivan, Edward T. *The Holocaust in Literature for Youth: A Guide and Resource Book*. Lanham, Md.: Scarecrow, 1999.

United States Holocaust Memorial Museum. *Remember the Children: "Daniel's Story"—A Teacher's Guide*. Washington, D.C.: Author, 1999.

Weisman, Kay. Review of *Daniel's Story*, by Carol Matas. *Booklist* 89, no. 18 (May 15, 1993): 1688.

—*R. Baird Shuman*

"Death Fugue"

Author: Paul Celan (1920-1970)
First published: "Todesfuge," 1952, in *Mohn und Gedächtnis* (English translation collected in *Poems of Paul Celan*, 1988)
Genre: Poetry
Subgenre: Lyric poetry

In this poem, Celan uses the musical structure of systematic repetition, along with allusions to music, in depicting the machinery of death in a Nazi concentration camp. The poem derives its effect as much from the irony of its musical aspects as it does from the juxtaposition of extreme opposites.

Overview

"Death Fugue" is structured like a musical fugue, in which a main idea or phrase is systematically repeated throughout the composition. The six irregular stanzas present the speaker's perspective on a Nazi concentration camp; the lack of punctuation between thoughts suggests the deterioration of the speaker's consciousness as he exposes the atrocities the crematorium has wreaked on those condemned to die. He also repeats incessantly, as if to suggest an urgent need to fill the void of death. Paul Celan's parents both were murdered in a concentration camp; Celan himself was taken to a forced-labor camp. Throughout his life he was haunted by their deaths and, in a sense, by his own survival.

The first stanza is an exposition of the time, space, and place of the death camp. The poem's narrator speaks for a collective and condemned "we" who dig graves from morning to night. The repetitiveness of time is revealed in the first two lines of the poem: "daybreak" is followed by "sundown," which is followed respectively by "noon," "morning," and "night" again. Time has ceased to flow with distinction for these workers of the death factory. Meanwhile, the officer who is responsible for keeping the gravediggers in line is seen writing letters home to Germany. That he corresponds nightly with the motherland indicates that the camps are outside Germany.

Each subsequent stanza reveals the cruelly civic and barbaric nature of the camps. Every image presented is "answered" by an opposing one. The golden hair of Margarete from Germany, for example, contrasts with the "ashen" hair of the Jew Shulamith. Daybreak soon becomes dusk or "sundown"; the sound of the spades hitting dirt is juxtaposed against the sound of Jews forced to sing and dance as they dig; the "black milk of daybreak" that characterizes the sky under which the Jews dig is contrasted with the starry and brilliant night under which the officer writes home.

The sharp distinctions between the condemned Jews and the Germans in the opening stanzas emphasize the relationship between the victims and their oppressors. As the poem progresses, the relationship intensifies. The officer "calls out more darkly" and demands that the condemned "jab deeper into the earth." The swifter the commands, the more quickly the condemned must act in their movements toward death. In order to hasten their final annihilation, the officer steps out of his house and moves closer to the condemned; he stops and gives himself the necessary distance to fire his "leaden bullets" at any who disobey him. The rest will be gassed to death in the crematorium.

In the last stanza, the separation between the dead and those responsible for death is expressed in the even number of lines describing each. The first half of the stanza reiterates the scene of the gravediggers, while the second half cruelly crowns death as "a master from Germany." This phrase is repeated as the speaker faces the point of death (signified by the point of the gun). The last lines shift back to contrasting the hair of Margarete with that of Shulamith; with the striking contrast of each with regard to life and death, this image expresses the final tendrils of death.

Paul Celan. (© A. Van Mangoldt)

The musical structure, as well as the allusion to music within the poem, belies the anguish of death, particularly the mass deaths in the concentration camps. Some have objected to the poet's "aestheticizing" the death camps, charging Celan with the audacity to write lyric poetry after the Holocaust. Others perceive that the death of

Celan's parents in Transnistria compelled the poet to transpose personal anguish into art, as this early poem suggests.

In fact, the systematic repetition and the musical aspects of the poem indicate that the condemned are no longer in control of life. Their activities are as mindless as their forced and mechanized behavior is soulless. They "speak" and "think" in run-on phrases, and the poem literally reflects their mental and physical deterioration. They dig graves and are forced to sing and dance even as they prepare for death; in the final coup de grâce, they beg for death so they can disappear into nothingness. Ironically, they sing for death in order to escape from death.

With the exception of stanzas 3 and 5 (which serve as the "counterpoint" in the musical fugue structure), the second half of each stanza shifts from the viewpoint of the condemned to the officer and what he represents—Nazi Germany. These sections reinforce the oppressiveness of the concentration camp. Each is as repetitive as the first section, but with a difference, since here, the officer acts as an agent of death. His power over the condemned can be seen in the variety of terrors he is capable of causing: "whistles his Jews," "commands us strike up for the dance," "grabs his iron," "plays with the serpents," "strikes you with leaden bullets," and "sets his pack on us." If the condemned have only one course available to them, it is the task of the officer to both hasten and torment them toward this end.

The poem's effect derives as much from the irony of the musical aspects as it does from the juxtaposition of extreme opposites. The first image, "black milk," is already suggestive of the deep taint of death. If the infant drinks of the mother's nourishment in its whiteness and purity, the condemned victims drink endlessly the dregs of their graves. They are doomed to the black smoke of the crematorium. Shulamith's "ashen hair" reinforces the results of cremation, while it contrasts with the "golden hair" of Margarete. The blond hair, as well as the officer's blue eyes, contrasts with the dark and black of the victims.

The shifts in opposing images, besides indicating the difference between the Germans and the Jews, also create the effect of heightened emotion and a sense of growing despair. The officer's perfunctory commands (reporting to Germany and keeping the prisoners in line) give way to increasingly cruel treatment and attitude.

In stanza 3, the speaker observes that the officer is noticeably more excited and animated. In stanza 5, "He calls out more sweetly play death death is a master from Germany," and he promises the condemned a space in the crematorium, "a grave you will have in the clouds."

In the next stanza, "he grants us a grave in the air" is a remark that expresses a twisted gratitude. These images serve as a counterpoint, an answer to the main theme of the men digging their own graves. As the condemned grow more mechanical and hopeless, the officer expresses a malicious glee at the pain he inflicts. In the end, it is death—as signified by the Nazis—that reigns supreme.

"Death Fugue" exposes the savage cruelty of the concentration camps by plainly describing the conditions. Everything that is human and active (working, singing, dancing, writing) is directed toward death. Without being didactic, the poet expresses the unforgettable conditions of the camps. The very vividness of the poem's first-person narration, however, also points to an incongruity within the poem: The poem's speaker, along with the other people in the camp, may be assumed to have been killed. Celan uses this incongruity to remind readers how far they will always be from knowing the full truth of the death camps.

The musical structure distances the reader from the events as they are presented in the poem. Rather than elicit an aesthetically pleased response from the reader, the poem achieves an opposite effect by making each episode tell what happened as directly as possible but in language that also reflects the progression toward death. The poet drives each point home with the repetition of images, especially the ones that lead from digging the graves to the final end, represented by the rising smoke.

In addition to the musical association of the word "fugue" (which comes from the Latin word meaning "to flee"), there is a psychological meaning, a state in which a patient suffers from a pathological amnesiac condition and has no recollection of incidents that occurred during the illness. Viewed from this perspective, the poem could also express the devastating historical fact of the Holocaust. It is impossible to forget the millions who were condemned to die by the Nazis, even though the full extent of what happened may never be known. Those involved have tried to flee from taking responsibility for their crimes. At the Nuremberg Trials, for example, the Nazis frequently claimed that what happened at the death camps was the result of their merely following orders.

Sources for Further Study

Baer, Ulrich. *Remnants of Song: Trauma and the Experience of Modernity in Charles Baudelaire and Paul Celan.* Stanford, Calif.: Stanford University Press, 2000.

Bernstein, Michael André. *Five Portraits: Modernity and Imagination in Twentieth-Century German Writing.* Evanston, Ill.: Northwestern University Press, 2000.

Chalfen, Israel. *Paul Celan: A Biography of His Youth.* Translated by Maximillian Bleyleben. New York: Persea Books, 1991.
Felstiner, John. *Paul Celan: Poet, Survivor, Jew.* New Haven, Conn.: Yale University Press, 1995.
Lyon, James K. *Paul Celan and Martin Heidegger: An Unresolved Conversation, 1951-1970.* Baltimore: The Johns Hopkins University Press, 2006.
Tobias, Rochelle. *The Discourse of Nature in the Poetry of Paul Celan: The Unnatural World.* Baltimore: The Johns Hopkins University Press, 2006.

—Cynthia Wong

The Deputy

Author: Rolf Hochhuth (1931-   )
First published: *Der Stellvertreter: Ein Christliches Trauerspiel*, 1963 (first produced, 1963; English translation, 1963)
Genre: Drama
Subgenre: Documentary drama

This controversial play addresses the failure of Western Christian civilization, as represented by Pope Pius XII, to act against one of the greatest crimes in human history—the Nazi extermination of six million innocent Jews. It ultimately warns what can happen when leaders fail to stand up against inhumanity.

Principal characters:
  Pius XII (1876-1958), controversial Roman Catholic pope during the years of Adolf Hitler's regime
  Father Riccardo Fontana, a Jesuit priest in the foreign office of the Vatican
  Kurt Gerstein, an officer in the Schutzstaffel (SS)
  The Doctor, director of the death selections at Auschwitz
  Jacobson, a Jewish prisoner

Overview

The Deputy begins in August, 1942, at the papal legation in Berlin. Riccardo Fontana, an idealistic Jesuit priest, pleads with the papal representative (the nuncio) of Germany to ask the pope to condemn publicly the Nazi extermination of the Jews of Europe. Kurt Gerstein, a German who joined the Schutzstaffel (SS) to gather information on the killings, and who has witnessed gassings of Jews in the Bełżec extermination camp, presents his graphic eyewitness account of the gassings and cremations to the nuncio. This confirms Fontana's worst fears.

The nuncio tells Gerstein that he is not authorized to deal with German officers and directs him to leave. Father Riccardo, however, continues to listen with horror to Gerstein's account. Gerstein says that at the Bełżec camp he saw 750 people crammed into each of four gas chambers, 3,000 people who were gassed in twenty-five minutes. Like Fontana, Gerstein has visited the nuncio to urge him to tell the pope to speak out against the mass murders in his capacity as Christ's deputy on earth.

The action shifts to Berlin, where Adolf Eichmann, the bureaucrat in charge of the deportations to the extermination camps, is relaxing, socializing, and casually discussing the extermination of the Jews with top industrialists and government officials. Also present is the cynical Doctor, who is in charge of selections for the gas chambers and medical experiments at the Auschwitz concentration camp. Pleased that most Europeans are indifferent to the exterminations, they express their concerns about possible negative reactions from the pope. The Nazi view that the extermination of the Jews is an idealistic and scientific necessity is expounded upon.

The final scene of the first act is set in Gerstein's Berlin apartment, where he has hidden a Jew named Jacobson. Gerstein and Riccardo will help the Jew escape by providing him with a false passport. The camp Doctor later enters Gerstein's apartment and expresses his cynical pride that one can exterminate Jews and still be accepted as a Christian. He is intent on challenging all categories of meaning by exterminating innocent people day after day without limit. The scene ends when Father Riccardo tells Gerstein that he will do everything in his power as a true Christian to beg the pope personally to speak out on behalf of Jews, who are being murdered all over Europe.

Act 2 reveals the spectrum of the reaction of Roman Catholic officialdom to the Holocaust. Riccardo tells his own father (who is a trusted counsel to the Holy See) about the extermination of the Jews. The elder Fontana first is incredulous, then tells his son that it would be impolite for the pope to speak out against Germany, for this would violate his policy of neutrality. Riccardo replies that the Deputy of Christ would be derelict in his duty not to take a moral stand before all Christian humanity. The father retorts that his son must be obedient to the Vatican and must respect the inter-

Rolf Hochhuth. (DPA/Landov)

ests of the Church. An important cardinal then enters and reminds Riccardo that Nazi Germany is a bulwark against the anti-Christian threat of Soviet Russia. He reproaches Riccardo for his unrealistic idealism, while further suggesting that the Jews have brought their grim fate on themselves.

Act 3 deals with the brutal seizure of the baptized Jews of Rome by the SS. When Father Riccardo expresses his outrage that the Jews are being seized under the very windows of the Vatican, the cardinal replies that the churches and monasteries around Rome have hidden large numbers of Jews. Riccardo holds to his belief that only a public statement from the pope can present a chance of saving the rest of Europe's Jews from the gas chambers—that only the Deputy of Christ can face down Adolf Hitler, the anti-Christ. The act ends at the headquarters of the Gestapo in Rome. SS officers reveal their sadistic brutality as they round up the Jews of Rome; they also demonstrate their contempt for Christianity.

Suspense builds as the pope finally makes his appearance in a meeting with Father Riccardo. The fourth act is the shortest of the five, for Riccardo's confrontation with the pope is intense and to the point. The pope is a cold, remote, formal, diplomatic, politically cautious, and calculating figure. He is neutral at best, favorable to Germany at worst, and completely unwilling to take the moral public stand that Fontana urges him to take. In a final gesture of extreme protest, Father Riccardo pins the Jewish Star of David to his cassock in the name of brotherly love and in solidarity with Christ's blood relatives. The pope is outraged by this gesture.

Act 5 is set in Auschwitz. True to his beliefs, Father Riccardo has chosen to accompany the Jewish victims in a railroad cattle car to Auschwitz. He meets the Doctor, who calls himself the "lord of life and death." The Doctor expresses extreme satisfaction in conducting "the boldest experiment that mankind has ever seen." He proclaims that "Auschwitz refutes creator, creation, and the creature" and declares that many of the leaders of the SS came from good Catholic backgrounds. Riccardo is put to work in the crematoria but does not relinquish his Christian faith. When he witnesses the Doctor sadistically driving a woman prisoner mad, Riccardo acts. In a last desperate gesture in which he affirms his faith in man and God, Riccardo tries to shoot the Doctor but is himself mortally wounded by a guard. The play ends as a German document about the pope's failure to act is read by an unemotional announcer. The spectator is left with a feeling of utter futility as the announcer concludes that the gas chambers continued to do their work until the end of 1944, when the Russians liberated the prisoners of Auschwitz.

The published text of the play includes a sixty-five page appendix titled "Sidelights on History" in which Hochhuth seeks to document the events dramatized. Hochhuth researched his topic for three years, and he provides a lengthy account of the policies of the Vatican during the Holocaust. He acknowledges that some characters, such as Father Riccardo, are fictional and that he conceived some scenes (such as Riccardo's confrontation with the pope) for dramatic effect. The main historical figures are real: Gerstein, the Doctor (modeled on the infamous Josef Mengele), and the pope were vital actors on the stage of history.

The Deputy is primarily a play about the failure of Western Christian civilization, centered in the person of the pope, to act against one of the greatest crimes in history—the Nazi extermination of six million innocent Jews for the crime of having been born. It is a drama about indifference and inaction, commitment and despair. During the Holocaust, Christians were perpetrators, bystanders, and victims. *The Deputy* is a Christian tragedy: Father Riccardo becomes the tragic hero by taking on the burden that should have belonged to the pope. In doing so, he is forced to be insubordinate to the pope and eventually to try to murder the viciously evil Doctor.

The Deputy is also a drama about the nature of evil and the choices that people must make in response to it. The SS officials and the Doctor have chosen to participate—to humiliate and to kill—while Father Riccardo and Kurt Gerstein choose to tell the civilized world about this evil. They strive to galvanize the pope into action and in the end give their lives for their Christian beliefs. According to Hochhuth, Pope Pius XII is particularly culpable, for he has chosen not to make a choice. He has therefore abdicated his role as the Deputy of Christ, which is to be a witness and sufferer for humanity and the truth. The play is also a reenactment of an extremely painful episode in modern history; its almost unbearable descriptions of life and death in the camps and its heartbreaking depictions of the suffering of innocent, abandoned people were intended to stir the conscience of the world.

The Deputy tries to answer the questions of why the pope kept silent, whether he should have kept silent, and what the consequences of his behavior were. Hochhuth attributes the pope's silence to his timid, cold personality, his sympathy for Germany, his fear of a schism in the Church, and above all his belief that the political, diplomatic, and financial interests of the Church had to be preserved at all costs. Some critics of the play, such as the future Pope Paul VI, believed the play to be an unfair attack on the pope. They argued that many church officials all over Europe tried to help Jews, while the pope himself approved of the hiding of Italian Jews and suffered great anguish over his inability to do more. Defenders of the play responded that the pope refused to recognize that the Nazis were really pagan apostates from Christianity. They pointed out that the pope did condemn the German invasion of neutral Belgium and Holland and condemned the Soviet aggression against Finland, while failing to take a public stand on an extermination campaign against innocent, helpless people. In addition, the pope failed to excommunicate top Nazis who were baptized Catholics and who never formally left the Church, such as Adolf Hitler, Joseph Goebbels, and Heinrich Himmler.

The last act deals not with the pope but with what the play calls the silence of God in Auschwitz. The play suggests that the answer to the meaningless universe of negation embodied in Auschwitz must come from humankind. In its view, Christianity failed in the person and institution of the papacy. Christian teachings must be lived and acted upon (as Riccardo and Gerstein act upon them) in order to be authentic.

The richness of dramatic devices, extreme length, overwhelming subject, and unusual appendix make this play difficult to categorize. It is a Christian tragedy, a drama of soaring heroism in the manner of Friedrich Schiller, an existentialist work on the struggle for meaning and human choices, and a historical docudrama with real characters. It is a polemic, a modern morality play, and a warning to the future. More than a play, it is a challenging book, a news story, a factual statement, and a philosophical tract. The original version of the play takes from six to eight hours to perform. Many shortened (three-hour) versions of *The Deputy* have been staged in Europe and the United States. All have failed to capture the complete texture of the original, for any serious cuts eliminate crucial episodes and therefore distort and trivialize the full meaning of the play.

In *The Deputy*, Hochhuth uses a wide variety of literary as well as dramatic devices. Each act is preceded by a few epigraphs and by a lengthy preface detailing its historical significance. In his preface to scene 2 of act 5, Hochhuth writes: "What took place in the interior of this underworld at the crematorium itself, exceeds imagination. There is no way of conveying it." Hochhuth was aware of the fact that the historical reality of the Holocaust threatens to exceed the imagination of the artist. However, he believed that it had to be dramatized to shock the spectator into an indignation that would lead to moral action.

The play is replete with irony. The pope is portrayed as a man who is shocked by the tactlessness of the Germans in carrying off the Jews of Rome within view of his windows, when he should be indignant about the murder of innocent people. He is also depicted as a man immersed in the trivia of religious observance instead of his moral duties as Christ's deputy. The supreme irony is that the evil Doctor, who mocks God and man, seems to triumph because the pope has not spoken out against him and the genocide he represents. Written in free verse, the play contains vivid narratives of historical events, stirring dialogues, pithy aphorisms, and dramatic irony. It forces the spectator to confront an unbearable but crucial episode in history.

Because of the great length of the play and the importance of the events with which it deals, it should be performed in its original version or not at all. Further, because of its lengthy appendix, it should be read and studied as well as performed. This drama thus imposes unique demands on performers, readers, and spectators. It is history as drama, a drama that calls for a scale as vast as its challenging subject.

The Deputy has been characterized as one of the most controversial plays of its time, perhaps of its century. When it premiered, it inspired a wealth of reactions—some negative, many favorable. It touched off demonstrations and angry debate, with responses to the play—in the form of reviews, essays, letters, and news reports—numbering in the thousands. *The Deputy* was written at a time when the Holocaust was being confronted by the West. The way had been prepared by the publication of Anne Frank's *Het Achterhuis* (1947; *The Diary of a Young Girl*, 1952) and the dramatization of that work as *The Diary of Anne Frank*, by Frances Goodrich and Albert Hackett (pr. 1955), the capture and trial of Adolf Eichmann in 1961 and 1962, and films and novels that had begun to deal with the Holocaust. Together with these developments, *The Deputy* was instrumental in forcing a wider awareness of the Holocaust. By dramatically centering his drama on the person and institution of the papacy, Hochhuth was able to provoke a controversy and awareness that a generalized criticism of Western civilization could never have accomplished.

Despite its flaws, *The Deputy* was a courageous and timely dramatization of a period of history that graphically demonstrated the expanding possibilities of evil and reiterated the necessity of facing and fighting that evil. The drama is ultimately a warning of what can happen when leaders and role models fail to act against inhumanity. It also, however, presents an inspiring example of those few ordinary yet heroic people who made the choice to confront overpowering forces. As Albert Schweitzer notes in his preface to the published edition of the play, *The Deputy* is a warning regarding the inhumanity that exists in the modern era.

SOURCES FOR FURTHER STUDY

Barasch-Rubinstein, Emanuela. *The Devil, the Saints, and the Church: Reading Hochhuth's "The Deputy."* New York: Peter Lang, 2004.

Bentley, Eric, ed. *The Storm over "The Deputy."* New York: Grove Press, 1964.

Bigsby, Christopher. *Remembering and Imagining the Holocaust: The Chain of Memory*. New York: Cambridge University Press, 2006.

Cochrane, Arthur C., ed. Special section on *The Deputy*. *Christianity and Crisis*, March 30, 1964, pp. 44-54.

Falconi, Carlo. *The Silence of Pius XII*. Translated by Bernard Wall. Boston: Little, Brown, 1970.

Friedländer, Saul. *Pius XII and the Third Reich*. New York: Octagon Books, 1980.

Lewy, Gunther. *The Catholic Church and Nazi Germany*. New York: McGraw-Hill, 1974.

Taëni, Rainer. *Rolf Hochhuth*. Translated by R. W. Last. London: Wolff, 1977.

Ward, Margaret E. *Rolf Hochhuth*. Boston: Twayne, 1977.

—Leon Stein

THE DESTRUCTION OF THE EUROPEAN JEWS

AUTHOR: Raul Hilberg (1926-2007)
FIRST PUBLISHED: 1961
GENRE: Nonfiction
SUBGENRE: History

Hilberg's determination to record every detail of the Holocaust accurately, his grim imperative to establish an orderly account of the greatest act of cruelty the world had ever known, results in a work of mesmerizing, often horrifying readability.

PRINCIPAL PERSONAGES:
    Adolf Hitler (1889-1945), the chancellor of Germany, 1933-1945
    Heinrich Himmler (1900-1945), the commander of the Schutzstaffel (SS) and the main organizer of the Nazi concentration camps
    Hans Frank (1900-1946), the governor-general of those parts of Poland not directly annexed to Germany
    Odilo Globocnik (1904-1945), an Austrian Nazi who carried out plans that killed more than one million Jews in Poland
    Bernhard Lösener, the doctor charged with formulating the specifications of who was and was not a Jew
    Rudolf Höss, the commandant of the Auschwitz concentration camp in Poland

OVERVIEW

The Destruction of the European Jews is a rare book in that it is both an objective account of history and a morality tale. The first history of the Holocaust to exert a thorough intellectual influence, Raul Hilberg's work immediately became the starting point for study and debate about the Nazi concentration camps and the policies that led up to them. Hilberg, however, could not place the book with a major press, and indeed it has never had a large New York publisher, even for the subsequent, expanded three-volume edition that appeared in 1985. Also, Hilberg, despite having a degree in history from Columbia University, was able to secure an academic position only in another discipline, political science, at the University of Vermont, where he spent his entire career.

Hilberg's work has never been universally popular, even among the Jewish community. It has often been said that this is the case because Hilberg concentrates on the perpetrators, not the victims; *The Destruction of the European Jews* stays within the viewpoint of the people who set and carried out the policy of extermination. Hilberg's procedure is documentary; scrupulous observation is, for him, a form of testimony. Despite his belief in historical objectivity, Hilberg is more than willing to make judgments, such as when he contends that a group of people who do something to somebody else also do that thing to themselves. Indeed, Hilberg gives dignity to the victims of the Holocaust by dwelling with minute sharpness on the malignant deeds of the perpetrators. Hilberg's tone may seem neutral and affectless, but it also possesses a deadpan quality, a barbed sarcasm toward the Nazis, whose every action he damningly describes.

Hilberg may be compared with Hannah Arendt in their shared emphasis on the relation of bureaucracy and totalitarianism. Arendt acknowledges Hilberg's work in *Eichmann in Jerusalem: A Report on the Banality of Evil* (1963), although, as Federico Finchelstein has noted, Arendt was an outside referee for Princeton University Press when the publisher originally turned down Hilberg's manuscript.

Perhaps the most controversial part of Hilberg's book is its initial argument that Nazi anti-Semitism drew on long-established European anti-Semitism. Hilberg asserts that modern technology enabled this literal application of anti-Semitic stereotypes. Others, however, have argued that, whatever the repugnance of traditional Christian anti-Semitism, modern totalitarian anti-Semitism was inspired by totalizing ideologies and was fundamentally different from its traditionalist predecessor in its thrust.

Every chapter of *The Destruction of the European Jews* describes a process whose enactment carries in its wake a historical destiny, intentional or unintentional. At first, the outcome of these processes is what the Nazis intend, and their own wishes seem to dovetail with historical inevitability. As World War II goes on and the totalitarian system convulses in defeat, however, the Nazis become the object of processes, not their agent. Their actions bring consequences, and Hilberg skillfully catalogs the reverberations of these consequences, such as postwar West Germany's agreeing to pay reparations to Israel. Hilberg has commented that his book has a musical structure, in which the deportations and killing-center operations are the central movement, flanked by the overtures of precedents, antecedents, expropriation, and concentration and followed by the successive codas of reflections, consequences, and implications. This is corollary to his understanding of the entire plan to wipe out the Jews as a deliberately conceived action whose roots and reverberations constituted a vast canvas, a feat of audacious daring and scope that the Nazis were almost able to carry off, until they were foiled by the Allied victory.

Much of the history Hilberg explores in *The Destruction of the European Jews* is economic history. One of the principal means the Nazis employed to destroy the Jews was the appropriation of their fiscal assets, whether commercial property, real estate, or cash deposits. This proved effective in the short term, as the expropriated money swelled Nazi coffers, but in the long term this strategy helped to denude the economic base of the German-ruled lands. Similarly, in the "general government" of Nazi-occupied Poland, administered by Hans Frank, Polish Jews provided much of the occupied land's skilled labor, and their conscription helped Nazi economic productivity. The persecution and killing of these people, as the ideological mandates of Nazi policy eventually demanded, substantially diminished the pool of labor available for the Nazis to exploit.

Hilberg also explores Nazi legal history. Bernhard Lösener formulated a law that defined individuals of half non-Jewish ancestry as *Mischlinge* and thus helped save many people who would otherwise have been killed. The *Mischlinge* constituted a third category, neither Jewish nor non-Jewish, that required a whole separate set of laws concerning their barely tolerated but nonetheless accepted status in Nazi society.

Step by step, Hilberg records the minutiae of Nazi regulations and their practical efforts. The Holocaust unfolds as microhistory, from detail to detail, and the accumulation of practical instances provides an anatomy of how the mammoth Nazi bureaucracy perpetrated appalling atrocity. Hilberg also describes the destruction process in Germany's allies and satellites—France, Italy, Bulgaria, Romania, and the two countries the Nazis conjured into existence during the war, Croatia and Slovakia. Some of these, such as Romania and Slovakia, tried to emulate the Nazis' systematic persecutions of the Jews; others went along out of opportunism or the necessity of cooperating with the policy preferences of the dominant power in Europe. The use of the word "European" in the title is thus justified—the book is not just about German Jews. Indeed, Hilberg notes, with bitter humor, that the Nazis despised the Polish Jews because they had so little money for the Nazis to expropriate; even though the Nazis saw the German Jews as subhuman, the Polish Jews were even lower on the social scale.

In the final section of the book, titled "Implication," Hilberg points out that even though postwar trends swung toward granting Jews full civil rights in Western countries, the ability of modern states to destroy Jews was still a theoretical possibility, as the Nazi example was now indelibly available. Conversely, Hilberg points to the increasing enfranchisement of African Americans in the United States (incomplete when his book was first published) as an important side effect of the destruction of the European Jews; the experience in Europe forced many Americans to realize that racial discrimination was no longer tenable in the world's leading democracy.

SOURCES FOR FURTHER STUDY

Finchelstein, Federico. "The Holocaust Canon: Rereading Raul Hilberg." *New German Critique* 96 (Fall, 2005): 3-48.

Hilberg, Raul. *The Politics of Memory: The Journey of a Holocaust Historian.* Chicago: Ivan R. Dee, 1996.

LaCapra, Dominick. *History and Memory After Auschwitz.* Ithaca, N.Y.: Cornell University Press, 1998.

Mieder, Wolfgang, and David Scrase, eds. *Reflections on the Holocaust: Festschrift for Raul Hilberg on His Seventy-Fifth Birthday.* Burlington: University of Vermont, 2001.

Pacy, James S., and Alan P. Wertheimer, eds. *Perspectives on the Holocaust: Essays in Honor of Raul Hilberg.* Boulder, Colo.: Westview Press, 1995.

Weinberg, Gerhard L. Review of *The Destruction of the European Jews*, by Raul Hilberg. *American Historical Review* 67, no. 3 (April, 1962): 694-695.

—Nicholas Birns

The Diary of a Young Girl

Author: Anne Frank (1929-1945)
First published: *Het Achterhuis*, 1947 (English translation, 1952)
Genre: Nonfiction
Subgenre: Diary

This diary, with entries written in the form of letters to an imagined friend, details the two years Anne Frank's family and four others spent in hiding after the Nazi invasion of Holland. The book combines Anne's coming-of-age reflections with descriptions of an everyday life of deprivation and the struggles, fears, and hopes of the group.

Principal personages:
 Anne Frank (1929-1945), a Jewish girl in hiding
 Otto Frank (1889-1980), Anne's father
 Edith Frank (1900-1945), Anne's mother
 Margot Frank (1926-1945), Anne's sister

Overview

Anne Frank's *The Diary of a Young Girl* recounts the two years during which the Frank family, who were Jewish, lived in hiding in Nazi-occupied Holland. In the intimate voice of an articulate, sensitive young girl, the diary details the harrowing experiences of life in a hiding place as well as the tumultuous emotions of an adolescent who knew that outside the window, bombs were falling and Jews were being marched off to death camps.

Anne Frank began her diary at age thirteen, having received the blank book as a birthday gift. A typical teenager, she was delighted at the prospect of writing down her most personal thoughts. Although she wrote her first few entries in the usual form for a diary, she soon decided to write as though she were addressing an imaginary best friend, Kitty, describing her experiences, her small group, and her thoughts in letter form. Her imagined audience facilitated a natural voice and a reason for describing her life and for exploring all that was in her heart.

The diary begins in Amsterdam, where Anne and her family lived after moving from Frankfurt, Germany, seven years earlier to escape the dangers of Nazi Germany. When the Nazis occupied the Netherlands in 1940, the same repression and fear that Jews had experienced in Germany became the reality. In June of 1942, Anne's sister, Margot, was ordered to report to the Dutch Nazi headquarters, and the family realized their lives were in imminent danger. One month after Anne began her diary, her family, along with her father's business associate, his wife, and their son Peter, moved into hiding. They were soon joined by a dentist, who took over Anne's bed; Anne had to sleep on a small divan extended by chairs. The group of eight occupied cramped, inconvenient rooms above a warehouse for a little more than two years before they were discovered.

Anne's diary testifies to her talent and potential as a writer as well as to her strength and character as a person. It reflects the strong family values and the personal qualities that enabled Anne to produce this moving and powerful document of the lives of her family members and the others in hiding as they experienced both terror and more mundane feelings of discomfort and boredom.

Before they went into hiding, the Franks had enjoyed a pleasant life, at least from the perspective of young person absorbed in school and friends. Although all German Jews endured increasing discrimination and restriction in the 1930's, the Frank family was able to maintain a comfortable, if anxious, lifestyle until they gave up and left the country. Anne recalled that for many years she and her sister enjoyed the benefits of an extended family, especially two uncles and two grandmothers, who doted on her and her sister.

While Anne's father, Otto Frank, a decorated veteran of World War I, chose to remain close to Germany, the other relatives emigrated to the United States and Switzerland. Otto Frank moved his family to Amsterdam in 1933 and established himself in business there. After the Nazi occupation of Holland, he maintained his business by representing company management through his Dutch business associates. He also prepared the secret space above the company's warehouse as a hiding place. His friends and business associates risked their lives providing the group with all their necessities and celebrating special occasions with them.

That the Frank family valued education is obvious in the diary. In Amsterdam, the young Anne and Margot attended Montessori schools until Jews were forced out, at which time they continued their studies at the Jewish lyceum. Anne was not the outstanding pupil Margot was, but she shone in other ways. Recognized by others and herself as a chatterbox, she was also a creative, enthusiastic organizer and leader. While she was in hiding, education became a preoccupation and a distraction from hunger, boredom, and anxiety. Otto Frank helped Margot, Anne, and Peter with

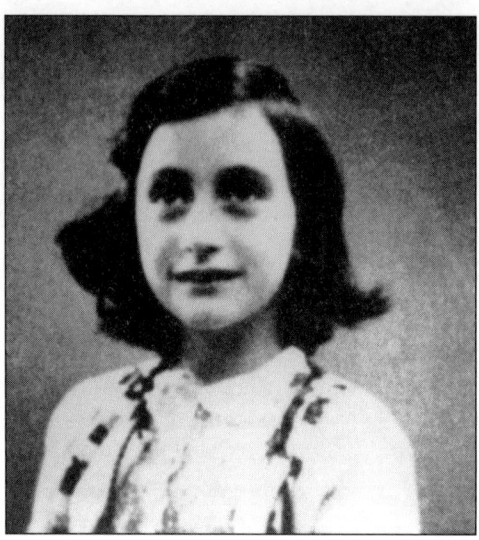
Anne Frank. (Library of Congress)

their lessons in their hiding place as they attempted to keep up with their peers in school. For Anne, her studies and writing—she wrote stories as well as her diary—provided the means to achieve her dream of becoming a writer, a goal that became dearer to her as her time in hiding grew longer.

The diary captures the details of life and Anne's personal reflections. It recounts the petty squabbles that often dominated the group's days in their cramped, deprived living conditions. It also demonstrates Anne's efforts to come to terms with her life. Her descriptions of herself show her petulant, adolescent attitudes toward her mother and her fondness for her father. She eagerly distinguishes herself from her mother, proclaiming that she will never be satisfied with life only as a mother and wife. She admits her antagonisms and her willful pronouncements, acknowledging at times that her own behavior has been rude and unkind, and promises to improve. She describes her growing awareness of her sexuality and her attraction to Peter, for whom she develops physical and emotional feelings. Her relationship with Peter takes her to a new level of emotion, provoking her to explore two very different aspects of her personality: her outgoing self and her deeper, meditative self, which matures as she grows.

The group had a radio and were able to tune in to British broadcasts, so all were aware of both the death camps and the progress of the Allies. Although Anne tired of the adult talk of politics, she did reflect on the state of the world. In words that would later be much quoted, she wrote that she still believed in the goodness of the human spirit, despite the horror around her. She also asserted that Adolf Hitler and the Nazis were not the only ones responsible for this reign of terror—ordinary people were culpable in their complicity.

Anne's self-analysis and her writing gave her life meaning and order. She set down her hopes and dreams and recorded her steps to realize them, despite the trauma that filled so many days. She acknowledged her spiritual beliefs and faith in God. She called this faith a gift and held it close.

Life became a vale of soul making for this young girl as she willed for herself an optimistic spirit. Developing wisdom beyond her years, she asserted that each person is responsible for who she becomes. She determined to be courageous and cheerful, to dream and to hope, and to act in every way as if her dreams and hopes would one day be a reality.

The hiding place was discovered two days after the diary's last entry, August 1, 1944. Anne and her sister died at the Bergen-Belsen concentration camp near Belsen, Germany, of typhoid fever in March of 1945. Their father was the only one of the group to survive. When he returned to Amsterdam after the war, he found Anne's diary, which the Nazis had left behind after the raid.

Anne Frank's diary is considered a classic of Holocaust and coming-of-age literature. Many other diaries of the period have been recovered, but this one has become the touchstone of the era. Translated into more than thirty languages, widely included in school reading lists in the United States, serialized by a newspaper syndicate, and adapted into a Pulitzer Prize-winning Broadway play (*The Diary of Anne Frank*, by Frances Goodrich and Albert Hackett, pr. 1955) as well as a film, the work fulfills Anne Frank's youthful longing to live on.

Sources for Further Study

Bettelheim, Bruno. "The Ignored Lesson of Anne Frank." In *Surviving, and Other Essays*. New York: Alfred A. Knopf, 1979.

Lee, Carol Ann. *Anne Frank and the Children of the Holocaust*. New York: Viking Press, 2006.

Levin, Meyer. "The Child Behind the Secret Door." *The New York Times Book Review*, June 15, 1952.

Schnabel, Ernst. *Anne Frank: A Profile in Courage*. Translated by Richard Winston and Clara Winston. New York: Harcourt Brace, 1958.

Swartz, Daniel. *Imagining the Holocaust*. New York: St. Martin's Griffin, 1999.

—*Bernadette Flynn Low*

The Double Bond
Primo Levi—A Biography

Author: Carole Angier (1943-   )
First published: 2002
Genre: Nonfiction
Subgenre: Biography

This biography traces the life of Primo Levi through the memories of his friends, his writings, his experiences as an author and as a survivor of Auschwitz, and his career as a chemist.

Principal personages:
 Primo Levi (1919-1987), Italian writer and chemist who survived the Auschwitz death camp
 Anna Maria Levi, Primo's sister
 Lucia Morpurgo Levi, Primo's wife
 Rina Luzzati Levi, Primo's mother
 Cesare Levi, Primo's father

Overview

Primo Levi would seem a curious subject for a biography, considering how excessively reticent, almost secretive, he was about his personal life, but as Carole Angier notes in her preface, for her as a writer, reserve intrigues—and the extreme reserve exhibited by her subject intrigued her extremely. In spite of her intrigue, however, Angier had to overcome not only Levi's reticence but also his family's high wall of reserve and privacy—made even higher, she discovered, by the traditional diffidence of Turinese—and the tragedy of his death by suicide. As biographer, therefore, Angier found herself confronting a peculiar dilemma, hence the title of her book, which she borrowed from Levi's last, incomplete novel: *Il doppio legame*. In Italian, the phrase has a double meaning: the double bonding in chemistry and the double bind in psychology, "a crippling conflict between contradictory or unfulfillable requirements, which you can neither escape nor win." Angier appropriated both meanings in order to take her biography into the personal and inward sides of Primo Levi. To do this, she structured her book on two levels: a rationally known, testable one and an irrational one, felt and imagined. In the end, Angier admits she does not know which turned out to be the more truthful and revealing of her subject, although finally the latter came to seem to her to be of greater significance.

Primo Levi was born on July 31, 1919, on the third floor at Corso de Umberto 75 in Turin, Italy, in a house owned by his mother and in which, except for a year in Milan and one in Auschwitz, he lived for all of his sixty-seven years. His father, Cesare, was an industrial engineer, and his mother, Rina, was a typical Italian housewife and mother. His sister, Anna Maria, was born a year and a half later. Although both sides of his family had been observant Jews, Primo's parents had ceased to be religious, as had most Italian Jews who were indebted to the Enlightenment ideas that had freed them to live in a predominantly Christian world. Nevertheless, Primo was bar mitzvahed, and for a brief period in his early teens he became intensely involved with his Jewishness; later in life, during the period of persecution by both the Italian and German fascists, he would again become acutely aware of his cultural and religious heritage.

Primo was a slight child, serious and shy, very unlike his sister, who was lively and outgoing. In spite of their differing personalities, she became his closest childhood companion. Primo's schooling started inauspiciously. During his primary years he was frequently absent because of various illnesses, which contributed to the impression that he was somewhat frail, an impression belied by his obvious strength of both body and will that allowed him to survive his experience at Auschwitz. As he progressed through the Italian educational system, he began to flourish, and by the time he attended the Gimnasio Liceo Massimo D'Azeglio, one of the best classical grammar schools in Turin, his intelligence and seriousness made him a model student. He also gradually overcame his shyness, enough at least to develop a number of lasting friendships among his schoolmates. At university, where he was allowed to indulge his passion for chemistry, he blossomed.

Levi's university experience allowed him to exploit his natural intellectual gifts, but Italy's anti-Jewish laws exerted enormous pressures. Jews could not fail a single examination, and they were forbidden to change their areas of interest, so when he grew disillusioned with chemistry and wanted to change to physics, he could not. As he was to write later, this restriction condemned him to a life as a technician rather than as a true research scientist. Angier demurs, suggesting that he chose not to pursue research, and that is what opened the world of letters for him. Levi secured a job as a chemist after graduation, largely because most of the non-Jewish chemists were in the military. His first job was at the mines of Balangero, north of Turin, where he worked on the extraction of nickel. He moved to Milan in July, 1942, to work for a Swiss company, a job that ceased with the armistice in September, 1943, when Italy surrendered to the Allies.

The euphoria that followed the collapse of Mussolini's government was curtailed when the Germans invaded Italy and set up Il Duce as the puppet dictator of the Republic of Salo. The occupation of northern Italy placed Turin and its environs under Nazi control, and, unlike the Italian fascists, the Germans strictly enforced the racial laws. Levi, out of a job, joined the partisans—who had already attracted many Italian Jews, some of them his friends—in the Val D'Aosta, and throughout the fall of 1943 and into the new year he ran guns for the resistance. Then he was picked up by the Gestapo and transported to Fossoli, a central staging point for Italian Jews. The short time he spent in the Fossoli camp, still nominally under Italian control, was relatively benign. However, on February 16 it was taken over by the Germans, and on February 22 Levi and the rest of the Jews began their journey to the concentration camps north of the Alps. The year he would spend as a prisoner would be the single most important event of his life.

Primo Levi arrived at Auschwitz on February 26, 1944. In less than ten minutes he had survived the first selection, the culling of those who would be gassed immediately and those who would be allowed to live and work in the camp. Although he was exhausted and weighed only a little over one hundred pounds—he was slightly built and always thin—he was saved from a summary death by the quick thinking of one of his friends, who declared that he and two others, including Levi, were experienced industrial chemists, occupations the Germans needed. Like all the others entering the camp, the Italian Jews who survived the selection were stripped of their clothing, had all of their hair shaved off, were showered, sprayed with disinfectant, and given a striped suit and coat, a shirt, underpants, foot rags, and a pair of wooden clogs. None of it was sized to the individual. Then they were tattooed with their camp number; Levi was number 174517. The process was designed to destroy both their dignity and their human personality, or as he was later to describe it, the demolition of man.

In the camp all the best died and the worst—that is, the fittest—survived, he would write in his last book. Angier speculates that by "the best" Levi meant the most civilized, the most delicate, the most innocent. Angier asks, But who was more civilized than Primo Levi? Who was more likely to die of the nakedness, of the bestiality? Who more needed rationality, predictability, faith, and hope? How, then, did he survive? At first he did so through his friendships, by being helped by others in the camp, by fitting himself for starvation, and ultimately by a sheer act of will. He looked on his experience as a chance to learn about human nature, and he treated the camp as a laboratory, a large biological and sociological experiment. Finally, by the end of 1943, when all able-bodied Germans were needed for the war machine, slave laborers became more valuable and the conditions in the camps improved slightly. These things kept him alive.

Auschwitz was abandoned by the Germans toward the end of January, 1944, and the prisoners, now free, were left to survive on their own until they were picked up by the invading Soviet Army, who moved many of them to a relocation camp at Katowicz, also in Poland. For the next nine months, Levi would undergo a journey both bizarre and comic that would take him as far north as Minsk, wending its way south to Romania and west through Hungary, Czechoslovakia, Austria, and Germany before he eventually returned to Italy. He arrived back in Turin on October 19, 1945, to find that miraculously both his mother and sister were alive and living in the family home only slightly damaged by the Allied bombing.

Primo Levi returned from the camps a sick and blasted man. All the suffering, grief, and memories he had postponed surfaced and he became seriously depressed, but he also was impelled to talk about his experiences and began to write about them. In the process, he overcame his preoccupation with death and embraced life. First, however, he needed a job, and after months of searching he secured one in January, 1946, as the assistant head of the research laboratory of Duco Avigliana, a manufacturer of paint. For the next thirty years of his life, he worked as an industrial chemist until his retirement as the director general of the SIVA paint company in 1977. During these years, Primo Levi lived two lives: one as an organic chemist and the other as a writer. He also rejoined life in the role of husband when he married Lucia Morpurgo early in December, 1946, and he became a father with the birth of a daughter, Lisa, in 1948 and a son, Renzo, in 1957.

Levi always remarked that if it had not been for Auschwitz, he never would have become a writer. Angier demurs. He was already a writer before the war, but he might not have become a truly great one if his natural Piedmontese reserve had not been overcome by the moral duty he felt to testify to the outrages of the Holocaust. *Se questo è un uomo* (1947; *If This Is a Man*, 1959; revised as *Survival in Auschwitz: The Nazi Assault on Humanity*, 1961) and *La tregua* (1963; *The Reawakening*, 1965) were books about his Auschwitz experiences that allowed him to break out as a writer.

In the years immediately before and following his retirement, Levi became world-renowned as a poet, fiction writer, journalist, and translator. If before he had been a respected figure, Angier writes, now he became a famous one with all the accolades and demands that fame demands. He was asked to do interviews by both Italian and foreign journalists, he spoke at schools and conferences, he gave lectures, and he received a growing number of prizes. Increasingly, he was also visited by periodic bouts of depression, and his health began to decline. Because he was now famous, he also became embroiled in various causes and controversies, which in turn increased his depression and depleted him physically. In spite of the demands made on him to travel, as Levi grew older he withdrew more and more into the safety of Corso de Umberto 75. On April 11, 1987, he was found dead at the bottom of the stairway there, having fallen from the third-floor landing above. The reasons for his death remain obscure: Was he murdered for his political views, was it an accident, or was it, as one Italian newspaper claimed, Auschwitz that claimed him forty years later? Angier believes it was suicide.

The critical reception of *The Double Bond* has been mixed. For example, Janet Maslin, reviewing the book for *The New York Times*, found Angier's literary analysis flimsy and her psychological insights mundane; on the other hand, Richard Eder, writing for *The New York Times Book Review*, described the biography as flawless and remarkable. However one finally judges the book, *The Double Bond* provides an extraordinary read. Although Levi's family refused its cooperation, Carole Angier interviewed an impressive number of those who knew him, many of them from his childhood, and these interviews helped her to construct the composite portrait of her subject. Furthermore, unlike many literary biographers, Angier devotes considerable space to analyzing the writings, often using them to fill in gaps in his life otherwise unavailable. In spite of its flaws, it is difficult to imagine a more challenging study of the life of Primo Levi being written anytime in the near future.

SOURCES FOR FURTHER STUDY

Acocella, Joan. "A Hard Case." *The New Yorker*, June 17, 2002, 162.
Anissimov, Myriam. *Primo Levi: Tragedy of an Optimist*. Translated by Steve Cox. London: Aurum, 1998.
Eder, Richard. "The Chemist and the Holocaust: Primo Levi 'Did Not Just Learn in Order to Survive,' His Biographer Says, 'He Survived in Order to Learn.'" *The New York Times Book Review*, June 16, 2002, p. 11.
Gornick, Vivian. "Life Sentence." *Los Angeles Times*, June 30, 2002, p. R13.
Klein, Julia M. "Searching for Primo Levi." *Chronicle of Higher Education* 49, no. 41 (June 21, 2002): 13.
Simpson, Thomas. "A New Life of Primo Levi Makes One Long for the Words of the Writer Himself." *Chicago Tribune*, May 19, 2002, p. 1.

—Charles L. P. Silet

The Drowned and the Saved

AUTHOR: Primo Levi (1919-1987)
FIRST PUBLISHED: *I sommersi e i salvati*, 1986 (English translation, 1988)
GENRE: Nonfiction
SUBGENRES: History; essays; meditation

In his last completed work, Levi provides a systematic analysis of the Nazi extermination camps in a series of vivid and meditative essays that display the author's penetrating insights and offer stunning conclusions.

Overview

Primo Levi died in Turin, Italy, on April 11, 1987, an apparent suicide. It was reported that he had been depressed following minor surgery. In reality, his suffering had been ever-present since the 1940's. His great works, beginning with *Se questo è un uomo* (1947; *If This Is a Man*, 1959; revised as *Survival in Auschwitz: The Nazi Assault on Humanity*, 1961) and culminating with *The Drowned and the Saved*, all dealt with the crucial task of analyzing and facing the Holocaust.

Levi was born in Turin in 1919. He was trained as a chemist, joined the antifascist resistance, and was captured. He was turned over to the Nazis when he identified himself as a Jew in a gesture of courageous, whimsical defiance. He was deported to Auschwitz in 1944. He owed his life to his training as a chemist, for he was put to work in one of the slave-labor industrial complexes in the camp. After liberation, he traversed Eastern Europe and wrote about his wanderings in his second book, *La tregua* (1963; *The Reawakening*, 1965). In 1977 he retired as the manager of a Turin chemical factory to devote himself to writing, a sign that he believed that the story and significance of the Holocaust could never be exhausted and that more than ever it had to be conveyed to a new generation far removed from the experience and even the memory of those events. His later works included *Il systema periodico* (1975; *The Periodic Table*, 1985), *Se non ora, quando?* (1982; *If Not Now, When?*, 1985), and *These Moments of Reprieve* (1986). He was awarded Italy's highest literary prize. The fires of Auschwitz had transformed a talented chemist into one of the greatest writers and most astute observers of his century.

The Drowned and the Saved was Levi's last completed work. It represents the summation of his life's work and refers to many of his previous writings. It is not a novel but a series of vivid and meditative essays that are a systematic analysis of the extermination camps. These essays are replete with penetrating insights and stunning conclusions.

What seems to have motivated the writing of this great work was Levi's fear that the memories of the Holocaust—the greatest single crime in human history—would dim with time and would ultimately become a legend. Levi sees himself as Samuel Taylor Coleridge's Ancient Mariner, having to retell and to clarify the terrible tale for a new generation.

The Drowned and the Saved is divided into a preface, eight concise chapters, and a powerful conclusion. Its overwhelming concern is the need to remember for the sake of justice. Levi recounts the story of the Nazi Schutzstaffel (SS) officers who told the Jewish concentration camp prisoners that no one would later believe their tales of horror because they were too horrible to be believed. This became one of the prisoners' worst nightmares.

In his second chapter, "The Gray Zone," Levi shows that there were degrees of evil in the camps, although the difference between the murderers and their victims was clear. The Nazis were guilty of murder, whereas the German bystanders were guilty of turning away and of refusing to help the victims. It is tragic, however, that some of the victims were forced to do things in the camps that they would never have done in normal life. For example, the *Sonderkommando*, or "Special Squad," those prisoners of Auschwitz who worked near the crematoria, were given more food and were kept alive for a short time so that they could do their horrendous work of disposing of the dead bodies. Also belonging to this "gray zone" were the functionaries of the Jewish councils appointed by the Nazis to administer the ghettos. Levi brilliantly characterizes Mordechai Chaim Rumkowski, the "Jewish elder" of the Łódź ghetto in Poland, as a man who was corrupted by power yet sought to save Jews.

Chapter 3 deals with the shame of the victims who survived. According to Levi, the prisoners who survived were privileged because of their skills, their knowledge of German, and their connections with the political underground. Many survivors felt guilty for having to look out for themselves and their close friends. Levi reminds the reader, however, that the greatest shame of all belongs to the murderers who planned the crime and to the civilized world that stood by.

Levi devotes a chapter to the importance of communication in human affairs. Those who understood some German in the camps might learn the skills of surviving. What could not be so easily grasped was the useless, gratuitous violence that the Nazis practiced. The extermination of the Jews was preceded by savage and calculated violence and humiliation. The prisoners were tattooed, stripped, and humiliated specifically to destroy their humanity before they were killed.

The final chapters of *The Drowned and the Saved* are devoted to the exploration of stereotypes of the Holocaust in the present generation and to the analysis of letters to Levi by German readers of his works. One question that is particularly troubling is why inmates did not revolt against such treatment. Levi poses a crucial question for a later generation to illustrate the plight of the Jews on the eve of the Holocaust: Why are people not leaving Europe now under the threat of a possible nuclear holocaust?

The Drowned and the Saved shows Primo Levi to be one of the great masters of modern prose. His style and tone produced a stunning combination of cool, dispassionate description, uncompromising honesty, righteous indignation, extremely vivid imagery, and an uncanny ability to relate the past to the present.

Levi clearly belongs in the classical tradition. He writes with great clarity without oversimplifying the complexities of his forbidding subject. His prose is concise, balanced, carefully molded, yet extremely powerful. Like the great Greek and Roman historians, he combines narrative with reflection. He also reflects the influence of his medieval forerunner Dante, who wrote the *Inferno* (c. 1320), that epic on punishment for sins and the portrayal of degrees of guilt. In the *Inferno*, however, those who have sinned have been punished as a result of their actions. In the Holocaust the Jews were exterminated because they had been born, something Dante would have had trouble imagining. Levi also acknowledges the Italian Romantic writers of the nineteenth century who strove to make patriotism a humane value rather than a doctrine of superiority and who glorified the individual human being. Levi was also influenced by the early twentieth century realist Italo Svevo. Levi quotes Svevo's remark that a dying man is too busy to think about death. Levi sees this as a valid statement about the camps.

Above all, Primo Levi stands in the tradition of the Enlightenment. He is a true moralist following in the footsteps of Jonathan Swift. His book is aimed primarily at the human intelligence as he constantly struggles to bring the reader back to the reality of the Holocaust and its implications for the present and the future.

Although influenced by his friend Jean Améry, Levi could not agree with the passion of his friend, who would uncompromisingly return blow for blow with the enemy and who would permit his life to be consumed by the memory of the tortures and humiliations he suffered. Levi preferred to trust in the laws of civilized society (however imperfectly applied) and to discourage feelings of revenge, as opposed to cheap forgiveness. The suicide of Améry seems to have haunted Levi, and a controlled anger smolders throughout this work and breaks out during key portions.

Levi's anger is directed primarily against those who would construct convenient truths about the terrible past, confuse the perpetrator with the victim, and oversimplify and stereotype reality. Like the ancient Greeks, Levi believes in the existence of the Furies, the ancient goddesses of the earth who would pursue tormentors and murderers and give them no rest. The sufferings of the Holocaust, however, gave the victims no peace. The only way to achieve any hope for justice is to cry out to anyone who would listen to the tales of injustice. Levi did this for forty years.

In the tradition of a true classic, *The Drowned and the Saved* is a treasure trove of unforgettable stories and eminently quotable, brilliant flashes of insight. Future editions of this work should be annotated in the manner of Dante's *Inferno* to identify the rich variety of literary and historical references.

At least three gripping stories are bound to remain with the reader. The first concerns an ordinary, but surrealistic, soccer game played by the Nazi SS and the special squad of prisoners they forced to tend the crematoria. What enabled such a game to happen at all was the bond of death—the mounds of dead bodies caused by the SS and disposed of by the special squad. Next comes a heartbreaking tale of a teenage girl found still alive after a mass killing in the gas chamber. She is no longer anonymous but a person. The prisoners try to save her, but the SS cannot let her live to tell her tale to the other inmates; the Third Reich was at war with memory itself. The third story shows how the memories of the Holocaust can be difficult to communicate to a later age. When Levi tried to tell the story of his life in the camp to a fifth-grade class, a boy drew a diagram to show how he would have escaped from the camp. Such is the difficulty of communicating the impossible situation faced by the Jews.

Levi had much less sympathy for a German who wrote to him saying that Adolf Hitler was a madman and a devil who misled the German people. Levi wrote back that no church gives indulgences to those who follow the devil. In addition, he noted that no one obliged the I. G. Farben Company to conscript thousands of slaves and work them to death and that no one forced the Topf Company of Wiesbaden to build the enormous multiple crematoria for Auschwitz. From where, he asks, did the average German think that the millions of children's clothes and shoes that flowed back to Germany during the war were coming?

Above all, Levi is most disturbed about the human frailties of self-deception and love of power. He finds that human beings today are distrustful of grand truths but are disposed to accept small truths. This is much too dangerous in the light of what happened during the Holocaust. Levi's statements on power and human corruptibility are reminiscent of Plato and Thucydides. Like Plato, Levi asserts that all tyrants go mad because they lose touch with reality. This was particularly true for Hitler. The goals of the Third Reich went far beyond an attempt to gain living space or to protect itself; Hitler's Germany sought to achieve immortality by killing and humiliating millions of innocent people. Such a society was bound to destroy itself.

The corruptibility of man is epitomized for Levi in the figure of Rumkowski, the head of the Łódź ghetto. Rumkowski was an elderly failed industrialist. He hoped that he could save the Jews of Łódź by working for the German army, but he became drunk with power, coining his likeness on the money of the ghetto and exhorting poets and schoolchildren to praise him. In 1944 the ghetto was liquidated, and Rumkowski was sent on a special train to Auschwitz, where he perished. Levi concludes:

> We are all mirrored in Rumkowski. . . . His fever is ours. . . . Willingly or not we come to terms with power, forgetting that we are all in the ghetto, that the ghetto is walled in, that outside the ghetto reign the lords of death and that close by the train is waiting.

Levi thus concludes that the human race is in the same boat, interdependent, vulnerable as ever.

As one of the tormented saved, Levi speaks for the drowned of his generation. It is hard to disagree with his findings and conclusions. He is not a professional historian or social scientist (although his reading is wide and his research accurate) but a supremely intelligent survivor and humanist. In his words, the camp "was a university. It taught us to look around and to measure man." More than many historians and social scientists, Levi has brilliantly captured and effectively communicated many of the crucial elements and implications of the human dimensions of the Holocaust.

If This Is a Man was Primo Levi's first work, and it remains one of the most perceptive eyewitness accounts of the Holocaust. Many fine works flowed from his pen in the course of the next forty years, but *The Drowned and the Saved* was his most condensed and powerful work. It distills the insights achieved during a lifetime of emotional struggle and intellectual reflection.

It is fitting and proper that Levi would set aside an important chapter for Jean Améry, his friend, fellow survivor, and creative thinker about Auschwitz. Améry's work *Jenseits von Schuld und Sühne: Bewältigungsver-*

suche eines Überwältigen (1966; *At The Mind's Limits: Contemplations by a Survivor on Auschwitz and Its Realities*, 1980) is a useful counterpart to Levi's last work. Améry's work is much more introspective, intensely angry, and militantly rebellious in tone and much more concerned with the problem of Jewish existence. Despite their differences and their disappointments, however, Levi and Améry kept their faith in the struggle for enlightenment and human decency. For them this is the only possibility for the salvation of humankind. Nevertheless, Levi is the better writer of the two, for he writes with great economy and controlled passion.

Like many Holocaust survivors who went on to become great writers, Primo Levi and Jean Améry took their own lives. Why they did so is open to many explanations, but these great souls who had suffered beyond all measure had made it clear that they feared that the Holocaust would be forgotten, would be obscured with convenient truths, and would lose its crucial lessons for humankind. These morally indefatigable men devoted their lives to telling their civilization about the mortal threats that lurk within it.

Primo Levi was the Dante of the twentieth century, the indispensable guide to the hell that was created on Earth. To read his works, particularly *The Drowned and the Saved*, is to be given some hope for an escape from the suffering from which he was not saved.

SOURCES FOR FURTHER STUDY

Angier, Carole. *The Double Bond: Primo Levi—A Biography*. New York: Farrar, Straus and Giroux, 2002.

———. "Second Opinion: Defender of the Memory of Auschwitz Gave Primo Levi His Subject, but Did That Make Him a Writer?" *The Guardian*, November 18, 1992.

Anissimov, Myriam. *Primo Levi: Tragedy of an Optimist*. Translated by Steve Cox. London: Aurum, 1998.

Hartley, James. *Suffering Witness: The Quandary of Responsibility After the Irreparable*. Albany: State University of New York Press, 2000.

Leiter, Robert. "The Science of Life: The Literary Insights of a Chemist Turned Survivor." *Jewish Exponent* 216, no. 14 (June 1, 2004): 20.

Thomson, Ian. *Primo Levi: A Life*. London: Hutchinson, 2002.

—*Leon Stein*

Eichmann in Jerusalem
A Report on the Banality of Evil

Author: Hannah Arendt (1906-1975)
First published: 1963
Genre: Nonfiction
Subgenres: Journalism; history

In addition to reporting on Adolf Eichmann's 1961 trial in Jerusalem for crimes the Nazi bureaucrat was accused of committing during the Holocaust, this controversial work presents Arendt's thesis that average people cannot be expected to recognize that they are doing wrong when their actions, no matter how heinous, clearly conform to prevailing social norms and gain them general approval.

Principal personage:
 Adolf Eichmann (1906-1962), Nazi officer who was in charge of transporting Jews to concentration camps

Overview

On May 11, 1960, Adolf Eichmann, who had been masquerading in Argentina as factory worker Ricardo Klement, was captured by Israeli agents and brought to Jerusalem for trial. During World War II, Eichmann, an obedient Nazi bureaucrat, had risen to Obersturmbannführer (a rank equivalent to lieutenant colonel) in the Schutzstaffel (SS), a branch of the state secret police, or Gestapo, headed by Heinrich Himmler. Eichmann became the "Jewish expert" of the branch known as the Head Office for Reich Security. In accordance with Adolf Hitler's plan for a "final solution" for the Jewish people, Eichmann was put in charge of arranging the mass deportations to the killing centers, which were mainly in Poland. After Germany's defeat in May, 1945, Eichmann was captured by the Americans but hid his true identity and, with the aid of Nazi sympathizers, eventually escaped to Argentina. For ten years, reunited with his family, he lived a quiet life until his capture.

When the news of Eichmann's capture and forthcoming trial was broadcast, Hannah Arendt proposed herself as a trial reporter to William Shawn, editor of *The New Yorker* magazine. Shawn gladly accepted Arendt's offer, as she had already earned a distinguished reputation as a political analyst through her work *The Origins of Totalitarianism* (1951). Also, as a Jew and an early refugee from Nazi Germany (she had escaped in 1933), Arendt was uniquely qualified to cover the trial.

The trial began before the District Court of Jerusalem on April 11, 1961, and continued until August 14. The court announced its judgment on December 11, 1961, declaring Eichmann guilty of most of the crimes in the fifteen-count indictment (including "crimes against the Jewish people, crimes against humanity, war crimes, and memberships in hostile organizations"). He was condemned to death and, after the rejection of his legal appeals, was executed by hanging at midnight on May 31, 1962.

Hannah Arendt attended most of Eichmann's district court sessions and then went home to New York, where she gathered her impressions of the defendant and formulated her analytic theses. The essential form of the book, according to Arendt, is that of "a trial report, and its main source is the transcript of the trial proceedings which was distributed to the press in Jerusalem." Of the book's fifteen chapters, the first few include descriptions of the Jerusalem courtroom, the judges, the prosecutor, and the defendant. The second chapter contains a perceptive brief biography of Eichmann, his "normality" (according to the Israeli psychiatric examiners), and his military loyalty. Eichmann had been a poor student and an unsuccessful worker. His last job (from which he was fired) before joining the Nazi Party and the SS in 1932 had been that of traveling salesman. "Already a failure in the eyes of his social class, of his family, and hence in his own eyes as well," Eichmann could now "still make a career" in the Nazi bureaucracy. Thus, over the course of thirteen years, he rose eagerly from the status of unemployed nonentity to that of SS Obersturmbannführer.

Chapter 3 begins the detailing of how Eichmann became "an expert on the Jewish question." He volunteered in 1934 for the Security Service of the SS and was put to work in the Information Department. After a few months, Eichmann began to work in the new section concerned exclusively with Jews. He then read Theodor Herzl's Zionist classic *Der Judenstaat* (1896; *The Jewish State*, 1896), which earned for him an assignment as the official spy on German Zionist organizations. Consequently, by March, 1938, Eichmann was appointed organizer of the forced emigration of Jews from Austria. Unfortunately for the victimized Jews, however, entry into British-ruled Palestine was very difficult. In any case, with the beginning of World War II in September, 1939, emigration anywhere for significant numbers of Jews became impossible, so Eichmann began to look for new avenues of career advancement. The opportunity came when the primary responsibility of his office was shifted from forced emigration of the Jews

Hannah Arendt. (Library of Congress)

to their deportation to concentration camps for forced labor and death.

By late 1941, the "final solution"—the killing of the Jews in the German-occupied areas—had begun, and Eichmann assumed significant responsibility for deportation of Jews to the extermination camps. He did it with the same diligence that he had previously used in trying to find a foreign country to which the Jews could emigrate. Such faint stirrings of conscience as Eichmann still possessed seemed to pertain only to German Jews and not to their more numerous coreligionists in the countries east of Germany.

At the important conference about the logistics of the "final solution" held in Wannsee, a suburb of Berlin, in January, 1942, Eichmann noted that none of his superiors, among the most prominent people in the Third Reich, had any hesitancy in embracing the policy of mass killing. At his trial he stated, "At that moment, I sensed a kind of Pontius Pilate feeling, for I felt free of all guilt." Buttressed by the approval of his social and military superiors, Eichmann became a master of the technique of appointing Jewish councils to fulfill his own ultimately murderous—but well-disguised—purposes. Thus, through deception and bureaucratic skill, he was often able to create a sense of administrative order out of the human chaos of forced deportation.

Helpful to Eichmann, according to his own testimony, was his version of the moral philosophy of Immanuel Kant, an eighteenth century German philosopher. Kant had maintained that a person should act as if the principle of his action were to become a universal law of nature. Eichmann seemed to follow a distortion of Kant's universalizing principle: "Act in such a way that the Führer, if he knew your action, would approve it." Eichmann clung tenaciously to this principle, even when the war was clearly lost and Heinrich Himmler had decided to put an end to the "final solution" in the vain hope of negotiating a postwar and post-Hitler position.

Chapters 9 through 13 detail the process of the "final solution" in the various German-occupied areas. Generally, the fate of the Jews in each country depended on the attitudes of the local populations toward them.

In the final chapters, Arendt notes the disparity between the small resources of the defendant and the vast resources of the prosecution (a condition that had also existed, she notes, at the original Nazi war crimes trials in Nuremberg, Germany). She doubts the relevance and accuracy of many of the statements made by the prosecution's witnesses, sixteen or more years after the fact. Although not disagreeing with the death sentence, Arendt suggests that an international tribunal would have been a more appropriate courtroom, given that genocide is a "crime against humanity."

Because the book began as a report on Eichmann's trial written for *The New Yorker*, it includes, in that magazine's characteristic style, detailed descriptions—in this case, of the physical appearance and legal rituals of the "House of Justice" in Jerusalem. It also includes an analysis of Eichmann's statements, the strategies of the prosecution and defense, and the final judgment. The book provides background descriptions of the Nazi bureaucracy involved in the "final solution," the part Eichmann played in it, and much of the sad history of the deportation and extermination of the European Jews. These details are explicated not only for their historical and legal relevance but also as a basis for Arendt's analytic propositions.

The intellectual heart of Arendt's thesis can be found in her subtitle, *A Report on the Banality of Evil*. Her portrayal of Eichmann after his capture is contrary to the popular opinion of him as a fanatical, sadistic anti-Semite. Rather, she analyzes his character as that of a bureaucratic careerist, a "banal" mediocrity, content to function as an advancing cog in an orderly totalitarian system. Tracing Eichmann's undistinguished career prior to becoming a Nazi and contrasting it to the heightened self-esteem he felt in his newly achieved status, Arendt states that Eichmann "might still have preferred . . . to be hanged as Obersturmbannführer . . . rather than living out his life quietly and normally as a traveling salesman."

Court psychiatrists had certified Eichmann as "normal," thus the central societal problem, according to Arendt, is that so many are like Eichmann: "terribly and terrifyingly normal." Such average people cannot be expected to recognize that they are, in fact, doing wrong in circumstances where their actions, clearly conforming to the prevailing social norms, gain general social approval and career advancement. Only Germany's losing of the war, Arendt believes, seemed to provoke in a few people any admissions of guilty conscience.

A second thesis developed by Arendt—even more inflammatory to many of her readers—was that the victims had cooperated in the destruction of their own communities and of themselves. Eichmann and his staff typically appointed Jewish councils from among the leaders of the occupied Jewish communities. The Nazis then held the councils responsible for maintaining order in the newly created ghettos, distributing rations and work assignments, compiling lists of Jewish property (for easy confiscation), and—especially—identifying the required number of Jews for deportation and "resettlement" to the concentration camps (destinations usually unknown to the leaders of the councils). According to Arendt:

> Wherever Jews lived, there were recognized Jewish leaders, and this leadership, almost without exception, cooperated . . . with the Nazis. The whole truth was that if the Jewish people had really been unorganized and leaderless, there would have been chaos and plenty of misery but the total number of victims would hardly have been between four and a half and six million people.

Depressed by her own analysis, Arendt notes, "To a Jew this role of the Jewish leaders in the destruction of their own people is undoubtedly the darkest chapter of the whole dark story."

Many of the reviews of *Eichmann in Jerusalem* were actually polemics directed against Arendt's style, her analytic tone and Olympian detachment from the dreadful events, her focus on the "aesthetics" rather than the moral depravity of Eichmann, and her obvious anti-Zionism. The most strident attacks focused on Arendt's two major theses: the routinely "banal" dullness of Eichmann's character and the collaborationist role of the Jewish leadership in occupied Europe. The varied positive and negative responses—often directed on a very personal level—were especially evident in the pages of *Partisan Review*, an influential intellectual quarterly.

Generally, the critics noted that Arendt accepts Eichmann's own projection of himself at the trial as a dutiful, law-abiding nonentity. She fails to imagine that same person as he had been when he committed his crimes— in uniform and in power. She sees him only as a "little man" transformed by a totalitarian system into an organizer of the "final solution." (Arendt's supporters believed that she had achieved an insight into the omnipotence of the totalitarian state over the average person.) In fact, Arendt is so certain of Eichmann's essential "banality" that when he is quoted as having told his men during the last days of the war, "I will jump into my grave laughing, because the fact that I have the death of five million Jews . . . on my conscience gives me extraordinary satisfaction," she attributes it merely to the lower-class vice of braggadocio rather than to any factual or legal reality.

Arendt's depiction of the Jewish councils as being treasonously destructive of the Jewish communities came under the most bitter attack. Critics noted that, among other historical omissions, Arendt does not address the killing of Jews in Russia. There, contrary to her thesis, Jewish councils were not appointed by the Nazis; mass killings were, nevertheless, carried out on the spot by firing squads. In addition, critics noted how few political and moral alternatives were really available to the Jewish leaders, how rational it seemed at first to cooperate, for the "civilized" Germans were not thought to be so illogical as to destroy a desperately needed labor force. (Mass resistance, after all, was impossible without outside support.) Reliable accounts exist of certain members of the councils who, having been informed of the destinations of the deportees, either committed suicide or refused to assist the Nazis further and were immediately killed.

Critics of Arendt's book also noted how the leaders of the Jewish councils begged the Allies to bomb the trains so that the deportees might have an opportunity to escape. Furthermore, they stressed that the most determinative factor in the saving or killing of the Jews was the attitude of the local population and the availability of a sanctuary—not the existence of a Jewish council. The death camps, for example, were established in Eastern Europe in the midst of hostile anti-Semitic populations, while virtually all the Jews of occupied Denmark were saved by the local citizens who ferried them in fishing boats to neutral Sweden.

The Eichmann trial, although conducted in Israel in the absence of any appropriate international tribunal, was actually a successor to the Nuremberg Trials, which had been organized during the years immediately following World War II. Eichmann had fled from judgment and so had not been available at Nuremberg. Sixteen years after the war's slaughter had ended, Arendt felt able to give a nonpartisan analysis of the procedures in Jerusalem and of the defendant's character and his crimes. She points out the Jerusalem court's failure, as well as that of the Nuremberg court, to resolve three fundamental issues: "the problem of impaired justice in the court of the victors; a valid definition of the 'crime against humanity'; and a clear recognition of the new criminal who commits this crime."

Arendt's "new criminal" is, as noted earlier, a "normal" individual who commits "administrative massacres" (the rationalized murder of entire populations) under circumstances that make it "impossible for him to know or to feel that he is doing wrong." This controversial insight is a direct application of Arendt's view of the state's power to shape the individual, expressed in her earlier *The Origins of Totalitarianism*. That is, in

Arendt's view, the Nazi genocide was not another chapter in the dismal history of anti-Semitism but rather a new kind of crime, an early chapter in the history of modern totalitarianism—"a system in which all men have become equally superfluous." The "banal, superfluous, average, normal" Eichmann was thus an efficient instrument for the Nazi totalitarian system.

Arendt's universalist views conflict with Zionism, a form of Jewish nationalism, so she is skeptical (unfairly so, according to her critics) of the validity of an Israeli (or any separate nation's) court's judgment of this new sort of crime committed by the modern totalitarian state, a "crime against humanity." Arendt's greatest contribution in *Eichmann in Jerusalem* lies in her demonstration of how a normal person can be brought, through a conditioned sense of duty, to serve the radically evil purposes of a totalitarian state.

SOURCES FOR FURTHER STUDY

Aschheim, Steven E., ed. *Hannah Arendt in Jerusalem*. Berkeley: University of California Press, 2001.

Bernstein, Richard J. *Hannah Arendt and the Jewish Question*. Malden, Mass.: Polity Press, 1996.

Birmingham, Peg. *Hannah Arendt and Human Rights: The Predicament of Common Responsibility*. Bloomington: Indiana University Press, 2006.

Hull, Margaret Betz. *The Hidden Philosophy of Hannah Arendt*. New York: RoutledgeCurzon, 2002.

Lang, Anthony F., Jr., and John Williams, eds. *Hannah Arendt and International Relations: Readings Across the Lines*. New York: Palgrave Macmillan, 2005.

Linn, Ruth. *Escaping Auschwitz: A Culture of Forgetting*. Ithaca, N.Y.: Cornell University Press, 2004.

May, Derwent. *Hannah Arendt*. New York: Penguin Books, 1986.

Whitfield, Stephen J. *Into the Dark: Hannah Arendt and Totalitarianism*. Philadelphia: Temple University Press, 1980.

Young-Bruehl, Elisabeth. *Hannah Arendt: For Love of the World*. 2d ed. New Haven, Conn.: Yale University Press, 2004.

—*Donald Gochberg*

"Elegy for N. N."

Author: Czesław Miłosz (1911-2004)
First published: "Elegia dla N. N.," 1974, in *Gdzie wschodzi słońce i kędy zapada* (English translation collected in *The Collected Poems, 1931-1987*, 1988)
Genre: Poetry
Subgenres: Elegy; meditation

Consisting of seven irregular verse-paragraphs on the general theme of human love, memory, and remorse, Miłosz's elegy includes a meditation on images and events of World War II, with suggestions of Holocaust atrocities and of anti-German violence.

Overview

Nobel laureate Czesław Miłosz, who witnessed the Nazi atrocities in Warsaw in his native Poland, became active as an anti-Nazi poet in the Resistance movement. In 1944, the Germans seized him and his wife as they attempted to leave Warsaw, but they were released after a brief detention in a makeshift camp. They spent the next few months wandering about as refugees until the Soviets' Red Army completed its annihilation of the German forces and Poland was at last liberated after more than five years of Nazi rule. These experiences no doubt laid the groundwork for much of Miłosz's later work, including "Elegy for N. N."

Written in free verse, "Elegy for N. N." consists of seven irregular verse-paragraphs that form an extended meditation on human love, remorse, and memory. It is addressed to "N. N.," a woman who is not so much the subject of the poem as its audience and who shares with the poet certain memories of youth in Lithuania. Elegies are traditionally occasioned by a death, but here it is not a person but the poet's sense of connection to his past that has been lost. The poem is composed in the first person, and the reader seems to be overhearing one side of a conversation between Miłosz and his friend on the subject of loss.

The poem begins with a considerate request regarding a journey: "Tell me if it is too far for you." Immediately, the themes of distance and human limitation are presented. The poem will attempt to bridge a widening gap between the poet and his addressee, an effort that, as Miłosz's hesitant, polite tone indicates, may prove insufficient. Miłosz proceeds to escort the reader on a flight of poetic imagination halfway around the globe, beginning at the Baltic Sea and swooping over Denmark, the Atlantic Ocean, Labrador, and the Sierra Mountains to arrive in California, where he waits in a eucalyptus grove. In his mind, Miłosz helps his listeners to make the same great journey that, in the course of his life, he had made himself. He had traversed whole continents on his path from Vilnius (also known as Vilna), Lithuania, his birthplace, to Berkeley, California, where he lived at the time of the composition of this poem.

In the second section, finding the distance enormous, Miłosz reverses direction, traveling "reluctantly" back through memory to the Lithuanian countryside where he knew "N. N." Yet the reality of that landscape, including its particular smells, contours, and features, has "changed forever into abstract crystal," oddly purified and idealized in the poet's mind.

He longs in the third section for such lost things "as they are in themselves" rather than for idealized images, but he finds that he "really can't say" how daily life there went on. He has lost touch with significant details, his "knowledge of fiery years"—perhaps the years of the Prussian and German occupations and the subsequent Soviet takeover—having scorched the elements of his pastoral and left him exiled and homeless.

The fourth and fifth sections recall images and events of World War II, with suggestions of Holocaust atrocities and of anti-German violence. Miłosz reflects on the impermanence of what he once believed to be immutable, on how "what could not be taken away/ is taken." He echoes the pre-Socratic philosopher Heraclitus, whose famous maxim that "one cannot step twice into the same river" is a depiction of restless change and eternal mutability.

Czesław Miłosz. (© The Nobel Foundation)

In the last two sections, Miłosz comes to terms with the failure of his sense of connection to his homeland through memory. He is cut off not because of physical distance, which he demonstrates can be bridged imaginatively in memory, but sadly because of his growing indifference to the world and to life around him.

At times, the poem uses a private vocabulary that contains certain personal "secrets." Clearly, the elegy is addressed to a close friend with whom alone Miłosz shares some of his memories. Experiences and feelings are described to which an impersonal reader could not possibly have access, even if Miłosz were to supply notes or commentaries. The reader is given no exact idea, for that matter, of the identity of "N. N." The features of the Lithuanian landscape and of Vilnius are given only in flashes—the bath cabin, the scent of leather, horses at the forge—without any overall picture emerging. This technique suggests fragmentation and discontinuity in the poet's mind as well as discrepancies in the reader's ability to read that mind. Some of those flashes use Germanic names, such as "Mama Fliegeltaub" and "Sachenhausen," names foreign to the Lithuanian landscape and language that make no sense either to the reader or to natives of Vilnius without an explanation, although Miłosz offers none. Consequently, the reader must piece together his or her own (necessarily flawed) sense of person and place. Some important figures in the poem, such as "the German owner," are unnamed, increasing their strangeness. Miłosz writes privately and exclusively in order to make the reader sense the opacity of distance and understand both Miłosz's sense of separation from the past and the growing impenetrability and sterility of his memories.

In Polish, from which Miłosz himself translated this poem along with Lawrence Davis, the tone of the poem is more aggressive and personal than in English, and the opening imperative is much more direct and informal: "Powiedz czy to dla siebie za daleko." Generally, Miłosz's Polish has a more concise, direct, and condensed effect than can be captured in English. "Skręcić na ocean," for example, must be rendered as "could have turned toward the ocean," a much more unwieldy phrase. Generally, however, the translation captures the imagistic fervor and sensuality of the original.

Miłosz verges at times on surrealism, juxtaposing unexpected images in a kind of cinematic jump-cutting or montage. He sees a bath cabin, for example, transformed into "abstract crystal," a metamorphosis that is difficult to imagine if one is limited by common sense. His peculiar vision and sensual counterpoint only increase the reader's sense of being a stranger in his world, helplessly dislocated and unable to make clear sense of what is seen and heard. Like Miłosz, the reader seems to be cut off from the comforts of stable knowledge and fulfilled expectations.

The poet laments not the death of "N. N."—which, if judged only from the content of the poem, may not even have occurred—but the loss of vitality in his imagination and memory. He mourns the failure of his spiritual connections both to an idyllic image of the past and to "things as they are in themselves," the self-sufficient world of creation around him. Miłosz's elegy, like many of his poems, deals with the loss of spiritual energy in the modern world and with his growing inability, as a poet and a human being, to remake the link between the spiritual and the physical in order to restore some sense of belonging and meaning to life. In the poem, Miłosz sees himself as indifferent and increasingly unwilling to make the effort to bridge the distances between the actual and the ideal through the medium of poetry.

Miłosz tries to come to terms with the insufficiency of poetic "greatness" and with the failure of his imagination to transcend the often trivial aspects of ordinary life. He finds, upon self-examination, that he has no "great secrets" to reveal. Indeed, this failure—which finds a correlative in the scorched, arid postwar landscape of his faraway homeland—becomes for Miłosz inevitable, fated, like a cancer growing within him from year to year "until it takes hold."

Miłosz is clearly pessimistic about the fate of humanity, and he condemns himself to gradual decline in the face of an inability to make sense of what he once thought were immutable values that "could not be taken away." Miłosz's thought, however, has been characterized—by various readers and critics as well as by himself—as an "ecstatic pessimism"; that is, in the midst of tribulation and decline, the poet is able to discover some ecstatic core, some essentially vital, energetic center on which he can draw for poetic inspiration. In this elegy, despite his apparent failure to connect to his homeland through memories, Miłosz can still imagine a sensuously dense landscape, rife with surprising juxtapositions and aesthetic promise. Though reluctant to face the possibility of failure again, Miłosz nevertheless undertakes his poetic work and, out of the scorched ashes of his memory, is able to make, if nothing else, a poignant tribute to his loss.

SOURCES FOR FURTHER STUDY

Fiut, Aleksander. *The Eternal Moment: The Poetry of Czesław Miłosz*. Translated by Theodosia S. Robertson. Berkeley: University of California Press, 1990.

Malinowska, Barbara. *Dynamics of Being, Space, and Time in the Poetry of Czesław Miłosz and John Ashbery*. New York: Peter Lang, 2000.

Miłosz, Czesław. *Czesław Miłosz: Conversations*. Edited by Cynthia L. Haven. Jackson: University Press of Mississippi, 2006.

Nathan, Leonard, and Arthur Quinn. *The Poet's Work: An Introduction to Czesław Miłosz*. Cambridge, Mass.: Harvard University Press, 1991.

—*Kevin McNeilly*

ENEMIES
A LOVE STORY

AUTHOR: Isaac Bashevis Singer (1904-1991)
FIRST PUBLISHED: *Sonim, de Geshichte fun a Liebe*, 1966 (English translation, 1972)
GENRE: Novel
SUBGENRE: Domestic realism

In this work, set in the postwar, post-Holocaust period, Singer uses the experiences of one man, Herman Broder, as well as the experiences of the various women in Broder's life to show some of the ways in which those who survived the Holocaust dealt with their memories and built new lives.

PRINCIPAL CHARACTERS:
Herman Broder, a young Jewish immigrant from Poland
Tamara Rachel Broder, his first wife
Yadwiga Pracz, his present wife
Masha Tortshiner, his mistress
Shifrah Puah Bloch, her mother
Rabbi Milton Lampert, Herman's wealthy employer

OVERVIEW

On a summer morning, Herman Broder stirs from his troubled dreams, wondering if he could be in Nazi-occupied Poland, perhaps in the hayloft where his parents' servant girl, Yadwiga, has concealed him to save his life. Then, fully awake, he realizes that he is in the apartment in Brooklyn that he shares with Yadwiga, whom he married after learning of the deaths of his wife and his children.

Herman tells Yadwiga that he must make another of his overnight train trips to sell books. Actually, he remains in New York City, spending the day in the office of Rabbi Milton Lampert, for whom Herman works as a ghostwriter, and the night at the apartment of his mistress, Masha Tortshiner, and her mother, Shifrah Puah Bloch, who are also Holocaust survivors. Although Masha knows that Herman is married, her mother does not. Shifrah Puah is determined to have Masha get a divorce from her husband, Leon, so that she can marry Herman.

One day, Shifrah Puah calls Herman's attention to a notice in the newspaper that names him and asks him to telephone a certain number. When he makes the call, Herman finds himself speaking to the uncle of his first wife, Tamara, who, it seems, is alive and in New York. When Herman and Tamara are reunited, he is surprised to find her prettier than ever and considerably easier to get along with than she had been in the past. Although Herman knows that he must choose between his two wives, he has to admit that he would like to keep them both, and the volatile Masha as well.

Herman's trips to see Tamara arouse Masha's suspicions, but she does not guess that Herman's first wife has come back from the dead. Herman thinks that he might be able to reassure Masha about his feelings for her during a vacation in the Adirondacks that they have been planning. At first, they do relax and enjoy themselves on their trip, but then Masha tells Herman that she is pregnant. Taken by surprise, Herman rashly promises to marry Masha.

Blithely ignoring the fact that Herman is already married—his wife is, after all, only a mere Gentile—Masha works on getting a divorce. Meanwhile, Herman's other two relationships with women are becoming ever more complicated. On an outing in the Catskills, he and Tamara, who had been merely friends since their reunion, find themselves making love and enjoying it. Then, Yadwiga decides that she can become closer to her husband if she converts to Judaism and gives him a Jewish child. Although Herman does not want to bring another child into a world so full of cruelty and suffering, he cannot refuse her.

Herman continues to manage to keep the three women apart, but he worries constantly about exposure, which he knows will cost him his job with the rabbi and might well

Isaac Bashevis Singer. (AP/Wide World Photos)

lead to his being imprisoned or deported. He has a little time to decide which of his present wives he will keep, because he married Yadwiga in all innocence, believing Tamara to be dead. However, he will have no excuse, moral or legal, for acquiring a third wife.

Quite unexpectedly, Leon Tortshiner offers Herman a way out. Leon meets with Herman to warn him that Masha is a promiscuous, deceitful woman. Leon tells Herman not only that Masha has been consistently unfaithful during their marriage but also that she has already betrayed Herman by sleeping with Leon as the price of obtaining her divorce. Herman's immediate response is to end his relationship with Masha, but she manages to convince him that Leon is lying, and the two are married after all.

By the time winter arrives, Herman is in serious financial trouble. Not only is Yadwiga expecting a baby, which means more bills in Brooklyn, but also Masha's pregnancy has turned out to be purely psychological. Masha has been left too depressed to work, and so Herman has to provide all the support for the Bronx household of Masha and her mother as well. As a new convert to Judaism, Yadwiga is also driving Herman crazy with her questions about a faith he no longer observes.

Finally, the inevitable happens. First, Tamara drops in at the Brooklyn apartment, and Yadwiga recognizes her. Then some neighbors bring a gossipy man named Nathan Pesheles to meet Mrs. Broder, and, although Tamara pretends to be Herman's cousin, Pesheles takes a good look at Yadwiga. When Rabbi Lampert finds out that Herman has recently married, he visits Masha and invites the newlyweds to a party. One of the rabbi's other guests at the party is the observant Pesheles, who promptly informs Masha that he met a Tamara Broder at Herman's apartment in Brooklyn, thus tipping Masha off to the fact that the dead wife is not dead. Pesheles then goes on to tell everyone else, including the rabbi, that, in addition to Masha, Herman also has a pretty, pregnant wife named Yadwiga.

Before the evening is over, the kindly rabbi offers Masha a job and both Masha and her mother a place to live. Masha accepts, telling Herman that she never wants to see him again. Tamara comes to Herman's rescue, taking him in, giving him a job in her uncle's bookstore, and even helping Yadwiga in any way she can.

Then, just when things are going well, Masha comes back into Herman's life. Now she wants him again, and he agrees to run away with her. However, she is delayed, first by finding that her apartment has been burglarized and then by her mother's death. Herman and Masha consider a double suicide, but finally Herman decides to leave not only Masha, but everyone else. Masha does kill herself, and Yadwiga moves in with

Tamara, who runs the bookstore while Yadwiga takes care of their place and her baby girl, little Masha. No one ever finds out what happened to Herman.

Generally considered the most important Yiddish writer of the twentieth century, Isaac Bashevis Singer received the Nobel Prize in Literature in 1978, in large part in recognition of his re-creation of a world that no longer exists. Singer often wrote about life in Polish Jewish villages before they and their inhabitants were destroyed by the Nazis. *Enemies*, however, is set in the postwar, post-Holocaust period. Its subject is serious: the ways in which those who survived the Holocaust dealt with their memories and built new lives.

Appropriately, *Enemies* begins with Herman Broder's reliving the past. Even though he is now safe, Herman has been forever changed by his experiences. He has lost his faith in God and in human life. While he has married again, Herman hedges his bets by also keeping a mistress and remaining open to other possibilities. He is adamantly opposed to having more children, for it is clear that one cannot count on a beneficent God to preserve them. In fact, all that Herman now believes in is lust, which existed even in the death camps, and deceit, which he believes is the only way one can make it through the world.

Singer also shows how his four major women characters have responded to the Holocaust. Shifrah Puah wears black to keep alive the memories of those who died and feels guilty because she is alive. However, Shifrah still believes in God and observes the Jewish rituals.

Masha hates God as much as her mother loves him. Now, the central reality in her life is the Holocaust. Masha finds sexual stimulation in telling stories of those days while she and Herman are making love. Masha is enchanted with death, and, indeed, she does finally commit suicide.

In a sense, Tamara did die in the Holocaust, for she has become a new person: more unselfish, more considerate, and far wiser than she was before the war. After she and Herman are reunited, Tamara asks nothing for herself, not even that he return to her. Ironically, it is Tamara who now becomes Herman's only real friend and confidant. Even when he tells her that he is running off with Masha, Tamara accepts his decision with grace, and it is she who will fill Herman's place at the bookstore and care for his wife and his child.

It is also ironic that it is a Polish Catholic, Yadwiga, who replaces Herman within the Jewish community. What begins as her attempt to please her husband by observing his rituals ends with her wholeheartedly accepting the faith in which he no longer believes. Although Herman would blame his Holocaust experience for his actions, Singer points out that

Herman's character was formed long before the Nazis came to power. It is appropriate that, at the end of the novel, the self-centered Herman, if not dead, is alone somewhere, while the generous Yadwiga is being cherished by her new community.

The tone of *Enemies* is not uniformly serious. Like the village storytellers from whom he drew his inspiration, Singer delights in the eccentricities of human behavior and in the capacity of human beings to make fools of themselves. Herman Broder's adventures in *Enemies* are essentially farcical, and Herman himself, though appealing, is devoid of common sense. After he has escaped from the Nazis by hiding from them and from God by denying him, Herman uses his new freedom to become the willing slave of lust, especially as it is embodied in the equally irrational Masha.

Of his three wives, Masha alone is as irrational and as self-destructive as Herman. While both Tamara and Yadwiga try to keep Herman out of trouble, Masha always encourages him to behave like a fool. She gets him to marry her at the risk of being imprisoned or deported, and eventually she causes him to lose his job. Then, after ending the relationship with him, she quits her job and persuades him to quit his so that they can run off together; she even agrees with him that, because of a slight hitch in their plans, they might as well commit suicide. Ironically, at that point Herman is saved by his own irrationality. When Masha confesses that she deceived him about sleeping with her husband, Herman fails to see the parallel with his lying about sleeping with his wife Tamara, and he decides not to kill himself after all. Like a thwarted child, he decides to quit the whole world.

As it is applied to Herman and Masha, Singer's subtitle, *A Love Story*, points to the accuracy of the title *Enemies*. Certainly these two lovers are each other's worst enemies. However, the epilogue suggests that love can be redemptive rather than destructive. Thus, after Herman has rejected their aid and turned his back on life, Yadwiga and Tamara find gratification in helping each other, in loving the child Herman left them, and in being a part of a community that, through this new Jewish child, will itself be renewed.

Sources for Further Study

Alexander, Edward. *Isaac Bashevis Singer: A Study of the Short Fiction*. Boston: Twayne, 1980.

Denman, Hugh, ed. *Isaac Bashevis Singer: His Work and His World*. Boston: Brill, 2002.

Farrell, Grace, ed. *Critical Essays on Isaac Bashevis Singer*. New York: G. K. Hall, 1996.

_____. *Isaac Bashevis Singer: Conversations.* Jackson: University Press of Mississippi, 1992.

Friedman, Lawrence S. *Understanding Isaac Bashevis Singer.* Columbia: University of South Carolina Press, 1988.

Hadda, Janet. *Isaac Bashevis Singer: A Life.* New York: Oxford University Press, 1997.

Lee, Grace Farrell. *From Exile to Redemption: The Fiction of Isaac Bashevis Singer.* Carbondale: Southern Illinois University Press, 1987.

Noiville, Florence. *Isaac B. Singer: A Life.* Translated by Catherine Temerson. New York: Farrar, Straus and Giroux, 2006.

Qiao, Guo Qiang. *The Jewishness of Isaac Bashevis Singer.* New York: Peter Lang, 2003.

Wirth-Nesher, Hana. *City Codes: Reading the Modern Urban Novel.* New York: Cambridge University Press, 1996.

Wolitz, Seth L., ed. *The Hidden Isaac Bashevis Singer.* Austin: University of Texas Press, 2001.

—*Rosemary M. Canfield Reisman*

Europe Central

Author: William T. Vollmann (1959-   )
First published: 2005
Genre: Novel
Subgenre: Historical fiction

In this novel, European political and military turmoil of the 1930's and 1940's is examined through the lives of several Germans and Russians.

Principal characters:
  Dimitri Dimintriyevich Shostakovich (1906-1975), Russian composer
  Nina Vasilyevna Shostakovich, Dimitri's wife, a physicist
  Elena Evseyevna Konstantinovskaya, the love of Shostakovich's life
  Roman Lazarevich Karmen, a Soviet filmmaker and one of Elena's husbands
  Isaak Davidovich Glickman, Shostakovich's best friend
  Kurt Gerstein, an officer in the Schutzstaffel (SS)
  Friedrich Paulus, a German general
  Andrei Vaslov, a Soviet general
  Anna Andreyevna Akhmatova, a Russian poet
  Käthe Kollwitz, a German lithographer
  Adolf Hitler (1889-1945), the chancellor of Germany, 1933-1945
  Vladimir Ilyich Lenin (1870-1924), Soviet leader
  Nadezhda Konstantinovna Krupskaya, Lenin's wife
  Fanya Kaplan, a would-be assassin of Lenin
  Joseph Stalin (1878-1953), Soviet leader

Overview

William T. Vollmann was born in Santa Monica, California, and educated at Deep Springs College and Cornell University, where he graduated summa cum laude. He has worked as a computer programmer and founded CoTangent Press, producing limited editions of his works and those of other writers. Vollmann received the Whiting Writers' Award in 1988 for *You Bright and Risen Angels: A Cartoon* and the Shiva Naipaul

Memorial Prize in 1989 for an excerpt from *Seven Dreams: A Book of North American Landscapes*.

William T. Vollmann's demanding, postmodern fiction has tackled a number of subjects, ranging from a war between insects and the inventors of electricity in *You Bright and Risen Angels: A Cartoon* (1987) to San Francisco prostitutes and drug addicts in *The Royal Family* (2000) to what Vollmann terms a "symbolic history" of North America in *Seven Dreams: A Book of North American Landscapes* (1990-2001). Vollmann offers another metahistorical fiction in *Europe Central*, a look at much of the twentieth century from German and Russian perspectives, with the emphasis on the events of World War II. A massive, ambitious, demanding work, *Europe Central* won the National Book Award but may put off some readers because of its bulk and its failure to adhere to a linear narrative. In addition to being a meditation on war and totalitarianism, *Europe Central* is also, through several sections dealing with artists, about the transforming nature of art: "Art does not so much derive from life as actually change the perception and appreciation of it, casting itself across existence *like a shadow*."

Vollmann has said that in his fiction he strives for a dreamlike effect. *Europe Central* resembles a slow-motion nightmare in which political conflict spins the lives of a large cast of characters out of control. Composed of thirty-seven stories, *Europe Central* looks at how artists, military leaders, and ordinary people struggle to understand the nature of evil. The central event, for which Vollmann has drawn a map, is Operation Barbarossa, the German advance into Russia in 1941, ending with the defeat of the invaders at Stalingrad. Vollmann employs both historical and fictional characters, all of whom exist at the petulant whims of Adolf Hitler and Joseph Stalin, who lurk in the background and occasionally make cameo appearances.

Europe Central is dedicated to Danilo Kiš, whose *A Tomb for Boris Davidovich* (1978) has a similar structure with interrelated stories and for a 2001 edition of which Vollmann wrote an afterword. (Kiš is also cited within the novel.) Both books also deal with anti-Semitism and Stalin's purges within the Soviet Union. With one exception, the stories appear as contrasting pairs from German and Russian points of view.

The longest set of pairs, "Breakout" and "The Last Field-Marshal," presents Soviet General Andrei Vaslov's capture and formation of a Russian Liberation Army to oppose Stalin and the efforts of German General Friedrich Paulus to complete his initially successful invasion of the Soviet Union. Vaslov first fights against Paulus's forces, only to join with the enemy after his capture. Paulus is likewise captured and used for propaganda purposes by his enemy. Both are good men doing what they must, and both their lives end badly. "Breakout" is the more effective story because Vollmann's Vaslov has greater psychological depth than does his Paulus. "The Last Field-Marshal" becomes bogged down a bit by the details of military maneuvering, one of several instances when Vollmann is seduced by his extensive research. He comes close to being a more literary version of James Michener who feels obligated to cram every bit of his research into the narrative.

One of the most affecting stories, "Clean Hands," tells of Kurt Gerstein's endeavors to alert the world to the horrors of the Holocaust. Beaten in 1936 and 1938 for opposing Nazi policies, Gerstein is a devout Christian whose beloved sister-in-law is killed by Nazis. Nevertheless, he becomes the Schutzstaffel (SS) officer responsible for supplying the toxic canisters used to exterminate Jews at Bełżec and other concentration camps in Poland. He tries to sabotage his own efforts and get word to the Allies. While everyone around him, including his father, supports Hitler and hates Jews, Gerstein just grits his teeth. The less known about his true feelings, the more likely he will find some way to help his victims. Because he does not believe in what he is doing, Gerstein keeps telling himself that he has clean hands.

Most of Vollmann's characters are protagonists in only one story, but many also appear briefly or are mentioned in other stories, creating the sense that all the people and events in *Europe Central* are inextricably linked by their fates. One character haunted by Vaslov is Dimitri Dimintriyevich Shostakovich, the Russian composer who comes closest to being the novel's principal character, appearing in several stories. Like Vaslov and Gerstein, Shostakovich is a patriot shaken by his nation's policies. Vollmann devotes considerable attention to Soviet efforts, especially those of Stalin himself, to convince Shostakovich to join the Communist Party. The composer's refusal results in constant denunciations despite his increasing international fame.

The Shostakovich stories, however, center less on politics than on his complicated love life. In 1934-1935, the composer has a passionate affair with Elena Konstantinovskaya and remains obsessed with her through his unhappy marriage to the long-suffering Nina, two more marriages, and many affairs. Ironically, Shostakovich eventually becomes friends with Roman Karmen, Elena's first husband, and writes scores for his films. Despite his devotion to propaganda filmmaking, Karmen feels that his love for Elena "is the only thing that's genuine about me." In a note, "An Imaginary Love Triangle: Shostakovich, Karmen, Konstantinovskaya," Vollmann admits that he has fictionalized this trio's relationship because there is no evidence that Elena was the love of the composer's life.

If Shostakovich cannot be faithful to Nina, at least he is true to his musical genius, composing symphonies, quartets, and operas that party-controlled critics attack as belonging to "that secret world of chromatic dissonance which everybody called 'formalism.'" Vollmann strives to show how Shostakovich's music, the string quartet Opus 110 in particular, with its "swarm of sorrows," reflects his inner turmoil about his love life, the war, and the pressure to conform to a political ideology he abhors. The composer's love for Elena becomes a metaphor for his inability to resolve his demons, and Elena herself, as Vollmann says in his postscript, represents the unfathomable enigma that is Europe.

The volume's first story, "Steel in Motion," sets up the theme of the interconnectedness of things, of the search for the meaning of Europe. Events in Germany influence those in the Soviet Union, whose countermeasures lead to additional countermeasures, all affecting numerous other countries. The political climate of the twentieth century creates an almost perpetual climate of vagueness, uncertainty, and fear throughout the continent. Vollmann sees Europe less as a victim than a coconspirator, full of self-delusions: "Europe's never burned a witch or laid hands on a Jew!"

Vollmann not only tells several stories but also writes them in different styles, using relatively straightforward, chronological narratives, stream of consciousness, and a dense, postmodernist, often elliptical technique. Each story is divided into chapters of varying lengths; for instance, several chapters are sometimes strung together on a page, followed by a much longer one. Only a moderate amount of dialogue appears, and several sentences go on for more than one hundred words, often interrupted by lengthy parenthetical remarks. Vollmann seems to be doing everything he can to engage his readers in the same sort of struggle for understanding that his characters are experiencing as they face complex social, political, psychological, romantic, and moral quandaries for which simple solutions are impossible.

In the early stories, Vollmann also calls attention to style as the essence of his aesthetic by having Vladimir Ilyich Lenin proclaim about a dictionary, "The alphabetical arrangement of words creates such a refreshing sort of chaos." There are meditations, as well, on the meanings of letters, some of which take on almost human characteristics. Vollmann's self-conscious method becomes obvious when he writes, "Most literary critics agree that fiction cannot be reduced to mere falsehood . . . the pretense that life is what we want it to be may conceivably bring about the desired condition. . . . [I]f this story . . . crawls with reactionary supernaturalism, that might be because its author longs to see letters scuttling across ceilings, cautiously beginning to reify themselves into angels."

Although Vollmann provides fifty-four pages of notes from his research into the complex historical background of his novel, his narrators still resort to explanatory, often scholarly footnotes. Vollmann wanted to provide a chronology to help his readers sort out events, but his publisher made him "cut it, on account of the wartime paper shortage."

One of the most fascinating aspects of *Europe Central* is the identity of the narrator or narrators. A first-person narrator pops up periodically throughout the novel. The narrator of the Russian stories is a member of the secret service who arrests and interrogates some characters, while the German stories are told from the perspective of someone from the signal corps. While these two narrators might be said simply to be spokesmen for their national sensibilities, they are specific characters with families and foibles they readily admit.

The German narrator is berated by his wife in 1962: "We all suffered in the war, even me whom you left alone while you were off raping Polish girls and shooting Ukrainians in the ditches." The self-conscious Russian narrator begs the reader's pardon for a digression and promises to exit the story, only to announce paragraphs later his preference for André Previn's conducting of Shostakovich's Tenth Symphony to Herbert von Karajan's and to confess his love for Elena. Vollmann himself seems to be the narrator at times: "I'm writing in the year 2002." Adding to the confusion is Vollmann's omission of quotation marks in his dialogue so that "I" has numerous identities. Vollmann employs his narrators, who often use "we" as well as "I," as unreliable interpreters who see events only from a political perspective.

The critical response to *Europe Central* was mixed. A surprising number of publications, including *Time*, *Newsweek*, *The New Yorker*, and the daily *New York Times* did not even review it. Not doing so did not keep *USA Today* from labeling the novel the year's most overrated. Michael Wood, in *The New York Review of Books*, wrote, "The book is always lucid, even as it hovers between the obvious and the recondite, and the under- and overexamined." In the *Village Voice*, Brandon Stosuy praised the work as "a visionary textbook on human suffering" but complained about the slackness of Vollmann's "sentence-to-sentence care." Many sentences, passages, and entire chapters fail to add anything to the novel's overall effect and could easily have been excised. Then there is the occasional sloppiness, as with misuses of "hopefully."

Yet the large themes, vivid characters, and frequent brilliant writing of *Europe Central* overshadow such flaws. At their best, Vollmann's sinuous sentences evoke both the complexity of the world they describe as well as the human misery at its core: "First the screaming of the enemy's Katyusha rockets, much shriller than the sirens of Wolf's Lair; then the explosions, followed after an interval by the crystal-clear cracklings of frozen rubble shivering to fragments, the cries of the survivors, each cry utterly sincere and wrapped up in itself, as if its own pain were the first pain which had ever come into this world."

SOURCES FOR FURTHER STUDY

Blythe, Will, ed. *Why I Write: Thoughts on the Practice of Writing*. Boston: Little, Brown, 1998.
Buckiet, Melvin Jules. "A Dark Gray Tapestry of Human Frailty." *Los Angeles Times*, March 20, 2005, p. R3.
Freeman, John. "Dazzling Reflections of a Murderous Century." *Boston Globe*, April 3, 2005, p. D7.
Kauffman, Linda S. *Bad Girls and Sick Boys: Fantasies in Contemporary Art and Culture*. Berkeley: University of California Press, 1998.
Leclair, Tom. "Party Line." *The New York Times Book Review*, April 3, 2005, p. 16.
Vollmann, William T. *Expelled from Eden: A William T. Vollmann Reader*. Edited by Larry McCaffery and Michael Hemmingson. New York: Thunder's Mouth Press, 2004.

—Michael Adams

Explaining Hitler
The Search for the Origins of His Evil

Author: Ron Rosenbaum (1946-   )
First published: 1998
Genre: Nonfiction
Subgenres: History; psychology

Rosenbaum explores the diverse and conflicting theories that attempt to explain Adolf Hitler's anti-Semitism and his unleashing of the Holocaust.

Principal personage:
  Adolf Hitler (1889-1945), the chancellor of Germany, 1933-1945

Overview

A writer named Milton Himmelfarb plays an important cameo role in Ron Rosenbaum's remarkable book *Explaining Hitler: The Search for the Origins of His Evil*. In March, 1984, Himmelfarb published "No Hitler, No Holocaust," an essay in which he contended that the decision to annihilate European Jewry was Adolf Hitler's alone, a view that has not been shared by every Holocaust scholar. Far from being impelled by historical, political, or cultural forces to murder the European Jews, Himmelfarb continued, Hitler wanted and chose to annihilate them.

More than anything else, links between Hitler (1889-1945) and the Holocaust explain why, as Rosenbaum says, "an enormous amount has been written" about him "but little has been *settled*." Persuaded by much of Himmelfarb's position, Rosenbaum keeps returning to it but also understands that, while Himmelfarb's position may explain a good deal about the Holocaust, it does not explain Hitler—at least not completely. How badly did Hitler want to destroy the Jews? When did he decide to do so? Even more basically, what made Hitler? Scholars have answered such questions differently, which makes the real Hitler elusive and the puzzles about him persistent.

Those questions and the diverse, even contradictory, responses to them persist partly because a photograph of Hitler was taken when he was probably less than two years old. Years later it was included in a Nazi book called *The Hitler Nobody Knows* (1932). In that context and others, Rosenbaum notes, the baby picture was used to build a wholesome image of Hitler, a tactic that helped to mask Hitler's identity in ways that still haunt us. The same baby picture also appears on the title page of Rosenbaum's book, which is one of the most comprehensive and provocative account of the dominant attempts to "explain" Hitler. The title page design centers on baby Hitler's eyes. Unavoidably drawn to them, the reader can also see the words *Explaining Hitler* and the book's subtitle, *The Search for the Origins of His Evil*.

As Rosenbaum understands, his title and Hitler's baby picture collide. Somehow the infant in the photo became Nazi Germany's führer. That normal-looking child became the leader of a regime that unleashed not only World War II but also an unprecedented genocidal attack on the Jewish people and millions of other defenseless people who were caught in the Holocaust, or Shoah, as it is also known (from the Hebrew word for "catastrophe"), which is arguably the quintessential evil of all human history. Hitler's baby picture raises a thousand questions that words must try to answer but perhaps never can. Starting his book with that tension-filled juxtaposition, Rosenbaum ends on a related point more than four hundred pages later. His concluding acknowledgments express special gratitude to the scholars and writers who granted him interviews. Rosenbaum honors their courageous and dedicated pursuit of what he knowingly calls "the impossible challenge of explaining Hitler."

A seasoned scholar-journalist who turned his disciplined and determined research into grippingly crafted, page-turning prose, Rosenbaum showed his own courage and dedication in writing this book, which was more than ten years in the making. He tracked down people who knew Hitler and got members of that dwindling number to share what they remembered. He traveled to obscure archives and located long-forgotten files that shed new light on Hitler research. He journeyed to remote Austrian sites in search of details about Hitler's ancestry and youth. All the while, he read voraciously and interviewed dozens of the most influential biographers, historians, philosophers, and theologians who have faced the challenge of bridging the abyss between baby Adolf and Auschwitz Hitler.

Rosenbaum reports the findings of those interpreters, but how he does so makes his book much more than a summary of other people's views. Rosenbaum's meetings with the Hitler scholars are charged with his penetrating questions, his insightful observations that complicate matters for all the writers he encounters, and his skeptical refusal to be overly impressed by the authority of any of the experts he meets. More specifically, Rosenbaum became intrigued by what he identifies as the "wishes and longings, the subtexts and agendas of Hitler explanations." When it comes to explaining Hitler, Rosenbaum asks, what do people want and why? How are the sometimes radical differences in interpretation best understood? What would it mean if Hitler could be explained definitively—or if he cannot?

Such questions concentrated Rosenbaum's attention as he met the major Hitler interpreters and then as he reflected deeply about what his investigations revealed. As the reader travels with him, Rosenbaum shows the strengths and weaknesses in the various Hitler "explanations." He finds the right questions to ask of each text he studies, every scholar he meets, and even any insight that more or less persuades him. While learning much about Hitler and the scholarship about him, the reader becomes a partner in Rosenbaum's inquiry, which entails coming to see that the challenge of "explaining" Hitler may be impossible. Even that conclusion, however, is driven home in Rosenbaum's distinctively inquisitive way. His reasons for thinking that it may be impossible to explain Hitler—and the implications that follow—are among the most important findings in this bold and instructive book.

At the outset, Rosenbaum pays tribute to largely forgotten German journalists who reported and opposed Hitler's rise to power. These anti-Hitler journalists—one named Fritz Gerlich receives Rosenbaum's special admiration—wrote for the *Munich Post* and *Der Gerade Weg* ("the right way" or "the straight path"). Before the Nazis brutally shut them down—Gerlich was sent to Dachau and then murdered in June, 1934—these courageous writers sensed Hitler's evil qualities and did their best, even in the early months after Hitler took power on January 30, 1933, to expose the blackmail and murder perpetrated by the Nazis. The German journalists planted seeds of suspicion about Hitler's sexual inclinations to subvert the deceptive wholesomeness of *The Hitler Nobody Knows*. They cast doubt on Hitler's ethnic origins and even his physical appearance to expose the irrationality of his racism and anti-Semitism. As soon as he could, Hitler ruthlessly crushed their dissent.

These anti-Hitler journalists wanted more to stop Hitler than to explain him, but Rosenbaum suggests that they set the stage for post-Holocaust explanations. Probing Hitler's background, they laid the groundwork for a key question in Hitler scholarship: Do Hitler's origins—psychological, familial, sociopolitical—explain him? Disclosing his corrupt and murderous deeds, they began to focus on whether Hitler was a cynical political opportunist or an "idealist" who thought that his policies, however deadly, were justified by the "right" and "good" ends they supposedly served. Emphasizing the virulence of his racism and anti-Semitism, the German journalists paved the way for explorations of Hitler's intentionality toward the Jews and, in particular, of whether his intentions were genocidal before he came to power or only afterward. The early anti-Hitler journalists had little doubt that Hitler did evil deeds and even that he was an evil man. They thus initiated inquiry about how Hitler's evil ought to be understood: Should Hitler be counted as an "ordinary man" or as an exception, an embodiment of demoniacally destructive power?

Rosenbaum shows that advocates for all of these positions—and many more—can be found among the leading scholars who have tried to explain Hitler. Biographer Hugh Trevor-Roper, for example, thinks that Hitler, thoroughly misguided though he was, sincerely believed in his anti-Semitism and thought that the destruction of the Jews was the right thing to do. Alan Bullock, another biographer, and theologian Emil Fackenheim disagree with Trevor-Roper, finding Hitler to be a cynical political opportunist who used anti-Semitism for his own advancement. Philosopher Berel Lang thinks that neither of those views does justice to the magnitude of Hitler's evil. Lang believes that Hitler was aware of his criminality and even reveled in it. Rosenbaum, who sees Hitler as "a vicious, cold-blooded hater," finds Lang's analysis impressive, if not conclusive. The scope, planning, and sheer brutality of the Holocaust suggest to Lang that Hitler's evil involved what Rosenbaum calls an "art of evil," which required intention, invention, and imagination that relished suffering and destruction. Nevertheless, Rosenbaum stops short of saying that Lang is absolutely right. To say that about any explanation of Hitler would go further than the available evidence permits, for too much time may have passed for anyone to find the key that can unlock the door to Hitler's identity once and for all.

Rosenbaum's conviction is that the yearning to explain Hitler often divulges a need that should be resisted, namely, the desire for closure, comfort, and consolation. Wanting an account that explains everything, we seem to await discovery of what Rosenbaum calls "a long-neglected safe-deposit box" that will grant final, irrefutable answers to the disturbing questions that Hitler raises. Rosenbaum doubts the existence of such a definitive source. His investigations of Hitler explanations—Robert Waite's psychohistorical account, Rudolph Binion's speculation about the importance of the Jewish doctor who treated Hitler's mother unsuccessfully, or Daniel Goldhagen's emphasis on Hitler's use of a pervasive German "eliminationist anti-Semitism," to name just a few—always leave him skeptical that final and complete answers will be found. This outcome, however, does not mean that Rosenbaum accepts the view of Claude Lanzmann, the filmmaker who produced *Shoah* (1985), an epic Holocaust documentary. Rosenbaum found Lanzmann asserting that it is wrong to seek explanation for Hitler and the Holocaust because answers lead to understanding, understanding leads to legitimation, and legitimation leads to exoneration. According to Lanzmann, one can confront the raw events of the Holocaust, but to "explain" how and why Hitler's power led to Auschwitz would be tantamount to forgiving the unforgivable, an outcome more obscene than rational.

While recognizing that some explanations reduce Hitler's responsibility by making him the pawn of social, political, or psychological determinants—a view that *Explaining Hitler* rejects—Rosenbaum disagrees with Lanzmann's extreme position and concurs instead with historian Yehuda Bauer. Holding that, in principle, Hitler can be explained, Bauer does not think it follows that Hitler has been or ever will be explained. Nevertheless, ongoing effort to explain him remains important. To stop trying would mean that, in principle, Hitler is beyond explanation, an outcome that takes him out of history and thereby promotes problematic mystification.

Rosenbaum thinks that Hitler was certainly human but not ordinary, for ordinary people do not do what Hitler did. Hitler was human, but he was also exceptional in the sense that he can rightly be called an evil man, even an evil genius. Rosenbaum's conclusions on these points—he says he holds them by "default" more than out of "a metaphysical conviction"—are influenced by Lucy Dawidowicz, author of *The War Against the Jews* (1975), who defended the thesis that Hitler formed his intention to destroy European Jewry as early as November, 1918. Coolly obsessed by that goal, Dawidowicz contended, Hitler orchestrated his opportunities until he could do what he wanted. Twenty-five years after Dawidowicz published her views, they are less accepted by scholars than those of Christopher R. Browning and others who place Hitler's decision to launch the "final solution" in the late summer or early autumn of 1941. Rosenbaum urges that Dawidowicz's position deserves renewed attention. Further inquiry will determine the scholarly status enjoyed by Dawidowicz and every other interpreter of Hitler, including Rosenbaum himself.

Explaining Hitler deals astutely with two of history's most important questions: Who was Adolf Hitler? How and why did the Holocaust happen? Rosenbaum's last word is that inquiry about those questions will be at its best to the extent that it involves resistance. Where Hitler and the Holocaust are concerned, explanatory inquiry should always resist temptations to misplace responsibility. Failure to resist "explanatory excuses" will grant Hitler "the posthumous victory of a last laugh." Not "faceless abstractions, inexorable forces, or irresistible compulsions," but Hitler's choices, Rosenbaum correctly argues, must be at the center of the effort to explain Hitler.

SOURCES FOR FURTHER STUDY

Boynton, Robert S. *The New New Journalism: Conversations with America's Best Nonfiction Writers on Their Craft*. New York: Vintage Books, 2005.

Fisher, Marc. "Anatomy of a Tyrant." *The Washington Post*, August 23, 1998, p. X7.

Katz, Fred E. "Casting a Wide Net." *New Leader* 81, no. 8 (June 29-July 12, 1998): 16.

Kaul, Arthur J. *American Literary Journalists, 1945-1995: First Series*. Vol. 185 in *Dictionary of Literary Biography*. Detroit: Gale Research, 1997.

Marrus, Michael. "The Enigma of the Century." *The New York Times Book Review*, July 19, 1998, p. 8.

Will, George. "The Hitler Explanation Industry." *The Washington Post*, October 29, 1998, p. 27.

—*John K. Roth*

The Fall of France
The Nazi Invasion of 1940

AUTHOR: Julian Jackson (1954-   )
FIRST PUBLISHED: 2003
GENRE: Nonfiction
SUBGENRE: History

Contesting conventional wisdom that Nazi Germany's 1940 defeat of France was unavoidable, Jackson maps the military campaign, explores the reasons for French failure, and assesses the consequences.

PRINCIPAL PERSONAGES:
   Philippe Pétain (1856-1951), premier of the Vichy government in
      unoccupied France
   Pierre Laval (1883-1945), successor to Pétain

OVERVIEW

On June 22, 1940, the French general Charles Huntziger sat opposite Adolf Hitler in a railway carriage in the forest of Compiègne. In 1918 that same French carriage and location had been the site of Germany's capitulation in World War I. Little more than two decades later, the tables were turned. The contrast, however, was not only that the Germans had supplanted the French as victors but also that the military conflict between these powers had been very different.

In the grim trench warfare of World War I, French and German forces had battled each other for four years. In 1940, the violence was often intense, but the fall of France came in six weeks. The sudden French defeat has been controversial ever since. Weighing in on that debate, historian Julian Jackson provides a detailed and lucid account that focuses on the May-June battle. He shows that the political and military circumstances were more complex than previous interpreters have said. That complexity, he urges, also helps to account for the multiple ways in which the 1940 defeat continues to mark French identity and culture.

World War II began with Nazi Germany's invasion of Poland on September 1, 1939. Having spent several months consolidating their gains in

Eastern Europe, German military forces made quick and successful strikes in the West. Following the invasions of Denmark and Norway in early April, 1940, the Germans attacked France, Belgium, Luxembourg, and the Netherlands on May 10. Just ten days later, German tanks had reached France's Atlantic coast. Only the massive sea evacuation of 340,000 British and French forces from Dunkirk at the end of the month prevented the Germans from destroying the main military forces that opposed them in the western parts of the European continent.

The Germans launched their final assault against France on June 5. Paris fell on June 14. Two days later, Marshal Philippe Pétain, the aging French hero of World War I, became head of the French government. He quickly asked for an armistice, which resulted in a two-zone division of the country. The Germans occupied the north, including Paris, and the western seaboard. Central and southern France, with governmental headquarters at the resort town of Vichy, remained unoccupied until November, 1942. Under these arrangements, the Germans allowed a collaborationist French government, led by Pétain and then by Pierre Laval, to remain in place in exchange for its cooperation, which included financial exploitation that benefited Germany, labor brigades sent to work in German industry, and punitive measures against Jews.

Meanwhile, Jackson reports, on June 17, 1940, the day after becoming prime minister, Pétain addressed the French people in a midday radio speech that praised the "magnificent resistance" of the French military "against an enemy superior in numbers and in arms." It was with "a heavy heart," he continued, "that I say to you today that it is necessary to cease fighting." Jackson does not deny that Pétain's judgments were widely shared in France, but he questions their factual status and unavoidability.

First, were the German forces overwhelmingly superior? To some extent they were but, Jackson argues, not necessarily in decisive ways. Although German tanks were bigger and faster than those commanded by the French, the French army still had its strengths, but they were compromised by more than German power alone. Jackson finds that French planning was inept, the execution of existing plans slow and uncoordinated, and there were failures to take advantage of exposed German lines as the enemy's Blitzkrieg tactics stretched its forces thin. With better leadership, more thorough troop preparation, swifter coordination of resources, and more aggressive plans, France need not have collapsed so suddenly. The unavoidability of France's defeat was not a foregone conclusion.

Furthermore, France's situation might have been much stronger if the Allied response to Hitler had been different, especially in regard to support for France. Jackson, however, does not press his counterfactual hypotheses too far. Instead, he sheds helpful light on the complexity of international relations at the time. European states had good reason to be fearful of renewed German power under Hitler, not least because the memory of World War I's devastation remained vivid.

France explored alliance possibilities with the Soviet Union and Italy as well as with Poland, but the viability of those prospects went from dim to nonexistent. The 1939 nonaggression pact between Hitler and Joseph Stalin enabled the partition of Poland between them. No help was available to France from Eastern Europe, nor was assistance from Italy in the cards, as Hitler and Benito Mussolini increasingly embraced each other.

Closer to home, the French counted on support from Belgium, but the French knew they faced problems when Belgium declared neutrality in 1936. Great Britain was France's best hope for a reliable ally, but relations between the two countries remained problematic after World War I and reached low points in the mid-1930's, when cooperation could have been extremely helpful. When the German onslaught came, France and Great Britain did not benefit each other as much as they could have. The Germans were not invincible when they invaded France, but strained relationships between Great Britain and France helped to give them the upper hand.

What about the "magnificent resistance" that Pétain emphasized in his June 17 radio address? By showing the situation's complexity, Jackson again sheds light on an important question. First, while memories of World War I did not make France a pacifistic nation, Jackson stresses that there was little enthusiasm for more military conflict. In the earlier war, 1.3 million Frenchmen had fallen; the bodies of 300,000 were never recovered or identified. More than a million veterans were invalids. War widows and orphans numbered in the hundreds of thousands.

Prior to the outbreak of war in 1939, most of the French people hoped that armed conflict could be avoided and reconciliation with Germany could be achieved. At the same time, and especially after Hitler invaded Poland, the French understood, however reluctantly, that the nation must be prepared to defend itself. Already in the second half of the 1930's, French rearmament had advanced, but it was hampered by production lags and inefficiencies, some of them caused by disagreements among the nation's military leaders, whose strategy preferences clashed. Nevertheless, by 1940 the French were fairly well equipped to do battle against the Germans—only fairly well equipped, however, because Jackson argues convincingly that "the French army was not a monolithic organization."

The French-German border was heavily fortified by France's Maginot line, which was intended to ensure that, if war came, it would not be

A Frenchman weeps as German soldiers march into Paris on June 14, 1940. (NARA)

fought primarily on French soil. Instead, even after the Belgians declared neutrality, the French anticipated that a German invasion would take place through Belgium. That judgment proved correct, but the French miscalculated by thinking that the German attack would repeat the strategy of 1914 by coming through central Belgium. Instead, the primary German offensive went farther south, taking routes through the Ardennes forest. It was evident to both sides that a thrust through the Ardennes was risky for the Germans, but the French did not overlook the possibility that the German advance would emerge from the forest. The French, however, did not regard that route as the most likely. Given that some French units were better equipped than others, the French generals committed the best forces to central and northern Belgium, leaving the weakest to cover the Ardennes.

Led by generals Heinz Guderian and Erwin Rommel, the Germans penetrated the Ardennes and then crossed the Meuse River on May 13, overcoming French resistance and establishing the bridgeheads that enabled German armor to flow into the breach. Prompt reinforcement could have slowed, if not stopped, the German advance, but that response did not materialize. Within days, it was too late for the French to recover. Civilians took flight to the south, while French forces found themselves increasingly on the losing side. Jackson reports that German losses in the battle against France "were remarkably light—27,074 killed, 111,034 wounded, 18,384 missing." He contends that the high number of French casualties, including between fifty thousand and ninety thousand dead, disproves charges that the French failed to fight. Although Jackson acknowledges that 1.5 million French prisoners of war might qualify that assessment, he notes mitigating circumstances by observing that half of the French troops "were captured in the six days between Pétain's 17 June broadcast, announcing that the government would be seeking an armistice, and the actual signing of the armistice itself on 22 June."

Pétain's claim that France resisted Nazi Germany magnificently in 1940 does not stand scrutiny. On the contrary, that French resistance, heroic though it was at times, proved insufficient to prevent what Jackson identifies as "the most humiliating military disaster in French history." Jackson also agrees with those who regard the fall of France as a pivotal point in twentieth century history. The French capitulation, which came earlier than necessary and at a relatively low cost to Nazi Germany thanks to the collaborationist policies of Pétain and his followers, turned a European conflict into a global war. Stiffer Allied and French resistance in 1940, Jackson thinks, might have resulted in "some kind of negotiated peace" with Germany. Nothing ensures that such a vague and counterfactual outcome would have been preferable to the unconditional surrender of Nazi Germany in May, 1945, but the fall of France remains a contender if one seeks to identify the twentieth century's most crucial events.

As for the French themselves, Jackson's summary is sound: "If 1940 figures less prominently in France's memory wars than one might expect," he writes, "this may be because it was an event too painful to contemplate." France's defeat led to the demoralizing experiences of occupation, collaboration, and deportation, including the destruction of eighty thousand Jews, mostly immigrants and refugees, who perished in Nazi death camps after being rounded up by French police who did the Germans' bidding. According to Jackson, Pétain and his Vichy regime enjoyed "moral authority" for a time because their "language of rootedness and authority, family and security, resonated with a nation traumatized by its recent experience of upheaval and dislocation." In retrospect, however, the Vichy regime gave France no reason for pride and joy.

After the war, when Pétain and Laval were convicted of treason and condemned to death, those actions were necessary to restore French honor but not enough to remove the stains of collaboration with the Nazis. When French sensibilities required Charles de Gaulle to commute Pétain's sentence to life imprisonment, that result inadvertently created a symbol for one legacy of the fall of France: A French hero from World War I, later compromised through defeat by and collaboration with Nazi Germany, became imprisoned for life by those events from World War II.

Jackson thinks that France deserves, and to a large measure has obtained, a better fate than that. What strikes him most about France in the second half of the twentieth century is "its capacity for survival and reinvention, its resilience, the continuing attraction of its culture." Nevertheless, debate about the fall of France and its consequences may never achieve closure. Even with the twenty-first century's arrival, Jackson concludes, it is too early to tell.

SOURCES FOR FURTHER STUDY

Jackson, Julian. "Historians and the Nation in Contemporary France." In *Writing National Histories: Western Europe Since 1800*, edited by Stefan Berger, Mark Donovan, and Kevin Passmore. New York: Routledge, 1999.

Johnson, Douglas. "When the Phoney War Ended." *The Spectator* 291, no. 9114 (April 12, 2003): 38.

McLynn, Frank. "Marianne in Chains." *New Statesman* 16, no. 747 (May 10, 2003): 54.

Wullschlager, Jackie. "Doomed by a Mutual Disdain." *Financial Times*, April 12, 2003, p. 4.

—*John K. Roth*

Fateless

Author: Imre Kertész (1929-   )
First published: *Sorstalanság*, 1975 (English translation, 1992)
Genre: Novel
Subgenres: Autobiographical fiction; philosophical realism

Based on Kertész's personal experiences, this book explores the meaning of the Holocaust through a detailed account of a crucial year in the life of a Hungarian Jewish adolescent, including his deportation from Hungry, his hard labor in the concentration camps, his near death, and his return home.

Principal characters:
 George Koves, the narrator, a fourteen-year-old Hungarian Jew and concentration camp prisoner
 Bandi Citrom, a fellow prisoner of George, a Hungarian Jew in his twenties

Overview

Imre Kertész's novel *Fateless* documents the episodes that make up the life of the young George Koves during a yearlong period in 1944-1945. The narrative proceeds in a linear way, but the account methodically builds to a larger, comprehensive meaning, eventually arriving at a complex philosophical perspective.

George's story begins in his home in Budapest, Hungary, where, added to the upset of his parents' recent divorce, a rapidly changing political situation requires his father, as a Jew, to give up his business and relocate to a Nazi labor camp. When George's uncle tells him that he must accept with forbearance a Jewish fate that includes such instances of persecution, George reacts with skepticism. Similarly, he reduces a playmate to tears by insisting that his identity as a Jew is cultural and not biological—biology, he explains, cannot determine his fate.

Despite George's resistance to what friends and family suggest is his fate as a Jew, it is as a Jew that he is forced into laboring at an oil refinery outside of Budapest. Soon, he is arrested and sent to the Auschwitz concentration camp in southern Poland. While going through the practical steps involved in this process, George finds that the dispassionate, self-contained, and watchful mode of consciousness he had already developed in Budapest protects him emotionally and provides him with the ability to see the big picture—namely, that everything that is happening to him is the predictable outcome of the totalitarian premises of Nazi Germany. He notes the efficiency and professionalism of the German soldiers, whose expectations of compliance are such that their prisoners can find no alternative but that of cooperation; when he finds shoes arranged and waiting for them in Auschwitz, it occurs to him that every detail has been taken into consideration. He realizes that people in leadership positions must have put their heads together in meetings to engineer everything in the camp, from the flower beds to the showers to the gas chambers, and that what is happening to him is the consequence of a powerful, sophisticated organization.

After brief stays at the Auschwitz and Buchenwald concentration camps, George is transferred to Zeitz, a work camp, where he is put to hard labor at a quarry. Despite the hardships of the camps, George understands that he and his fellow prisoners still retain the freedom to dissent from the Nazi perspective, and he documents a number of different forms of resistance—or, as he calls it, stubbornness. His cool, detached perspective, for instance, becomes an important way of refusing to acquiesce to the Nazi juggernaut. The prisoners also do their best to help one another—for instance, a fellow prisoner makes sure the young George does not have his food ration purloined, and a fellow Hungarian, a resilient man in his twenties named Bandi Citrom, takes George under his wing and teaches him various important survival strategies. Additionally, George finds that his imagination remains free even while he is in captivity and that he can travel in his mind backward in time to a safe haven or forward to future happiness. In fact, he holds on to the recognition that the future can always bring new possibilities and alternatives that could change everything.

By the time George is imprisoned at Zeitz, the other adolescent boys with whom he was arrested have dispersed. They have long since lost the youthful sense of adventure with which they began their life in the camps, and they have either died or become prematurely aged. As time goes on, food rations become scarce, and the feeble and emaciated George is further weakened by a leg wound, his health deteriorating to such an extent that he lingers near death. Even in this condition, however, he realizes that the Nazis cannot take away his wish to live or his appreciation for the value of life. On the verge of being sent to the crematorium, George is instead removed to the infirmary, where a male nurse helps him to regain his health and another attendant brings him extra food. Added to this near-

Imre Kertész. (AP/Wide World Photos)

miraculous change in George's fortunes is the sudden collapse of the Nazi regime, which had seemed unassailable; American soldiers will soon liberate the camp.

George's return home following his liberation, however, is not jubilant. He fears that the good and admirable Bandi may not have survived, and he is vexed by an encounter with an unnamed journalist who is shocked when George tells him that what he feels after a year in the camps is simply hatred, of everything and everyone. Even more shocking to the journalist is the way George uses the word "naturally" to describe his experience, because to the journalist it seems far from natural. George has realized, however, that the concentration camps were the natural, logical outcome of the Nazi system and that the journalist himself, by refusing to understand this, demonstrates the kind of false consciousness that unwittingly allowed the camps to come about.

No longer the child he was a year earlier, George cannot return to life as usual. The story culminates in a confrontation between George and two of his uncles, who, having remained safely in Budapest, fail to comprehend the meaning of the camps or the level of suffering George has undergone in them. He tries to explain to his uncles that what happened was not a horrible deviation from normal life or a bit of bad luck; rather, it was an expression of a systemic disorder in European society. He also suggests to his uncles that the camps were a continuation of a system of which they were all a part and that, as with the journalist, their lack of understanding means they cannot appreciate the terrible meaning of George's experience there.

George especially brings up the issue of fate, pointing out that his "fate" was in fact the product of an intentional institutional malevolence. As he works out his ideas of fate and freedom for his uncles, he concludes that if there is freedom, there is no fate. As he suspected before his experience in the camps, George affirms that he is free and, ultimately, fateless. Noting that nothing had to be the way it was, George nevertheless will honestly face what happened to him and make it a part of his own journey; he will never forget, and he will make his experience in the camps the core of his own developing view of the world and his own identity.

In one way, George's identity was taken from him when he became simply a number in the camps; in this same period, however, his identity as a Jew became paramount. Coming from a family of nonbelievers, George did not speak Yiddish or Hebrew and knew no prayers when he became a prisoner, but although being a Jew meant nothing to him, his identity as a Jew was the reason he became part of the Nazis' systematic persecution. He concludes, however, that only he himself can choose to be a Jew; the Nazis did not make that choice for him—he made it for himself.

George's conversation with his uncles is a victory of sorts; the camps were not able to take his soul, his free spirit. Despite his liberation from the camps and his return home, however, he maintains a skeptical distance from his family and a bitter distance from the rest of his society. Ironically, he finds himself remembering intense moments of happiness he experienced back in the camps with prisoners with whom he was in solidarity and whose basic humanity and decency he shared. It was also within the awful circumstances of the camps that he was able to affirm the beauty and value of life itself. This refusal to surrender to despair will become a source of strength for George as he faces the future.

Kertész is a unique and important contributor to the literature of the Holocaust. His writing is comparable to the work of such major authors as Primo Levi and Elie Wiesel both in terms of high literary merit and in terms of the authority that derives from his having suffered and survived the experience of the Nazi concentration camps. Although aspects of *Fateless* suggest a memoir, Kertész's choice of fiction points to a type of Holocaust literature that is regarded as having received true recognition only with the awarding of the Nobel Prize in Literature to Kertész in 2002.

Kertész also inferentially extends his examination of the effects of the Nazi worldview beyond World War II; this speaks to his ideas about the evil tendencies of the modern state in general and about the importance of maintaining the conditions of freedom. Because of these ideas, Kertész was virtually ignored for nearly his entire writing life by the Hungarian literary establishment under Communism; it was not until the 1990's that his work was discovered and acclaimed in Germany, France, and Scandinavia. With the collapse of Communism, *Fateless* found recognition in Hungary and in the rest of the world as well. A new English translation of the novel was published in 2004 under the title *Fatelessness*.

Sources for Further Study

Adelman, Gary. "Getting Started with Imre Kertész." *New England Review: Middlebury Series* 25, nos. 1/2 (2004): 261-278.
Kertész, Imre. "Eureka! The 2002 Nobel Lecture." *World Literature Today* 77, no. 1. (April-June, 2003): 4-8.
Nádas, Péter. "Imre Kertész's Work and His Subject." *Hungarian Quarterly* 43, no. 168 (Winter, 2002): 38-40.
Vasvári, Louise O., and Steven Tötösy de Zepetnek, eds. *Imre Kertész and Holocaust Literature*. West Lafayette, Ind.: Purdue University Press, 2005.

—Margaret Boe Birns

THE FIFTH SON

AUTHOR: Elie Wiesel (1928-   )
FIRST PUBLISHED: *Le Cinquième Fils*, 1983 (English translation, 1985)
GENRE: Novel
SUBGENRES: Historical fiction; psychological realism

This novel employs strong imagery and terse language in presenting a sympathetic treatment of a sensitive subject: the feelings of the children of Holocaust survivors. Wiesel also provides a valuable portrayal of the survivors themselves, whose experiences often isolate them from the rest of society.

PRINCIPAL CHARACTERS:
   The narrator, the Brooklyn-born son of Holocaust survivors
   Reuven Tamiroff, the narrator's father
   Simha-the-Dark, a Holocaust survivor and Reuven's companion in philosophical discussions
   Bontchek, another survivor, excluded from the discussions
   Lisa, the narrator's girlfriend
   The Angel, a sadistic Nazi officer
   Ariel, an older Tamiroff son, who is killed by The Angel

OVERVIEW

The Fifth Son describes a journey into the past, a pilgrimage that leads the narrator, the son of Holocaust survivors, to an understanding of his father. Although written from the narrator's point of view, the novel has three other voices: Reuven Tamiroff, the narrator's father, whose reminiscences and letters provide glimpses of a tortured man; Bontchek, another survivor, whose recollections reveal more about Reuven; and Simha-the-Dark, also a survivor, who finally unlocks Reuven's past.

The novel begins with the narrator's dream; in Reshastadt, he sees his father, who tells him that the trip to Germany is a mistake. The dream fades, and the narrator begins to piece together twenty years of reminiscences about his attempts to understand his father's silence.

As the narrator assembles the vignettes about his life, he remembers his father as silent and his mother as an unhappy woman who withdrew into a private world when he was only six. He is reminded of a Passover during which Simha demanded that Reuven remember his duty to the living. Simha then told the folktale about the four sons and The Question. The first son knows and assumes The Question, the second knows and rejects it, the third is indifferent to it, and the fourth is ignorant of it. The fifth son, not mentioned in the tale, is gone.

Few vignettes involve Reuven's descriptions of his own life, but the narrator recalls that Bontchek "brought to life . . . an entire society with its heroes and villains, its giants and its dwarfs." He particularly remembered the sadistic Nazi called The Angel and recalled The Angel's murder of fifty men, an act that the survivors protested by going on strike. In retaliation, The Angel executed half of the Jewish Council, sparing Simha and Reuven. Intermittently, the narrator analyzes his relationship with Lisa, a banker's daughter whom he met in a philosophy class. He recounts his seduction by Lisa, his obsession with her sensuality, her frenetic existence, and her political activism. Simha completes Reuven's story by remembering the shooting of more than two hundred people (among them, Simha's wife, Hanna) for defying The Angel's orders that they pray in public so that he could prove that God did not hear them. Several men swore that if they survived the war, they would execute The Angel.

Throughout *The Fifth Son* are Reuven's secret letters to an absent son named Ariel. In them, Reuven questions God and existence and reveals his remorse at the deaths of his fellow councillors. (He admits that he feels responsible because he supported the strike.) Finally, he tells Ariel that he and several others found The Angel after the war and killed him. Reuven confides that he and Simha are still disturbed by their action; revenge is the sole topic of their monthly discussions. He wonders how he would have acted in different circumstances.

The narrator eventually remembers his discovery of the Ariel letters, his reading of the letter in which Reuven relived Ariel's last day. The letter contained Reuven's cry to Ariel: "That night you left us, you were six years old; you are still six years old." Ariel, son of Reuven and Regina, was tortured to death by The Angel. Obsessed with Ariel, the narrator attempted to learn everything about The Angel and finally discovered that The Angel, still alive, became Wolfgang Berger, a businessman and a respected citizen of Reshastadt. In his own attempt at revenge, the narrator traveled to Reshastadt, but the encounter between former Nazi and survivors' son was anticlimactic: The narrator could only tell Berger who he was and threaten Berger with the curse of the dead. Assassination was impossible.

Years later, the narrator ends his quest with a meditation on his life. He has assimilated his father's lost years and Ariel's lost life into his own existence; he has finally connected with his father. His life has purpose and form but no meaning: "When," he asks, "yes, when, shall I finally begin to live my life, my own?"

Although the narrator provides brief physical descriptions of the other characters, he himself remains indistinct, exhibiting the same absence from life that he deplores in his father. Content to watch rather than to experience life, the narrator spends his childhood and adolescence as his father's assistant, instead of participating in games with his peers. In college, he drifts into philosophy, again demonstrating his preference for abstractions. With Lisa, he is passive, allowing her to initiate him into new experiences. Despite (or maybe because of) the barriers he has erected between himself and life, he is attracted to those who are his opposites—Lisa and Bontchek—perhaps hoping to discover life through them.

Trained in economy of emotion, the narrator reveals his capacity for passion only in his persistent attempts to know his father. Convinced that his father's history has the answers to his questions, he searches for information about his parents and their life before him. Later, having exhausted Bontchek's and Simha's store of recollections and having heard his father's vague tales, the narrator turns to libraries for information that will substantiate his family history.

Reuven Tamiroff shares himself only minimally with his son, slightly more with Simha. Reuven lives a narrow life defined by two concerns: his act of revenge and his attempt to write a commentary on the work of Paritus.

The other major characters are little more than substantial shadows. Simha-the-Dark and Bontchek are figures from Reuven's past, survivors of The Angel's regime. Bontchek is more talkative, more practical; he inhabits the world of action rather than the world of discussion. While in the ghetto, he traveled secretly, smuggling Jews to friendly countries. Bontchek's stories reveal the events that shaped the brooding man that Reuven has become. It is significant that the narrator provides a vivid description of this garrulous man: "a mixture of martyr and hedonist. A black . . . face as though covered with soot, flattened nose, powerful neck, square chest." Simha is "a nocturnal character attracted by darkness and its ghosts. . . . He buys and sells shadows." A shadow himself, Simha lives alone and spends his free hours calculating the time that separates the Jews from messianic deliverance. He and Reuven spend hours together in philosophical debates, from which they exclude Bontchek.

At one point, the narrator remembers Simha's explanation of his occupation as a merchant of shadows: "Most people think that shadows follow, precede, or surround beings or objects; the truth is that they also surround words, ideas, desires, deeds, impulses, and memories." *The Fifth Son* is about shadows: shadows of the Holocaust, of Ariel and of others who died at The Angel's orders. The characters are all shadows, their lives outlined by the past. Reuven, in particular, cannot separate himself from the past, and he passes on his preoccupations to his son.

Two concerns inform the novel. First is the narrator's story; second is the question of revenge. The two concerns intersect and parallel, often forming one narrative thread. As he becomes acquainted with his father's past, the narrator learns that Reuven is obsessed with revenge because he is guilty of it. Overcome with the enormity of his action, Reuven engages in endless discussions with Simha, always on the same question: Is revenge ever justified? The theme of revenge comes full circle when, discovering that The Angel is not dead, the narrator decides to finish what his father started.

Although Ariel clearly is the "fifth son" of both folktale and novel, Simha's reminder to Reuven of his duty to the living indicates that the narrator is also a "fifth son." Indeed, in the epilogue, the narrator reveals that his name is Ariel; he represents both the dead and the living.

The Fifth Son has elicited mixed commentary. Critics generally agree that the work is almost a poem, with its strong imagery, its terseness, and its carefully handled language. Praised for its sympathetic treatment of a sensitive subject—the feelings of children born to Holocaust survivors—Elie Wiesel's novel has also been hailed for its ambition of purpose, its poetry, its spare characterization, its brilliant use of novelistic techniques, and its masterly construction.

It is ironic that *The Fifth Son* has also been strongly criticized for those qualities often singled out as its strengths, but there are elements of truth in the criticism. To a certain extent, the structure is ill conceived, the characters are almost faceless, and the novel's ambition goes largely unrealized. Occasionally, the novel is overwhelmed by its own technique. Oddest of all is the suspenseful unveiling of Ariel's identity and fate. Reuven's letters to Ariel slowly become more specific, slowly provide more information about who Ariel is; yet the final revelation is only a vague reference to the execution of a child.

Flaws of construction aside, what Elie Wiesel has produced in *The Fifth Son* is a thoughtful study of the least-known Holocaust victims: the children of survivors. How accurate that study is, only those children can say. Wiesel's book, however, is valuable because it makes all readers "children" of the Holocaust through its sympathetic portrayal of the feelings that isolate the survivors from the rest of society.

SOURCES FOR FURTHER STUDY

Abrahamson, Irving, ed. *Against Silence: The Voice and Vision of Elie Wiesel.* 3 vols. New York: Holocaust Library, 1985.

Brown, Robert McAfee. *Elie Wiesel: Messenger to All Humanity.* Notre Dame, Ind.: University of Notre Dame Press, 1983.

Drainie, Bronwyn. "The Guilt of the Next Generation." *Toronto Globe and Mail*, April 20, 1985, p. E17.

Fine, Ellen S. *Legacy of "Night": The Literary Universe of Elie Wiesel.* Albany: State University of New York Press, 1982.

Kolbert, Jack. *The Worlds of Elie Wiesel: An Overview of His Career and His Major Themes.* Selinsgrove, Pa.: Susquehanna University Press, 2001.

Mano, D. Keith. "An Omen or Three." *The National Review* 37 (July 12, 1985): 57-59.

Morton, Frederic. "Execution as an Act of Intimacy." *The New York Times Book Review*, March 24, 1985, p. 8.

Rosen, Alan, ed. *Celebrating Elie Wiesel: Stories, Essays, Reflections.* Notre Dame, Ind.: University of Notre Dame Press, 1998.

Wiesel, Elie, and Richard D. Heffner. *Conversations with Elie Wiesel.* Edited by Thomas J. Vinciguerra. New York: Schocken Books, 2001.

—Edelma Huntley

Friedrich

Author: Hans Peter Richter (1925-1993)
First published: *Damals war es Friedrich*, 1961 (English translation, 1970)
Genre: Novel
Subgenres: Historical fiction; young adult literature

Fritz, a German born in 1925, objectively recounts his close friendship and experiences with Friedrich Schneider, a Jewish boy, from the time they are both four years old until 1942, when all Jews still in German concentration camps are to be transferred to the Auschwitz extermination camp.

Principal characters:
  Fritz, the narrator of the story, a German boy whose upstairs neighbor and closest friend is the Jewish protagonist
  Friedrich Schneider, the Jewish boy through whose experiences Fritz learns what it means to be a Jew during the Holocaust
  Fritz's parents, who sympathize somewhat with the plight of Jews but join the Nazi Party primarily to secure better living conditions and secondarily for fear of possible reprisals
  Herr and *Frau Schneider*, Friedrich's educated but naïve parents, who do not heed warnings to leave Germany
  Herr Johann Resch, the malevolent and sadistic apartment landlord, who is also warden of the local air-raid shelter
  Herr Neudorf, the sympathetic teacher, who explains why Friedrich may no longer attend school

Overview

In *Friedrich*, Fritz, the adult German narrator, describes the experiences he shared with his Jewish best friend and upstairs neighbor, Friedrich Schneider, from their births in 1925 until 1942. The plot is shown through the eyes of the innocent, youthful narrator, who offers only objective descriptions of dialogue and of events that culminate in the "final solution" in Nazi Germany. Although they have lived in the same apartment building for more than four years, from 1925 until 1929, Fritz's parents scarcely know the Schneiders. Yet, as Fritz narrates, the boys become friends when one day Mrs. Schneider must go to the city hall and asks if she can leave her son with Fritz's mother. In spite of her father's violent anti-Semitism, Fritz's mother welcomes the four-year-old Friedrich but makes a point of his Jewishness. As time passes, Fritz learns about Jewish customs, and Herr Schneider, a post office official, in small ways aids Fritz's family, whose only income since Fritz's father became unemployed is support from the retired grandfather and what Fritz's mother earns washing clothes.

Times are hard when Adolf Hitler becomes chancellor of the Third Reich in 1933, and the boys witness the beginnings of overt hostility toward Jews, exemplified by the appearance of swastikas and by boycotts against Fritz's Jewish doctor and the local stationer. Friedrich, not understanding why his father forbids him to attend the Jungvolk with Fritz, sneaks in with his friend but leaves alone, humiliated after he is forced to recite, "The Jews are our affliction."

Although the Schneiders are frightened when their landlord, Herr Resch, orders the family to move from his building and Friedrich's father is fired from the post office, the family is temporarily relieved when a judge decrees that the family may remain in their apartment and Herr Schneider is hired as department manager in a Jewish merchant's store. Nevertheless, ominous warnings escalate as Fritz's father encourages his son's participation in the Jungvolk, Herr Neudorf explains to the class why Friedrich may no longer attend school, and the Schneiders' cleaning lady is intimidated into quitting.

In 1936, Fritz's father, in a rare conversation with Herr Schneider, explains why as a German he joined the National Socialist German Workers' Party (the Nazi Party), and he warns the Jew to leave Germany immediately. Blinded by his naïve faith in civilization and strong German chauvinism, and inured to threats by memories of two thousand years of anti-Semitic persecution, Herr Schneider chooses to ignore the warning but begs Fritz's father to care for Friedrich and Frau Schneider should it become necessary. In spite of their fervent handshake sealing an unspoken promise, Fritz's father does nothing when the time for action arrives.

Violent pogroms envelop German Jews in 1938, and even Fritz participates in a destructive rampage once, as if it were a game. The Schneiders' apartment is destroyed, and Frau Schneider dies. Friedrich and his father barely manage to obtain a little food through doing odd jobs and leave their apartment only under cover. Yet one night in 1941 when Friedrich is away, Herr Resch discovers that the Schneiders are harboring an aged rabbi, and he informs the Gestapo, who arrive and drag the men off into the night.

Friedrich goes into hiding until one evening in 1941, when he furtively visits Fritz to obtain a picture of his parents. When bombing begins, Herr

Resch tells Friedrich to remain in the apartment and not even attempt to enter the bomb shelter. Terrified, Friedrich bangs on the door of the shelter and begs to come in. Herr Resch refuses, despite the pleas of those inside. After the raid, Friedrich is found dead, and in ironic truth Herr Resch proclaims, "His luck that he died this way."

Purpose and theme mesh in *Friedrich* as readers must search their own identities and clarify their own personal values in reading this book. Richter's recounting of the events leading to the Holocaust leaves the ultimate universal question, one that has been asked repeatedly but cannot be answered: How could educated, "civilized" adults have tolerated, accepted, and even participated in, much less created, such barbarism? William Golding proposed the same theme in his fiction, but he made the question even more basic by using sheltered, innocent children in *Lord of the Flies* (1954) to question the validity of "civilization."

The book also explores what can be done to prevent the senseless hatred that causes and the complacency that permits continuing barbarism that may ultimately threaten the very existence of humankind. Although the answers may never be found, the importance of dealing with these themes is paramount. What Richter does point out, in his innocent but chilling narrative, is that there can be no tolerance of governmental or personal hatred directed toward any member of a group simply because he or she is a member of that group. He indicates that tolerating even the first simple inroads of general bigotry without speaking out and destroying it immediately can lead to utter debasement of personal and governmental character and self-respect.

Friedrich is, in Hans Richter's own words, a "somewhat autobiographical," painfully accurate chronological documentation of the events in Germany leading to Hitler's "final solution"—the extermination of Jews during the Holocaust. Beginning in 1925, when nonviolent but deep and historically ubiquitous anti-Semitism boiled below the surface throughout Europe, the archetypal hatred appeared as a physical outlet against the economic depression in Germany and enabled Hitler to vent his own personal hatreds and create a focus for uniting the German people.

Most of the characters in *Friedrich* are rounded, and they represent a realistic cross section of the German populace, through whose actions and words the German people's involvement with the genocide of World War II can be explained. Herr Resch is the recognizable prototype of the realistic absolute archvillain that exists in all societies. His ability to control a sizable group of law-abiding citizens through intimidation is representative of the many villains recorded in all literature. Without corresponding prototypical heroes willing to act and ready to sacrifice themselves, evil can rule. Because arch villains were present, and because not enough heroes appeared, a minority of activists were able to urge groups, already primed from infancy to dislike Jews, to perform acts together that, as individuals, might be unthinkable. The reader sees even young Fritz, who has had only positive experiences with Jews, join mob rule and senselessly destroy Jewish property.

The succeeding tragedies endured by the Schneiders follow the actual dates of laws, decrees, and regulations dealing with Jews, and the reader can begin to recognize how basically "good" non-Jews were induced to conform. Fritz's father joins the party primarily to help his family financially, and later, when he realizes fully all that joining the party entails, even though he disagrees with the "rules," he believes that he must continue his loyalty to ensure his family's safety. Additionally, he rationalizes the inhumanity that he witnesses by saying that no government can be perfect, and one must go along with what provides the greatest benefits.

Friedrich is painful but important reading. It won two German prizes, one in 1961, when it was first published, and another in 1964. It was also awarded the Mildred L. Batchelder Award of the American Library Association in 1972. It is a tribute to Richter's sensitivity that both German and American professionals and readers have responded with similar praise to this treatment of the Holocaust, as witnessed by an author, who, ironically, fought in the German army from 1942 to 1945 and won medals for bravery during that time.

With discussion, this book can provide young readers with much-needed information about the Holocaust, a period of history that should not be forgotten so that it will not be repeated. If the voids created by the objective, unemotional narrative style can evoke empathetic understanding of Fritz and Friedrich and their families, answers to the past and prescriptions for the future may become possible.

Sources for Further Study

Brown, Robert McAfee. *Elie Wiesel: Messenger to All Humanity*. Notre Dame, Ind.: University of Notre Dame Press, 1983.

Kokkola, Lydia. *Representing the Holocaust in Children's Literature*. New York: Routledge, 2003.

Sullivan, Edward T. *The Holocaust in Literature for Youth: A Guide and Resource Book*. Lanham, Md.: Scarecrow, 1999.

Wiesel, Elie. Interview by John S. Friedman. *Paris Review* 26 (Spring, 1984): 130-178.

—*June H. Schlessinger*

THE GATES OF THE FOREST

AUTHOR: Elie Wiesel (1928-   )
FIRST PUBLISHED: *Les Portes de la forêt*, 1964 (English translation, 1966)
GENRE: Novel
SUBGENRE: Psychological realism

Wiesel's fourth novel tells the story of Gregor, who loses his family in the Holocaust, survives the genocide, and experiences the suffering and guilt common to many Holocaust survivors. Because these experiences parallel Wiesel's own, the novel seems to be more than a work of fiction, and its characters seem more than figures from the author's imagination.

PRINCIPAL CHARACTERS:
   Gregor, whose real name is Gavriel, a young Hungarian Jew who has escaped the Holocaust
   Gavriel, a mysterious, unnamed Jew who borrows Gregor's real name and sacrifices himself for Gregor
   Maria, a former servant in the home of Gregor's family
   Leib the Lion, the leader of the Jewish partisans
   Clara, Leib's lover and, after his death, Gregor's wife

OVERVIEW

Beginning with spring and ending with winter, *The Gates of the Forest* is divided into four parts, each standing for a season in its natural order. The first and last parts concentrate on the inner self and the middle two on action. The novel first introduces Gregor, a Hungarian Jew in his late teens who, without his family, has escaped the Holocaust. While Gregor hides from the Nazis in a village forest, another Jew, a mysterious man of about thirty, happens onto his hiding place. As this stranger has no name, Gregor gives him his own name, Gavriel, which Gregor had abandoned because it was too conspicuously Jewish. The two Jews hide in a cave whose entrance is concealed by a large boulder. There, they pass many days together, sharing their beliefs and stories with each other. From Gavriel, Gregor learns of the hideous facts of the war, especially information about the cruelties of the Nazis against the Jews. Gavriel comes to be seen as a lunatic philosopher-saint who sometimes reacts to the Holocaust with insane laughter.

The search by the Nazis intensifies outside the hideout; getting away from them seems impossible to the two men. Just as the Nazis are upon the site, Gavriel gives himself up. The Nazis have no reason to believe that there is more than one Jew in the forest area, and so they are satisfied. The sacrifice of Gavriel leaves Gregor with a moral obligation to which he totally commits himself.

In a nearby village, he finds refuge in the home of Maria, a Christian and an old servant of his family. She has him pretend to be a deaf-mute and the son of her sister Ileana, who has departed the village, leaving behind a reputation for looseness. Unaware of Gregor's pretense, the village folk take him into their confidences, many of the men confessing to illicit relations with Ileana. The parish priest, "against sin, but not against crime," confesses to having betrayed a Jew because the Jew refused to accept Christianity as a condition of refuge. What is for Elie Wiesel a thematic analogy between the Crucifixion of Jesus and the annihilation of the Jews is brought out dramatically. Against Maria's protests, Gregor is cast as Judas in a school play about the Passion of Christ. Becoming caught up in the drama as it is performed, members of the cast and the audience, also, verbally and then physically attack Gregor. He stuns them to temporary inaction by declaring, first, that he is not Judas and second, that he is not the son of Ileana. When at last he tells them that he is not Gregor, that he is a Jew whose name is Gavriel, the villagers are prepared to cut out his tongue. They despise him because he is a Jew and fear him because he knows their secrets. The mayor of the town, Petruskanu, who suspects that he may have fathered Gregor, rescues him and helps him make contact with Jewish partisans in the forest.

As Gavriel had informed Gregor about the concentration camps and the crematoria, Gregor now tells the partisans. They are led by Leib the Lion, who was a boyhood friend of Gregor; at ten years of age, the two stood up against Christian bullies. Hearing from Gregor of Gavriel's imprisonment, Leib says that the prisoner must be set free in order for him to communicate what he has seen as a victim of the Holocaust. The plan to get Gavriel out of prison backfires, however, and Leib is captured by the Nazis. Once more, Gregor, who was the central figure in the escape plan, believes that he has betrayed another. The partisans, suspicious of him, put him through an intense grilling that ends only when Clara, Leib's lover, intervenes.

Yehuda, a young partisan, now befriends Gregor. Putting aside his feeling that his own death is imminent, Yehuda tells Gregor that he should make known to Clara the obvious truth that he loves her. In an inhumane world, Yehuda declares, love is a protection against solitude. It is the great reward, the greatest victory. Gregor admits to Yehuda that indeed he does love Clara. A few days later, Yehuda is stabbed to death, the partisans shoot his killer, and Gregor tells Clara that he loves her.

After a chance meeting in Paris following the war, Gregor and Clara are married. The marriage is a failure, however, because Clara, haunted by a past of death and destruction, acts as if Gregor is Leib, her dead lover. Just when Gregor is about to give up on his marriage and leave Clara, he is drawn into a relationship with a rebbe who helps him rediscover his Jewish past. A man who may or may not be Gavriel appears at the rebbe's synagogue. After a long conversation with this mysterious man, Gregor comes to realize that he cannot, after all, leave Clara. To do so would be to return to solitude and thus betray her as he has, at least by omission, betrayed others. Once more, Gregor assumes the name of Gavriel. Asked by a young boy to serve as the tenth man necessary to say morning prayers, Gregor consents. While reciting the prayer for the dead, he turns the moment into an occasion to pray for the soul of Leib and to ask God to arrange an end to the suffering of those who loved, and still love, the dead hero.

The central character, Gavriel, changes his name to Gregor and then, at the end of the novel, back to Gavriel. Furthermore, he uses the name Judas temporarily, if only for the purpose of a play. For Wiesel, the name choices and name exchanges in his novel clearly serve as devices that underscore the themes of sacrifice and suffering. An angel, Gabriel, comes to earth in the person of the mysterious Gavriel, who risks his life for Gregor. Gregor, in turn, takes on the suffering of all the Jews of history by becoming Judas. Other biblical names—notably, Maria and Petruskanu (Peter)—are given to characters who, although Christian, take great risks for the Jews.

Elie Wiesel himself is very much a part of his story. Like his protagonist, he lost his family in the Holocaust, and, like Gregor, he survived it and experienced the suffering and guilt that many Holocaust survivors have felt. Wiesel's story allows him, a witness to Nazi crimes, to be a messenger to the world; *The Gates of the Forest* thus seems more than a mere work of fiction, and its characters seem more than figures from the author's imagination.

The Gates of the Forest begins with a Jewish tale, essentially an epigraph, illustrating the vitality of storytelling. The facts of the Holocaust, all the horrors, must be told as many times and in as many ways as are necessary to make the story known; Wiesel's novel is another attempt to convey that story so that readers will be as haunted by it, as unable to forget it as he himself has been. Leib the Lion, as the last line of the novel indicates, is a messenger to heaven just as, in Wiesel's *Le Jour* (1961; *The Accident*, 1962),

Eliezer is a living messenger from the dead. A central theme of *The Gates of the Forest* is that the Jews, although deserted by God during the Holocaust, have no alternative but to tell their tragic story and to recover their faith. "After what has happened, how believe in God?" is answered by "After what has happened, how not believe in God?"

Along with the theme of faith is that of friendship, oneness, and community. If the Messiah has not come to the Jews, the novel says, then let every Jew, every individual, be the Messiah to everyone else. Christians must do their part to bring humanity together; one way is to end their persecution of Jews as descendants of Judas, to cease making Jews take the place of Christ on the Cross.

Like Eliezer in *The Accident*, Clara in *The Gates of the Forest* is immobilized by the dead, by the past. She gives her love to Gregor only when she pretends that he is Leib the Lion, the lover she has lost to the Holocaust. Symbolically, Leib not only defends Gregor but also sacrifices himself for him, as Gavriel does at the beginning of the novel. Sacrifice, or courageous and unselfish risk taking such as that of Maria or Petruskanu, is a recurring theme of great substance in this novel. Guilt—both in the survivor and in the recipient of another's sacrifice—is still another controlling and pervasive theme. Instead of living with guilt, Gregor learns to love, to affirm the present and put the past behind. He even learns to change places with another, which is something like returning one's life to both the giver and the receiver. To love the living is not to forget the dead; to pay homage to the dead is not to lay aside an obligation to the living.

The Gates of the Forest, Wiesel's fourth novel, should be read after his *L'Aube* (1960; *Dawn*, 1961), *The Accident*, and *La Ville de la chance* (1962; *The Town Beyond the Wall*, 1964) and before *Le Mendiant de Jerusalem* (1968; *A Beggar in Jerusalem*, 1970). This order is important because of the thematic development in Wiesel's first five novels—from annihilation to affirmation, from solitude to community. Having lost his entire family and many other loved ones in the monstrous Holocaust, Wiesel came to know that there are countless ways to record or interpret such an event. Each of Wiesel's novels may be seen, then, as a circle that shares a center with the other novels; that center is the Holocaust. Along with other writers—notably, Primo Levi, Nelly Sachs, Robert Donat, Paul Celan, Ernst Weichert, Vladka Meed, Pierre Gascar, André Schwarz-Bart, and Tadeusz Borowski—Wiesel is a sensitive and bold interpreter of the Jewish experience. With his receipt of the Nobel Peace Prize in 1986, Wiesel enhanced an already considerable reputation worldwide. He has given his life to creating a literature assuring his readers that victims of inhumanity, both living and dead, will never be forgotten.

Sources for Further Study

Berger, Alan L. Review of *The Judges*, by Elie Wiesel. *Shofar* 21, no. 3 (Spring, 2003): 151-153.

Bosmajian, Hamida. *Sparing the Child: Grief and the Unspeakable in Youth Literature About Nazism and the Holocaust*. New York: Routledge, 2002.

Freedman, Samuel G. "Bearing Witness." *The New York Times*, October 23, 1983, p. A32.

Kokkola, Lydia. *Representing the Holocaust in Children's Literature*. New York: Routledge, 2003.

Kolbert, Jack. *The Worlds of Elie Wiesel: An Overview of His Career and His Major Themes*. Selinsgrove, Pa.: Susquehanna University Press, 2001.

May, Jill P. "The Impossible Legacy: Identity and Purpose in Autobiographical Children's Literature Set in the Third Reich and the Second World War." *Shofar* 19, no. 3 (April 30, 2001): 165-168.

Rosen, Alan, ed. *Celebrating Elie Wiesel: Stories, Essays, Reflections*. Notre Dame, Ind.: University of Notre Dame Press, 1998.

Wiesel, Elie, and Richard D. Heffner. *Conversations with Elie Wiesel*. Edited by Thomas J. Vinciguerra. New York: Schocken Books, 2001.

Williams, Thomas. "Wiesel: A Holocaust Survivor Turns Horror into Art." *Chicago Tribune*, March 24, 1985, p. 35.

—David Powell

Ghetto

Author: Joshua Sobol (1939-   )
First published: *Geto*, 1984 (first produced, 1984; English translation, 1986)
Genre: Drama
Subgenre: Documentary drama

Sobol's controversial play depicts the events surrounding the production of a drama staged by Jews in the ethnic ghetto of Vilna during the time the Nazis occupied Lithuania during World War II.

Principal characters:
  Srulik, a puppeteer and singer
  Srulik's dummy, a puppet who utters subversive sentiments that the principals in the play dare not utter
  Hans Kittel, a Nazi Schutzstaffel (SS) officer, an Austrian native, and commandant of the Vilna ghetto
  Jakob Gens, a Jew, the Nazi-appointed head of the ghetto
  Weiskopf, the manager of a tailoring factory in the ghetto
  Chaya, a singer
  Herman Kruk, head of the library and keeper of a diary

Overview

Controversial though it is, Joshua Sobol's *Ghetto* is a remarkable documentary about the actual staging of a play within the Jewish ghetto of Vilna (spelled "Wilna" in Sobol's text), Lithuania, in the period 1941-1943. This production is mounted with the full consent and support of Hans Kittel, the Nazi commandant who oversees the ghetto with the cooperation—many would say collaboration—of Jakob Gens, a former police officer and a Jew whom the Nazis have appointed to be head of the ghetto. Both of these characters, like many others in the play, were actual people who, during the Nazi occupation, served in the capacities in which Sobol casts them.

Gens has been forced to select many of his fellow Jews within the ghetto to be deported and to face certain execution in nearby Ponar, where five thousand Jews were killed on a single Sunday in 1943, or in one of the other Nazi death camps. The play opened in the ghetto on June 18, 1942, some four months after Vilna's Jews were consigned to the ghetto and only two months after the annihilation of more than fifty thousand of the seventy thousand Jews whom the Nazis rounded up. The play subsequently was performed in the ghetto 111 times. Some 34,804 tickets were sold, mostly to Jews who, even on the eve of their deportation, dressed in their finery to attend the performances.

Gens, who can legitimately be considered a traitor to his people, justifies his actions by saying, "If the Germans want a thousand Jews from me, they get them. Because if we don't do it their way, they'll march in here and take a thousand Tuesday, a thousand Thursday. And a thousand Saturday. And ten thousand next week." Gens is buying time for himself and for many other Jews in the ghetto by cooperating with the Nazis, settling for what little he can get from them in order at least to minimize their bloodthirsty demands.

Sobol depicts a ghetto where most of the people confined there face certain death at the hands of their captors. Still, a clear social structure exists within the ghetto, and life goes on. The Nazi regime reigns supreme but is criticized through the comments of Srulik's puppet, who utters sentiments that, if uttered openly by any of the inmates, would lead to their immediate deportation to death camps. Much of the background of Jews in Lithuania is presented in the many ballads, sung by a Jewish chanteuse named Chaya, that are integral to the play.

Kittel has an amicable relationship with those who run the ghetto, although he is capable of doing swift about-faces, making it evident that he cannot be trusted. Gens, with the help and financial support of Weiskopf (the Jewish owner of a tailoring factory who is growing rich on refurbishing uniforms for the Nazi troops), has a working relationship with Kittel. Gens seeks permission from Kittel to expand Weiskopf's factory and to turn it into a training facility for textile workers, a ploy that he devises in order to spare the lives of many Jews by persuading the Nazis that their labor is vital to the Nazi cause.

Gens and Weiskopf host a lavish party for the Nazis, providing them with food, liquor, and prostitutes. Weiskopf participates primarily to increase his business, which has turned him into a millionaire, while Gens participates in the hope of saving himself and sparing as many Jewish lives as his proposed training program can justify.

Ghetto, which opened in Haifa, Israel, in the spring of 1984 and soon was translated into both English and German, won Israel's David Harp Award for best play in 1984. In its German translation, it won the Theatre Heute

Award for the best play and best production of 1984. The Nicholas Hytner production at the Royal National Theatre in London won the Evening Standard and London Critics Award for best play in 1989 and was also a finalist for the Olivier Award in that year.

The play was subsequently translated into more than twenty languages and presented in some thirty countries throughout the world. One play in what Sobol conceived of as a triptych, *Ghetto* was followed by *Adam*, produced in 1989, and *Underground*, produced in 1991. Of Sobol's many plays, *Ghetto* is certainly the best known and most frequently performed.

The critical reception of the play was varied. Some critics (including Hans Sahl) complained about the depiction of the Jews who helped run the ghetto as manipulative and self-seeking. Others objected that the dialogue is turgid and that the musical selections—a fundamental part of the play's production—are not placed advantageously within the play's framework. Certainly it is evident that Sobol's script contains many soliloquies that sometimes border on the didactic. Nevertheless, the serious subject matter of the play, which lends itself to didacticism, is lightened by the frequent irreverent critical comments of the puppet, who serves a function somewhat like that of the fool in medieval literature or the chorus in ancient Greek plays.

Ghetto was particularly popular in Germany, where audiences often were not fully aware of the atrocities that were perpetrated during World War II by the Nazi government and probably, in many cases, by their ancestors. Critic Henry Kamm wrote about a performance of *Ghetto* at the Volkstheater in Vienna, Austria, in 1985, reminding his readers that Hans Kittel—the Schutzstaffel (SS) commandant who in actuality used his machine gun to murder hundreds of Jews in the ghetto over which he presided—was an Austrian and that Austrians voted almost unanimously to join forces with Adolf Hitler in 1938. Kamm noted that young Austrians had not been exposed to the sad history of the Holocaust in their schools. The Volkstheater, founded in 1889, has considered its major objective through the years to instruct through drama. It was with this objective in mind that the Volkstheater production of *Ghetto* was approved, although even some forty years after the end of World War II, a reliable survey of Austrians revealed that 85 percent of them admitted to being somewhat anti-Semitic, and 7 percent admitted to being strongly anti-Semitic.

Many of the details relating to the production of a play within the Vilna ghetto were provided by some of the few survivors. Most significant in piecing together what took place there, however, was the discovery of a diary kept by Herman Kruk, the ghetto librarian who did not survive but whose journal was hidden and later uncovered.

Sources for Further Study

Gordon, Harry. *The Shadow of Death: The Holocaust in Lithuania*. Lexington: University of Kentucky Press, 1992.

Kamm, Henry. "Drama Warns Vienna About Anti-Semitism." *The New York Times*, May 28, 1985, p. C12.

Langer, Lawrence L., ed. *Art from the Ashes: A Holocaust Anthology*. New York: Oxford University Press, 1995.

Sahl, Hans. "*Ghetto*, a Deplorable Play." *The New York Times*, May 14, 1989, p. H3.

Seibert, Gary. "A Conversation with Israeli Playwright Joshua Sobol." *America* 160, no. 22 (June 10, 1989): 559-563.

Tory, Avraham. *Surviving the Holocaust: The Kovno Ghetto Diary*. Cambridge, Mass.: Harvard University Press, 1990.

—*R. Baird Shuman*

God's Presence in History
Jewish Affirmations and Philosophical Reflections

AUTHOR: Emil L. Fackenheim (1916-2003)
FIRST PUBLISHED: 1970
GENRE: Nonfiction
SUBGENRES: Ethics; philosophy; religion and spirituality

Fackenheim uses Jewish resources to interpret non-Jewish philosophy and Western techniques on Jewish texts and history. He defines an authentic Jewish philosopher—and an authentic Jew—as one who has opened the self to the historical uniqueness of the Holocaust and one who actively supports the building of the State of Israel as past, present, and future home for the Jews.

OVERVIEW

The text of *God's Presence in History* is a revision of three lectures delivered by Emil L. Fackenheim as the Charles F. Deems Lectures at New York University in 1968; the volume addresses how world historical Jewish events such as the Holocaust and the establishment of the modern State of Israel categorically entail concrete responses by Jews to ensure Jewish survival. The event that directly precipitated this work was the 1967 surprise attack by the Arab states surrounding Israel (the Six-Day War) and the total lack of support for Israel by any other nation in the world. An additional impetus was Fackenheim's assertion that responses to the Holocaust, such as the "death of God" movement of the 1960's and the rise of secular and nonobservant Jews, were threatening the future existence of the Jewish people as a whole. However, it could easily be argued that Fackenheim was working toward just such an apologetic response his entire life.

Fackenheim begins his text by dedicating it to Holocaust survivor and activist Elie Wiesel, to whom he credits his use of a midrashic method in exploring the faith-commitment of Jews post-Holocaust and their support of the modern State of Israel. His opening, a Midrashic interpretation of a scriptural passage, provides the cornerstone of his argument that post-Holocaust Jews have the right and duty to judge others because they survived the attack on their ongoing existence as a people. Hence Fackenheim begins with his telling of an "ancient Midrash [that] affirms God's presence in history" and demonstrates how that presence becomes historically effective through Jewish witness. However, modernity challenges such testimony in two ways: First, the modern scientist has to expel God from nature because of a lack of verifiable proof, and the modern historian expels God from history because of the incompatibility of the supernatural with natural history. Second, and consequently, modern Jewish and Christian theologians can only affirm a provident God who uses nature and humans but is absent from history. Adding to the modern rejections, Fackenheim challenges a commitment of faith by asking: After Auschwitz and Hiroshima, who can still believe in a God who manifests himself as a superintending providence, or in an ideal kind of progress based on the promises of modern, enlightened technological advances?

In wake of the Holocaust, the Jewish people must still believe because they have a unique status based on the phenomenon of collective survival, a claim that serves as the key term for understanding Fackenheim's entire thought. Fackenheim argues that this collective survival has significance for both Jewish people and the rest of humanity because the God of Israel is not a mere tribal god but is someone who is Creator of the world and is concerned for universal humanity. However, Fackenheim's conception of God is nonetheless of one who does not have a presence-in-general but is, rather, present to particular people in particular situations. For Fackenheim, these "implications, however, are manifest only in the particular; and they make of the men to whom they are manifest, not universalistic philosophers who rise above their situations, but rather witnesses, in, through, and because of their particularity to the nations." He then asks, How is the modern Jew today, after Auschwitz, able to be a witness to the world?

His answer is that Jews can continue to draw on their foundational root experiences, that is, the historical events of Exodus and Sinai that ensure continuity in how they are relived in rituals. Accordingly, Fackenheim contends that the past is able to be relived in the present; the root experience is a public event in which there is a transformation of the earth and which decisively affects all future Jewish generations. Later generations have access to the founding event and can and do reenact them as present reality.

Fackenheim links philosophy to his religious heritage via the congruence of starting points that he establishes between the religious experience and the philosophical experience of the world, principally the historical concept of wonder. For Fackenheim, the religious experience is an astonishing experience of an event that enters the system of cause and effect and becomes transparent, thus allowing a glimpse of the sole power at work that is not limited by any other. Moreover, he draws on Martin Buber to support his claim that, like the philosophical experience of wonder, the religious experience is an "event which can be fully included in the objective, scientific nexus of nature and history" with the proviso that it includes a "vital meaning" that, "for the person to whom it occurs, destroys the security of the whole nexus of knowledge for him, and explodes the fixity of the fields of experience named 'Nature' and 'History.'"

Based on such historical effectiveness, for example, the believer in and practitioner of ritual relates to the Red Sea event during the Jewish ritual of Passover. By reenacting the event, practitioners reenact the abiding astonishment and make, thereby, the historical event their own, which results in a continuation of the sole power that is God. Hence, memory enacted becomes living faith and hope, and the root experience is able to legislate from the past to the present and future.

Questions arise, however, about the nature of God as one that is on the one hand transcendent and on the other involved. In short, the question of human control of the earth leads to judgments of the nature and relationship of an historically effective God to such an earth. If God were present at that particular moment of the Exodus and exercised power on behalf of the Jewish people, as sole power, God necessarily should be able to fight oppressive evil once again, demonstrating God's status as Creator and as absolute sovereign of the world. Fackenheim accepts this paradox and responds with a recourse to traditional Jewish thought that God does act and is involved in history and is not merely the consummation or transfiguration of history; that is, God does not stand over the entirety of the historical continuum.

Such a present God is the object of messianic faith where the believing Jew responds to historical instances of evil and threats to existence by pointing to the future where evil will ultimately be vanquished and human freedom and divine freedom are reconciled. Furthermore, such a future is anticipated in a reenacted past, that is, the reenactment of the root experiences through ritual. Such reenactment is what Fackenheim understands as the Midrashic experience, which he argues is "consciously fragmentary" and "yet destined to an ultimate resolution."

As Fackenheim relates at the end of the first part of the work, two of the strongest criticisms of God's presence in history have to do with the Holocaust. Given the actuality of God's presence as it is affirmed in Judaism and Christianity, to still believe in God post-Holocaust entails that Auschwitz is punishment for Jewish sins, which slanders a million innocent children in an abortive defense of God, and that any God connected with Auschwitz must have decreed Auschwitz, and such a God must be dead.

Fackenheim takes these criticisms seriously and spends the next two parts of his text in elaborating his rejection. In his analysis, the metaphysical foundations for such a rejection are based on how the Jewish people are rooted in the actuality of history. Because of their dialectical balance and playing out of the oppositions of the particular and the universal facets of their own lives, they are concretely situated within the overarching temporal framework of past, present, and future relations with other nations and their God.

Specifically, Fackenheim confronts a series of philosophical challenges, the greatest coming from modern positivists such as Auguste Comte, who reject God as a hypothesis that is empirically unverifiable. Fackenheim rejects the reduction of religious experience to scientific explanation and the positivist's assertion that a resort to absolutes is a mere logical mistake by contending that such a reduction eliminates wonder and ongoing historical effectiveness of abiding astonishment. The alternative is to replace that wonder with mere scientific or historical curiosity. What Fackenheim argues is that faith and modern secularism are irreconcilable because they are mutually irrefutable and that in order for historians, secular and Jewish, to exercise genuine impartiality, they should be required to suspend judgment between faith and secularism, resulting in a more nuanced philosophical stance of "criticism of criticism."

Fackenheim criticizes those who spoke out against the Jews, including German philosopher Friedrich Nietzsche, because of his predilection for Hellenic aristocracy and aestheticism, and the Marxists who, based on a kind of Jewish messianic expectation, nonetheless preached that Jews had a universal duty to assimilate into general humanity. Philosopher Ludwig Feuerbach taught that Jews are nothing more than egoists projecting an idea of God to themselves as an instance of self-worship. Karl Marx, for the sake of ideological consistency, claimed that Jews are merely self-interested hucksters who worship money and are dialectically false because they are so bound up with capitalism.

Fackenheim reserves his final critique for Ernst Bloch's philosophy of hope. He tempers his critique with a generally sympathetic reading of Bloch because of his affirmative acceptance of the survival of the Jewish people. The problem, however, is that Bloch relocates his version of messianism to Moscow, not Palestine, thus committing a very old Jewish act, namely, premature messianism.

Finally, the shortfall of all modern philosophers is their iterations of various versions of the "death of God" theme. Consequently, Fackenheim ends part 2 of the work by referring approvingly of philosopher Martin Buber's conceptualization of an eclipse of God rather than the death of

God, viewing it as an authentic messianic response to the unique challenge of Auschwitz and the abiding human experience of horror.

The culmination of Fackenheim's own dialectic is fueled by his Jewish faith, as quintessential good, which is confronted by Adolf Hitler, as quintessential evil. Fackenheim asks, post-Auschwitz: Although Hitler failed to kill all the Jews, did he ultimately succeed postmortem by destroying Jewish faith? Fackenheim responds: "Yet we protest against a negative answer, for we protest against allowing Hitler to dictate the terms of our religious life. If not martyrdom, there can be a faithfulness resembling it, when a man has no choice between life and death but only between faith and despair."

After Auschwitz, Jews are left with existential fragments related to the problems of being uniquely targeted for destruction and yet, as part of their destiny with God, are demanded to survive. Moreover, such survival must be existentially grounded and faith-committed. After Auschwitz, he argues, the defiant success of the Jews to survive despite many challenges, especially the ultimate challenge of extermination, testifies to their endurance. Mere survival is not enough, however, and in order to avoid madness, Jews desire to endure precisely because of the testimony to the voices of the prophets of their heritage with the living presence of God in history. Hence Jews must continue to pray, after Auschwitz, as proof against madness in defiant particularity and as witnesses.

Fackenheim's analysis of modern philosophical and psychological perspectives and certain forms of social theory continues to provide powerful arguments that other philosophers of religion have continued to debate. Fackenheim continued to publish refined versions of his argument, eventually resulting in his most philosophically systematic work, *To Mend the World: Foundations of Future Jewish Thought* (1982). However, even this text carries on the basic insights about the Holocaust, the State of Israel, and the failure of philosophy that Fackenheim initially presented in *God's Presence in History*. According to Fackenheim, the reason for the surprising success of the Israeli defense forces against the attack by the surrounding Arab states in 1967 was that the Israelis responded with "a new song of defiance in the midst of hopelessness—the song of the Warsaw Ghetto Jewish Underground." For many Jews, both inside and outside Israel, Fackenheim provides a voice for their general concerns regarding the inexplicable horror of the Holocaust. Indeed, his call for a renewed defense of Israel was in tune with a general move not only by Jews the world over to resist further attacks on Israel but also especially by the initiation of the support of the U.S. government, which emerged in the second half of the twentieth century as a strong and faithful ally of Israel.

Sources for Further Study

Berger, Alan L. *Children of Job: American Second-Generation Witnesses to the Holocaust*. Albany: State University of New York Press, 1997.

Braiterman, Zachary. "Fideism Redux: Emil Fackenheim and the State of Israel." *Jewish Social Studies* 4, no. 1 (October 31, 1997): 61.

Doidge, Norman. "Thinking Through Radical Evil." *National Post*, September 27, 2003, p. A24.

Fackenheim, Emil L. *Jewish Philosophers and Jewish Philosophy*. Edited by Michael L. Morgan. Bloomington: Indiana University Press, 1996.

Greenspan, Louis, and Graeme Nicholson, eds. *Fackenheim: German Philosophy and Jewish Thought*. Toronto: University of Toronto Press, 1992.

Haberman, Joshua O. *The God I Believe In*. New York: Free Press, 1994.

Joffe, Lawrence. "Obituary: Emil Fackenheim, Addressing Great Philosophical Questions for the Jewish People." *The Guardian*, October 10, 2003, p. 31.

Oppenheim, Michael. *What Does Revelation Mean for the Modern Jew? Rosenzweig, Buber, Fackenheim*. Lewiston, N.Y.: Edwin Mellen Press, 1985.

Seeskin, Kenneth. *Jewish Philosophy in a Secular Age*. Albany: State University of New York Press, 1990.

—Julius J. Simon

Gone to Soldiers

AUTHOR: Marge Piercy (1936-   )
FIRST PUBLISHED: 1987
GENRE: Novel
SUBGENRES: Psychological fiction; war fiction

To tell this story of women's experiences during World War II and beyond, Piercy uses ten different voices in a decentered format that weaves multiple threads of human existence into a unified whole. Through her characters, Piercy explores the answers to Albert Einstein's question "Why war?"

PRINCIPAL CHARACTERS:
  Louise Kahan, a popular writer of women's fiction
  Daniel Balaban, the child of immigrant Jewish parents living in the Bronx
  Jacqueline Lévy-Monot, a woman known by her Jewish name of Yakova, as Jacqueline Porell in order to disguise her heritage, and as Gingembre, her nom de guerre
  Abra, a graduate student at Columbia University and the lover of Oscar Kahan, Louise's former husband
  Naomi Siegal, Jacqueline's sister, a twelve-year-old at the beginning of the novel
  Bernice Coates, an unmarried woman who joins the Army Air Corps as a pilot
  Jeff Coates, the artistic brother of Bernice and a member of the Jewish Resistance in France
  Ruthie Siegel, a woman who works in a plant and attends school at night
  Duvey Siegel, the brother of Ruthie
  Murray Feldstein, a Marine who comes home to marry Ruthie

OVERVIEW

Gone to Soldiers offers an answer to the question that Albert Einstein asked in a July 30, 1932, letter to Sigmund Freud regarding the topic "Why war?" As the lives of ten major characters are played out against the backdrop of World War II, "man's inhumanity to man" is revealed in the horrors of prejudice against Jews and women. War, whether against an oppressive society or within oneself, is fought and won only against overwhelming odds.

Dedicated to Marge Piercy's grandmother, Hannah, *Gone to Soldiers* memorializes her as a storyteller who has a "gift for making the past walk through the present." The importance of memory in preserving the lessons of the past makes Jacqueline Lévy-Monot's mission a religious one as she affirms her identity as a women and as a Jew.

Jacqueline, whose stories are told in the form of a diary, is not the only character in the novel who is a teller of tales. Louise Kahan, the war correspondent, and Abra, in a series of interviews, mark their own quests for identity in the stories they tell. Recounting the experience of her bleak childhood, Louise recalls being raped and having an abortion at the age of fifteen. Later, mired in dull wifehood, she finds it hard to juggle the demands of her daughter and philandering husband. When Louise divorces Oscar and strives to live as a single mother in a war-torn society, she learns that women in that society have no military status, no privileges, no protection, and no insurance. It is only at the end of the novel that Louise learns that the lessons of the past enable her to reunite with Oscar and be healed. In one of the book's more important passages, Louise comes to several realizations:

> Miracles came seldom and rebirth more rarely yet and for countless and uncountable and never to be counted women like herself, her age, her body type, death had come from a machine gun, from blows of the butt end of a rifle, from poison gas, from poison injections, from starvation and typhus and neglect, from all the nasty ways to die warped minds in a violent and relentless system could devise. They had died of a lack of common respect and common love. They cried out to her, take him back and go live in peace as husband and wife and as Jews. Go make a home again and give thanks. Life is the first gift, love is the second, and understanding the third.

Abra, on the other hand, has to give up the role of mistress and separate from Oscar in order to find herself and to learn that a relationship of equals brings fulfillment rather than subservient dependency. This is a hard lesson to learn—for men as well as for women. After the United States has dropped the atomic bomb on Hiroshima, Abra's beloved Daniel tells her, "I feel as if I looked out through a vast eye and saw the future of the world in a plain of ashes, of sand turned to glass, flesh vaporized, time itself burned up." When asked what can be done, Daniel replies, "First, put our opinions in the report if we can." *Gone to Soldiers* is the report and the answer to the question "Why war?" as each character reveals her or his own experiences of intolerance, misunderstanding, failures of communication, powerlessness, subjugation, and abuse.

In an interview published in the anthology *Ways of Knowing* (edited by Sue Walker and Eugenie Hamner, 1991), Piercy stated that, among all her works up to that time, *Gone to Soldiers* was the novel that caused her the most problems as she was writing it. Because the book uses ten viewpoints and moves regularly from one to another, Piercy noted, she views it as a cantata. Each character has her or his own social world, history, milieu, loved ones, and problems, and as Piercy moves in the work from the world of one character to another, the reader is also moved forcefully. The novel is separated into segments as first one and then another character appears, disappears, and comes back again in various sections. The disjointed result is part of the author's technique. Piercy rejects the Aristotelian notion of plot as progressive movement from beginning to middle to end; instead, she selects a decentering format that weaves multiple threads of human existence into a unified whole. Men as well as women redefine their attitudes and adjust their ways of functioning in order to heal the abuses of the past. The novel is not intended to invoke comfort or ease; it is designed to disrupt the reader's inner and outer worlds as the characters challenge and fight over ideals and value systems.

As a major feminist writer, Piercy often espouses the causes of women; she is also perhaps the leading female Jewish novelist in the United States. The great-granddaughter of a rabbi, Piercy recounts in *Gone to Soldiers* the horrors of anti-Semitism, so that, in Daniel's words, "No one will ever again call us dirty Jews. No one will make laws against us, ever again." The wars that take place in the novel extend beyond World War II; they are fought on American as well as foreign soil and concern the misuse of women, by society in general and by men in particular. Louise undergoes an abortion that almost kills her. Naomi is raped by Leib, her friend Trudi's husband—a soldier who was shipped home because he lost a foot in the war—and finds herself pregnant. Bernice is told by her father that grown women do not run around in airports and that "real" women should not want to fly planes. "Real" women get married and exist to please their men; they do not pursue higher degrees. They want to bring babies into the world. Jacqueline comments that "a family is an accidental construct, a group of people brought together by chance and forced to cohabit in insufficient space." Even being Jewish is a matter of accident. "I was born Jewish," Jacqueline says, "but what does that mean?" She is unable to communicate with her Polish refugee aunt, uncle, and cousins—even about things as simple as tables and chairs, let alone her aspirations, feelings, and dreams.

The novel notes both the treatment of women in a prison camp—where they are forced to march and are clubbed to death if they stumble from exhaustion, where they are fed only soup every other day and take on the appearance of genderless, starved specters rather than human beings—and the routine subjugation of women in a society that lacks tolerance of lesbians, blacks, and Jews, and where women are deprived of employment and pay equal to those available to men. This insidious misuse of females results in women at war with themselves as they struggle to find their identity and sense of self-worth, not only in war-torn France or bombed London but also in Detroit and Alabama and throughout the United States, where prejudices make people victims and deny them their human rights.

Einstein's question "Why war?" has a multitude of answers that are as complex as the lives of Louise, Daniel, Jacqueline, Abra, Naomi, Bernice, Jeff, Ruthie, Duvey, Murray, and the other characters in *Gone to Soldiers*. These characters' experiences, both separate and intertwined, touch on the issues of women's rights, the psychology of mother-daughter and father-daughter relationships, and the need to claim one's past on individual, local, and global scales. Through an anatomy of war, Piercy shows that what Einstein called humanity's "lust for hatred and destruction" can be overcome only when men and women learn to heal, to have relationships of equals instead of victimizing one another, whether on the level of nation, country, religion, class, or law. Through storytelling, perhaps, this lesson may be learned. As Naomi goes off to bear Leib's daughter, joy is brought back into the world, along with hope. Misfortune can be instructive, even though the end of one set of troubles is but the beginning of another.

Piercy examines the situations of women in relation to marriage, education, work, and wealth, especially in terms of gender divisions of labor in employment, authority, leadership, and ethnic issues of race and religion. At the beginning of *Gone to Soldiers*, Louise begins the chronicle of issues that oppress women, and Jacqueline laments the fact that people bring babies into the world so casually that often a birth is celebrated when it should be mourned.

Throughout her fiction, Piercy raises the question of what it is to be a "real" woman. In *Gone to Soldiers*, as in Piercy's earlier work *Small Changes* (1973), men insist that a real woman directs her energy to, and derives her identity from, a relationship with a man. A real woman should not want to pursue higher education; a real woman should not want to fly airplanes. Rather, a woman's duty is to stay at home and care for her family members. The repression and abuse of women in *Gone to Soldiers* exist in many places, not only in the concentration camp. Women suffer within the family, in the workplace, and in interpersonal relationships. Women in the military can be dishonorably discharged for being lesbians, and Bernice finds herself forced to adopt a masculine identity in order to find a job in which she can support herself and live with her beloved, Flo.

Piercy shows that a "real" woman is one who can take control of her life and wrest it from any man who believes he needs to subjugate her for his own selfish desires. Being real means being able to form a relationship with whomever one loves without fear of losing a job or being court-martialed. It means that a woman can feel secure within herself and be assured of her own individual worth without having to do things she dislikes in order to keep a man. Real women can earn higher degrees and pay equal to that earned by men; they can obtain positions of influence regardless of race and religion.

Piercy's feminist stance extends into a mission to affirm her Jewish heritage. *Gone to Soldiers* engages the place of memory in keeping the past alive as a deterrent to future abuse. As Jacqueline promises, "I will live and tell the world about this. I will live and make them pay." Piercy's concerns enjoin social, ethical, and political wrongs in regard to the treatment of women and envision a society characterized by wholeness, without barriers created by sex, race, religion, age, or class.

SOURCES FOR FURTHER STUDY

Foster, David L. "Women on the Edge of Narrative: Language in Marge Piercy's Utopia." In *Patterns of the Fantastic II*, edited by Donald M. Hassler. San Bernardino, Calif.: Borgo Press, 1985.

Giles, James R, and Wanda H. Giles, ed. *American Novelists Since World War II: Sixth Series*. Vol. 227 in *Dictionary of Literary Biography*. Detroit: Gale Research, 2000.

Jones, Libby Falk. "Gilman, Bradley, Piercy, and the Evolving Rhetoric of Feminist Utopias." In *Feminism, Utopia, and Narrative*, edited by Libby Falk Jones and Sarah Webster Goodwin. Knoxville: University of Tennessee Press, 1990.

Kramer, S. Lillian. "A Feminist Interpretation of Jewish History and Spirituality: Collision and Fusion in Marge Piercy's Later Poetry and Fiction." In *Connections and Collisions: Identities in Contemporary Jewish-American Women's Writing*, edited by Lois E. Rubin. Newark: University of Delaware Press, 2005.

Pacernick, Gary. *Meaning and Memory: Interviews with Fourteen Jewish Poets*. Columbus: Ohio State University Press, 2001.

Piercy, Marge. *Parti-Colored Blocks for a Quilt*. Ann Arbor: University of Michigan Press, 1982.

Ratiner, Steven. "Marge Piercy: The Communal Voice." In *Giving Their Word: Conversations with Contemporary Poets*, edited by Steven Ratiner. Amherst: University of Massachusetts Press, 2002.

See, Carolyn. "A Great Novel That Examines the Great War." *Los Angeles Times*, June 15, 1987.

Shands, Kerstin W. *The Repair of the World: The Novels of Marge Piercy*. Westport, Conn.: Greenwood Press, 1994.

Walker, Sue, and Eugenie Hamner, eds. *Ways of Knowing*. Mobile, Ala.: Negative Capability Press, 1991.

Yardley, Jonathan. Review of *Gone to Soldiers*, by Marge Piercy. *The Washington Post Book World*, May 3, 1987, p. X3.

—*Sue Brannan Walker*

The Hiding Place

AUTHORS: Corrie ten Boom (1892-1983), with John and Elizabeth Sherrill
FIRST PUBLISHED: 1971
GENRE: Nonfiction
SUBGENRE: Autobiography

This autobiography details Ten Boom's upbringing, her trials in a concentration camp during World War II, and the Christian beliefs that helped her survive. Her subsequent work and her willingness not only to forgive but also to embrace her enemies stand as one of the twentieth century's great testimonies to the power of faith.

PRINCIPAL PERSONAGES:
   Corrie ten Boom (1892-1983), a Christian Dutch watchmaker whose family hid Jews from the Nazis
   Betsie ten Boom, Corrie's older sister

OVERVIEW

Corrie (Cornelia) ten Boom first published her heart-wrenching memoir, *A Prisoner and Yet . . .* , in 1954. John and Elizabeth Sherrill, editors of *Guideposts,* a religious magazine, read the book, heard Corrie recount her experiences in Nazi concentration camps, and assisted her in writing the Christian spiritual classic *The Hiding Place,* knowing that Corrie had a bigger story to tell. The "hiding place" refers to two places: a Bible passage calling on God as a protector and shield from danger, and the Ten Booms' secret room, where Jews were hidden from the Nazis.

Corrie begins her autobiography with the celebration of the one hundredth anniversary, in 1937, of the Ten Booms' watch shop and home at 19 Barteljorisstraat, Haarlem, Holland, known as the Beje. Corrie, the first female watchmaker in Holland, is single and lives above the shop with her older, attractive sister, Betsie, also unmarried, and their father, Casper. Brother Willem's and sister Nollie's families live nearby. Casper is a devout Christian who twice daily prays and reads the Bible. He loves and respects the Jewish people, considering them to be God's chosen people. The women of the Ten Boom family took care of German orphans during

World War I and have cared for Haarlem's sick and poor. Their home is a virtual social service agency, where Jews are welcomed and their holidays celebrated. With Adolf Hitler's rise to power as German chancellor, anti-Semitism is increasing in Germany, and the nursing home in Hilversum that is run by Willem ten Boom, a Dutch Reformed minister, is overflowing with Jewish refugees. German Jewish suppliers of watchmaking parts are disappearing.

During World War II, the Germans invade Holland and harass Jews. Everybody must have ration cards to buy food. In November, 1941, German soldiers rob Corrie's neighbor's store and throw the neighbor into the street. At night, Corrie's nephew takes the neighbor into hiding. Casper declares that it is an honor to risk one's life to save Jews. Consequently, Jews, resistance workers, and men trying to avoid Nazi forced labor come to the Ten Booms for help. Resistance workers build a tiny, secret room in Corrie's third-floor bedroom and install an alarm system. Fearful of Gestapo raids, the Ten Booms conduct drills to get Jews to the hiding place. Corrie obtains food cards and safe hiding places for Jews outside the Beje from people whom her family has previously helped, and she coordinates a network of underground workers.

On February 28, 1944, a Dutchman comes asking for help. Corrie agrees to help him, and the Nazis raid the Beje. The Ten Booms' guests who are in the secret room are not caught, but Corrie, Casper, Willem, Nollie, and Betsie are hauled away in a wagon drawn by black horses. They are interrogated and sent to Scheveningen, a Dutch prison. Ten days later, Casper dies. All the Ten Booms but Betsie and Corrie are released. A nurse gives Corrie a copy of the Gospels, which help sustain her spirit while she is being held in solitary confinement. Then, Betsie and Corrie are sent to Ravensbrück, one of the worst death camps. Corrie is able to smuggle her Bible and vitamin drops into Ravensbrück. Betsie's unfailing trust in Jesus and the sisters' hope that, one day, their story of joy in suffering will turn people to Jesus sustain them. Saintly Betsie consistently insists that Corrie be thankful for their trials and tribulations and pray for their abusers and forgive them. In the midst of all the horrors of the camp, God provides for Corrie and Betsie. They share the vitamin drops, and miraculously the bottle does not go dry. The fleas in the barracks keep the guards from confiscating their Bible. The prisoners suffer humiliation, overwork, freezing cold, starvation, beatings, the leering guards' eyes when they shower, lack of space and sanitation, odors of burning flesh, black lice, and death; in response, they become belligerent and selfish. The Ten Booms change the women in their barracks through intercessory prayer and Bible readings; they encourage the women to pray for their captors.

Corrie is forced to see her beloved Betsie suffer and finally die, joyfully and peacefully, at age fifty-nine, after revealing three visions and telling Corrie that they will be out of the camp before New Year's Day. A clerical error leads to Corrie's release from Ravensbrück, but she cannot leave the camp because she has edema. Hospitalized, she hears Betsie remind her that God's will is a "hiding place." Despite her status as a patient and disregarding her swollen feet, Corrie takes bedpans to the other women who are ill. When she finally leaves the camp, all the women her age or older have been killed. Later, at a Berlin train station, a starving Corrie realizes that she was discharged and thus liberated on New Year's Day, 1945, just as Betsie had envisioned. After an exhausting trip to Holland and care at a Dutch hospital, Corrie reunites with her family. Her joy is tempered with sadness, however: Willem is dying from a crippling spinal tuberculosis contracted in Scheveningen.

Now age fifty-three, Corrie is unhappy with watchmaking, and she decides to spend the rest of her life fulfilling Betsie's visions. The Beje eventually becomes a home for the healing of Holland's most hated people, the Dutch people who collaborated with the Nazis. Betsie's first vision comes to fruition when a wealthy Dutch woman gives Corrie a mansion at Bloemendaal, which Corrie, with the help of volunteers, transforms into a rehabilitation center where she teaches refugees, former prisoners of concentration camps, and people who were in hiding to forgive and love their enemies. Betsie's second vision becomes a reality when Corrie turns Darmstadt, a former Nazi concentration camp, into a home for the reconciliation and healing of Germans. Corrie fulfills Betsie's third vision when she travels the world telling audiences that Jesus became the victor in the concentration camps. On a speaking tour, Corrie meets one of the cruelest former

Ravensbrück camp guards and immediately feels hate for him; she begs God to help her forgive him, and instantly she is able to forgive him. Corrie has never known God's love so intensely as she does at that moment. She also forgives the man who betrayed her family and other camp personnel she meets.

Ten Boom's storytelling skills made her a reluctant celebrity who humbly insisted that Jesus, not she, was responsible for her accomplishments. She wrote thirty-two books and remained in demand as a speaker until paralysis stopped her in 1978. She died on April 15, 1983, her birthday, at the age of ninety-one. The proceeds from her books continue to finance missionaries.

The Ten Booms' Calvinist beliefs in God's love, the Bible, positive affirmations, charitable acts, and willingness to risk their safety for that of their neighbors fill this story. The Ten Booms' trust in and love of Jesus is evident throughout the narrative not only in their words but also in their actions. Corrie's parents set the example for their children, practicing the Golden Rule and passing that belief and practice on to Betsie and Corrie as well as their siblings. As a Christian evangelist, Corrie traveled to more than sixty nations preaching and bringing people to Jesus. She refused donations, preferring to avoid influence, depending totally on God's goodness and the kindness of strangers for her shelter, food, and daily needs. Corrie's faith in God never failed her. She not only preached but also lived love and forgiveness, gratitude for trials, and joy in suffering. Her example stands in stark contrast to many in modern society, whose stony indifference to human suffering—whether that of a neighbor or that of an enemy—is humanity's most fatal disease. Her message is that of Jesus: To forgive one's enemies is to free the prisoner, you.

The Hiding Place is one of the best-selling true Holocaust stories, a testimony that serves as a warning for future generations not to deny the Holcaust and never to allow such persecution to occur again. Frequently used in schools for teaching students about the Holocaust and character education, it was made into a successful film (released by World Wide Pictures in 1975) and continues to provide hope and inspiration. Corrie ten Boom has been honored in Israel with a tree planted near that of Oskar Schindler, another Holocaust hero, along the Avenue of the Righteous Gentiles near Jerusalem.

SOURCES FOR FURTHER STUDY

Baron, Lawrence. "Supercessionism Without Contempt: The Holocaust Evangelism of Corrie ten Boom." In *Christian Responses to the Holocaust:*

Moral and Ethical Issues, edited by Donald J. Dietrich. Syracuse, N.Y.: Syracuse University Press, 2003.

Carlson, Carole C. *Corrie ten Boom, Her Life, Her Faith: A Biography.* Old Tappan, N.J.: Fleming H. Revell, 1983.

"Corrie ten Boom Was Imprisoned by Nazis for Sheltering Jews." *Boston Globe*, April 17, 1983, p. 1.

Ten Boom, Corrie, and Jamie Buckingham. *Tramp for the Lord.* Old Tappan, N.J.: Fleming H. Revell, 1974.

—*Margaret T. Sacco*

The History of Love

AUTHOR: Nicole Krauss (1975-   )
FIRST PUBLISHED: 2005
GENRE: Novel
SUBGENRE: Psychological fiction

Krauss's sophomore novel concerns survivors of the Holocaust and the impact of a book about true love on the lives of people connected beyond time and space.

PRINCIPAL CHARACTERS:
  Leopold Gursky, a retired locksmith and reclusive octogenarian writer, survivor of the Holocaust
  Alma Mereminski-Moritz, Leopold's love since childhood, mother of two sons, one of whom is Leopold's
  Isaac Moritz, Leo and Alma's son, a renowned writer
  Alma Singer, a teenage girl named after Alma as Leo wrote about her in *The History of Love*
  Charlotte Singer, a widowed translator, young Alma's mother
  Bird Singer, Charlotte's seven-year-old son, who believes he may be a messiah
  Zvi Litvinoff, Leo's childhood friend, exiled in Chile, who published Leo's manuscript as his own

OVERVIEW

Nicole Krauss, an acclaimed poet who has worked on her verses with Joseph Brodsky, negotiated a six-figure deal to write two books after her first novel, *A Man Walks into a Room* (2002), garnered rave reviews. An excerpt from *The History of Love*, called "The Last Words on Earth," was published in *The New Yorker* in February, 2004; subsequently, Krauss sold the book rights to *The History of Love* in almost twenty countries and the film rights to Warner Bros. studios.

The History of Love is the title of a book within a book. Some people's lives have been wrapped by the book, which has shaped their destinies. The reader enters that magical world, and it opens views to other worlds. The novel is about reading and writing, the way a book can change lives, love, and loss. Witty and emotional, it is also about nostalgia for the places one cannot revisit because they are lost forever. In the end, however, it is about living and survival, often creatively accomplished.

This ambitious and remarkable work depicts unconventional life journeys; its themes include love lost but never forgotten, human destiny charted by the atrocities of war, and loneliness of the "invisible" people. Leopold Gursky survives the massacre of the Jews in his native village of Slonim, in Poland, by hiding in the woods for more than three years. His girlfriend Alma Mereminski, the love of his life, escapes to the United States. Leo follows and finds her, but he arrives too late. Because his letters did not reach her, she thought he was dead, like many others. Now she is married, with two sons. One is Leo's.

A locksmith and a writer, Leo lives in Manhattan, not far from Alma and her family but without any physical contact with them. After having lost his parents, his native land, his only love, his son, and the book he wrote while a young man—inspired by his first and only love—he is now retired. The book opens with him at eighty years old, brooding over his wasted life and approaching death. He often wonders who will be the last to see him alive. He makes a point of being "seen" and sits as a model in a nude drawing class. Most of the time, however, he is alone and philosophizing: "Put even a fool in front of a window and you'll get a Spinoza."

Leo and Alma's son, Isaac Moritz, a famous writer, dies at age sixty from Hodgkin's disease. Until Isaac's death, Leo wonders if Isaac knew who his own father was. Once, in order to attend his son's book reading, Leo had obtained tickets months in advance. He joined Isaac's fans in lining up to meet the writer. Once face-to-face with Isaac, however, he could not say a word. Isaac was kind and patient, but a security guard firmly grasped Leo's elbow and escorted him out. Only after Isaac's death does Leo find himself in his son's home, touching and sniffing his clothes, trying on his shoes, which are larger than his own.

There are two major, and several minor, life stories flowing, like blood, through this book. Unknown to one another, and Leo, the characters all meet in the heart, symbolized by his book. Leo had given his old manuscript to his childhood friend, Zvi Litvinoff, in Minsk. Since then, Litvinoff has lived a refugee's life in Chile. A young woman, Rosa, falls in love with him and marries "her dark crow." He reads the manuscript to her, and she helps him translate it into Spanish, assuming it is his. After it is published, the book takes on its own life, touching people with its powerful energy of love. Litvinoff gains notoriety, which improves his life. He lives with his secret, never finding a suitable moment to tell Rosa, unaware that she had found out and deliberately destroyed the evidence. She had even informed Gursky that the manuscript had been lost when their home flooded.

In addition to Leo's first-person, earthy, eccentrically witty narration, there is another voice, that of another Alma, the teenage Alma Singer, named after the book's heroine. Her voice is counterpointed with Leo's, bringing with it youthful imagination, curiosity, and wonder with life. Her journal successfully portrays the lives of all her family members. The book *History of Love* has great significance for the Singer family: Her father gave it to her mother at the time of their courting. Now he is dead, her mother a widow faithfully dedicated to his memory. She is stacking books and dictionaries between her and the outside world. Unexpectedly, she receives a commission from a Jacob Markus, wanting her to translate *The History of Love* from Spanish.

With the book to aid in her secret quest, young Alma Singer looks for a man who could change her mother's solitary life. Alma also helps her dreamy, out-of-touch mother in raising Bird, Alma's younger brother, another dreamer. He believes he is a Lamed-Vovnik—that is, one of the Lamed Vov, who are, according to Jewish tradition, the thirty-six righteous individuals in the world—and that he can fly. He jumps from the second floor (at age six), breaking his arm and earning his nickname. In keeping with Jewish tradition, he avoids writing God's name and spells it G-d. He believes he just may be a messiah. Secretly, he reads his sister's writing and gets into the mystery of the lost book, unknowingly adding to its resolution. While recording the "real" but awkward exchange of kisses with her first love, Misha, Alma is secretly but strongly dedicated to finding out more about her namesake.

Numerous supporting characters are lush and picturesque: Bruno, born out of Leo's loneliness and undying love; Litvinoff's wife, Rosa; Alma's Uncle Julian (with his lopsided smile and a passion for Alberto Giacometti). All of them are intelligent and unusual but vibrantly true to life. Just as one sympathizes with Leo Tolstoy's character Anna Karenina in spite of her transgression, one cannot harshly judge Litwinoff and Rosa for stealing Leo's book. The circumstances of their lives make it understandable. Love is brimming in the book as a motivating force behind human actions, spilling into the world through the readers.

In an interview, Krauss admitted she had decided to write a book based on her knowledge, not research. She enjoyed writing it and therefore expected that readers would enjoy it too. Krauss pays homage to many of her favorite writers within the work, such as Antoine de Saint-Exupéry, Pablo Neruda, Miguel de Cervantes, Jorge Luis Borges, and Franz Kafka. She also honors composers, painters, and numerous others among the great, gifted, and famous. The creative spirit, with the message, resonates in the reader.

Through her devoted, passionate search, young Alma finds out that Jacob Markus is only a character from the book her mother is translating. The real man behind the commission is Isaac Moritz, son of the original Alma. It is too late to meet Alma or Isaac in person, Alma soon finds; instead, she connects with Leo. His years of longing end when the two of them meet. Ready to join his loved ones, Leo sees young Alma as the embodiment of his long-awaited love, young and beautiful as he has always remembered her from their blissful youth. Their separate voices now unite in a powerful duet in an ode to joy of life and love (*Amor omnia vincit*). It is a happy ending that life gives, as a well-deserved gift, to Leo, gentle and touching as a mother's lullaby or a last kiss.

The History of Love defies a thorough summary. The work examines the place of love in human lives, the invisible golden thread connecting all people through the most powerful energy in the universe. It celebrates the magic of life and love through some extraordinary episodes in the lives of remarkable people. Perhaps all people are remarkable when their most intimate stories are known. Of these, most often the words not spoken—although there are words for everything in life, Krauss tells the reader through Leo.

At almost fifteen, Alma seems to embody what is known about the young Nicole Krauss, yet the character confesses feeling more comfortable expressing Leo's point of view. Dedicated to Krauss's grandparents, who taught her "the opposite of disappearing," this novel is an immigrant story, teaching empathy with the "invisible" people around the world and around the corner—one's neighbors, one's sisters and brothers.

It is worth noting the author's diction: almost scientific precision coupled with sensitivity, emotion, and gentleness. Her sense of wonder turns her story into a roller-coaster ride of excitement, revealing the unknown sides of human lives. She uses many stories within the novel and many characters of all ages, from an earthy old man or a dreamy middle-aged widow to her idiosyncratic son and curious, level-headed teenage daughter. Krauss employs letters, journals, diagrams, different languages and orthographies, even the words that stay unsaid, with images and almost-blank pages that speak louder than the busy ones.

SOURCES FOR FURTHER STUDY

Eder, Richard. "A Life of Mixed Connections." *Los Angeles Times*, May 1, 2005, p. R5.

Jackson, Devon. "Some Cracks Are Showing in a Novel That Got All the Hype." *Santa Fe New Mexican*, July 17, 2005, p. G5.

Long, Colleen. "Weaving Losses into a Fable: *The History of Love* Author Braces for Success." *Bergen County Record*, June 21, 2005, p. F7.

MacGillis, Alec. "Krauss Can't Translate Grand Passions to the Page." *Baltimore Sun*, May 22, 2005, p. 8F.

Maslin, Janet. "The Story of a Book Within a Book." *The New York Times*, April 25, 2005, p. E1.

Miller, Laura. "Under the Influence." *The New York Times Book Review*, May 1, 2005, p. 19.

—Mira N. Mataric

History on Trial
My Day in Court with David Irving

AUTHOR: Deborah E. Lipstadt (1947-   )
FIRST PUBLISHED: 2005
GENRE: Nonfiction
SUBGENRES: History; current affairs

Lipstadt presents a compelling firsthand account of the libel case that prominent British historian David Irving brought against her and her publisher, Penguin Books, when Lipstadt, in an earlier book, accused Irving of being a Holocaust denier. The trial addressed the issues of intellectual honesty in historical scholarship, the reality of the Holocaust, and the significance of the Holocaust denial movement for the rise of neofascism.

PRINCIPAL PERSONAGES:
  Deborah E. Lipstadt (b. 1947), an author and professor of Jewish Studies at Emory University
  David Irving (b. 1938), a British World War II historian
  Anthony Julius, a literary scholar and Lipstadt's solicitor
  Richard Rampton, a barrister selected by Penguin Books to present Lipstadt's case
  Charles Gray, the judge at Lipstadt's trial
  Robert Jan van Pelt, an architectural historian who appeared as an expert witness for the defense
  Richard Evans, a historian who served as chief historical adviser to Penguin Books and appeared as an expert witness for the defense
  Hajo Funke, a German professor of politics who appeared as an expert witness for the defense

OVERVIEW

History on Trial: My Day in Court with David Irving is Deborah E. Lipstadt's very personal account of her legal battle with the prominent British historian David Irving in 2000 and the behind-the-scenes events associated with the trial and the key persons involved. When her previous book, *Denying the Holocaust: The Growing Assault on Truth and Memory*, was published by Penguin Books in 1993, Lipstadt never expected that Irving would sue her and her publisher for libel. In that comprehensive history of the Holocaust denial movement, Lipstadt accused Irving of being a dangerous Holocaust denier who distorted historical evidence to support his biased conclusions.

Few believed the libel case would go to trial—Irving probably expected that Lipstadt would apologize and retract her criticism of him, as fighting a libel suit in England, where the trial would take place, is a difficult and costly business. The burden of proof in English law is on the defendant—Lipstadt would have to prove the truth of her statements. Often called "the Irving trial," the case was actually the Penguin/Lipstadt trial, given that Irving was the plaintiff. Lipstadt's right to free speech, not Irving's, was the core of the case.

Because she believed Holocaust denial to be a growing danger and thought that Irving would gain increased credibility if she did not contest the lawsuit, Lipstadt responded vigorously. She raised $1.5 million for the defense (Irving claimed there was a global conspiracy to destroy him, funded by Jewish financiers). To the credit of Penguin Books—given that the trial would cost millions of pounds—Lipstadt's publisher stood by her. The defense assembled a formidable legal team that included Anthony Julius (Lipstadt's solicitor) and Richard Rampton (a leading barrister). Irving represented himself. It was agreed that the proceedings would not be a jury trial, because the quantity of original source material to be presented would be too much for a jury to examine.

In 2000, Justice Charles Gray presided over the sensational trial, which lasted ten weeks. Auschwitz survivors and Nazi sympathizers were among those in the packed courtroom. Much to Irving's chagrin, the defense team refused to call Lipstadt to testify in her own behalf. They also refused to call eyewitnesses, both to spare them the unpleasant experience of cross-examination and, more important, to keep the focus on Irving. The defense's strategy was to emphasize Irving's methodology and his association with right-wing radical groups. Rampton sought to prove Irving a liar and a bigot who had deliberately distorted and falsified history to serve his anti-Semitic agenda. Julius had asked the court to require Irving to disclose a vast quantity of materials relevant to the case, and the defense engaged a number of respected historians to research Irving's work and write expert reports. Their preparations took four years. At the trial, the defense experts provided documentation supporting Lipstadt's assertions that Irving had not been objective, had connections with extremist political groups, and had falsified the historical record.

Central to the trial was the issue of the function of the Nazi concentration camp at Auschwitz, where more than one million people, mostly Jews, were alleged to have died in gas chambers. Irving tried to create doubts about the gas chambers at Auschwitz because Auschwitz has become almost a synonym for the Holocaust. While conceding there were mass murders by gassing at other camps, he said that Auschwitz was "baloney" and a "legend." He claimed the gas chambers at Auschwitz-Birkenau were used for gassing objects and cadavers. Irving's conclusions were influenced by a report by Fred Leuchter, an American execution specialist, who found higher residue of hydrogen cyanide gas in the delousing rooms at Auschwitz than in the gas chambers and assumed that humans were not killed in the gas chambers. (He did not know that humans are less resistant to cyanide than vermin are.)

Rampton questioned why a room for gassing objects would have a spy hole in the door, with a heavy metal grill on the inside. He also questioned why the chutes for sliding bodies to the morgue were replaced with steps when the crematoria buildings at Auschwitz were transformed in 1942 to gas chambers. Irving claimed that the gas chambers were air-raid shelters—although this meant that the Nazi Schutzstaffel (SS) personnel would have to run more than a mile from their barracks to the supposed

Deborah E. Lipstadt celebrates outside London's High Court after winning the case brought against her and her publisher, Penguin Books, by British historian David Irving. (AP/Wide World Photos)

shelters—and asserted there was not enough fuel at Auschwitz to incinerate all of the alleged victims. He challenged the authenticity of a letter from the head of Auschwitz's building program that indicated the potential incineration capacity was more than sufficient. Robert Jan van Pelt, an architectural historian, prepared a seven-hundred-page expert report for the court that documented the evidence for the existence of an extermination camp at Auschwitz; he successfully defended his findings under cross-examination by Irving.

In *Denying the Holocaust*, Lipstadt had asserted that Irving was an admirer of Adolf Hitler and an apologist for the Nazi leader's actions. Irving claimed that Hitler never ordered the murder of Jews, was unaware of their extermination until late 1943, and tried to mitigate the anti-Semitic actions of his subordinates. Richard Evans, a Cambridge historian who produced an expert report more than seven hundred pages long that was critical of Irving's methodology, maintained that Irving deliberately misinterpreted and distorted documents, suppressing evidence at will. For example, Evans made it clear that the diary of Joseph Goebbels, the Nazi propaganda minister, and other documents proved that Hitler authorized the "demonstrations" of Kristallnacht—the "night of broken glass" in Germany, when Jews were attacked and killed, their homes and shops were vandalized, and synagogues were set on fire. Irving maintained that Hitler was ignorant of the pogrom and tried to stop "the madness." Hajo Funke, a German professor, presented videos of Irving's speeches to far-right extremists to show Irving's associations with neo-Nazis and leading Holocaust deniers.

Rampton argued that Irving's "mistakes"—more than twenty had been raised in the trial—could not be inadvertent given that they all led to excusing Hitler and denying the Holocaust. Justice Gray agreed. In a ruling for Penguin Books and Lipstadt, he declared Irving to be a right-wing pro-Nazi polemicist and a racist anti-Semite who had deliberately falsified history in order to excuse Hitler and disseminate anti-Semitic propaganda. Irving was required to pay the defendants' legal expenses.

Although the Irving trial produced other books by well-known authors, Lipstadt's firsthand account is significant because it presents the most comprehensive narrative of the trial. It deals with the emotional and personal cost of the trial for Lipstadt as well as with the moral issues that were at stake and the trial's significance for Holocaust survivors and Jews worldwide.

It is doubtful that Lipstadt's criticisms seriously damaged Irving's career, but the trial cost Irving his reputation as a serious scholar. The kind of scrutiny to which his work was subjected durng the trial created a fear of censorship among some historians and raised questions as to whether Irving's unacceptable agenda prejudiced the court. All historians approach evidence with some degree of subjectivity and bias, but a heightened awareness of the need for objectivity and accountability was certainly an outcome of this case. The ways in which historians use evidence were very much on trial in the Penguin/Lipstadt trial.

A more serious issue for Lipstadt was the reality of the Holocaust. As an editorial in Britain's *Daily Telegraph* stated, the trial had "done for the new century what the Nuremberg tribunals or the Eichmann trial did for earlier generations." The trial made it clear that sufficient historical data exist to demonstrate that the Holocaust really happened and was not invented by politically motivated Jews, that the gas chambers at Auschwitz were a reality, and that Hitler, even if he was not directly responsible, had been aware of what was happening.

Sources for Further Study

Evans, Richard J. *Lying About Hitler: History, Holocaust, and the David Irving Trial*. New York: Basic Books, 2001.

Guttenplan, D. D. *The Holocaust on Trial*. New York: W. W. Norton, 2001.

Lipstadt, Deborah E. *Denying the Holocaust: The Growing Assault on Truth and Memory*. New York: Penguin Books, 1993.

Shermer, Michael, and Alex Grobman. *Denying History: Who Says the Holocaust Never Happened and Why Do They Say It?* Berkeley: University of California Press, 2000.

Van Pelt, Robert Jan. *The Case for Auschwitz: Evidence from the Irving Trial*. Bloomington: Indiana University Press, 2002.

—*Edna B. Quinn*

Hitler

Author: Ian Kershaw (1943-   )
First published: *Hitler, 1889-1936: Hubris*, 1998; *Hitler, 1936-1945: Nemesis*, 2000
Genre: Nonfiction
Subgenres: Biography; history

Kershaw's two-volume biography explains why despairing and angry Germans turned to Adolf Hitler to restore their nation's order and pride, why conservative nationalists and the army thought they could manipulate Hitler, and what responsibility Hitler bore for the Holocaust.

Principal personages:
 Adolf Hitler (1889-1945), the chancellor of Germany, 1933-1945
 Ernst Röhm (1887-1934), the head of the Nazi Sturm Abteilung (SA, or storm troopers)
 Rudolf Hess (1894-1987), one of Hitler's earliest followers, ineffective head of the Nazi Party until 1941
 Hermann Göring (1893-1946), the most powerful figure in Hitler's inner circle, 1936-1938, later merely the head of the German air force
 Joseph Goebbels (1897-1945), the Nazi propaganda minister who served as Hitler's spokesman to the world
 Heinrich Himmler (1900-1945), the head of the Schutzstaffel (SS)
 Joachim von Ribbentrop (1893-1946), Germany's foreign minister and one of the foremost advocates for war

Overview

In his two-volume biography of Adolf Hitler, Ian Kershaw takes on the biographer's ultimate questions: What makes a man become what he is? Does an individual control events, or is he a prisoner of his times? Previous biographers have struggled with Hitler, sifting the records relating to him and his times to try to make sense of the events of his life. The myths have been so strong, however, and the evidence so contradictory that not until a half century after Hitler's death was it possible for Kershaw to collect the scattered information on the man and analyze it calmly, if not dispassion-

Adolf Hitler reviews a parade of SA troops. (Charles Russell Collection, NARA)

ately. It seems that nobody can remain emotionally detached from the times and career of Adolf Hitler.

In his first volume, *Hitler, 1889-1936: Hubris*, Kershaw offers a conventional portrait of the young Adolf—the future führer was an unhappy boy, an unremarkable youth, and a frustrated young artist. He grew up in Austria, on the German border, in a somewhat dysfunctional family, then spent his inheritance in Vienna, pretending to be an art student. His drawings were good enough for him to make a modest living, but he preferred talking to drawing, and he seemed destined to die in some obscure flophouse in a multicultural city he detested except for its architecture and its productions of Richard Wagner's operas. There was nothing particularly notable about any of this, Kershaw observes. Many boys are unhappy, and every city has drifters and bums.

Anti-Semitism and racism were present at all levels of European society, but especially in Vienna, where Jews had opportunities to advance as far as their talents permitted. Hitler was little different from others in his attitudes, but his indolence and indecision could turn suddenly to anger and impulsive action. It was World War I, Kershaw notes, or rather Germany's loss of the war, that made Hitler's rise possible. None of these observations is new, but Kershaw presents new confirmation of these judgments from people who had been reluctant to talk earlier, and he devotes more pages to Hitler's early years than have most other historians and biographers.

Kershaw illustrates how Hitler became an effective demagogue and propagandist, attracting crowds of political cranks and malcontents to his speeches in Munich, filling beer halls and employing toughs to keep order. He had no original ideas; rather, he reflected popular stereotypes and prejudices about the Versailles treaty, Jews, and communists. As postwar inflation wrecked the German economy, radical movements appeared from the political Right as well as the Left. The National Socialists (Nazis) constituted a small party and would have remained obscure except for the bizarre event in 1923 known as the Beer Hall Putsch. It was a total fiasco, but Hitler was willing to take the entire blame on himself. Kershaw posits that this gave him national publicity as well as the thanks of those who escaped justice. He received an extremely light sentence for his role in the failed coup, and his brief incarceration in the Landsberg Prison gave him the opportunity to dictate *Mein Kampf* (1925-1926; English translation, 1939), a mendacious account of his life and struggles that laid the basis for the future Hitler myth.

Little is known about Hitler's private life, probably because there was little to know. Kershaw reports that he had simple tastes and little if any sex life, did not drink alcohol or eat meat, read only to reinforce his own beliefs, and relaxed only by watching movies or by listening to recordings of Wagner's music. He changed moods almost instantaneously, politeness turning to fury, then back again. He considered himself an expert on everything worth knowing about—art, music, the military—and had a good memory for details.

Kershaw explains why Hitler attracted the men whose names would become almost as familiar as his—Joseph Goebbels, Hermann Göring, Heinrich Himmler, and Ernst Röhm—and made his political rivals underestimate him. Although his Sturm Abteilung (SA), or storm troopers, were useful for street and alley fights against communists and socialists, there seemed little future for the Nazis until political feuds and posturing, along with an economic crisis of catastrophic proportions, paralyzed the Weimar Republic.

Kershaw asserts that Hitler was greatly helped by important groups in Germany that hated democracy. The Left had always favored a Soviet model, and the Right wanted a return to a monarchy or rule by the military. Hitler was useful to the Right in countering the Left, but he was despised by the Right's leaders—and underestimated.

As the Left came to believe that Hitler was merely a tool of capitalists, industrialists, landowners, and the army, the members of those very groups came to the same conclusion. Both were mistaken. Hitler wanted only power. He had no detailed program, but he could speak with passion for hours, swaying audiences that were ready to believe that capitalism and the Jews were the sources of their troubles and that national unity was the solution. The situation was critical—the Weimar Republic was despised and essentially dead, the Right had already introduced government by decree, and the Left anticipated picking up the pieces after everything fell apart.

Without the political machinations of the Right, Kershaw observes, Hitler would never have come to power or, once in office, could not have established himself as dictator. Once in control, his storm troopers and the Nazi-dominated police ruthlessly smashed all organized opposition, killing some, driving others into exile, and imprisoning many in hastily erected concentration camps. Social organizations were dissolved or incorporated into Nazi equivalents. Only one political party remained—Hitler's.

That party, however, was still divided. Röhm had his own plans—more radical and violent than Hitler's—which caused conservatives and the army to insist that Hitler bring his party under control. Hitler delayed and dithered—as was his practice in all matters—then acted impulsively and decisively. In mid-1934, in the "Night of the Long Knives," he personally led the raid that captured Röhm, then ordered his execution along with other troublemakers, potential rivals, and political enemies. It seemed, briefly, that Nazism was evolving into a more moderate movement.

With Germany at last stable, businessmen could proceed without worrying about strikes or leftist legislation, but rearmament was soaking up government income, and unemployment remained serious. Hitler was able to say without contradiction that the situation was improving, but only because nobody dared disagree; the economy continued to lag, with high unemployment and low wages. Hitler's response was political—in 1935 and 1936 he moved to abolish the terms of the 1919 Treaty of Versailles and sent troops into the Rhineland, which had been a demilitarized zone. Britain and France, which had refused to aid the Weimar Republic, capitulated to Hitler's bullying. Germany passed laws that called for the sterilization of mental incompetents as well as laws that prohibited marriages between Jews and Germans. In 1936, the Olympic Games were held in Berlin, and Hitler took this opportunity to show his country to the world as a place of peace, prosperity, and national renewal.

There was nothing organized about the Hitler regime, Kershaw argues. Hitler was the leader, but he gave few orders, and he allowed neither party nor bureaucracy to provide stability and give clear guidelines for implementing policies. At the bottom, petty bullying and corruption flourished. At the top, chaos and indecision were followed by swift and unexpected action, with Hitler then declaring that the crisis had been overcome.

The first volume of Kershaw's biography closes with Hitler having restored a sense of pride and national purpose in Germany. He had been so successful that he came to believe he could never make a mistake. The second volume of the work illustrates how wrong Hitler was, and why he failed to see it.

Hitler began to treat neighboring nations as brutally as he had his domestic opposition, and as successfully. Kershaw posits that Hitler's hypochondria made him believe that he was aging quickly and that he had to act while his physical powers were still good and before the corruption and incompetence of his regime caused a public reaction. Also, the internal dynamism of fascism required ever swifter forward momentum. To stand still was to die.

Hitler's intuition in seizing the right moment, his contempt for his opponents, and the public's reluctance to believe that anyone could want another war made his well-advertised program of aggression possible. Hitler did want a war—and soon. Göring's moderation at Munich, where Hitler intimidated France and Britain, led to his replacement by other henchmen, who vied with one another in proposing ever more radical steps against Jews and for war. Hitler, who felt that the Munich Agreement had prevented his making a triumphal march into Prague, was determined never to be frustrated again. The German occupation of the Czech lands was followed by demands on Poland.

From this point on, Kershaw's story is familiar—Hitler used threats, blackmail, and bribery (most important was his pact with Joseph Stalin), only to discover that he could not shake Polish and British resolve. Frustrated and angry, he slept little, ranted, and demanded immediate action; his henchmen scurried to respond. Even his most random comments were now taken as commands for action. Joachim von Ribbentrop was the most enthusiastic, but no one held back, not even the army.

While the German army smashed through Poland, Britain and France massed forces on the western front but did nothing. All the initiative was Hitler's—victory in Poland, the occupation of Denmark and Norway, then the swift conquest of France. Kershaw does not credit the invasion of Yugoslavia with having a significant effect on the Russian campaign, and he notes that Germany's conquest of Greece had been long planned to keep British bombers far from the Romanian oil fields.

The Nazis' euthanasia program, the roundup of Jews and their murder, and other programs required no action by Hitler, whose attention was in any case totally given to the war. Also, military decisions once attributed to Hitler—such as stopping the armored columns short of Dunkirk—were made by the professionals. Hitler had set up, or allowed to come into being, a state that ran without central direction, a state that would collapse if it did not have a crisis to confront.

The attack on Russia was based on geopolitical judgments, especially Hitler's perception that Germany needed land in the east. He now despised Bolshevism more than he feared it—the Soviet Union would be an easy victim, his commanders assured him. Afterward, Britain would come to terms.

Kershaw notes that Hitler's well-known interference in the Russian campaign did take place, but it was later exaggerated by military commanders eager to excuse their failures. Moreover, his order to troops to stand fast against the Soviet winter offensive of 1941 proved so sound that he became even more persuaded of his infallibility. Hitler's public support decreased sharply after the Battle of Stalingrad (1942-1943), but no one saw a way of escaping the foreseeable disaster. Only Hitler remained optimistic, living in a fantasy world. He viewed all setbacks as the results of either betrayals or weakness, but he believed that everything would be well in the end—something would come to his rescue, either his secret weapons or a falling out among the Allies.

By 1944, Hitler was a sick man—Parkinson's disease, pills and injections, and exhaustion took their toll. After a nearly fatal assassination attempt on July 20, Hitler tightened the screws on his perceived enemies, on the army, and on the entire German society. Nothing helped for long, and with Hitler's belief that the only choices were victory or death, it was clear which was coming. He ignored military advice, overruled his henchmen's efforts to make peace, and in general lost touch with reality. The end was coming both for him and Germany.

In spite of everything, Hitler held on to power. His generals or his associates could have assassinated him and seized power, but they were held back by his myth of infallible judgment, their memory of his having pulled victory out of apparent defeats, their jealousy of one another, and their fear of sudden and horrible death. As hope vanished, Hitler's henchmen and true believers awaited their fate. Some followed him in suicide, some fled, and some surrendered. For the German public, the shame and humiliation of losing the war were profound, made bearable only by the pressing need to dig out of the physical ruins and find some way to survive. Fifty million persons, however, did not live to see the end of the war. Stalin's troops occupied half of Germany; the Western powers took charge of the rest.

In these volumes on Hitler's life, Kershaw presents both more and less than other biographers have done. He draws on new sources and surpasses previous scholars in his use of old sources and in his analysis. He also discards much of the earlier speculation around Hitler, dismissing inaccurate stories and implausible explanations. Kershaw's scholarship is impeccable, his analysis persuasive, and his style compelling.

As Kershaw notes, never in history before Hitler was so much ruination associated with one name. A beer-hall demagogue, bigot, and racist led a once-great country with a historically great culture to destruction, and much of Europe with it. Hitler's only positive contribution was that he demonstrated the consequences of hypernationalism, racism, and ambitions for world power. Kershaw's work is essential reading for those who seek to understand the Nazi version of totalitarianism—how ambitious and jealous underlings sought to advance themselves by proposing ever more radical policies to a leader who rarely gave direct orders but approved those that fit best into his own nationalist/racial views and the political possibilities of the moment. When war removed all restraints, the unthinkable—the Holocaust—became reality.

Sources for Further Study

Fest, Joachim. *Hitler*. Translated by Richard Winston and Clara Winston. New York: Harcourt Brace Jovanovich, 1974.

Haffner, Sebastian. *The Meaning of Hitler*. Cambridge, Mass.: Harvard University Press, 1979.

Kershaw, Ian. *The Nazi Dictatorship: Problems and Perspectives of Interpretation*. 4th ed. New York: Oxford University Press, 2000.

Lukacs, John. *The Hitler of History*. New York: Random House, 1997.

Rosenbaum, Ron. *Explaining Hitler: The Search for the Origins of His Evil*. New York: Random House, 1998.

Victor, George. *Hitler: The Pathology of Evil*. Dulles, Va.: Brassey's, 1998.

—*William L. Urban*

The Hitler of History

Author: John Lukacs (1924-   )
First published: 1997
Genre: Nonfiction
Subgenres: History; biography

In this long bibliographical essay, Lukacs examines how historians have interpreted various aspects of the life and career of Adolf Hitler.

Principal personages:
  Adolf Hitler (1889-1945), the chancellor of Germany, 1933-1945
  Martin Broszat,
  Sebastian Haffner,
  Helmut Heiber,
  Andreas Hillgruber,
  Eberhard Jaeckel,
  Werner Maser,
  Ernst Nolte,
  Gerhard Schreiber, and
  Ranier Zitelmann, German historians and biographers of Hitler
  Joachim Fest and
  Konrad Heiden, German journalists and biographers of Hitler
  Alan Bullock,
  William Carr,
  David Irving,
  Ian Kershaw, and
  Robert C. L. Waite, English historians and biographers of Hitler
  Harold Gordon, Jr.,
  Bradley F. Smith, and
  John Toland, American historians and biographers of Hitler

Overview

In *The Hitler of History*, John Lukacs surveys the most important works that have appeared in German and English concerning several aspects of the life and career of Adolf Hitler, offering critiques of the works and his own interpretations. A consistent theme that runs throughout the book is a plea for the "historicization" of Hitler. By "historicization," Lukacs refers to the tendency of many historians who have written about Hitler to demonize him, to portray him as something other than a man, as something completely outside human experience. Lukacs calls for objective research into the life of Hitler that examines the Nazi leader's virtues as well as his faults. Lukacs carefully points out that he is not calling for a "rehabilitation" of Hitler and that the essentially evil nature of the man and his regime must always be noted. (Here the author shows that he is not immune to the tendency of modern historians to make Hitler the scapegoat for most of the ills of the twentieth century.)

An introductory chapter examines most of the important biographies of Hitler as well as many monographs on aspects of his life and career. The authors of those works include German historians and journalists Martin Broszat, Joachim Fest, Sebastian Haffner, Helmut Heiber, Konrad Heiden, Andreas Hillgruber, Eberhard Jaeckel, Werner Maser, Ernst Nolte, Gerhard Schreiber, and Ranier Zitelmann; British historians and journalists Alan Bullock, William Carr, David Irving, Ian Kershaw, and Robert C. L. Waite; and American historians and journalists Harold Gordon, Jr., Bradley F. Smith, and John Toland. Lukacs finds nits to pick with all these authors, but he reserves his most critical remarks for British historian David Irving and American historian and journalist John Toland.

Lukacs accuses Irving of being a secret admirer of Hitler who tries to rehabilitate him through destroying the reputations of his three most implacable foes: Winston Churchill, Franklin Roosevelt, and Joseph Stalin. Lukacs also casts serious doubts on Irving's reliability as an historian, pointing out that many of Irving's references are either misrepresented or nonexistent. Lukacs dismisses Irving's contention in *Hitler's War* (1977) that Hitler did not order the mass murder of the Jews and did not learn of it until 1943-1944 as fantasy. Lukacs also indicts Toland as an admirer of Hitler, dismisses his research as the efforts of a "popular" historian, and insists that there exists no evidence for several of the anecdotes Toland relates about Hitler. Exactly why Lukacs concludes that Toland "admires" Hitler never becomes entirely clear.

The introductory chapter also notes a number of controversies in Hitler studies swirling at the time of the book's publication, such as the so-called *Historikerstreit* (historians' quarrel) in Germany. Exactly what the issues in the *Historikerstreit* are, Lukacs never makes entirely clear, which is not surprising given that many of the historians involved seem unsure of those issues. He also notes the "intentionalist"/"functionalist" debate (whether Hitler intended the murder of the Jews from the beginning of his assumption of power or whether the murders were the result of the functioning of a huge bureaucracy run amok). He also examines the many problems associated with any attempt to get at the "real" Hitler, such as the dearth of written documents he left and the highly emotionalized and sensationalized accounts of most people who knew him.

Lukacs addresses a problem apparently dear to his own heart in chapter 2: whether Hitler's ideas crystallized in Vienna—as Hitler himself said in *Mein Kampf* (1925-1927) and as most historians have uncritically accepted—or whether they actually solidified in Munich, as Lukacs believes. He examines all the relevant works in English and German to arrive at the conclusion that Hitler's *Weltanschauung* (worldview) did not form fully until after he returned to Munich after World War I. The chapter also explores what Lukacs calls the turning points of Hitler's life. The author again critiques most of the major biographies of Hitler to arrive at the conclusion that there were four, possibly five, such points: Hitler's arrival in Vienna in 1908, his move to Munich in 1919, his release from prison in 1924, and his obsession with the idea that he did not have long to live that he developed in 1937-1938. Lukacs thinks that the fifth turning point may have been in November, 1941, when he realized he could no longer win the war on his own terms. Lukacs believes that it was at this point that Hitler decided on the mass murder of Jews.

Lukacs raises the question in chapter 3 of whether Hitler was a reactionary, as some historians have concluded, or a revolutionary, as other biographers have argued. After a thorough examination of the literature on the subject, Lukacs concludes that Hitler was a "populist revolutionary" who led a party made up of representatives from all classes of society, all religious persuasions, and all regions of Germany (a true *volkspartei*). He also argues that Hitler had a demonstrable genius for politics and an instinctive genius for economics that led to the economic miracle in Germany between 1933 and 1938, and that Hitler's programs were modern, looking toward the future rather than the past. Lukacs makes the curious observation in this chapter that Hitler used anti-Marxist rhetoric in his speeches without actually being an anti-Marxist, rejecting the contentions of Ernst Nolte that, reduced to its essentials, Nazism was nothing more or less than militant opposition to Marxism.

Chapters 4 and 5 explore Hitler's relationship to the state and the people of the Third Reich and Hitler's abilities as a statesman and as a military commander, again through an examination of the historical literature on the subjects and Hitler biographies. In these chapters, Lukacs comes to several unorthodox conclusions, such as that Hitler never intended to exercise dictatorial/totalitarian power but wanted to rule with the consent of his people, that Hitler was *not* a racist but an extreme nationalist, and that Hitler's aim was to unify the German people into one Reich that would become the greatest power in Europe, not, as some historians have maintained, to conquer the world. The author also unoriginally identifies the drive for *lebensraum* (living space) and judeophobia as the most consistent parts of Hitler's policies. (Lukacs does not explain how one can be a judeophobe without being a racist.) Almost alone of all the historians whose works he surveys, Lukacs praises Hitler's skills as a military commander, identifying him as an instinctual strategist. Lukacs apparently attributes Hitler's military setbacks to bad luck and the actions of his generals.

In chapter 5, Lukacs argues that Hitler underwent a psychological and physiological transformation in 1937-1938, when he became convinced that his health was deteriorating and that he did not have many years left to live. Lukacs observes that Hitler became obsessed with accomplishing his foreign policy objectives quickly, risking war if necessary, but never actually *wanting* war. In this chapter, Lukacs indulges in much speculation about Hitler's diplomatic and military strategy based on very limited evidence.

Chapter 6 ruminates (again through the prism of what other historians have written about the subject) on Hitler's strange obsession with the "Jewish problem." After noting that the subject remains highly emotional, Lukacs proceeds to try to get at the reasons for this obsession. After examining the voluminous literature that has attempted to psychoanalyze Hitler (in particular Waite's *The Psychopathic God: Adolf Hitler*, 1977), Lukacs concludes that the true reasons for the obsession may never be known but that they had their roots in Hitler's autodidactic education and the huge gaps in his knowledge of the world. Lukacs maintains convincingly that Hitler was not intent on murdering the Jews from the beginning of his regime; rather, the mass murders resulted from military reverses on the eastern front. According to this interpretation, the "final solution" to the Jewish problem was the deportation of all Jews living in German-occupied Europe to regions conquered from the Soviet Union. There the Jews would become either tenant farmers, on estates overseen by Germans, or small craftsmen and skilled laborers in the villages and cities. The process of rounding up Jews and transporting them to transit camps in Poland had already begun when the war turned against Germany during the winter of 1941-1942. As more and more Jews poured into these transit camps, which were unequipped to feed them or see to their medical and physical needs, Germans began their systematic program of mass murder. Lukacs also argues that Hitler must have ordered the mass murders either in writing or by verbal instructions, regardless of the lack of a paper trail leading directly to him.

Lukacs tackles the contentious problem in chapter 7 of whether Hitler and the Third Reich represent the logical outcome of previous German history or whether they were in fact aberrations made possible by a very special set of circumstances. After examining most of the relevant literature on the subject, Lukacs concludes that Hitler was not the *sole* logical outcome of previous German history, but one possibility out of many. Lukacs acknowledges that Hitler could never have come to power without the widespread resentment engendered in Germans by the Treaty of Versailles and the recurrent economic dislocations in German society caused by such calamities as the great inflation of 1922-1924 and the Great Depression.

Lukacs devotes chapter 8 to condemning admirers and defenders (open and secret) of Hitler. He surveys the literature produced by those he perceives to be Hitler apologists such as David Irving, John Toland, and Ernst Nolte (how Nolte could possibly fit into this category is not at all clear), finding this literature unconvincing in its entirety though not in some of its particulars. Lukacs seems prepared to acknowledge that Hitler was a human with virtues as well as faults, but he nevertheless insists on the underlying evil of Hitler's nature.

In the final chapter, Lukacs speculates on Hitler's place in history. Was Hitler a "great" man? Here Lukacs argues that one's answer to that question will depend on one's definition of "greatness." The author points out that Hitler's many accomplishments must be weighed against the results of his rule—the almost total destruction of Germany and the permanent scar left on the psyches of people everywhere that resulted from the revelation of Auschwitz. Lukacs concludes that the observation that if "great" should be applied to men who had an abiding influence on the society of their time, then Hitler surely must be called great. If by "great," however, is meant a man who has had a *beneficial* influence on his society and his time, then Hitler is surely the antithesis of great.

SOURCES FOR FURTHER STUDY

Ledford, Kenneth. "Seeking the Real Hitler: Survey Winnows Literature for Truth." *Cleveland Plain Dealer*, October 19, 1997, p. 13.

Lehmann-Haupt, Christopher. "Reconciling Madman and Patriot." *The New York Times*, October 30, 1997, p. E8.

Lukacs, John. *Confessions of an Original Sinner*. 1990. Reprint. South Bend, Ind.: St. Augustine's Press, 2000.

———. *Remembered Past: John Lukacs on History, Historians, and Historical Knowledge.* Edited by Mark G. Malvasi and Jeffrey O. Nelson. Wilmington, Del.: ISI Books, 2005.

Rosenbaum, Ron. "Springtime for Hitler." *Los Angeles Times*, November 23, 1997, p. 12.

—*Paul Madden*

HITLER'S WILLING EXECUTIONERS
ORDINARY GERMANS AND THE HOLOCAUST

AUTHOR: Daniel Jonah Goldhagen (1959-   )
FIRST PUBLISHED: 1996
GENRE: Nonfiction
SUBGENRE: History

Touting his book as a much-needed revision of Holocaust scholarship, Goldhagen argues that German anti-Semitism was the central cause that induced thousands of "ordinary Germans" to slaughter European Jewry while millions more of them actively collaborated in the Holocaust or at least gave their compliant approval for that genocide.

OVERVIEW

Begin with a young Harvard professor of government who is as bright as he is brash and whose ways with words are as pretentious as they are perplexing. Take his doctoral dissertation and turn it into a book whose methodology, tone, and content intentionally collide with judgments of the major scholars in the field. Promote the book in ways that propel it to international best-seller status and hurl its largely unknown author into the media spotlight. Such ingredients are bound to cause a stir. Focus them on a topic charged with intense feeling and profound implications—the Holocaust, the annihilation of the European Jews by Nazi Germany and its collaborators—and the resulting controversy will come to a boil. So it has been with Daniel Jonah Goldhagen and *Hitler's Willing Executioners: Ordinary Germans and the Holocaust*.

Even when they are about immensely important subjects such as the Holocaust, six-hundred-page history books rarely get the attention that Goldhagen's has received. Repeatedly finding his research at odds with their own, most Holocaust scholars in the United States, Europe, and Israel do not give Goldhagen marks to match the high sales figures that his book has enjoyed. For mainly good reasons, the leading scholars whom Goldhagen vies to supplant take his methodology to be suspect, the tone of his writing to be arrogant and disdainful of even the best work in Holocaust studies, and his research results to be either far less original than Goldhagen claims or perniciously incorrect to the point of being destructive because they reignite undeserved prejudices against Germans and Jews alike.

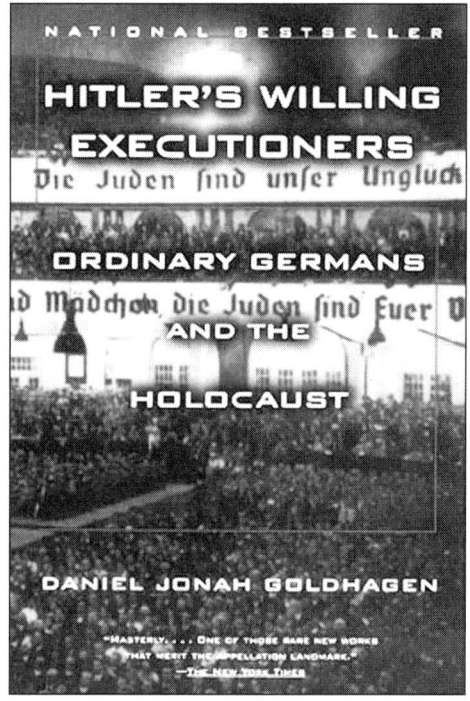

What did Goldhagen say—and how did he say it—to provoke such critical reactions, which, ironically, call even greater attention to his book? Note, first, that *Hitler's Willing Executioners* was preceded, even scooped, by the work of Christopher R. Browning, a distinguished historian who published a 1992 work that has achieved classic status in Holocaust studies. Browning called his book *Ordinary Men*. It analyzed the postwar judicial interrogations of 210 members of Reserve Police Battalion 101, a 500-man killing squadron of the German Order Police that was responsible for 83,000 Jewish deaths in Poland during the so-called final solution.

Goldhagen targeted Browning's book when he chose *Ordinary Germans and the Holocaust* as the subtitle for *Hitler's Willing Executioners*. Having probed the same archival material about Reserve Police Battalion 101 that Browning had investigated, Goldhagen believed that Browning mishandled and misinterpreted the data. Specifically, Goldhagen contended that Browning underestimated the extent and depth of anti-Semitism in Germany and played down its tenacious grip and deadly influence on the German people. Furthermore, Goldhagen charged that Browning wrongly advanced a universalistic perspective about the Holocaust. In Goldhagen's judgment, that outlook inadequately explained the killing behavior of the men in Reserve Police Battalion 101 by taking conformity to peer pressure, blind acceptance of current political norms, and careerism to be among its chief motivational causes.

Browning's interpretation did stress that the reserve policemen, German though they were and anti-Semitic though they may have been, were of special significance because they were also very ordinary human beings. He maintained that the story of Reserve Police Battalion 101 should cause, at the very least, discomfort for men and women everywhere. For as post-Holocaust history shows, people in other times and places—people like *us*—are also capable of complicity in genocide. Goldhagen was not impressed, let alone persuaded. He found fault with Browning's book because it missed what he regarded as the essential point about the Holocaust: Only the deep-seated racist anti-Semitism that infested the German people could motivate, and thus account for, the behavior of particular Germans who committed the atrocities that advanced the "final solution."

Making his case, however, obliged Goldhagen to do more than disagree with Browning's interpretation of the archival records about Reserve Police Battalion 101. He would have to show, first, that "Germans' anti-Semitic beliefs about Jews were the central causal agent of the Holocaust," a claim that required him not only to trace the history of German anti-Semitism but also to document how that history involved authority and power fatal enough to account for the Holocaust's vast destruction. In addition, Goldhagen's case would hinge on demonstrating that "ordinary Germans"—not just rabidly anti-Semitic Nazis who had the political power to define social reality and to dominate a German population that might be more ambivalent about the so-called Jewish question—either willingly engaged in the slaughter or were so willing to let it go forward that they would have become active killers if called on to do so. In short, Goldhagen had to show that the Holocaust, contrary to Browning's "ordinary men" hypothesis, was essentially the willful act of "ordinary Germans," who were much more lethally anti-Semitic than previous scholarship admitted.

To establish these positions, Goldhagen's book argues in two directions that govern its organization. Beginning with the history of German anti-Semitism, Goldhagen aims to show how, in particular, a potentially lethal anti-Jewish racism had a powerful influence in pre-Nazi Germany. Then he focuses on the actual German perpetrators of the Holocaust, studying specifically the personnel and work of killing squadrons such as Reserve Police Battalion 101 and the parts played by other "ordinary Germans" in the huge system of concentration, labor, and death camps that was, as he correctly puts it, "the emblematic institution of Germany during its Nazi period." To these perspectives, he adds detail, as hideous as it is valuable, about a lesser-known aspect of the Holocaust, namely, the brutal "death marches" that took place from late 1939 until the end of World War II.

As it moves in both of these directions—one looking toward a Holocaust that had not yet taken place, the other looking back from the "final solution" to determine how it happened—Goldhagen's basic argument can be summarized in two syllogisms. They reason as follows: First, ordinary Germans were anti-Semitic. Their anti-Semitism entailed elimination of the Jews. Therefore, ordinary Germans were prepared to be willing executioners. Second, far from being reluctant murderers, some Germans actually became willing executioners of the European Jews. Typically, those same Germans were a representative cross section of the German population. Therefore, with exceptions that only prove the rule, ordinary Germans stand indicted for the destruction of the European Jews.

Goldhagen's evidence for these claims derives initially from an appraisal of the history of anti-Semitism in Germany. According to his reading of that history, venomous forms of cultural and racist anti-Semitism became normative in Germany in the nineteenth and twentieth centuries, well before Hitler and the Nazi Party gained power in 1933. Such anti-Semitism called for the elimination of Jews and Jewish influence in Germany. In one way or another, then, the vast majority of the German populace was prepared to destroy Jews.

When the Nazis came to power, they advocated an overtly *exterminationist* anti-Semitism. Crucial to Goldhagen's argument is his claim that this exterminationist ideology was only a variation on the already *eliminationist* anti-Semitism that had existed in Germany for some time. During the Nazi period, 1933-1945, German perpetrators of the Holocaust willingly persecuted and destroyed Jews because they basically shared the Nazis' anti-Semitic perspective. This perspective held that the annihilation of the Jews was necessary and just because they were an unremitting pestilence threatening the racial superiority and political prerogatives that properly belonged to Germans.

Given legitimacy by the Nazi regime, the German killers, according to Goldhagen, were not an extraordinary minority. Instead, they were representative of the German populace. Goldhagen's logic entails this relationship to mean that the vast majority of Germans were not only willing to let the Holocaust happen but also would have participated directly in the killing if the need enjoined them to do so.

Goldhagen's reading of the pre-Holocaust history of German anti-Semitism musters his evidence that ordinary Germans were possible perpetrators and accomplices in a potential but not yet real "final solution." This part of his account makes it no surprise, however, that the potential elimination of German Jews became the actual destruction of the European Jews. While recognizing that this movement from potential to actual annihilation has many dimensions and multiple causes, Goldhagen holds that too many scholars have agonized needlessly, often to the point of confusion, in their misguided efforts to show why and how the Holocaust happened.

Ever confident of the superiority of his own judgment, Goldhagen thinks that few puzzles remain about the Holocaust's causes. Although explaining how the Holocaust happened remains a long story, he believes that there is no need to dwell on most of the complexities that so much causal analysis of the Holocaust has produced. As Goldhagen sees it, the Holocaust had one cause that outweighed the others. Direct and straightforward, it involved the motivation without which the Holocaust was unthinkable, namely, the Germans' anti-Semitic beliefs about Jews. Remove that factor and the Holocaust that actually happened would not have taken place. On the other hand, to realize the "final solution," the anti-Semitism of Goldhagen's ordinary Germans did need the catalyst that Hitler and the Nazi Party provided. Nevertheless, by themselves Hitler and the Nazi Party alone could not have made the Holocaust happen as it did. The actual Holocaust required willing, ordinary Germans to effect it.

Fanatically anti-Semitic as they were, Goldhagen suggests, Hitler and the Nazi Party had a reciprocal relationship with ordinary Germans when it came to the Jewish question. In Hitler and the Nazi Party, ordinary Germans got the organization, determination, and legitimation to carry out their latent, if not active, will to destroy European Jewry. In ordinary Germans, Hitler and the Nazi Party found a people who were well prepared to carry out the plan for a Third Reich that would be *judenrein* ("cleansed of Jews"). Thus, when Goldhagen reckons with the actuality of the Holocaust, his book becomes much more than an explanation of how he thinks the Holocaust took place. With his view that the Germans' anti-Semitic motivation was the most crucial condition—necessary though not alone sufficient—for the Holocaust, Goldhagen indicts "ordinary Germans," a category as broad as it is undiscriminating, and renders a sweeping verdict of collective German guilt.

Goldhagen's book has its merits. They exist primarily in his expansion of some details about the "final solution," but not in the book's specious promise to achieve a groundbreaking analysis that meets a need—more imagined than real—for "radical revision" of nearly all previous scholarship on the Holocaust. Nowhere is this appraisal of his book more apt than in regard to his claim that "German's antisemitic beliefs about Jews were the central causal agent of the Holocaust."

Goldhagen is wrong when he implies that scholars such as Raul Hilberg, Yehuda Bauer, and Christopher Browning have "denied or obscured" the importance of German anti-Semitism. What they and other leading Holocaust scholars have done, however, is to avoid the oversimplifications that make and break Goldhagen's book. Anti-semitism, for example, was a major current in pre-Nazi times. Nevertheless, while Goldhagen's work fills in empirical details about that ugly picture, pre-Nazi anti-Semitism in Germany was not primarily the essentially lethal variety that Goldhagen requires to make his claims hold. Conveniently dismissing any evidence to the contrary as insufficient or inadequate, failing to do the comparative work that ought to modify his extreme views about German anti-Semitism by placing it in a larger European context, Goldhagen relies too much on an assumed German uniformity to buttress his case.

At times Goldhagen emphasizes that his "ordinary Germans" must not be caricatured as a slavish, order-obeying people and that their freedom of choice should be recognized as crucial if they are to be held responsible for their Holocaust-related actions. To cite one of Christopher Browning's succinct rebuttals, however, Goldhagen ignores his own principles by describing ordinary Germans as basically "undifferentiated, unchanging, possessed by a single, monolithic cognitive outlook," especially as far as Jews were concerned before and during the Holocaust.

How will Goldhagen's work stand the test of time? Will it be more than a 1996 international book sensation? In deliberately provocative ways, Goldhagen has raised issues about Germans, Jews, anti-Semitism, and Holocaust scholarship that will not be taken lightly by any of the parties involved. At least for a time, his book will continue to be the subject of impassioned debate. In the long run, however, *Hitler's Willing Executioners* is likely to be much less than it was hyped to be. More than anything else, it will be remembered in the history of Holocaust studies as a phenomenon that did more harm than good.

Sources for Further Study

Eley, Geoff, ed. *The "Goldhagen Effect": History, Memory, Nazism—Facing the German Past*. Ann Arbor: University of Michigan Press, 2000.

Finkelstein, Norman G., and Ruth Bettina Birn. *A Nation on Trial: The Goldhagen Thesis and Historical Truth*. New York: Henry Holt, 1998.

Kautz, Fred. *The German Historians: "Hitler's Willing Executioners" and Daniel Goldhagen*. New York: Black Rose, 2003.

Shandley, Robert R., ed. *Unwilling Germans? The Goldhagen Debate*. With essays translated by Jeremiah Riemer. Minneapolis: University of Minnesota Press, 1998.

Wesley, Frank. *The Holocaust and Anti-Semitism: The Goldhagen Argument and Its Effects*. San Francisco: International Scholars, 1999.

—*John K. Roth*

The Holocaust in American Life

Author: Peter Novick (1934-   )
First published: 1999
Genre: Nonfiction
Subgenres: History; current affairs

Analyzing the importance given to the Holocaust in the United States at the end of the twentieth century, Novick assesses the policies of American Jewish leaders, disputes the Holocaust's usefulness as a source of moral lessons, and questions the wisdom of the American emphasis on the Holocaust.

Overview

The Holocaust, Nazi Germany's destruction of the European Jews, took place far away from the United States where the Jewish population—about 3 percent—is a relatively small part of the total. By the 1990's, however, this event loomed large in American life. Curious about that prominence and skeptical about its desirability, Peter Novick, an American Jewish scholar who is a prizewinning historian at the University of Chicago, went to work on *The Holocaust in American Life*. As contentious and controversial as it is diligently researched and lucidly written, Novick's unrelenting arguments debunk conventional wisdom about Holocaust memorialization in the United States. Persistently provocative, Novick's polemical book makes enough unpopular claims to guarantee that debate about it will not end any time soon.

"Why now?" Novick asks about Americans' growing consciousness of the Holocaust. Right off, his response advances an arguable proposition: Shortly after they occur, historical events are usually talked about the most; then they gradually recede from the spotlight. The Holocaust, he thinks, defies that trend. For twenty years after World War II, the Holocaust was barely named as such, let alone discussed much in the United States. From the 1970's on, however, it became "ever more central in American public discourse." A key reason for the Holocaust's relatively late impact on the American scene, Novick contends, is that reference to "the Holocaust" as a distinct event is "largely a retrospective construction."

Novick does not deny that the Holocaust happened. To the contrary, he stresses the reality of Nazi Germany's genocidal attack on European Jewry. Therefore, he distinguishes between "the *historicity* of events" and "collective memory" about them. Awareness of the former, Novick explains, entails understanding historical events in their "messy complexity," which involves "circumstances different from those that now obtain." Following the French sociologist Maurice Halbwachs, Novick claims that collective memory, which he finds dominating Holocaust remembrance, may be "ahistorical, even anti-historical," for it tends to simplify and mythologize history as "present concerns determine what of the past we remember and how we remember it."

At the beginning of the twenty-first century, Americans of all kinds memorialize the Holocaust, but when Germans were actually shooting and gassing Europe's Jews en masse, American attention was understandably occupied by the overall course of World War II and especially the war against Japan in the Pacific. In government circles, let alone the public mind, nothing like contemporary awareness of the Holocaust existed. According to Novick, only in the late 1960's, after the 1961 Israeli trial of Nazi war criminal Adolf Eichmann increased Holocaust news, did many Americans consider the Holocaust as "a distinct—and distinctively Jewish—entity." Even this American awareness was far removed from what the power of collective memory would make of the Holocaust during the next thirty years.

Unsatisfied, Novick's curiosity relates one question, "Why now?" to another, "Why here?" How did awareness of the Holocaust, an event so distant from most American experience, take root in the United States at all? Novick responds that Holocaust consciousness in the United States would not have caught on apart from American Jewry's self-interested choices. Far from a Jewish conspiracy to impose Holocaust consciousness on the United States, these choices, "shaped and constrained by circumstances," were primarily about American Jewry's "collective self-understanding and self-representation." Nevertheless, despite the relatively small number of people who advanced them, those decisions became sufficiently powerful to affect a much larger American public.

Rejecting the often-repeated theory that the Holocaust's trauma was so severe that testimony about it was repressed for years, Novick stresses that postwar attention to the Holocaust grew in the United States only when Jewish interests dictated that it should. Until the late 1960's, the American "market" for Holocaust interests was small. True, American sympathy for the plight of Holocaust survivors helped to support the 1948 establishment of the State of Israel, but, on the whole, American Jewish leadership saw no advantage in promoting widespread attention to the Holocaust's horror.

Doing so would underwrite an image of the Jew as victim, an outcome sure to create unwanted dissonance with the postwar American optimism shared by most Jewish Americans. Jewish promotion of Holocaust consciousness also would have conflicted with the American need to rehabilitate West Germany as a Cold War buttress against the Soviet Union. It followed that most of the recently arrived Holocaust survivors in the United States—Novick estimates that they numbered about 100,000—accepted the message that American Jewry would get along best if they kept their Holocaust experiences to themselves, put the past behind them, and got on with their new American lives.

Still underscoring that American Jewry's interests led the way, Novick's account continues by arguing that decisive changes in Americans' Holocaust consciousness emerged not only from two Israeli wars—the 1967 Six-Day War and especially the Yom Kippur War of 1973—but also from domestic developments. Although the Israelis prevailed in both wars, a threatened Israel, isolated in the Middle East, produced renewed Holocaust fears as well as efforts to ensure that memory of the Holocaust would not fade, a movement accompanied, Novick thinks, by a real but unwarranted suspicion that American Jews themselves faced the isolating effects of renewed anti-Semitism in the United States.

Holding the debatable position that there was not much to hold Jewish identity together in the increasingly secular American culture, where intermarriage and other assimilationist forces were also at work, Novick contends that the Jewish leadership in the United States increasingly linked Jewish identity to Holocaust memory and memorialization. As changing perceptions of Jewish need caused the Holocaust to be remembered anew, the chosen approach reversed earlier trends by stressing that even American Jews were potentially, if not actually, victims of processes that would dilute, diminish, and perhaps destroy the vitality of Jewish life. Novick adds that these Holocaust-related appeals were bolstered by complementary cultural changes in American life that highlighted the diversity of ethnic identities in the United States by acknowledging and even celebrating the victimization that various minority groups had experienced in their histories. All these factors combined to stimulate an intensified Jewish accent on the "sacralization" and uniqueness of the Holocaust. This burgeoning emphasis on the Holocaust, Novick suggests, then spread into the American mainstream largely because American Jewry's "influential role in Hollywood, the television industry, and the newspaper, magazine, and book publishing worlds" worked in that direction.

Although Novick stresses again that no "Jewish conspiracy" governed these developments, he focuses on an expanding Jewish awareness that

"Americans could be made more sympathetic to Israel, or to American Jews, through awareness of the Holocaust." NBC's four-part, nine and one-half hour *Holocaust* miniseries provided evidence to support that belief by drawing an audience of almost one hundred million American viewers when it aired in 1978, the same year in which President Jimmy Carter established the President's Commission of the Holocaust to explore the creation of a national Holocaust memorial. The result of this initiative eventually included the observance of "Days of Remembrance of Victims of the Holocaust" (ceremonies are held annually in the Capitol rotunda) and the building of the United States Holocaust Memorial Museum in Washington, D.C. Since it opened in 1993, the same year in which filmgoers jammed theaters to see Steven Spielberg's Academy Award-winning adaptation of Thomas Keneally's *Schindler's List* (1983; first published in 1982 as *Schindler's Ark*), the museum has received millions of American visitors—most of them Gentiles—every year.

As the twenty-first century begins, Novick observes that the Holocaust has entered American life to such a degree that it has become, "except for hermits, inescapable." He finds this outcome more harmful than beneficial. American Jewish identity, he claims, has become too Holocaust-dependent, a lightning-rod thesis that has drawn reaction both supportive and critical. Novick also believes that the Holocaust's impact on Americans' consciousness has been less than many people think, an evaluation that produces more clashing rejoinders, especially when Novick finds it dubious that attention to the Holocaust teaches moral lessons.

Peter Novick. (© Fredric Stein)

Empty, unnecessary, irrelevant, ineffective—these are only some of the faultfinding barbs that Novick hurls at "lessons of the Holocaust." Convinced both that the Holocaust was so extreme that it has little connection to ordinary life and that the Holocaust could be no more nor less a source of "lessons" than, say, the Irish potato famine—views subject to criticism for trivializing the Holocaust—Novick thinks that the Holocaust's supposedly "universal" lessons (for example, society must not be indifferent to evil) are so obvious as to be clichés, so general as to be empty, and too vague to be relevant or effective. Although Novick admits that visits to Holocaust museums and courses about the Holocaust may "sensitize" people about other atrocities, he doubts that this payoff actually occurs. For most Americans, he complains, "contemplating the Holocaust is virtually cost-free: a few cheap tears." In his judgment, however, the price of such contemplation is very high indeed, for he suspects that it promotes "*evasion* of moral and historical responsibility." Although Novick provides no empirical evidence to support these allegations, he vigorously presses his indictments nonetheless.

Novick protests too much. Insisting that he is "skeptical about the so-called lessons of history," Novick obviously thinks it is good to study historical events, especially when they are confronted in all their complexity and contradictions. His reasoning implies, moreover, that such work is fundamentally ethical, and he compares it to that of a medical researcher who studies diseases knowing that expressions of moral outrage or clinging to unexamined preconceptions will not be very helpful in achieving the goal of checking, if not eliminating them. If Novick takes his medical research analogy seriously, then his historical work, which emphasizes the Holocaust, surely involves an analogous goal—namely, to limit, if not to cure, the genocidal ills that afflict humanity. Insights about progress in that direction, if they can be found, are not going to be of Novick's straw-man variety—ones that fit on bumper stickers or that shape and shade the past so that inspiring lessons emerge. Nevertheless, his chosen analogy does not suggest that historical study is an end in itself. People study disease—and, at least in part, the Holocaust—for the sake of future prevention and cure. In the case of the Holocaust, to do otherwise would be tantamount to indifference to the awe and horror that Novick finds always appropriate when one confronts the Holocaust.

Apparently Novick loathes lessons. Nevertheless, ironically if not inconsistently, he prescribes one Holocaust-related lesson after another. His lessons are virtually imperatives: Focus on the historicity of the Holocaust. Approach collective memory of the Holocaust with skepticism. Do not link Jewish identity too closely to the Holocaust. Be cautious in assuming that the Holocaust's impact on Gentile Americans is as deep as it is broad. Novick rejects some "lessons of the Holocaust" only to advance his own versions of them.

Novick's long list of Holocaust-related lessons contains one of special importance: Americans—Gentiles and Jews—should be realistic about the future of the Holocaust in American life. Holocaust consciousness has grown immensely in the United States, but without much regret Novick argues that current trends in American culture, and in American Jewish life particularly, are unlikely to sustain the dubious centrality that the Holocaust achieved at the twentieth century's end. Many will disagree, but he affirms that expanded emphasis on the Holocaust is no longer needed to defend Israel, to check anti-Semitism, to fortify Jewish religious and cultural identity, or even to combat the dangers of Holocaust denial.

According to Novick, American Jewish interests can now live optimistically, flourishing in a post-Holocaust age whose times will include the demystifying effect that the passing of the last survivors will entail and a reduction of Holocaust-related news as the event recedes further into the past. Novick neither hopes nor believes, however, that the Holocaust will be forgotten. He offers reassurance that commemoration and memory of the Holocaust have been successfully institutionalized. Professionalized Holocaust scholarship and teaching will continue to ensure the Holocaust's presence in American culture. If the outcome is a more moderate Holocaust presence in the United States, Novick suggests, that result is one that Americans—Jews in particular—should embrace, because, among other things, it will deny Hitler the posthumous victory that would be his if Jews make Holocaust victimhood "the emblematic Jewish experience."

At times misguidedly contentious, *The Holocaust in American Life* deserves a place among the noteworthy books of 1999 because it raises so many fundamental challenges about how the Holocaust should be remembered in the United States. Novick's basic argument is that it would be better for American Jewry, more honest for Americans generally, and more respectful for the Holocaust itself if that event had a less hyped and a more modest part in American culture. In a book full of ironies, however, the final one may turn out to be that Novick's work will have the opposite effect.

Sources for Further Study

Bresnick, Adam. "Is It Good for the Jews?" *Los Angeles Times*, September 5, 1999, p. 6.
Kakutani, Michiko. "Taking Aim at the Symbolism of the Holocaust." *The New York Times*, August 17, 1999, p. E6.
Lang, Berel. "On Peter Novick's *The Holocaust in American Life*." *Jewish Social Studies* 7, no. 3 (Spring, 2001): 149.
Lederhendler, Eli. "On Peter Novick's *The Holocaust in American Life*." *Jewish Social Studies* 7, no. 3 (Spring, 2001): 159.

Popkin, Jeremy D. "Holocaust Memory: Bad for the Jews?" *Judaism* 50, no. 1 (Winter, 2001): 112.

Stone, Marla. "Holocaust Infatuation." *Tikkun* 14, no. 5 (September/October, 1999): 75.

Wolf, Arnold Jacob. "The Shoah in America." *Judaism* 48, no. 4 (Fall, 1999): 490.

—*John K. Roth*

Holocaust Politics

Author: John K. Roth (1940-   )
First published: 2001
Genre: Nonfiction
Subgenres: History; religion and spirituality

This work asserts that we must teach, study, learn, "own," and commemorate the Holocaust if we are to prevent the recurrence of such genocide and become more deeply empathic and sensitive humans, responsible for our own actions and their effects on others. Roth notes that, although the Catholic Church's anti-Jewish teachings helped create the environment for the Holocaust, Christians and Jews are positively interconnected.

Overview

In his prologue, "What Is Holocaust Politics?" John K. Roth recognizes our lack of intellectual, emotional, and spiritual closure over the Holocaust, the torture and killings of Jews and others by the Nazi regime in the 1930's and 1940's during World War II. We will never comprehend the "how" or "why" of this atrocity because the depth and breadth of its evil defy all of our assumptions about civilized human behavior. Holocaust politics involves such issues as Holocaust denial, memorializing, and financial restitution to survivors. In arguing that ethics needs to be an integral part of Holocaust politics, Roth insists that Holocaust study should be done not as an end in itself but solely as a means to an end: human betterment.

In chapter 1, "Who Owns the Holocaust?" Roth points out how difficult it is to provide restitution for survivors when such debts are incalculable. Do Jews "own" the Holocaust, or does it belong to the Germans or others (Gypsies, homosexuals, Jehovah's Witnesses) who were slaughtered? Roth concludes that all humanity "owns" the burdens, lessons, and responsibilities of the Holocaust as well as the necessity to become more deeply caring and loving humans.

In chapter 2, "What Can and Cannot Be Said About the Holocaust?" Roth debates whether the Holocaust (the conscious, systematic annihilation of an innocent people) is unique and exceeds the bounds of historical comparison. It is a chilling irony that German chancellor Adolf Hitler was *Time* magazine's Man of the Year in 1938, and was considered for Man of the Century in 1999. Although historians have researched details of Hitler's life and the Holocaust, we will never fully understand or explain the man or the genocide; clearly, we must study both with deep commitment to truth.

In chapter 3, "How Is the Holocaust Best Remembered?" Roth explains our obligation to study and teach the particularity of the Holocaust, since eventually no living witness will remain. We must also study what happened before the Holocaust—such as Pope Pius XI's failure in 1938 to condemn Nazi racism—and after it: Only 12 of 142 defendants found guilty were actually executed, despite the best efforts of the Nuremberg tribunal.

In chapter 4, "How Is the Holocaust a Warning?" Roth insists that the Holocaust warns us to reevaluate all human knowledge, philosophy, and assumptions about values. Holocaust politics exhorts us not to take our freedom or dreams for granted and not to practice a xenophobic "us" versus "them" mentality. Indeed, we must remember Holocaust researcher Gitta Sereny's caveat that we are responsible for ourselves as well as others because of "the fatal interdependence of all human actions."

In chapter 5, "Holocaust Politics and Post-Holocaust Christianity," Roth explains that the Papal Concert to Commemorate the Holocaust in 1994 did not go far enough to acknowledge Catholic anti-Semitism before and during the Holocaust; however, during Pope John Paul II's 2000 visit to Israel, he prayed for God's "forgiveness for Jewish suffering caused by Christians." Christian anti-Jewish teachings throughout history created "dry kindling" that facilitated the conflagration of the Holocaust; Hitler had but to "light" the fateful "match." Absent Christian dissent to Nazi sadism, the flames of hate incinerated six million Jews. After Auschwitz, Christians need to focus on the "good news" that God's grace allows and live "full of Grace and Truth."

In chapter 6, "Ethics After Auschwitz," Roth avers that some historians feel that nothing is to be learned from the Holocaust, since all that we thought we knew of morality and ethics evaporates in such immeasurable hate. For example, destruction of the handicapped and other "undesirables" led quickly to the extermination of an "inferior race": Jews. None of this could have occurred, however, without the Catholic Church's demonizing of the Jews. By contrast, Jehovah's Witnesses, whose allegiance was only to God, were destroyed by the Nazis in part because they opposed Jewish persecution. Moreover, the good Christians of the French village Le Chambon-sur-Lignon, inspired by their pastor, André Trocmé, and his wife, Magda, successfully practiced active nonviolent resistance by sheltering some five thousand Jews and others from Nazi destruction. To counteract post-Holocaust ethical despair, we must look to God, demand human rights worldwide, and celebrate those rescuers and resisters who oppose the treachery of the perpetrators and bystanders.

In his epilogue, "Where Does Holocaust Politics Lead?" Roth concludes that there is more to be learned and remembered from the Holocaust than the historical event itself. Teachers of the Holocaust believe that a humane future world depends on the power of ethical education. We must keep our memory of the Holocaust potent, focused, moral, detailed, and unclouded so that we may speak out loudly and clearly to condemn the destructiveness of racism, to celebrate those who did good and remained human in the midst of sociopathy and inhumanity, and to assert the inherent dignity of each human.

In playwright Arthur Miller's 1980 teleplay adaptation of Fania Fénelon's Holocaust memoir *Sursis pour l'orchestre*, 1976 (*Playing for Time*, 1981), Fénelon, just before liberation from Auschwitz, says, "We have changed . . . we know a little something about the human race that we didn't know before. And it's not good news." While Roth does not disagree, he counters that even after the Holocaust, there is "good news": "The Word became Flesh and lived among us, full of Grace and Truth" (John 1:14). Roth argues that there would be no Christianity without Judaism. Sadly, the Church has historically betrayed Jews by pronouncing them killers of Christ, sacrilegious, and descendants of Satan. While the Church did not implement the Holocaust, its false and defamatory teachings facilitated Hitler's "final solution to the Jewish question." While some Christians bravely imperiled their own and their families' safety by rescuing Jews, too many stood by or participated in the destruction.

However, Roth finds hope in the controversial Gospel of John, which has often been cited to justify anti-Semitism. In historical context, Roth argues that this Gospel, written during the bifurcation of traditional Jews and Jewish Christians, should never have created an adversarial relationship between Christians and Jews: In John 15:12, Jesus exhorts us to "love one another as I have loved you." Christians and Jews are clearly interrelated, as is clear in John 4:22 when Jesus says, "Salvation is from the Jews."

So brilliant and warming is God's light that, Roth writes, "in spite of the Holocaust, God abides." In the Gospel of John, Jesus' healing, feeding, and protecting of the sick, poor, and vulnerable—along with his resurrection—prove "that evil, despair, suffering and death do not have the last word." Grace is a gift from God. God's Hebrew name, "Yahweh," was translated into Greek as "I Am." In the Gospel of John, Jesus, too, "embodied God" when he said, "I am the light of the world," meaning that, like God, Jesus "does not permit darkness to prevail." Therefore Jesus, full of grace, the "good news" in a post-Holocaust world, should be a model of and conduit for compassion, love, and godly behavior.

By contrast with the godless lie emblazoned over the gates of Auschwitz, "Arbeit Macht Frei" ("Work Makes You Free"), Roth counters with the godliness of John 8:32, "The Truth will make you free." Le Chambon's pastor André Trocmé understood God's grace and truth and "the Word made Flesh"; the admonition "Love One Another" appeared at the entrance to his church.

Sources for Further Study

Beck, Norman A. *Mature Christianity in the Twenty-First Century: The Recognition and Repudiation of the Anti-Jewish Polemic of the New Testament.* New York: American Interfaith Institute/World Alliance, 1994.

Cargas, Harry James. *Shadows of Auschwitz: A Christian Response to the Holocaust.* New York: Crossroad, 1990.

Garber, Zev. Review of *Holocaust Politics*, by John K. Roth. *Shofar* 23, no. 1 (Fall, 2004): 141-143.

Hallie, Philip P. *Lest Innocent Blood Be Shed: The Story of the Village of Le Chambon, and How Goodness Happened There.* New York: Harper & Row, 1979.

Henschel, Stepanie N. "Ethics During the Holocaust: Professor Studies Effects of Anti-Semitism." *Jewish News of Greater Phoenix*, January 28, 2005, p. 17.

Rittner, Carol, and John K. Roth, eds. *"Good News" After Auschwitz? Christian Faith in a Post-Holocaust World.* Macon, Ga.: Mercer University Press, 2001.

Rittner, Carol, Stephen D. Smith, and Irena Steinfeldt, eds. *The Holocaust and the Christian World.* New York: Continuum, 2000.

Roth, John K. "Converting Dreams into Realities: Reflections on the Shadow of Birkenau." In *History, Religion, and Meaning: American Reflections on the Holocaust and Israel*, edited by Julius Simon. Westport, Conn.: Greenwood Press, 2000.

_____. "Good News After Auschwitz: Does Christianity Have Any?" In *"Good News" After Auschwitz? Christian Faith in a Post-Holocaust World*, edited by Carol Rittner and John K. Roth. Macon, Ga.: Mercer University Press, 2001.

Roth, John K., and Michael Berenbaum, eds. *Holocaust: Religion and Philosophical Implications.* St. Paul, Minn.: Paragon House, 1989.

—*Howard A. Kerner*

Holocaust Testimonies
The Ruins of Memory

Author: Lawrence L. Langer (1929-   )
First published: 1991
Genre: Nonfiction
Subgenres: History; oral history

Utilizing the Fortunoff Video Archive for Holocaust Testimonies at Yale University, Langer explores the oral histories of former victims of the Holocaust and shows how their testimonies affect understanding of that disaster.

Overview

Elie Wiesel survived Auschwitz, became a distinguished author, and, in 1986, was awarded the Nobel Peace Prize. In April, 1977, Wiesel gave an address at Northwestern University titled "The Holocaust as Literary Inspiration." Although he and other noted writers have made that disaster a fundamental dimension of their work, Wiesel contended that his talk's title contained a contradiction. His point was that the Holocaust, Nazi Germany's planned total destruction of the Jewish people and the actual murder of nearly six million of them, outstrips, overwhelms, and negates "literary inspiration." What happened then to Jewish children, women, and men—and to millions of non-Jewish victims who also were caught in the Holocaust—eludes complete expression, to say nothing of full comprehension, now.

Such claims involve no mystification. Nor do they deny that the Holocaust is an explicable historical event that was unleashed by human beings for human reasons. Yet, as disclosed by the testimony of those who survived it, the Holocaust remains at the depths of personal experience a disaster that no description can equal. Tempting though silence may be, it provides no refuge from this condition. Words to cry out of those depths must be found. Therefore, Wiesel's address at Northwestern underscored how significant it was that there were writers in every ghetto, witnesses in every camp, who did their best to testify.

In particular, Wiesel called attention to the diaries of Zalman Gradowski, Leib Langfuss, and Yankiel Wiernik. Trapped by what Lawrence L.

Langer calls "choice-less choices," those *Sonderkommando* members were condemned to burn the bodies of their Jewish brothers and sisters at Auschwitz-Birkenau and Treblinka. Listen, Wiesel urged, and then he read their words to his audience. Listen, listen—at one point, gripped by his own listening, Wiesel interrupted himself. "You must listen more," he insisted, "you must listen to more. I repeat, if Wiernik had the courage to write, you must listen." And then he read on.

No one has listened more or better than Lawrence Langer, a professor of English at Simmons College in Boston who had long been a leading interpreter of literature about the Holocaust. The proof is his *Holocaust Testimonies*. Profoundly, this book takes its readers into a region that Langer's subtitle aptly identifies as "the ruins of memory." Langer borrowed that phrase from another powerful writer, Ida Fink, whose personal Holocaust experiences led her to speak not about time "measured in months and years" but about time measured in scraps—separations, selections, silences—that forever fragment life and thwart its wholeness.

Langer's book results from years of painstaking excavation in the ruins of memory at the Fortunoff Video Archive for Holocaust Testimonies, established at Yale University in 1982. Its holdings—more than forty-three hundred testimonies that range in length from thirty minutes to more than four fours—are available for viewing. *Holocaust Testimonies* compels one to witness these moving accounts.

Langer himself conducted many of the archive's interviews with Holocaust survivors or "former victims," as he prefers to call them. But Langer's exceptional accomplishment goes much further than that. Few people, if any, have witnessed more Holocaust testimonies. Nor has anyone observed so many of them so carefully. Definitely no one has written about these testimonies with more intensity, honesty, and telling impact.

A governing theme in Langer's findings comes from Maurice Blanchot, the author of *L'Écriture du désastre* (1980; *The Writing of the Disaster*, 1986), a study that helped to inform Langer's listening. "The disaster ruins everything," Blanchot's first sentence says, "all the while leaving everything intact." Like nature's changing seasons, the rising and setting of the sun, apparently life goes on for the Holocaust's former victims. Many testify, for example, how they married after liberation from the German camps, built homes in new surroundings, reared children, and advanced careers. Apparently their survival led to living lives that left everything intact.

Only apparently, however, because the disaster leaves everything intact in another, far more devastating, sense. Leaving the survivors alone, it removes—takes the former victims away from—the stability and coherence that normal life assumes. Thus, for those who stayed alive after Auschwitz, life does anything but just go on. For the Holocaust's former victims, the disaster that came upon them so often pivoted around disorienting/orienting scraps of time, crucial moments involving what Blanchot calls the "sovereignty of the accidental," a tyranny that ruled and destroyed life with systematic capriciousness. Its disruptive impact makes the Holocaust a past ever present and always to be reencountered in the future.

Only one of the many testimonies that Langer sensitively weaves into his account, Philip K.'s epitomizes how "the disaster ruins everything." Resisting the reassurance of people "who pretend or seem to be marveling at the fact that I seem to be so normal, so unperturbed and so capable of functioning," Philip K. concludes *Holocaust Testimonies* by denying that "the Holocaust passed over and it's done with." No, he stresses, "it's my *skin*. This is not a coat. You can't take it off. And it's there, and it will be there until I die."

Ghettoized, starved, deported, tattooed, beaten, raped, gassed, burned, callously scattered to the winds, but some of it left permanently scarred to live—Holocaust skin both covers and recovers what Langer calls "an anatomy of melancholy." Physically rooted in the disaster, that anatomy is much more than skin-deep. Often buried deeply but incompletely by an impossible necessity to forget, the memory resurrected—but not triumphantly—by the anatomy of melancholy is laden with what another former victim, Charlotte Delbo, calls "useless knowledge." Dissenting from the conventional wisdom that knowledge is always useful, Delbo's phrase is another that echoes in Langer's listening, for *Holocaust Testimonies* shows how survival in Auschwitz did little to unify, edify, or dignify the lives of former victims. It divided, besieged, and diminished them instead.

Langer's account, it must be emphasized, protests against any impulse that would judge and find wanting what the former victims did in their conditions of Holocaust extremity. On the contrary, the entire book is an expression of esteem and admiration "to all the hundreds of men and women who told their stories before the camera." Judgment, to be sure, does speak in these pages—it seethes in quiet rage between the lines as one hears silently Langer's writing of the disaster—but that judgment is properly reserved for the German policies that systematized the Holocaust's choiceless choices and the perpetrators who administered them. The disaster that came upon the Holocaust's victims was designed to make evident what Nazi ideology proclaimed, namely, that Jews were subhuman or even nonhuman, and its plan for doing so was to create conditions of domination so extreme that normal human life could not go on within them. That plan did not succeed entirely, but in the Nazi camps, as Leon H. puts it, "human life was like a fly." Hunger, to mention but one of the Holocaust's hells, was not only "devastating to the human body," as George S. testifies, but also "devastating to the human spirit, . . . and you didn't know how to function."

The victims of *l'univers concentrationnaire* did what they had to do—"This wasn't good and that wasn't good," remembers Hannah F., "so what choice did we have?" Sidney L. adds to that realization when his testimony begins with the fact that he was one of nine children. The Holocaust's desolation left him as his family's lone survivor. One glimpses how far life under German domination was removed from usual human expectations about choice and responsibility when, with disarming simplicity, he recalls, "I was never asked 'Do you want to do such and such?'" The glimpse, however, remains incomplete—"Well, how shall I describe to you how Auschwitz was?" puzzles Edith P. Her question, which is asked in one way or another by many of the Holocaust witnesses Langer heard, seems addressed to herself as much as to her audience.

Speaking from his own experience, Langer rightly insists that listening to these testimonies requires extraordinary effort. They can easily be distorted and falsified by the imposition of moral, philosophical, psychological, or religious categories—including what Langer calls "the grammar of heroism and martyrdom"—that are inappropriate because they belong to a universe of normal discourse that the Holocaust eclipsed. After Auschwitz, the human mind would naturally like to reduce the dissonance that Holocaust testimonies introduce, heal the heartbreak left intact in their wake. The yearning runs deep—especially as one reads *Holocaust Testimonies*—for justice to prevail, wholeness to be restored, moral expectation to be vindicated, and the human spirit to be triumphant. But that yearning collides with Langer's convincing insistence that the anatomy of melancholy does not forecast a high probability in favor of those hopes. The reader is split by Langer's book. In the ruins of memory, expectation diminishes and yearning intensifies at once. As those feelings, conflicted and conflicting, resound in the testimony he has heard, Langer moves his reader to encounter them and to let the resulting tension remain as it must: unreconciled and unreconciling.

The stark bleakness of Langer's anatomy of melancholy calls for coming to terms, if one can, with a condition that recalls Blanchot once more. As though he had heard Helen K.'s lament ("I can't believe what my eyes have seen") and pondered the question posed by Edith P. and so many others ("Do you understand what I'm trying to tell you?"), Blanchot invites meditation on circumstances in which "there is a question and yet no doubt; there is a question, but no desire for an answer; there is a question, and nothing that can be said, but just this nothing, to say. This is a query, a probe that surpasses the very possibility of questions."

Optimism is scarce in the ruins of memory, but what Langer does find and carefully guard is "unshielded truth," an honesty that underscores what must be faced: "How overwhelming, and perhaps insurmountable," as he puts it, "is the task of reversing [the Holocaust's] legacy." That legacy dwells in memory that is deep, anguished, humiliated, tainted, and unheroic. Correspondingly, that memory disturbingly uncovers selves who are buried, divided, besieged, impromptu, and diminished. Such is the taxonomy that Langer's anatomy of melancholy requires.

Often with greater penetration than written narratives by former victims, Langer is convinced, their oral testimony divulges the disruptions within these dimensions of the Holocaust's legacy. Written words can be polished, edited, and revised; they can become art in ways that oral testimonies cannot. Langer wants both oral and written testimony to have the respect each kind deserves. So he stresses that written accounts by former victims typically have a narrative quality—beginning, middle, and end—that eludes their oral counterparts even when the latter move from pre-Holocaust events to those that occurred after liberation. Importantly, and thanks to the camera's eye, the oral testimonies that Langer heard are also visual. Spoken and unspoken, they communicate significantly through body language. In them hands and faces, especially eyes, have much to say. Such expressions, like the spoken thoughts they help to convey, are less controlled and controllable than written words.

Thus, even oral testimonies that start as chronological narratives are usually interrupted and disrupted by memories buried deep within—such as the one that constrains Edith P. to wonder, "Is there such a thing as love?" So harshly different from the world outside the ghettos and camps, such deep remembrances expose selves divided by the anguish they contain. "I talk to you," Isabella L. tells her interviewer, "and I am not only here, but I see Mengele [she lived in a barrack from which he chose women, including her sister, for his experiments] and I see the crematorium and I see all of that.... I am not like you. You have one vision of life and I have two. I—you know—I lived on two planets.... We have these... these double lives. We can't cancel out. It just won't go away.... It's very hard."

Within such anguish may be recollections of humiliation that besiege— "I left [my brother] there," laments Viktor C., "and I survived [prolonged weeping]. If I forget anything, this I will never forget." Even the present's recovered moral sensibility can taint memory by disapproving the impromptu acts one had to improvise—or failed to improvise—in the past: "How can you, how can you *enjoy* yourself?" Leo G. questions himself. The vulnerability that remains is intensified by recognition that Holocaust survival is less a heroic victory than a matter of chance. At times, Helen K. grieves, "I don't know if it was worth it."

These strains are not the only ones Langer heard. Some of the former victims tell about their determination to survive; they "knew" they would come out alive. Others accent their defiance against German brutality. There are also many who emphasize how important it has been for them to make their lives worthwhile and to retain some hope after Auschwitz. Philip K. speaks for many of his fellow survivors when he affirms, "We lost.... And yet we won, we're going on." Langer concludes that "several currents flow at differing depths in Holocaust testimonies." All of them, he adds, are "telling a version of the truth."

It would have been an immense contribution if Langer had only let those multiple truths be told. But the work he has done with such distinction—and it goes without saying how deeply he wishes history had not placed the task before him—required more. He met that demand by refusing the consolation that "a vocabulary of chronology and conjunction" could provide if it were permitted to transcend "a lexicon of disruption, absence, and irreversible loss." Declining that consolation, *Holocaust Testimonies* may make possible a greater sharing of the burden that goes with Langer's refusal. As this superb book helps its readers to understand, such sharing is awesome because it must contain all that Elie Wiesel meant when he testified that "the Holocaust demands interrogation and calls everything into question. Traditional ideas and acquired values, philosophical systems and social theories—all must be revised in the shadow of Birkenau."

SOURCES FOR FURTHER STUDY

Langer, Lawrence L. "Damaged Childhood in Holocaust Fact and Fiction." In *Humanity at the Limit: The Impact of the Holocaust Experience on Jews and Christians*, edited by Michael A. Signer. Bloomington: Indiana University Press, 2000.

_____. "Redefining Heroic Behavior: The Impromptu Self and the Holocaust Experience." In *Holocaust: Origins, Implementation, Aftermath*, edited by Omer Bartov. New York: Routledge, 2000.

Volf, Miroslav. "Redeeming the Past?" *The Christian Century* 119, no. 4 (February 13-20, 2002): 44.

—*John K. Roth*

House of Dolls

AUTHOR: Ka-tzetnik 135633 (Yehiel Feiner, also known as Yehiel Dinur or Yehiel De-Nur; 1909-2001)
FIRST PUBLISHED: *Bet ha-bubot*, 1953 (English translation, 1955)
GENRE: Novel
SUBGENRE: Psychological realism

This important work by a Holocaust survivor follows the lives of a Jewish sister and brother in Poland from the Kraków ghetto through their time in a Nazi concentration camp. Although bleak, the novel is ultimately uplifting.

PRINCIPAL CHARACTERS:
Daniella Preleshnik, a Polish teenager
Harrick Preleshnik, known as Harry, Daniella's older brother
Fella, Daniella's flirtatious friend
Vevke, a Jewish cobbler and technical supervisor of the shoe factory in the Kraków ghetto
Tedek, Vevke's son, who loves Daniella
Schultze, the chief German supervisor of the shoe factory
Elsa, the overseer of the brothel called the House of Dolls

OVERVIEW

House of Dolls is the second of a quintet of Holocaust novels published by Ka-tzetnik 135633. Born Yehiel Feiner and later known as Yehiel Dinur or De-Nur (from the word for "fire" in Hebrew), the writer took his pseudonym from his inmate number while he was captive at Auschwitz and a slang version of the German word *Konzentrationslager*, meaning concentration camp prisoner. Reviewing *House of Dolls* in *The New York Times Book Review*, Meyer Levin acclaimed it as the most important Holocaust story published up to that time. Ka-tzetnik's only book to achieve fame outside Israel, it has been translated into more than twenty languages and has sold more than five million copies. Its vivid, poetic treatment of horrific events led Israeli writer Gershon Shofman to call *House of Dolls* a holy book, and it has been required reading in Israeli schools. The Israeli Ministry of Education issued a special edition of the novel in 1994.

The novel begins in 1942, with teenage Daniella Preleshnik working in the rag room at Camp Breslau in Poland, repairing clothing that has been taken from Jews sent to the Nazi concentration camps. The rag room establishes the novel's theme of chance or fate: The workers have to take whatever clothing is on top of the pile, and the lucky ones find concealed coins. Likewise, it is all a matter of chance who gets sent to what camp for what duties and what destiny.

Other workers at Breslau are jealous of the blond, beautiful Daniella, suspecting that Vevke, the supervisor of the shoe factory, is looking after her. Vevke's main goal, however, is to try to protect all the workers by seeing that they do not commit offenses that would get them transported to Auschwitz. Daniella feels responsibility toward Vevke because his son, Tedek, has been arrested while trying to find an escape route to the Slovakian border. Tedek is in love with Daniella and wants to take her to Palestine. Vevke rescues Daniella from the Jewish militia and from being sent to another camp by promising to replace the leather soles on a militiaman's shoes. Working at the shoe factory is seen as highly desirable because having a labor card saves a worker from worse fates. Vevke is considered a savior for rescuing doctors, lawyers, rabbis, and others who have no skills as laborers. His antagonist is the German supervisor, Schultze, who delights in sending inferior workers to Auschwitz.

House of Dolls alternates between the story of Daniella and that of her older brother Harrick, known as Harry, the autobiographical hero of Ka-tzetnik's first novel, *Salamandra* (1946; *Sunrise over Hell*, 1977). At Camp Niederwalden, Harry, who had begun studying medicine before the war, is designated a physician. Having a sick bay in a concentration camp is one of dozens of bitter ironies found in Ka-tzetnik's work. The camp commander maintains the sick bay only so he can brag about it to other commanders. Harry's true duty is not to care for the ill but to oversee mass burials.

Daniella, who is reportedly based on the writer's sister, is eventually sent to this labor camp but is spared the normal duties because of her beauty. She and her flirtatious friend Fella join the ironically named Joy Division, becoming prostitutes for German soldiers on leave. (The novel is the source of the name of the 1970's British rock group Joy Division.) The brothel, known as the House of Dolls, is overseen by the brutal "Master-Kalefactress" Elsa, who resents the young women for their beauty. Daniella keeps a secret record of her experiences, hoping that her notebook will help the rest of the world understand what has happened in the Jewish ghettos and the camps. Fella maneuvers her way into becoming a servant in the commander's quarters, praying she can use her influence to protect her friends.

Some have criticized *House of Dolls* as an exploitative, even pornographic, novel, but the work is in fact a catalog of Holocaust horrors presented in a surprisingly objective manner, with little melodrama. Ka-tzetnik depicts the crowded living conditions in the Kraków ghetto, with the Jews burning not only their furniture but also their beloved books for heat. When she arrives in the camp, Daniella cannot at first determine whether the people she sees are fellow prisoners or corpses, so emaciated are they. When women prisoners undergo "Sin Purgation," the others are forced to watch their flogging. Cruel medical experiments are conducted at the Institute for Hygiene and Scientific Research. Seeing a truck loaded with corpses, Harry desperately tries to identify the bodies, hoping his friends are not among the dead. The camp prisoners have no true identities any longer; they are only Jews.

Ka-tzetnik includes many ironies in the novel. For example, one of the most prized commodities in the ghetto canteen is cyanide. A woman thinks that her oven would be an ideal place to hide from the Germans. Flowers cultivated by the Blossom Platoon give the labor camp an idyllic appearance that masks its harsh reality. The camp commander's mistress thinks that Harry looks like Christ, underscoring the novel's theme of sacrifice for the greater good.

The characters feel they are living borrowed lives. One minute there is the illusion of limited freedom, the next minute the death camps. Ka-tzetnik writes in an impressionistic style, with occasional stream of consciousness, creating a hypnotic, slow-motion effect that accentuates the dreamlike quality of Daniella's experience—a nightmare from which no one awakes. Characters constantly ask themselves and others whether the entire experience is a dream. As camp physician, Harry feels as if he is dreaming of a dream. Seeing a friend being taken away, Daniella thinks that everything is happening under water.

Ka-tzetnik's style includes long passages of sentence fragments, not just in keeping with modernist literary techniques but especially fitting for his subject. Bombarded by loss and deprivation, his characters struggle to maintain complete thoughts. The fragmented narrative conveys their chaotic existences. Ka-tzetnik was a poet before the war, and *House of Dolls* is more self-consciously literary than most autobiographical Holocaust writings (with the notable exception of the works of Elie Wiesel).

Because the characters are reduced to the basics, Ka-tzetnik frequently uses sensual imagery. The inhabitants of the ghetto and the camps cannot make sense of what is happening to them, but they can still respond to heat and cold, sight and sound, smell and taste. A particularly beautiful description of the moonlight outside Daniella's window contrasts the normality of her previous existence with this new world, where glimmers of light teasingly try to draw her away from the darkness that is her fate.

Harry identifies with a sapling growing beside the camp wall. It becomes a symbol of stunted possibilities, of his confinement, struggling for breath, for freedom. For all its bleakness, *House of Dolls* is also an uplifting tale of survival. Ka-tzetnik's goal is to show how his characters maintain their sanity and dignity, as well as their commitment to family and friends, against great odds. At the end, Fella abandons her plans for revenge. After what she has seen, she can hate no more. As Omer Bartov has observed, Ka-tzetnik's fiction represents a struggle to understand Jewish faith and fate.

The true identity of Ka-tzetnik 135633 was not publicly known until the author testified in the 1961 Israeli trial of Nazi war criminal Adolf Eichmann. Ka-tzetnik, who emigrated to Palestine after the war, and his wife, Nina Asherman De-Nur, also a writer, worked to promote understanding between Israelis and Palestinians, the subject of the final novel about Harry, *Ke-hol me-efer* (1966; *Phoenix over the Galilee*, 1969; published again as *House of Love*, 1971).

SOURCES FOR FURTHER STUDY

Bartov, Omer. "Kitsch and Sadism in Ka-Tzetnik's Other Planet: Israeli Youth Imagine the Holocaust." *Jewish Social Studies* 3, no. 2 (1997): 42-76.
Brierley, William D. "Memory in the Work of Yehiel Dinur (Ka-tzetnik 135633)." In *Hebrew Literature in the Wake of the Holocaust*, edited by Leon I. Yudkin. Rutherford, N.J.: Fairleigh Dickinson University Press, 1993.
Needler, Howard. "Red Fire upon Black Fire: Hebrew in the Holocaust Novels of K. Tsetnik." In *Writing and the Holocaust*, edited by Berel Lang. New York: Holmes & Meier, 1988.
Popkin, Jeremy D. "Ka-tzetnik 135633: The Survivor as Pseudonym." *New Literary History* 33, no. 2 (Spring, 2002): 343-355.

—*Michael Adams*

I WILL BEAR WITNESS
A Diary of the Nazi Years, 1942-1945

AUTHOR: Victor Klemperer (1881-1960)
FIRST PUBLISHED: *Ich will Zeugnis ablegen bis zum letzten: Tagebücher 1933-1945 von Victor Klemperer*, 1995 (English translation, 2000)
GENRE: Nonfiction
SUBGENRE: Diary

The second volume of Klemperer's diary depicts the Jewish scholar's increasingly precarious wartime life in Nazi Germany as he experiences intensified persecution and narrowly escapes death when he and his Gentile wife, Eva, reach Allied lines after the bombing of Dresden destroys their home city in February, 1945.

OVERVIEW

The first volume of *I Will Bear Witness*, Victor Klemperer's diary about his life as an endangered Jew in Nazi Germany, ends with the New Year's Eve observation that 1941 was the most dreadful year that he and Eva, his non-Jewish wife, had experienced. On Klemperer's mind were the ever more constrained and dangerous conditions that the intensification of war and Nazi anti-Semitism inflicted on them. In late June, the Germans had invaded the Soviet Union. That autumn, German Jews were ordered to wear the "yellow star," and the Nazis halted all Jewish emigration from Germany and German-occupied territory. Klemperer was among the 163,000 remaining German Jews who were trapped in a regime that was rapidly moving to implement its murderous "final solution."

At the time, dependent as he was on rumors and secondhand reports from foreign news broadcasts, Klemperer could not have known the details of those developments. They included Chełmno, the Nazi death camp that become operational on December 8, and construction projects at Bełżec and Auschwitz-Birkenau, two other Polish sites where millions of Jews would be gassed to death. Klemperer's last words for 1941 refer to murder and deportations—often he speaks of "evacuation" instead—but as his diary's second volume reveals, it took time for Klemperer to realize that the worst was yet to come.

The Holocaust destroyed about 2.7 million Jews in 1942, making that year the most lethal in Jewish history. Primarily because of his "mixed" marriage, which gave him fragile privileges as the Jewish spouse of an "Aryan" woman, Klemperer remained alive. Unbeknownst to him, while Klemperer dealt with his personal dilemmas in Dresden's severe winter cold, the fate of Jews in such marriages was being discussed during an important meeting in the Berlin suburb of Wannsee on January 20, 1942. There, under the leadership of Reinhard Heydrich, the Schutzstaffel (SS) lieutenant general who was also chief of the Reich security main office, fifteen government and SS officials, many with doctorates from German universities, convened at a comfortable lakeside villa to coordinate the "final solution." One proposal at the Wannsee Conference was to dissolve mixed marriages so that the Jewish spouses could be targeted more easily, but at that time no further action was taken on the matter.

While the Wannsee Conference took place, Klemperer's diary entry indicates that he was spending time with Paul Kreidl, a Jewish resident in the special Dresden Jews' house where the Klemperers were also forced to live. A week earlier, Kreidl had shared a disturbing rumor: Jews sent from Germany to Riga, Latvia, had been shot. The rumor was true. On January 21, Kreidl was one of 224 Dresden Jews deported to the Riga ghetto, a victim caught in a power struggle between Nazis who were willing to postpone Jewish death while Jews did labor in key wartime industries and those who wanted to make Germany *judenrein* (free of Jews) immediately.

Klemperer's reflections reveal the forlorn mixture of anxiety and ambiguity, gossiped information and nonsensical incongruity, and immediate need and tentative hope that makes his diary compelling because of the desperate plight it conveys. On March 16, 1942, he writes about the Hitler jokes he heard during a morning work break, the hearsay about the military situation at the eastern front, a report about lenient anti-Jewish policies in Hungary, a new ban in Germany that prohibited Jews from buying flowers, and the growing scarcity of food and fuel. In his eclectic list of experiences mentioned on this date, Klemperer writes that he has also heard of a place called Auschwitz, which was described to him as "the most dreadful concentration camp." How dreadful Auschwitz was he could not know, but within days of his Auschwitz reference, while he notes the latest rations reductions in Dresden, gas chambers are put into operation in a renovated farmhouse at Auschwitz-Birkenau, the main killing center in the Auschwitz complex, with Polish Jews as the victims.

Six months later, on September 19, Klemperer observes that the decree requiring German Jews to wear the yellow star is one year old. "What indescribable misery has descended upon us during this year," he writes. "Everything that preceded it appears petty by comparison." Two days later, on Yom Kippur, the sacred Day of Atonement, he describes visits to the Pinkowitzes and Neumanns, who will soon be deported. "Going into a beyond," as Klemperer puts it, his friends' situation is grim, and yet the diarist resists the direst conclusion, for the available reports have been "no more than supposition." By this time, however, with the turning-point Battle of Stalingrad under way but far from decided against Nazi Germany, more than 250,000 Jews from the Warsaw ghetto had been murdered in the gas chambers at Treblinka.

On New Year's Eve, Klemperer again takes stock. The year 1942, he notes, has been the worst of the ten years he has experienced under Nazi rule. Apart from some reading, he has not been able to do any of the scholarly work that means so much to him. The people with whom the Klemperers spent last New Year's Eve have all been "blotted out by murder, suicide, and evacuation." With no end in sight, he constantly feels in "mortal danger." As the year draws to its close, Klemperer can only conclude that 1942 has been the worst year "thus far." For him and many other European Jews, he expects that the terror will increase, and it does. Consider, for example, what took place on February 27, 1943.

That morning, Jews remaining in Germany, even those in armaments industries, were rounded up at their workplaces and assembled for deportation. Even mixed marriages seemed to provide protection no longer, but then something remarkable happened in Berlin. At the Rosenstrasse Jewish community center, where several hundred Jewish men were interned, their non-Jewish wives appeared and protested publicly against the impending deportation. Ordered to disperse, threatened with violence if they did not, the women persisted. Uneasy about the unrest that might spread, the Nazi officials relented and released the Jewish men in mixed marriages. The next day Klemperer makes no comment about the Rosenstrasse protest—probably no news of it reached him—but he does record that "the current action did *not* concern the mixed marriages."

Although no further action against Jews in mixed marriages would be taken until the war's final months, Klemperer saw that his safety was ever more precarious. On February 28, 1943, he recalls that his wife recently heard a German woman's account of a postcard message sent by her son from the eastern front. "I'm still alive"—repeated three times—is all it said. "That is also how far my feelings go," writes Klemperer, "depending on my mood, and changing from hour to hour, the emphasis is now on 'alive,' now on 'still.'" About four months later, on June 12, Klemperer estimates that only a handful of Jews remain in Dresden. He hears contradictory rumors: Mixed marriages will be broken up; mixed marriages will still be safe havens. His mood, he says, keeps shifting "between fear, hope, indifference." Still, as the Klemperers hold out, the reader becomes increasingly aware that despite the threats of despair and death, the husband-and-wife team are expanding and deepening the meaning of "resistance."

Back on May 27, 1942—it was the same day that Czech resistance fighters fatally wounded Heydrich in Prague—Klemperer noted once again how hunger exhausted him. Although he had fought for Germany during World War I, armed resistance against the Third Reich was scarcely a wartime option for a Jew in Dresden. Writing would be Klemperer's chosen form of resistance instead. "I will bear witness," he vows, "precise witness!" Although he could not know that his diary would achieve bestseller status more than fifty years later, there are moments when he senses that he may be writing for history, that it is crucial to record his everyday existence because that detail will be essential to document what Nazi Germany did to the world and to the Jews in particular.

On June 8, 1942, Klemperer mentions that he has heard about Heydrich's death, but the diarist's personal situation remains the focus. The result is that his diary becomes an extended lamentation for the Jews of Dresden, an anguished indictment of the Germany he still loves in spite of its Nazi ways, and a sustained record of the efforts that he and his wife make to endure, to preserve the semblance of a decent life in inhuman circumstances, and to survive for better times. Whether those times will be theirs remains unclear, for in addition to his jeopardized existence as a Jew under Nazi rule, German civilians are endangered as the war is brought close to home by the Allies' air raids, which intensify in 1942 and reach devastating proportions by the end of 1943. The end of that year finds Klemperer observing that Dresden has not yet been hit; nevertheless, it is a place of fear for all the city's inhabitants, not only its very few Jews.

Six months later, Klemperer's wife brings him news that the Allies' D-day invasion at Normandy is under way, but on that day, June 6, 1944, he is "no longer or not yet able to hope." His ambivalence was not misplaced, for even though the war had definitely turned against Nazi Germany, the Holocaust still raged in 1944. On March 19, for example, while Klemperer did air-raid duty, German troops occupied the territory of their faltering Hungarian ally, and the last large group of European Jews came under the Nazis' genocidal control. By July 9, when Klemperer wrote that he could "no longer imagine myself transformed back into a human being," some 437,000 Hungarian Jews had been deported to Auschwitz, where most of them were gassed. On September 3, as Klemperer reports that Dresden's Hitler Youth is marching and singing, another diarist, a young Jewish woman named Anne Frank, is deported to Auschwitz from the Netherlands with her family and hundreds of other Dutch Jews. Klemperer knows nothing of her, but his September 1 judgment—written on the fifth anniversary of World War II's beginning—sums up the situation: "no safety anywhere." The year ends with air-raid alerts in Dresden, with the numbed feeling that the war will end "perhaps in a couple of months, perhaps in a couple of years."

On February 12, 1945, the last of the Dresden Jews learn that they must report for special labor duty. No illusions remain; the orders are a death sentence. Klemperer is not included in the first groups, but he carries the orders to others and expects no mixed-marriage reprieve. Then, on the night of February 13, the situation changes. The Allied air raids begin. The resulting firestorm reduces Dresden to rubble, enabling the city's surviving Jews to destroy the documents and yellow stars that identify them and perhaps eventually to rebuild their lives in the Third Reich's ruins. The Klemperers managed to do so.

Of all the documents from World War II and the Holocaust, Klemperer's diary is among the most unusual. Few others chart day-to-day life in Nazi Germany from the Third Reich's start to finish. From a German Jew's perspective, none does so as thoroughly. Bearing precise witness, Klemperer not only recalls how much was lost but also warns that human beings forget at tremendous peril.

SOURCES FOR FURTHER STUDY

Bartov, Omer. *Germany's War and the Holocaust: Disputed Histories*. Ithaca, N.Y.: Cornell University Press, 2003.

Heim, Susanne. "The German-Jewish Relationship in the Diaries of Victor Klemperer." In *Probing the Depths of German Anti-Semitism: German Society and the Persecution of the Jews, 1933-1941*, edited by David Bankier. New York: Berghahn Books, 2000.

Klemperer, Victor. *I Shall Bear Witness: The Diaries of Victor Klemperer, 1933-1941*. Abridged and translated by Martin Chalmers. London: Weidenfeld & Nicolson, 1998.

_____. *To the Bitter End: The Diaries of Victor Klemperer, 1942-1945*. Abridged and translated by Martin Chalmers. London: Weidenfeld & Nicolson, 1999.

_____. *The Lesser Evil: The Diaries of Victor Klemperer, 1945-1949*. Abridged and translated by Martin Chalmers. London: Weidenfeld & Nicolson, 2003.

Meider, Wolfgang. "'In Lingua Veritas': Proverbial Rhetoric in Victor Klemperer's Diaries of the Nazi Years, 1933-1945." In *Language, Poetry, and Memory Reflections on National Socialism: Harry H. Kahn Memorial Lec-*

tures, 2000-2004, edited by Wolfgang Meider and David Scrase. Burlington: University of Vermont, Center for Holocaust Studies, 2004.

Niven, Bill. *Facing the Nazi Past: United Germany and the Legacy of the Third Reich*. New York: Routledge, 2002.

—*John K. Roth*

IN KINDLING FLAME
THE STORY OF HANNAH SENESH, 1921-1944

AUTHOR: Linda Atkinson (1941-   )
FIRST PUBLISHED: 1985
GENRE: Nonfiction
SUBGENRES: Biography; young adult literature

Through her account of the life and death of the young Jewish freedom fighter Senesh, Atkinson personalizes the Holocaust for young readers.

PRINCIPAL PERSONAGES:
    Hannah Senesh (1921-1944), a young Hungarian Jew who emigrates to Palestine and returns to Hungary to help rescue other Jews
    Catherine Senesh, Hannah's mother, who remains in Budapest throughout the war and is imprisoned with her captured daughter
    George Senesh, Hannah's brother, who leaves Hungary for France and, later, Palestine
    Reuven Dafne, a young Yugoslav member of the parachute rescue team from Palestine that includes Hannah
    Yoel Palgi, a member of the rescue team who, like Hannah, is captured and imprisoned in Budapest
    Miryam, Hannah's roommate and best friend at the agricultural school in Palestine
    Margit Dayka, a Hungarian actress and friend of Catherine Senesh
    Captain Simon, the judge advocate at Hannah's trial, who sentences and executes her

OVERVIEW

Linda Atkinson's *In Kindling Flame: The Story of Hannah Senesh, 1921-1944* recounts the cycle of a young Hungarian Jewish woman's life against the backdrop of the events of the mid-1930's through the end of World War II known as the Holocaust. Senesh is an insightful, talented, yet unsure young woman whose desire to become a writer is altered by the extraordinary circumstances surrounding the resurgence of anti-Semitism in her native Hungary and throughout Europe. The account documents her decision to embrace Zionism and to emigrate to Palestine. Senesh ultimately asks to take part in a rescue mission that will allow her to return to her homeland in order to help Jews escape and to rescue her mother and bring her to Palestine. Upon her return to Hungary via Yugoslavia, Senesh is captured and executed.

Atkinson organizes the book chronologically into three main parts. The first is 1935 to 1944, the period of Senesh's adolescence in Budapest, emigration to Palestine, and training for a return to Adolf Hitler's Europe to help organize resistance. The second is 1944, the year of Senesh's return to Yugoslavia and Hungary as a member of a parachute team to collect intelligence, establish escape routes, and rescue Jews, culminating in her capture and execution. The third section is 1945 and after, which contains a brief history of those Jews, both victims and survivors, who resisted or bore witness to the Holocaust. Throughout the biography, Atkinson conveys to the young adult reader the larger historical record of Jewish resistance by interspersing specific events, such as the Warsaw Ghetto Uprising, with the personal experiences of her subject, Hannah Senesh.

In its description of a young woman's search to understand herself and her place in the world, and the circular nature of her life's journey from Budapest to Palestine to Hungary, *In Kindling Flame* imparts the quality of the classic quest or hero tale to Senesh's life. Atkinson portrays that life through the use of excerpts from Senesh's diary and correspondence and of the recollections of her mother, her brother, and members of her rescue team. Atkinson carefully places this individual life in the broader contexts of a Europe dominated by anti-Semitism that would culminate in the Holocaust and the creation of Israel, the Jewish homeland in Palestine. She does not, however, permit the setting to overwhelm the sensitively drawn picture of a young woman's emerging maturity and search for the meaning in her life. The use of photographs, some of which depict Senesh's personal life in Budapest and Palestine and others of which show the atrocities visited upon the Jewish population of Europe, visually complements the author's presentation.

It is clear that Atkinson's motivation in writing *In Kindling Flame* and the nature of the content itself are both highly emotionally charged. As she indicates in her acknowledgments, writing the biography of Senesh followed the example of those European Jews who resisted and recorded the events of the Holocaust. One of Atkinson's primary goals in the book is to dispel the misconception that European Jews were unresisting and submissive to the policies and actions directed against them. By portraying a young woman who grows up in a world hostile to Jews and whose final years embody opposition to Hitler's plans to make Europe *Judenfrei* (free of

Hannah Senesh.

Jews), Atkinson is able to personalize the record of Jewish resistance within the framework of the complex political and military events underlying the Holocaust.

Senesh's own perception of her life's work, and that adopted by Atkinson, is conveyed in the line of Senesh's poetry from which the title of the biography is taken: "Blessed is the match consumed/ in kindling flame." Atkinson's unifying focus is the gradual development of Senesh's search for the meaning of her life, which culminates in her single-minded commitment to return to Hungary to rescue Jews. The strength of the author's portrayal lies in the use of Senesh's own diary as a primary source; the introspective entries and poems help the reader to follow Senesh's search for self. There are striking parallels between Senesh's description of her own adolescent development and that provided by Anne Frank in her diary, *Het Achterhuis* (1947; *The Diary of a Young Girl*, 1952). Senesh's own perceptions are broadened by the views of her mother, her brother, and members of her rescue team, rendering a well-rounded portrait. Despite the obvious empathy of the author for her subject, Atkinson is fair in her portrayal of Senesh. While clearly conveying to the reader that Senesh achieved her desire "to be a great soul," Atkinson addresses her subject's adolescent self-doubts, difficulties in adjusting to kibbutz life in Palestine, and impatience and unwillingness to submit to good advice and authority during training.

In the process of interweaving an individual life with the sociopolitical events of a significant historical period, it is important that the biographer achieve a balance between these two factors that will not sacrifice the subject to the events or use her simply as a vehicle for historical commentary. Atkinson handles this balance well; she is able to maintain a focus on Senesh while providing the reader with pertinent information about the larger context in which she lived and died. This information, primarily concerned with Jewish resistance to the German process of extermination, strengthens Atkinson's description of Senesh's decision to return to Europe to rescue Jews. In the final section of the book, Atkinson deals specifically with the misconception that European Jews submitted to the policy of extermination. She accurately portrays the many acts of Jewish resistance, ranging from failing to comply with German directives regulating daily life to armed rebellion. For many victims, the act of resistance was to produce a written record of their suffering.

In this section, Atkinson also condemns the failure of the rest of the world to come to the aid of European Jewry, with harshest criticism reserved for Allied governments. She does not, however, cite the numerous acts of personal courage by individuals across Europe who committed themselves to save Jews from the Holocaust. While such an examination is not the focus of her book, its inclusion would have been helpful to balance the historical record.

In Kindling Flame is one of a significant body of works for young adults—biography, autobiography, historical fiction, and information books—that address the issue of the Holocaust. These books collectively bear witness to one of the most cataclysmic events of human history and seek to ensure that, through knowledge and understanding provided in the written record, such events can never happen again. Senesh's life story, as recorded in Atkinson's biography, is a singular example of European Jewry's resistance to the policy of genocide. It is in Senesh's response to the particular circumstances of her adolescence, shaped by her Jewishness and the rise of anti-Semitism, that her life becomes a transcendent experience to be shared with young adult readers. This biography fills the need for adolescents to learn about individuals who have the capacity for believing in something and acting on that belief.

It was in the act of having her life extinguished by the Holocaust (a term that originally referred to an offering to God consumed by fire) that Senesh became one of those individuals whom she herself described as "people whose brilliance continues to light the world though they are no longer among the living." Atkinson's work is a testament to the good in the face of evil that a single life can offer.

SOURCES FOR FURTHER STUDY

Kellman, Amy, and Trevelyn E. Jones. Review of *In Kindling Flame: The Story of Hannah Senesh, 1921-1944*, by Linda Atkinson. *School Library Journal* 31, no. 9 (May, 1985): 98.

Kokkola, Lydia. *Representing the Holocaust in Children's Literature*. New York: Routledge, 2003.

Sullivan, Edward T. *The Holocaust in Literature for Youth: A Guide and Resource Book*. Lanham, Md.: Scarecrow, 1999.

Torres, Nellie. "Young Adult Works Put to Test by Youth." *San Diego Union*, May 5, 1985, p. Books 4.

—John J. Carney

"In the Blue Distance"

AUTHOR: Nelly Sachs (1891-1970)
FIRST PUBLISHED: "In der blauen Ferne," 1957, in *Und niemand weiss weiter* (English translation collected in *O the Chimneys*, 1967)
GENRE: Poetry
SUBGENRES: Lyric poetry; meditation

Sachs addresses the theme of the Holocaust in this poem through earthy images presented in sure, quiet steps. The transformation depicted signifies that out of suffering, upheaval, and even death can come a spiritual insistence on life and beauty.

Overview

"In the Blue Distance" is a haunting meditative lyric poem that presents intense images in free verse. Like most of Nelly Sachs's painfully beautiful poems, it is a variation on the basic theme of the Holocaust. This poem searches for a way to go on afterward, reflecting the theme revealed in the title of the collection in which it first appeared, *Und niemand weiss weiter*, which translates as "and no one knows how to go on." The poem's travelers look toward "the blue distance," where "longing is distilled" or where one can recognize and find deliverance from longing. Exactly what one longs for (peace, forgiveness, love, death?) is not specified in the poem, but the mood of the work is one of acceptance. The mood of quiet reconciliation in the last stanza offers the possibility of transcendence from hate and bitterness. That offer is perhaps made with reference to the suffering of the Holocaust, if only implicitly.

The first stanza presents a vista—a metaphorical view from a valley. Those who live below can see far away a row of apple trees with "rooted feet climbing the sky." In this image, the juxtaposition of "rooted" and "climbing" suggests a tension between two longings, perhaps. One is to remain earthbound, and the other looks toward the blue distance, skyward. In Sachs's vocabulary, flying—one way to interpret "climbing the sky"—often signifies transcendence or re-creation. "Those who live in the valley" might feel some comfort knowing that a higher realm exists.

The apple trees in one sense signify the hope and abundance of such a spiritual place. Perhaps it can be as simple as those on earth wishing to see heaven, or simply to know one exists. The poem in stanza 1 thus seems to consider another way (among all the ways in Sachs's poetry) for those hurt by the insanity of the war to expiate their terrors and to relieve longings intensified by the losses they suffered.

"Rooted" and "climbing" may also allude to the magic of organic growth—the magic that all plants possess. Such organic growth, or regeneration, would mean, in human terms, spiritual healing. Apple trees also are heavily laden with mythology: Apples have long been equated with the forbidden fruit of the tree of knowledge, but apple trees also bring blossoms in spring, and thus hope. Stanza 1 thus suggests the necessity for those who are suffering from their pasts to find some way to regenerate their spiritual balance and inner peace, the way plants grow anew after they have been cut back. There seems to be a yearning for some way to grow toward the sky, out of the low valley.

The image of "the sun, lying by the roadside" in stanza 2 is, on one hand, a simple description of the sun lying low on the horizon, at sunset; on the other hand, this image may be seen as frightening: If the sun really lay by the roadside, like some suffering or ambushed traveler, such eerie displacement would suggest the worst kind of chaos. The "magic wands" mentioned in this stanza could suggest that this sun is an impostor, a prankster, or a sorcerer. If this is so, perhaps the travelers are being deceived; perhaps even nature is not to be trusted in a world so prone to chaos and pain.

In a lighter and more positive interpretation, these magic wands could simply suggest the regenerative magic of the natural world, of which the sun is a part. It provides light, so basic to life, and, in a figurative sense, knowledge. Perhaps the stanza reflects the wrenching uncertainty of life during the Holocaust—the command "to halt" could come at any time, from any quarter. Life during the Holocaust had become so unpredictable, so unnatural, one might not be surprised to see the sun collapse and become earthbound.

In stanza 3, the travelers have halted, although they seem alone "in the glassy nightmare." One cannot be sure why or for whom they have stopped. This lack of certainty compounds the eeriness that arose in the second stanza. "Glassy" lends an apt sense of distortion and again, uncertainty, to the poem's increasingly nightmarish atmosphere.

An image from the natural world characteristically rescues people from the nightmare and barely breaks the silence of this poem. A cricket "scratches softly at the invisible"—a beautiful and redeeming, although practically inexplicable, image. The mystical quality of Sachs's work is exemplified here in that the relief this profound image bestows on the reader must be felt rather than understood. No easy explanation exists for "the invisible" (eternity? the unknown? the deity?), and any attempt at explanation dilutes the power of the image itself, which is effective primarily in its emotional impact.

The poem ends with a second such image, which, again characteristic of Sachs's poetry, relies on emotion to complete what it communicates. "Stone" and "dust" reverberate in their earthboundness back to the tension in stanza 1 between being rooted and "climbing the sky." In Sachs's poetry, images of earth, dust, and sand often signify the past—specifically, here, the human suffering of years past. In the transcendent spirit-filled final lines of this poem, the stone does fly—it dances and "changes its dust to music." The transformation signifies that out of suffering, upheaval, or even death can come a spiritual insistence on life and beauty, only two ideas that "music" might suggest here. The stone thus dances a dance of renewal and life, not of death.

"In the Blue Distance" is highly imagistic. Its impact comes from the visual intensity of its metaphors as well as from their eerie, mystical reverberations. In this sense it is similar to most of Sachs's work.

Known for its enigmatic quality, Sachs's poetry is not "easy" to read. Whatever difficulty the reader confronts, however, is not attributable to the technical devices of the poems. They are not written in encoded language, nor are they riddles to be solved. Readers may experience difficulty laying aside their demands to have the "meaning" of "In the Blue Distance" made easily comprehensible. Sachs's concentrated and emotional language, its allusions and metaphors, unfold only slowly, and the reader must be prepared not to rely on a need for explicit meaning but to experience the mystery of the poem. That is, as with the cricket image, one feels Sachs's poetry better than one can hope to understand it in the analytic sense.

Sachs uses masterful craftsmanship in her poetry. The earthy images in "In the Blue Distance" manage to root the poem as though in good warm soil. The poem's movement from section to section seems almost, again inexplicably, like natural growth. Each stanza has an image central to its movement and to the "narrative" movement of the poem. The climbing apple trees, the "lying" sun, the cricket scratching, and the dancing stone are simple pictures, yet they are profoundly intriguing and suggestive. These images, one to a stanza, move the poem forward with sure, quiet steps, as if the delicate thread of emotion spun stronger by each new line is being handed carefully along.

Sachs also employs personification; it lends an eerie yet somehow friendly quality to otherwise mysterious images—the cricket scratching "at the invisible" and the stone dancing. As the stanzas are not regular in number of lines or line length, the images that reside within the poem provide its form. The interplay among the images unifies the poem.

Sachs speaks in simple language, and the rhythm of "In the Blue Distance" is relaxed and unassuming. In fact, the low-key, conversational tone of the poem is amazing given the otherworldly intensity of the images. That the work breaks down into three relatively simple sentences shows Sachs's ability to comb away the wool surrounding an emotion she wishes to convey and to find a beautifully simple correlation in the imagery. The poem's concrete images are the key to this fertile simplicity.

"Death gave me my language," Sachs said. "My metaphors are my wounds." Such a statement implies an intensely private poetry, and there is perhaps a sort of arrogant folly in searching for "meanings" in images whose very strength comes from their wildly errant suggestiveness. Sachs's images suggest many directions, many meanings, but her statement also simplifies a discussion of meaning. The poet's basic theme, the Holocaust, leads her to explore all avenues of thought and emotion in terms of the great mystery, death.

One may read "In the Blue Distance" as a meditation on arriving at the edge of death. The stillness, approaching silence, at the heart of this poem certainly suggests that the travelers teeter between worlds—where language becomes unnecessary. The momentary yet strong break in movement after stanza 2 ("The sun . . . commands the travelers to halt") suggests an interface between the worlds of life and death. In the "glassy nightmare," the travelers are fairly on the edge of a world. The "invisible" at which the cricket scratches suggests an entrance point, if one follows this theme, into the next world.

Death, however, is neither fearsome nor terrible in this poem. In a sense, it has already happened, for there is no escape from the sun. The poem is really a reckoning, an acceptance of the inevitable event of death, which seems to approach almost tenderly—as softly as the cricket scratches at the door. Sachs wrote a number of harshly accusatory poems about the Holocaust, but this is not one of them. Her work has been called forgiving, and the calm lyricism of this poem certainly demonstrates that quality. In it, even death seems forgiving. The stone is cold and hard, but "dancing," transforming dust, and the past with all its anguish, to music.

SOURCES FOR FURTHER STUDY

Bahti, Timothy, and Marilyn Sibley Fries, eds. *Jewish Writers, German Literature: The Uneasy Examples of Nelly Sachs and Walter Benjamin*. Ann Arbor: University of Michigan Press, 1995.

Bower, Kathrin M. *Ethics and Remembrance in the Poetry of Nelly Sachs and Rose Ausländer*. Rochester, N.Y.: Camden House, 2000.
Dove, Rita. "Poet's Choice." *The Washington Post*, May 28, 2000, p. X12.
Hirsch, Edward. "Nelly Sachs, 1891-1970." *The Washington Post*, August 15, 2004, p. T12.
Myers, Ida. "Nelly Sachs: Neglected Nobelist." *Jerusalem Post*, May 12, 1995, p. 25.

—JoAnn Balingit

Incident at Vichy

Author: Arthur Miller (1915-2005)
First published: 1965 (first produced, 1964)
Genre: Drama
Subgenre: Social realism

Miller's play questions the tendency of human beings to evade complexity and elude confrontations with evil and thus to avoid responsibility for that complexity and evil. The words and actions of each character in the work reveal some aspect of this moral dilemma.

Principal characters:
 Lebeau, a painter
 Bayard, an electrician
 Marchand, a businessman
 Monceau, an actor
 Leduc, a psychoanalyst
 Von Berg, an Austrian prince

Overview

Incident at Vichy is a one-act play that takes place in a detention room in Vichy, France, during the German occupation. When the curtain opens, the stage reveals a grim setting with little furniture except for a long bench on which sit six men and a young boy. In the playwright's words, these characters are "frozen there like members of a small orchestra at the moment before they begin to play." In the course of the drama, each man anticipates and experiences a dreaded event: his being called into the office of the Nazi captain who is conducting an interrogation and checking identification papers to determine whether the detainee is Jewish. Before each summons, the characters demonstrate their mounting terror, fearful that the interrogation will result in their slaughter.

During the tense moments between interrogations, the detainees discuss their fears, their disbelief that their countrymen are detaining them, their alternating desire to flee and inability to escape for fear of being killed in the process. Each character reveals his own value system, from Marchand and his capitalistic businessman's attitude to Prince Von Berg, who had fled Austria and rejected Nazism because of its vulgarity. Marchand's and Von Berg's summonses produce the same result: a white pass that means freedom. The reasons for the passes and the uses of those passes, however, are radically different.

Marchand's words and actions suggest that, just as he had lived by a mercenary, heartless value system, so he was able to save his life by resorting to that same system and purchasing his freedom. When he leaves the place of detention, displaying his white pass, he leaves behind detainees who, except for Von Berg, can neither buy their freedom nor talk their way out of their eventual destruction.

Arthur Miller. (Inge Morath/Magnum)

Von Berg, a nobleman who had been detained because of his accent, is different from Marchand and also from the other captives. He is neither a heartless individual nor a Jew; he is a person who is struggling with the question of guilt and responsibility. He is troubled by the comments of the psychiatrist Leduc, who challenges him to assume responsibility for the atrocities being perpetrated by the Nazis. Von Berg insists that he has never said a word against the Jewish people, but Leduc asserts that it is not only verbal abuse that leads to culpability; the very human condition, according to Leduc, requires all people to assume responsibility for human brutality.

When Von Berg emerges from his interrogation with a white pass in his hand, he gives the doctor his pass, thus sacrificing himself to free the psychiatrist. As he leaves, Leduc's gestures reveal that he is aware of his own guilt, indicating that both he and Von Berg recognize that human beings share responsibility and guilt for their actions and the actions of other human beings. In the last moment of the play, a new group of detainees arrives to occupy the bench and observe Von Berg silently staring into the eyes of his Nazi captor and murderer.

Incident at Vichy is a morality play that questions the tendency among human beings to evade complexity and elude confrontations with evil and thus to avoid responsibility for that complexity and evil. The words and actions of each character reveal some aspect of this moral dilemma.

The businessman Marchand views the process of detention and interrogation not as a prelude to human destruction but as a simple procedure for identifying people with false papers. The painter Lebeau announces that the measuring of people's noses on the streets has to do with a labor shortage: The Occupied Forces need people to carry stones. The actor Monceau explains that trains carrying Jews are simply transporting volunteers to work in Germany. Even Prince Von Berg, who recognizes the vulgarity and brutality of the Nazis, does not see his cousin Baron Kessler as the person whom Leduc knows—a Nazi who helped remove all the Jewish doctors from a medical school. Collectively, the detainees represent those human beings who, for various reasons, refuse to see evil and destruction in the world around them and therefore avoid responsibility for that evil and destruction.

Blinded to this reality, the characters participate in a victimizer/victim syndrome in which the entrapped victim seeks out another person to entrap and victimize. Thus, two nameless characters—the Gypsy and the Old Jew—are victimized by their fellow detainees, and the Major who is guarding the detainees speaks of his own entrapment. Holding a revolver to the head of Leduc, the Major speaks to the loss of humanity when all people are simultaneously victims and victimizers: "Tell me how . . . how there can be persons any more. I have you at the end of this revolver—*indicates the Professor*—he has me—and somebody has him—and somebody has somebody else."

Part of the difficulty in destroying this syndrome of victim becoming victimizer is that the characters rely too heavily on logic and rationality in their efforts to understand the nature of the syndrome and the presence of evil. Two characters whose professions force them to deal with intuition and the unconscious—the painter Lebeau and the psychiatrist Leduc—speak often of the need to recognize the absurd illogic of suffering and the limitations of reason and intellect. Lebeau compares the meaninglessness of suffering to the lack of logical meaning in his painting. Instead of asking what his paintings mean, he says, people should look at them. In other words, instead of seeking neat, reasonable explanations, they should see with the mind's eye that not all paintings have meanings, not all problems have solutions. Similarly, Leduc comments that logic can be immobilizing and warns his fellow detainees of that paralysis: "You cannot wager your life on a purely rational analysis of this situation. Listen to your feelings: you must certainly *feel* the danger here."

Prince Von Berg ultimately feels the danger and acts with nobility and idealism when he sacrifices his life for Leduc's. He announces his belief in ideals before he goes into the interrogation. He asserts this belief angrily: "There are people who would find it easier to die than stain one finger with this murder. They exist. I swear it to you. People for whom everything is *not* permitted, foolish people and ineffectual, but they do exist and will not dishonor their tradition."

Von Berg does not dishonor his tradition. He courageously identifies the need for idealism and the fact that this idealism is, in a tragic sense, both noble and "ineffectual." The nobility is clear: One man sacrifices his life for another. This sacrifice has no effect, however, on the perpetual victim/victimizer syndrome that is dramatically represented by the final moments of *Incident at Vichy*. One man is saved through the sacrifice of another, but another line of detainees arrives, none of whom will likely have a Prince Von Berg who will die for them. Thus, this morality play both affirms and questions idealism, leaving its audience with sacrificial gain and sacrificial loss, with hope for a human race that produces a Prince Von Berg but despair over human beings who detain and destroy one another.

Incident at Vichy is a modern morality play. Like a medieval morality play, Arthur Miller's drama has characters who are allegorical, embodying abstract virtues and vices. Thus, when Dr. Leduc acknowledges that he and his fellow detainees are "symbols," he is speaking about the qualities they embody and represent. This representation is presented most dramatically when the curtain falls, and good and evil, in the characters of the idealistic prince and the brutal Nazi, are staring at each other, symbolizing the confrontational duality of humankind.

In addition to these two characters—and others—who represent virtues and vices, *Incident at Vichy* includes the symbolic use of objects, not all of which have single explanations. The Gypsy and the Old Jew, themselves symbols of universal victims, refuse to divest themselves of, respectively, a pot and a bundle when they are called in for interrogation. Each object seems to be representative of a value that these oppressed detainees cherish: The Gypsy has fixed the pot, and so it is his, and the Old Jew has likely plucked the feathers from his own chickens, and so the bundle of feathers is similarly his. In a universe in which characters are displaced from their property and distanced from their family and friends, these objects represent futile efforts to cling to the familiar and the beloved. The pot is broken and the bundle of feathers is torn open by a Nazi, in one more demonstration of the destructive power of human force.

Incident at Vichy follows the pattern Arthur Miller established in his earlier and greatest play, *Death of a Salesman* (pr., pb. 1949), and developed in subsequent dramas such as *The Crucible* (pr., pb. 1953) and *A View from the*

Bridge (pr., pb. 1955). In these plays, Miller takes up the theme of individual guilt and commitment within the tradition of Greek tragedy. Concerned with creating tragic drama in an age that appears to have no classical tragic heroes, Miller explored the possibilities of bourgeois tragedy. In an essay titled "Tragedy and the Common Man," he argued that the modern age called for a new kind of tragic drama, which he aimed to produce.

While *Incident at Vichy* may not be considered his best example of such modern tragedy, it is an excellent demonstration of Miller's ongoing attempt to redefine the classical genre in terms of contemporary issues. Thus, his effort to examine Nazi genocide through the actions of his tragic heroes and villains has an important place in his artistic canon.

Miller's plays and essays continually call attention to the moral dilemmas facing contemporary society. His essay "On Social Plays," his introduction to the 1955 version of *A View from the Bridge*, and his introduction to his *Collected Plays* (1957) all give voice to the clarion call to view drama as a public way to raise questions at the heart of twentieth century civilization.

Sources for Further Study

Bigsby, Christopher. *Arthur Miller: A Critical Study*. New York: Cambridge University Press, 2005.

Brater, Enoch. *Arthur Miller: A Playwright's Life and Works*. London: Thames and Hudson, 2005.

Centola, Steve R., and Michelle Cirulli, eds. *The Critical Response to Arthur Miller*. Westport, Conn.: Praeger, 2006.

Gottfried, Martin. *Arthur Miller: His Life and Work*. Cambridge, Mass.: Da Capo Press, 2004.

Gussow, Mel. *Conversations with Miller*. New York: Applause Theatre and Cinema Books, 2002.

Miller, Arthur. *Timebends: A Life*. New York: Grove Press, 1987.

Roudane, Matthew C., ed. *Conversations with Arthur Miller*. Jackson: University of Mississippi Press, 1987.

Rousuck, J. Wynn. "Blatantly Political: A Rarely Produced 1964 Play by Arthur Miller Suffers from Didactic Writing." *Baltimore Sun*, March 22, 1999, p. 8E.

Schlueter, June, and James K. Flanagan. *Arthur Miller*. New York: Ungar, 1987.

Welland, Dennis. *Miller: The Playwright*. 3d rev. ed. London: Methuen, 1985.

—Marjorie Smelstor

An Interrupted Life
The Diaries of Etty Hillesum, 1941-1943

AUTHOR: Etty Hillesum (1914-1943)
FIRST PUBLISHED: *Het verstoorde leven: Dagboek van Etty Hillesum, 1941-1943*, 1981 (English translation, 1983)
GENRE: Nonfiction
SUBGENRES: Diary; letters

These diaries, written by a young Jewish woman who would not survive the Holocaust, are directed from an unbearable present to the hope of a better future. The author knew that she would not live to tell her story, and she left her writings behind to share with others the solutions she had found for the problems of her own life.

PRINCIPAL PERSONAGES:
  Etty Hillesum (1914-1943), a student of philosophy and law and a teacher of Russian who died in the Auschwitz concentration camp
  Julius Spier, Etty's psychotherapist and lover
  Han Wegerif, Etty's lover, a widower of sixty-two
  Maria Tuinzing, Etty's friend, who saved her diaries
  Mischa Hillesum, Etty's brother, a pianist
  Jaap Hillesum, Etty's brother, a scientist

OVERVIEW

On November 30, 1943, a twenty-nine-year-old Dutch Jewish woman named Etty Hillesum died in Auschwitz. Hillesum had known that she would not survive and had asked her friend Maria Tuinzing to save her diaries and give them to Klaas Smelik, a writer and a member of the Dutch Resistance. The diaries, which filled eight exercise books and came to more than four hundred pages, were rediscovered almost forty years later. J. G. Gaarlandt edited the diaries for publication and wrote an informative introduction to them.

Etty Hillesum was born in 1914 into a cultivated and assimilated Dutch Jewish family. Her father was a classical scholar and headmaster of a college-preparatory secondary school. One of her brothers, Mischa, was an accomplished pianist, and other brother, Jaap, was an outstanding scientist. A brilliant student herself, Hillesum took a degree in law and went on to study Slavic languages, philosophy, and psychology. The entire Hillesum family perished at the hands of the Nazis, a fact underscoring not only the overwhelming human tragedy of the Holocaust but also the inestimable loss of countless talented and decent individuals.

The diaries begin on March 9, 1941, in Amsterdam and end on December 11, 1942. The letters from Westerbork collection camp cover the period from July 3 to August 24, 1943. The last two years of Hillesum's life as revealed in the diaries were a time of intense personal growth. She underwent a transformation from an intelligent but somewhat hedonistic protégé to an independent woman who faced her fate with courage.

It is no accident that the diaries begin at a point when Hillesum sought spiritual and psychological direction. She had begun psychoanalysis with Julius Spier, a German Jewish refugee and the founder of psychochirology (the study and classification of palm prints). Spier had trained under the distinguished psychologist Carl Jung and was almost twenty years older than Hillesum. She fell in love with Spier while she was involved with Han Wegerif, a widower of sixty-two. Her circle of friends included a variety of interesting people who were active in the Resistance.

While Hillesum was seeking her identity and the meaning of her life, the German occupation of the Netherlands was closing in on the Dutch Jews. In 1942, the Jews were subjected to increasing restrictions and humiliations. They were not permitted to ride bicycles, play the piano, shop for food during the day, or travel on the streetcars.

Hillesum chose to record her struggles by writing in her diaries. The entries begin with a statement acknowledging that she is taking the momentous step of describing her innermost feelings about herself and about the horror that is surrounding her. Her diaries discuss her lovers, her friends and family, her search for God, and her renewed sense of Jewishness.

In 1942, Hillesum became a typist for the Jewish Council of Amsterdam, but she refused to be hidden or to be granted exemptions. She decided to accompany a group of Jews to Westerbork. During this time Spier died; Hillesum was now completely on her own.

The final portion of *An Interrupted Life* contains a number of heartbreaking letters from Westerbork, letters written in Hillesum's last months. These letters reveal what Gaarlandt calls Hillesum's "radical altruism," her devotion to the wretched prisoners, particularly the children, who were facing extinction.

The book ends with a letter of September 7, 1943, written by Hillesum's friend Jopie Vleeschower, who witnessed her departure for Auschwitz.

This letter serves as an epitaph for the courage of Etty Hillesum and others like her. After her departure for Auschwitz, Dutch farmers found a postcard she had thrown out of the train. Her final message was that the Jews had left Westerbork singing.

The diaries of Etty Hillesum reveal an intense struggle for personal independence against the backdrop of unprecedented threats from without. Writing was Hillesum's outlet, and it became the vehicle her spiritual liberation. By the end of 1941, the issues of life and death had taken precedence over all else. Rumors reached the Netherlands that the Jews were being sent to concentration camps in Poland. In her entry of November 10, 1941, Hillesum confesses "mortal fear in every fibre" and the collapse of her self-confidence. Yet as the diaries unfold, she continues to struggle for personal liberation as a woman, a Jew, and a human being. She rejects the resignation of her father, a scholar who withdrew into the rarefied world of pure ideas. She also begins to reject the pleasures of life as the main way to happiness. She is inspired by the works of the German lyric poet Rainer Maria Rilke and the novels of the Russian author Fyodor Dostoevski. By the spring of 1942 she discovers her destiny: the courageous acceptance of her fate. She will rebel against radical evil with moral indignation but without feelings of indiscriminate hatred and revenge, and she will draw on the sources of her faith in God and her faith in humankind.

Hillesum's evocation of the details and the atmosphere of the times is remarkable throughout the diaries. For example, she describes listening to the music of Johann Sebastian Bach with the accompaniment of noise from an air raid. As the situation around her grows more desperate, Hillesum becomes intensely aware of the small comforts of life: a cup of coffee, a few good friends, a vase of freshly cut flowers on her desk. As the diaries progress, her writing begins to acquire a near-mystical intensity; every word is essential.

In April of 1942, the Dutch Jews were forced by the Nazis to wear the yellow star. Hillesum responds with a sense of pride in her Jewish identity. In a remarkable entry dated July 3, 1942, she accepts a "new certainty," that the Germans were now intent on the total destruction of the Jewish people. Hillesum's premonition is all the more amazing because the destruction of the Dutch Jews took a more subtle form than the open reign of terror carried out by the Nazis in faraway Poland. Although confronted with this vision of her own extinction, Hillesum affirms her struggle for a meaningful life. Above all, she vows to persevere and to remain productive. Like so many victims of the Holocaust, she strove to keep her inner dignity intact: "I have already died a thousand deaths in a thousand concentration camps. And yet I find life beautiful and meaningful."

Her descriptions of the details of everyday life under the Nazi occupation are so vivid that the reader is made to see the value of each moment of her remaining days. Hillesum's entries also convey the fragility of the human body in the face of the Nazi assault. When the Nazis prohibit the Jews from traveling on streetcars, she develops blisters on her feet from the constant walking. Hillesum reports the range of human behavior during this time. She describes the rare kindness of a German soldier and tells of a Dutch civilian who viciously asked her whether as a Jew she was allowed to purchase toothpaste in a pharmacy. She resolves to wield her fountain pen as a weapon and to bear witness for the sake of the future.

By the summer of 1942, rumors began to circulate that the Germans were exterminating the Jews by gas. Hillesum refused, however, to go into hiding. She turned to the Psalms and prayed to be able to help God, to safeguard what was left of God in man. Indeed, she composed new psalms appropriate for the times. Meanwhile, her health was undermined by the reduction in food rations. In a powerful passage, she likens her heart to a sparrow caught in a vise. Despite the interdependence of mind and body, Hillesum's spirit refuses to be destroyed. She believes that the crushed sparrow that is her heart will take wing as she writes. Like other victims of the Holocaust, Hillesum believed that she would have to find a new language to convey the horrors of her experiences. Her diary closes with an affirmation of her mature philosophy: "We should be willing to act as a balm for all wounds."

Etty Hillesum's closing letters from Westerbork document her confrontation with death. Like Primo Levi, an Italian writer and a survivor of Auschwitz, she remarks that one would need a new language to describe the hell that she has witnessed. Her portrait of the camp commandant who professes sympathy with a smirk while he sends people off to die is unforgettable, as is her description of the starving children who tell her of their suffering. Hillesum's quiet heroism prevailed at the end, as she joined her family in a wagon bound for Auschwitz. Survivors of Westerbork would later marvel that Etty Hillesum had kept her humanity and courage to the end.

Above all, the focus of *An Interrupted Life* is directed from an unbearable present to the hope of a better future. Etty Hillesum knew that she would not live to tell her story. She wanted to leave her writings behind for future generations to share with others the solutions she had found for the problems of her own life. Herein lies the ultimate gift of Hillesum's interrupted life. Her eloquent words and deeds reflect and reinforce one another.

An Interrupted Life takes its place alongside such classics of Holocaust literature as Anne Frank's *Het Achterhuis* (1947; *The Diary of a Young Girl*,

1952), Primo Levi's *Se questo è un uomo* (1947; *If This Is a Man*, 1959; revised as *Survival in Auschwitz: The Nazi Assault on Humanity*, 1961), and Elie Wiesel's *Un di Velt hot geshvign* (1956; *Night*, 1960). Like Anne Frank, Hillesum retained her faith in God and man throughout her struggle. Because of Hillesum's age and education, her work addresses the subjects of identity, femininity, religion, and personal fulfillment. Unlike the narratives of Primo Levi and Elie Wiesel, which unforgettably re-create the atmosphere of Auschwitz, Hillesum's diaries emphasize the difficulty of living and loving while in the shadow of the most merciless system of destruction conceived by man.

The diaries of Etty Hillesum represent the coming-of-age of a sensitive young adult caught between the culture and charms of Amsterdam on one hand and the horrors of Auschwitz on the other. Her courageous and creative response to her suffering is portrayed with awe-inspiring eloquence. *An Interrupted Life* is a testimony to the great inner resources of the human spirit. Also available in English translation is Hillesum's *Letters from Westerbork* (1986), a full volume of the letters from which a few examples were chosen to supplement the diaries in *An Interrupted Life*.

SOURCES FOR FURTHER STUDY

Brenner, Rachel Feldhay. *Writing as Resistance: Four Women Confronting the Holocaust—Edith Stein, Simone Weil, Anne Frank, Etty Hillesum*. University Park: Pennsylvania State University Press, 1997.

Costa, Denise de. *Anne Frank and Etty Hillesum: Inscribing Spirituality and Sexuality*. Translated by Mischa F. C. Hoyinck and Robert E. Chesal. New Brunswick, N.J.: Rutgers University Press, 1998.

Ergas, Yasmine. "Growing up Banished: A Reading of Anne Frank and Etty Hillesum." In *Behind the Lines: Gender and the Two World Wars*, edited by Margaret Randolph Higonnet, Jane Jenson, Sonya Michel, and Margaret Collins Weitz. New Haven, Conn.: Yale University Press, 1987.

Figes, Eva. "Thou Shalt Not Kill, Not Even to Save Your Own Life? Eva Figes on the Terrible Dilemmas Faced by Victims of the Holocaust." *The Guardian*, December 11, 1999, p. 10.

Flinders, Carol. *Enduring Lives: Portraits of Women and Faith in Action*. New York: Jeremy P. Tarcher/Penguin Books, 2006.

Pleshoyano, Alexandra. "Etty Hillesum: A Theological Hermeneutic in the Midst of Evil." *Literature and Theology* 19, no. 3 (September, 2005): 221.

—Leon Stein

INTO THAT DARKNESS
FROM MERCY KILLING TO MASS MURDER

AUTHOR: Gitta Sereny (1921-   )
FIRST PUBLISHED: 1974
GENRE: Nonfiction
SUBGENRES: Biography; history

Sereny's work provides a thoroughly documented glimpse into the mind of Franz Stangl, the man who commanded the largest of the five Nazi death camps during World War II.

PRINCIPAL PERSONAGES:
  Franz Stangl (1908-1971), commandant of the Nazi execution camp Treblinka, 1942-1943
  Theresa Stangl, Franz's wife
  Franz Suchomel, a Schutzstaffel (SS) officer who worked alongside Stangl
  Richard Glazar, a survivor of Treblinka
  Dieter Allers, a lawyer and unrepentant Nazi

OVERVIEW

Although Gitta Sereny's *Into that Darkness: From Mercy Killing to Mass Murder* is an insightful book, it has been overshadowed by Hannah Arendt's much more famous *Eichmann in Jerusalem: A Report on the Banality of Evil* (1963). That this is the case is unfortunate, because apart from a few surface similarities, the two books ultimately reach very different conclusions about how ordinary humans can commit the most enormously evil acts.

A political philosopher, Arendt had been hired to cover the 1961 war crimes trial of Adolf Eichmann, a leading Nazi who oversaw the transportation of millions to death camps during World War II (1939-1945). The trial drew worldwide attention, in part because of the dramatic story of how Eichmann had been kidnapped from Argentina and taken to Jerusalem and in part because Eichmann repudiated any characterization of himself as a Nazi true believer, instead arguing that he was simply a bureaucrat, a nondescript little man. Accepting this self-characterization at face value, Arendt subsequently coined the famous proposition of the "banality of evil": Modern evil is frequently committed by ordinary people dutifully following monstrous laws. The uncomfortable implication is that almost anyone could become Eichmann given similar contexts. Since 1963, criticism of Arendt's book has centered on the claim that Arendt ignored ample evidence that Eichmann was, indeed, a devoted Nazi who understood the moral dimensions of what he was doing.

In contrast, *Into That Darkness* tells the story of an opportunistic and self-righteous man who cooperated with the dark events of his time. It offers the perspective that Franz Stangl was responsible for his choices, but we all are responsible for social conditions that encourage the development of conscience and the repudiation of evil.

Told in six parts, *Into That Darkness* focuses on a "gradual process of . . . corruption" that began in the mid-1930's. Various sections of the book examine Stangl's increasing responsibility for mass murder, as he administered a Nazi euthanasia facility as well as two execution camps. Interspersed in the narrative are sections that cross-check Stangl's versions of events and offer perspective on his actions; these sections usually draw from interviews with Stangl's wife, with an accomplice of Stangl, or with one of the survivors of the extermination camps. Other sections of the book argue that various Roman Catholic officials—especially Pope Pius XII—should have spoken out more forcefully against the Holocaust.

Born and raised in Austria, Stangl developed an authoritarian mind-set and a sense of entitlement early on. Unhappy in his first career because it gave him limited economic opportunity, Stangl became a police officer. Medals and promotions soon followed as Stangl found himself increasingly busy investigating political crimes. In Austria during the mid-1930's, German agitators were importing National Socialist (Nazi) ideology, particularly spreading the idea that all German-speaking peoples should be part of a larger Germanic state. Tasked with investigating Nazi infiltration, Stangl found their authoritarianism to his taste and may have joined the Nazi Party while it was still illegal in Austria. This was his first step toward corruption.

Certainly, by the time of the Anschluss—the 1938 annexation of Austria by Germany—Stangl was a card-carrying member of the Nazi Party. At first, he said that he joined the party to protect himself and his young family against revenge for his previous police work, but those closest to Stangl believed that he joined the party because it afforded him greater privilege and increased opportunities. In actuality, his joining the party drove a wedge between Stangl and his wife. In separate chapters of *Into That Dark-*

ness, both describe a bitter argument over the steps he was willing to take to demonstrate his loyalty to the party. By 1939, Stangl had signed a document rejecting his loyalty to the Roman Catholic Church, in which he had been raised and to which his wife was still loyal. This was his second step toward corruption.

Mass murder has to begin somewhere. For Nazi Germany, it began with the decision to murder the mentally ill and developmentally delayed. In the early to mid-twentieth century, many Western nations were considering legislation that would promote the health of the human species through various medical and social interventions. In Germany, such eugenics measures included forced sterilization and the killing of "unfit" persons. Hidden from the general public and even denied as unconstitutional by the Nazi Ministry of Justice, the euthanasia program in Germany was, Sereny states, nothing less than "legalized murder, undertaken for starkly economic—and later political—reasons." There was no concern for mercy: Victims of the euthanasia program were sent to institutes and murdered in batches with poison gas, often within hours of their arrival.

Taking an administrative position in the Nazi euthanasia program was the final step in Stangl's corruption. From the late 1930's to the end of his life, Stangl would avoid moral reflection and would instead focus on efficiency. As he described it, he was seduced into the euthanasia program with the promise that his was merely a security position and that doctors had the responsibility for examining and killing the unwanted. Stangl argued that other leaders within the community, including priests and ministers, supported euthanasia. Sereny notes that, to the contrary, the Roman Catholic Church was vociferous in opposition to this early Nazi program.

Able to rationalize his own actions, Stangl worked with such efficiency that he was asked in 1942 to administer one of the new extermination camps being built in Poland. In administering the camp, Stangl worked not just with efficiency but also with imagination. Much of *Into That Darkness* describes how large groups of unwitting victims would arrive by train and it would be the job of men like Stangl to keep the new arrivals mildly anxious but not agitated, ready to move when ordered and unaware that most of them were about to die. Stangl did this by building a pretty railway station in Treblinka with false timetables displayed that listed numbers for trains going to various locations. The timetables were intended to reassure new arrivals that Treblinka was only a way station and not a place of execution. Camp survivors interviewed for *Into That Darkness* told of the quiet but confident Schutzstaffel (SS) officer, in a white uniform and carrying a riding crop, who calmly watched thousands being "processed."

Like other Nazis, Stangl engaged in actions in 1945 that demonstrated his awareness of the criminality of his actions and his eagerness to escape justice. Those German military men who believed that they were innocent kept their identities and returned home following the war. Stangl, in contrast, according to his own account, wandered through Italy until he made contact with various relief workers, including a Catholic bishop, who helped him obtain a Red Cross passport for the Middle East. From 1946 to 1967, Stangl and his family lived abroad, in Syria and in Brazil. Almost twenty years after the war ended, Stangl was finally extradited to West Germany, where he was tried and convicted of murdering approximately 900,000 people.

At one point in *Into That Darkness*, Sereny relates the remarks of a young guard at the prison where Sereny interviewed Stangl; the man wonders how a person could know of the murders being committed—let alone be responsible for them—and yet "consent to remain alive." Near the end of her book, Sereny suggests that as a result of their series of interviews, Stangl reached the end of his obfuscations and rationalizations and grudgingly accepted responsibility before he died of a heart attack.

SOURCES FOR FURTHER STUDY

Arad, Yitzhak. *Belzec, Sobibor, Treblinka: The Operation Reinhard Death Camps*. Bloomington: Indiana University Press, 1987.
Arendt, Hannah. *Eichmann in Jerusalem: A Report on the Banality of Evil*. 1963. Reprint. New York: Penguin Books, 2006.
Friedlander, Henry. *The Origins of Nazi Genocide: From Euthanasia to the Final Solution*. Chapel Hill: University of North Carolina Press, 1995.
Sánchez, José M. *Pius XII and the Holocaust: Understanding the Controversy*. Washington, D.C.: Catholic University of America Press, 2002.

—Michael R. Meyers

JEWS
THE ESSENCE AND CHARACTER OF A PEOPLE

AUTHORS: Arthur Hertzberg (1921-2006) and Aron Hirt-Manheimer (1948-)
FIRST PUBLISHED: 1998
GENRE: Nonfiction
SUBGENRES: History; religion and spirituality

This history of the Jewish people examines the uniqueness and perseverance of Jews and Jewish culture around the world despite the pressures of assimilation and persecution.

OVERVIEW

Arthur Hertzberg was Bronfman Visiting Professor of the Humanities at New York University and Professor Emeritus of Religion at Dartmouth. He also had served as president of the American Jewish Policy Foundation and the American Jewish Congress. In addition to *Jews: the Essence and Character of a People*, he wrote several other books on Judaism, including *The Zionist Idea* (1959) and *Being Jewish in America* (1987). Aron Hirt-Manheimer has served as editor of *Reform Judaism* magazine and was the 1988 recipient of the Anne Frank Medal. In the preface to *Jews: The Essence and Character of a People*, Hirt-Manheimer explains that Hertzberg dictated the entire first draft of the manuscript to him, which Hirt-Manheimer then "rendered into a workable text." Hertzberg and Hirt-Manheimer accomplished further revision and editing of the work together. Therefore, the book is defined by Hertzberg's "viewpoint and scholarship."

Hertzberg attempts a difficult task, even a provocative one, in his search for the defining characteristics of the Jewish people. His stated aim is to provide a means to embrace all types of Jews, rather than taking a position that narrowly defines Jewishness. Hertzberg himself was descended from Hasidic scholars and rabbis, yet he considered himself to have grown up in the mainstream of Jewish experience. His father, the rabbi of the Hasidic community in Baltimore, Maryland, hosted Jews from varied sects and viewpoints in his home, and the young Hertzberg experienced firsthand the endless discussion and debate of Jewish scholars. He believed that this experience allowed him to be particularly accepting of all brands of Judaism.

In *Jews*, Hertzberg poses the question, What is a Jew? The simplest answer would be a religious one: that a Jew is someone who believes in the one God of Abraham, the God of the Hebrews. This is too simple, however. In the first chapter, "The Chosen," Hertzberg proposes the psychological consequences of being a chosen people. He does not believe that Jews invented the concept of chosenness, but he asserts that they have clung to it in their fierce determination to remain distinct from other peoples. They are different because they believe that God has required them to be different, to stand apart from other peoples and at the same time to serve as a moral beacon to the world.

In chapter 3, "The Outsider," Hertzberg examines a second characteristic, that of "otherness." The insistence of Jews in maintaining their culture and beliefs throughout the history of the Diaspora, or Jewish exile from the Holy Land, has caused them to remain outside the dominant cultures of their geographic homes. In chapter 4, "The Wild Streak," Hertzberg identifies a facet of the Jewish character, most often expressed as martyrdom, that causes them to rise up in the face of persecution. Jews fought back in Masada in 73 B.C.E., slaughtering themselves and their families rather than submit to the Romans, and fought back in the Warsaw Ghetto Uprising in 1943, when the Nazis were exterminating Jews. Hertzberg mentions many other examples of this "wild streak" in this chapter and throughout the book.

Having stated these three major points in his analysis of Jewish character, Hertzberg goes on to provide a detailed history of Judaism and the Jewish people. He uses the biographies of individual scholars and influential Jews to illustrate how these characteristics had impacts on the experiences of all Jews as they left Israel and spread throughout the world.

In chapter 5, "The Synagogue of Satan," Hertzberg examines the relationship of the Catholic Church and Protestantism to the Jews. He finds in the writings of Jules Isaac an answer to the anti-Semitism expressed so violently in the Holocaust, or Shoah. Isaac revealed that the Church had taught contempt for the Jews from its beginnings, and the Church's subsequent influence in Europe rooted this hatred in all European Christian cultures. Hertzberg acknowledges the role that Isaac's writings have played in moving the Catholic Church toward a reconciliation of this prejudice, beginning with the reforms of the mid-1960's.

The history of the Jews in Spain is discussed in chapter 6, "The Terrible Choice." A large and prosperous community of Jews had existed in Spain during the Middle Ages and had prospered under Muslim rule. They "had achieved prominence in every sphere of society, from the affairs of state and commerce to art and science." It was a complete shock, then, when in 1492 the Jews were given an ultimatum: They had four months to convert to Christianity, or they were to leave the country forever, leaving all of their property and possessions behind. Certainly, Jews had been persecuted since the return of Spain to Christian rule between the thirteenth and fifteenth centuries. There had been other choices to make between conversion and death, but this complete exile proved that Jews were not safe anywhere. The population was evenly divided, with half choosing exile, half converting. Among the converts, however, were many who converted in name only and sought to continue their unique worship in secret; these were known as crypto-Jews. Hertzberg examines the nature of Jewish worship, study of the Torah and the Talmud, as being the ultimate goal of Jewish life. Examination of the Word is a never-ceasing task that Jews will perform until the "end of days." Following the period of the Spanish expulsion, a new study began of the Kabbala, an apocalyptic message that taught that the end of the world was near, when Jews would return to Zion (Israel). The focus of the new Kabbalists was to use supernatural means to bring about the end times and the redemption of the world.

The phenomenon of messianic leaders is examined in "Messianic Mania." Hertzberg recounts the story from the 1660's of Shabbetai Zvi, who was touted as the Messiah returned to lead his people to freedom and usher in the last days. Half the Jewish world chose to believe in Shabbetai Zvi, but when the would-be Messiah announced a specific date of redemption, he was arrested by the Turks and forced to convert to Islam or die. Shabbetai chose conversion. Hertzberg speaks of other messianic pretenders arising in nearly every generation, finding ready followers eager to believe that the redemption of the Jews is at hand.

In "The Age of Dissent," Hertzberg discusses the rise of Protestantism and the renewed attempts on the part of these new sects of Christianity to convert the Jews. Martin Luther, especially, reacted viciously when his overtures were rejected. Hertzberg believes that Luther's condemnation of the Jews had a lasting effect, both in Protestant Christianity and in German culture. Hertzberg also discusses the subject of money and the jealousies of the majority culture regarding the financial success of the Jews. This effect of Jewish success can be traced back to the Spanish experience and forward to Germany of the 1930's. Hertzberg looks at many reformers, including Baruch Spinoza, who was excommunicated by the Jewish community in Amsterdam for his heresies. Skeptical Spinoza identified all religious texts as having human origin and, therefore, human error; he chose to identify reason as superior to faith. Spinoza himself redefined the concept of chosenness as reserved for those who lead virtuous lives.

During this time, many Jews were assimilating, but Jewish culture, tradition, and worship continued. Hertzberg does not abandon his examination of character in these historical snapshots; he relates the lives of these influential Jews and shows how chosenness, otherness, and the wild streak play a part. Even Jews who assimilated found that they were not accepted fully into the majority society; despite all of their efforts to renounce their Jewishness, they were still perceived as "other." Spinoza wrongly asserted, according to Hertzberg, that Jews "continued to exist by a defiant act of will." Hertzberg claims that it was not the doctrine of chosenness that influenced Abraham but the act of defiance in breaking the idols of his father, and thus choosing God, that continues to operate even in Spinoza, who criticized Western society.

Chapter 10 contains a history of the Hasidic movement. Although Hertzberg was reared in this tradition, he notes that he is uncomfortable with the "partisan and usually polemical usurpation" of the Hasidim. Hertzberg relates a personal anecdote of his meeting, at the age of twenty-eight, with Martin Buber, an important and culturally celebrated Jewish philosopher. Buber's stories about the Hasidim, including some of Hertzberg's ancestors, did not strike Hertzberg as accurate portrayals of the descriptions handed down to him. Hertzberg challenged Buber's claim to be a Hasid, which affronted the philosopher. Hertzberg believes that Buber failed to notice the "profound and absolute obedience of the Hasidim to the religious practices and laws in the Talmud." Hertzberg goes on to link the Hasidic movement with an increased interest in returning to Zion and leaving the life of the Diaspora behind.

A chapter titled "Unrequited Love" deals with the yearning of some Jews to assimilate into the dominant culture, mainly through conversion to the majority faith. Hertzberg roots this desire in self-contempt brought on by widespread and persistent anti-Semitism in the age of Enlightenment in the eighteenth century. Jewish educational reform often meant an abandonment of Torah and Talmud for study of the language and literature of the dominant European cultures. A call to universal morality, which meant for Jews a conversion to Christianity, gained adherents but failed to destroy the community of Jewish believers. Karl Marx, son of a German rabbi who had become a Deist (a believer in reason over faith), attacked the Jews as parasites, as representatives of the bourgeois merchant class who lived off the labor of the workers.

In chapter 12, "Reinventing Jewishness," Hertzberg examines the experience of Jews in the United States. Jews found a more open society than they ever had, without the exclusionary laws that Jews had been forced to live under in European societies. Although anti-Semitism was still present, Jews were able to prosper and to live freely as Jews. This led to a lessening of the messianic message and even to a loss of interest in the return to Zion. Hertzberg traces the rise of the three main branches of Judaism in existence at the end of the twentieth century: Orthodox, Reform, and Conservative. He seeks to show how, even in their differences, these movements retain the essential identification of Jews as a unique people.

Hertzberg examines Jews who do not believe in God and decides that the character traits of the Jews still operate within them and move them to act as moral examples to the world. He addresses the crisis of faith that many Jews experienced as a result of the Holocaust. He explains that to the Orthodox, the Holocaust was no surprise, because they "had never doubted that Jews were other." It did not matter to the Nazis that any Jews had converted; the Nazis were bent on exterminating anyone who could be identified as Jewish by blood. Hertzberg calls for a full self-examination of all nations that were complicit in the slaughter and plunder of the Jews before these nations can be at peace. Hertzberg shows how, paradoxically, the Holocaust served to stimulate renewed pride in Jewish identity and a beginning to Jewish studies programs in colleges and universities.

Hertzberg concludes with a look at the future, specifically, the future of the State of Israel. He decries the actions of those on the religious right who have impeded peace efforts and cautions against the "wild streak" that has brought destruction on the Jews before. He admonishes the Israelis to continue to be examples of morality by learning to live with and to accept their Palestinian Arab neighbors. He provides a "Chronology of Jewish History," along with notes to the text.

As the Jews and the Palestinians in Israel continue to move toward a peaceful solution to their decades-long conflict, this book provides insight into the fierce Jewish will to endure as a people and the historical experiences that have shaped the desire for a Jewish homeland. As Hertzberg shows, historically Jews have not been safe anywhere in the world from persecution or expulsion. He writes longingly of the "port of Haifa and Ben-Gurion airport near Tel Aviv" as places where "the young women and men in uniform who are inspecting passports will never say that Israel already has too many Jews." Through centuries of exile from their homeland, Jews have looked forward to the day when they did not have to live under the rule of an alien culture. Hertzberg's assertion that Jews exist to provide a moral guide to the rest of the world is a worthy goal of an admirable people. Not everyone, however, will agree that there is a definable Jewish character.

SOURCES FOR FURTHER STUDY

Fischel, Jack. "A Definable Jewish Character." Review of *Jews: The Essence and Character of a People*, by Arthur Hertzberg and Aron Hirt-Manheimer. *Virginia Quarterly Review* 75, no. 4 (Fall, 1999): 782-783.

Hertzberg, Arthur. *A Jew in America: My Life and a People's Struggle for Identity*. San Francisco: HarperSanFrancisco, 2002.

Nadell, Pamela S. Review of *Jews: The Essence and Character of a People*, by Arthur Hertzberg and Aron Hirt-Manheimer. *Shofar* 19, no. 2 (January 31, 2001): 137-139.

Silk, Mark. "Styles of Jewish Identity: *Jews*." *The New York Times Book Review*, May 17, 1998, p. 36.

Tigay, Chanan. "A Man of Influence." *Jewish Chronicle* 46, no. 50 (April 20, 2006): 12.

—*Patricia Masserman*

The Journey Back

AUTHOR: Johanna Reiss (1932-   )
FIRST PUBLISHED: 1976
GENRE: Nonfiction
SUBGENRES: Autobiography; young adult literature

In a sequel to her first autobiography, Reiss chronicles her family members' attempts to rebuild their interrupted lives after they emerge from hiding at the end of World War II.

PRINCIPAL PERSONAGES:
   Annie de Leeuw (later Johanna Reiss; b. 1932), the youngest member of the reunited family
   Sini de Leeuw, Annie's sister who has been in hiding with her
   Rachel de Leeuw, Annie's oldest sister
   Ies de Leeuw, Annie's father, a Winterswijk cattle dealer
   Magda Vos, the widowed neighbor who becomes Annie's stepmother
   Johan Oosterveld, the Usselo farmer who hid Annie and Sini during the war
   Dientje Oosterveld, Johan's wife
   Opoe Oosterveld, Johan's elderly mother

OVERVIEW

In the foreword to *The Journey Back*, Johanna Reiss (who had grown up with the name Annie de Leeuw) explains that her second book is the sequel to the earlier *The Upstairs Room* (1972), which describes how she and her sister Sini were hidden for three years by a simple farm family while Adolf Hitler's armies rounded up European Jews for deportation and death. So that the sequel is not dependent on the first book, Reiss begins the story of her journey back by describing what the three years of hiding were like for her, her sister, and the Oostervelds, who sheltered them. In the first and briefest of four parts, Reiss recalls the tedium of her days in hiding, the paralyzing monotony broken only by the warm presence of the Oostervelds each night. Then, in the spring of 1945, the war in Europe ended and Annie and Sini began the journey back to their Winterswijk home.

In part 2 (Summer) and part 3 (Fall and Winter), Reiss tells of the reunited de Leeuws' attempts to become a family again. They began their new life without their mother, who had died a few weeks after the younger girls went into hiding. Because their father was consumed with rebuilding his business in the aftermath of the war, Rachel tried to play the role of parent for her younger sisters. Yet Sini wanted only freedom after three years of confinement, and Annie was increasingly left alone with a changed Rachel. No longer the carefree oldest sister content to entertain the family's youngest, Rachel was preoccupied with remaking the home ravaged by war and caught up in the conversion to Christianity that she had experienced in hiding. With their father away much of the time, and with Sini and Rachel no longer the same people that they were, a confused Annie found comfort only in a visit back to the Oostervelds in Usselo. Like the rest of her family, she was caught between two worlds, unable to live fully in either.

As summer turned to fall, the older members of the family began to make decisions, choosing the new worlds in which they wished to live and leaving Annie even more isolated. Sini left home to begin a nursing course in a nearby town. Mr. de Leeuw unexpectedly announced his intention to remarry, choosing for his second wife Magda Vos, a Winterswijk Jew widowed by the Germans. Before the wedding, Rachel returned to the family that had hidden her during the war. Annie also found herself once again stepping into a new world. Fall and winter were dominated by Annie's attempts to please her perfectionist stepmother, to take the place of Magda's daughter, Nel, who was away at boarding school, and to reconcile the presence of a refined but cold Magda with the memory of the simple but loving Oostervelds.

After a year of struggling with emotional scars that healed more slowly than physical ones, Annie revisited the Oostervelds in the spring of 1946 and found her first sense of direction. Like the Oostervelds and like the other members of her family, she began to understand that life means change. "Me, too. Move on, go places, see things," she told herself, reaching out to what was ahead. Thus, for Annie, the hope of spring overcame the cold of winter.

Like *The Upstairs Room, The Journey Back* is an autobiographical memoir, chronicling the impact of World War II and its aftermath on Reiss and her family. As in the earlier book, Reiss tells her story in a highly personal style that lends a journal-like quality to her writing. Especially in part 1, describing the months and years of hiding, she moves freely from actual event to personal impression, from organized thought to dreamlike imaginings. It is an effective stylistic choice, conveying how the life of the mind continued even as Annie herself sat noiselessly in the darkened upstairs room of the Oosterveld farmhouse day after endless day. When Annie left her hiding place and returned to Winterswijk, she resumed a more active life, and Reiss's style shifts to a traditional first-person narration of events in parts 2 and 3. In part 4, with Annie emerging from a winter of confusion into a springtime of hope, imagination again interweaves with reality as she begins to look toward the future and what it might hold.

While *The Upstairs Room* centers on the most visible losses incurred by Jewish victims of the war—the loss of freedom, home, and family–*The Journey Back* explores even deeper losses. Annie learned that time lost cannot be reclaimed. Her family was irrevocably changed by the years apart. Annie returned from hiding a different person, reuniting with family members who had become different people. Even Annie's place in the community was changed. The Winterswijk Jewish community had been decimated, only a handful of survivors straggling back from Hitler's concentration camps. Among the many Gentile children, Annie had become an oddity. While they were spurred by curiosity to question her about the years in hiding, Annie remained outside the friendships forged during her absence. Isolated at home and in the community, Annie felt a sense of belonging only with the Oostervelds in Usselo, and yet she knew that she could not stay there, that she must reclaim something of her Winterswijk life.

In reflecting on the war years and their aftermath, Reiss relies on metaphor. In the same way that her legs were left weak and crooked from the years of confinement, Annie's spirit was also weakened. Her joy in being alive was obscured by uncertainty and confusion. Like the legs too weak to carry her far, Annie's sense of hope was so circumscribed by her experience that she could not look to the future with confidence. Her crooked legs became a metaphor for the convoluted life to which she returned. Physical disability mirrored Annie's inability to relate to those around her. Yet crooked legs straighten, weakened spirits strengthen, disjointed lives find direction, and winter's cold gives way to the hope of spring.

By reliving the memories of her days in hiding in part 1, Reiss creates a sequel that continues the story of *The Upstairs Room* effectively but also stands alone for the reader who comes to the second book without having read the first. After experiencing the tedium of Annie's years in hiding, the reader can sense her anxiety at leaving the Oostervelds' upstairs room, stepping out onto the streets of Usselo after three years and returning to war-ravaged Winterswijk. Within the context of that anxiety, the reader can understand—with or without having read *The Upstairs Room*—the emotional turmoil that Annie encountered during her first year back in Winterswijk. Thus Reiss achieves a criterion essential for an effective sequel.

By writing a sequel to the earlier account of her war years, Reiss explores aspects of war's consequences that are largely untouched in literature for children and young adults. While *The Upstairs Room* joins many World War II memoirs, *The Journey Back* stands virtually alone as an account of the war's aftermath. In writing of her motivation for telling this story, Reiss stated that "there was still something I wanted to say, something that was as meaningful to me as the story I had told in the first book. . . . From a political point of view, the war was over, but in another sense it has not really ended."

Reiss's second book thus not only complements her first but also provides in itself a unique contribution to autobiographical accounts of war and war's aftermath, especially as experienced by children. As such, this autobiography carries an important message, reminding its young readers that the wounds of war extend beyond the battlefield, beyond the prisoner-of-war compounds and refugee camps, and beyond the hiding places of the persecuted. Reiss reflects that "wars leave emotional scars that take a long time to heal, generations perhaps. I know this to be true of myself, and of others." By sharing her own struggle to overcome those emotional scars, Reiss provides another valuable contribution to the world of young adult biography.

Sources for Further Study

Day, Frances Ann. *Multicultural Voices in Contemporary Literature: A Resource for Teachers*. Rev. ed. Portsmouth, N.H.: Heinemann, 1999.

Kokkola, Lydia. *Representing the Holocaust in Children's Literature*. New York: Routledge, 2003.

Riede, Paul. "Human Rights, Human Wrongs: Teachers Learn How to Explain the Lessons of Holocaust." *Syracuse Post-Standard*, December 22, 1998, p. B2.

Sadler, Dave. "Author Spent Holocaust in Hiding: Johanna Reiss Tells Children How She Survived as a Child in WWII Europe." *Syracuse Post-Standard*, April 22, 1999, p. 19.

Sullivan, Edward T. *The Holocaust in Literature for Youth: A Guide and Resource Book*. Lanham, Md.: Scarecrow, 1999.

—*Diane L. Chapman*

"Journey Through the Night"

Author: Jakov Lind (1927-2007)
First published: "Reise durch die Nacht," 1962 (English translation, 1964)
Genre: Short fiction
Subgenres: Psychological realism; parable

Lind's brief story, which never mentions the Holocaust directly or indirectly, develops the morbid interplay of victimizer and intended victim through the motif of cannibalism. Given the fact that the author was a survivor of Nazi persecution, many have interpreted this story as a Holocaust parable.

Principal Characters:
 An unnamed traveler
 His fellow passenger

Overview

Between three and four o'clock in the morning, on a train traveling between Nice and Paris, two Austrians are seated opposite each other in a locked compartment, to which the narrator's fellow passenger has somehow obtained a key. Describing his unexpected companion, the narrator uneasily likens him to a seal and wonders why he does not show his tusks. This partly comical, partly anxious description grows menacing when he pictures the contents of the other's small black suitcase. He correctly conjectures that it contains carpenter's tools—a hammer, saw, chisel, and drill. What he has guessed earlier has now become undeniable: The owner of the black bag is a cannibal, intent on murdering and eating him.

Although the friendly cannibal appears sure that he will accomplish his aim, the protagonist expresses his determination to thwart him. Having gotten fair warning, he insists that he will remain awake through the night's journey. The cannibal persists in his confidence, however, and matter-of-factly describes how he will dismember and consume his fellow traveler. The narrator's resistance yields to curiosity, and he asks if the ears can be digested or if they have bones in them. Soon convinced that his life truly is endangered, he attempts to ward off the threat by maintaining a steady stream of conversation. This leads to a detailed account of dismemberment by the cannibal as he opens his black bag.

The narrator slowly succumbs to his companion's perverse logic and mentally accepts the inevitability, even the reasonableness, of the violent end that awaits him. Only hesitantly and feebly does he manage to express his will to live, asking that he be spared long enough to go for a walk in Paris. The cannibal asserts himself still more sardonically and reopens his bag of tools. The narrator instinctively leaps to his feet and pulls the emergency cord. The train screeches to a halt, and the cannibal speedily disembarks, bitterly chiding his intended prey for the foolishness that will now cost him a huge fine. As several upset passengers crowd into the compartment, the cannibal disappears into the darkness, still shouting invectives.

"Journey Through the Night" is the second of seven stories in Jakov Lind's debut book *Eine Seele aus Holz* (1962; *Soul of Wood, and Other Stories*, 1964). Although only three stories deal directly with the Holocaust, the collection immediately gained its Austrian-born author international fame as a savagely inventive, often grotesquely humorous portrayer of the Nazi extermination of the Jews. Given the atmosphere of horror that pervades the book, along with Lind's biography as a survivor of Nazi persecution, a sweeping view of his early stories as Holocaust parables was widely espoused, and "Journey Through the Night" has often been cited as such a parable. Lind himself appeared to suggest reading the story in this vein. Writing on the annihilation of the Jews in his native Vienna as a result of Nazi racism, he expressly linked the central motif of the story with the Jewish catastrophe. "Vienna died," he said, "when it destroyed its [Jewish] spirit in an act of autocannibalism."

An analogy with the Holocaust will, however, appear less evident to readers unacquainted with Lind's larger work and the forces that motivated it. If the Nazi universe of industrialized genocide can be imagined at all, it is only in terms of its own singular realities. These, however, were so enormous as to defy both objective historical portrayal and literary representation through metaphor or symbol. However Lind may have intended his decidedly elusive tale, it is bare of any reference to the Holocaust. The reader may thus legitimately view its central theme in more universal terms: as humanity's endless capacity for evil or, alternately, as the insanity of a world in which evil has seemingly become normal. Lind's success in conveying his theme depends, in turn, on the psychological plausibility of the story's uneventful plot, the morbid interplay of victimizer and intended victim as developed through the motif of cannibalism.

Within the locked train compartment, Lind's narrator discovers that the social codes that regulate interpersonal behavior and guard human society from physical assault have been suspended. His fellow passenger claims the right to commit the unthinkable—to murder, dissect, and consume him. His Paris vacation trip, which promised some degree of civilized enjoyment, turns into a nightmare of brutality. At first disbelieving his would-be killer, or perhaps in order to shield himself against believing him, the narrator attempts to dismiss the man's evil intent jokingly. This can be accepted as the normal, if anxious, response of a person educated to respect the sanctity of human life and thereby to expect the safety of his own.

When the cannibal tauntingly opens his black bag, the mere sight of the tools seems to convince the narrator that he is hopelessly trapped. He capitulates intellectually to the immorality of brute power and, without prompting by his captor, begins to accept his impending gruesome death as reasonable: "Every animal eats every other just to stay alive, men eat men, what's so unnatural about that?" Although comically distorted, this sympathy on the part of the victim with the aims of his tormentor validly reflects a psychological phenomenon well documented in the literature on captivity and imprisonment. Only at the last second, when the cannibal wields his mallet, does the succumbing narrator almost miraculously spring to his feet and pull the emergency cord.

In his autobiographical writing, Lind has spoken of his own deep shame at the helplessness and, as he saw it, the passivity of the Jews as they were rounded up by the Germans and deported to their deaths. Possibly he wished, in "Journey Through the Night," to provide a moral corrective to the depravity that holds sway in the train compartment by having the narrator overcome his psychological torpor and save his own life. Nevertheless, it is the embodiment of evil, the cannibal, who has the last word in the story. Although his murderous hand was stayed, his potential to wreak evil remains undiminished, and the irate passengers who crowd into the compartment—among them, as representatives of public order, a conductor and a police officer—will hardly believe the narrator's unlikely tale. As the cannibal charges as he scurries off, his intended victim has made a fool of himself for life.

Lind's story is slightly more than six pages long. Narrated in the first person by the protagonist, it consists primarily of his thoughts and descriptions and the dialogue between him and his fellow passenger. To the extent that the story can claim a plot, in the sense of a series of connected events rising to a climax, the plot is skeletal. It consists entirely of a few key actions and gestures: the cannibal's opening of his black bag to reveal its contents, his wielding of the mallet, the protagonist's last-second tug on the emergency cord, and the appearance of other travelers as the cannibal escapes. Lind has reduced the setting and time of his story to the barest minimum. Such drastic reduction places the burden of artistic success on the persuasiveness of the psychological conflict that unfolds between the two characters within a single hour and a space whose sole attribute is its seemingly inescapable confinement.

It is a tribute to Lind's artistry that he has rendered believable a situation so utterly bizarre as the one around which his story is constructed. In large part this results from the subtly disquieting atmosphere that he creates at the very outset. The eerie bluish light of the train compartment, the view into a darkness relieved only by a few scattered lights of unclear origin, the nocturnal hour between half wakefulness and deep sleep, and the unidentified hovering voice of the first lines dissolve reality and allow the presence of a cannibal to become plausible. What remains problematic, however, is the narrator's quick acceptance of his doom. Rather than motivating this submission through a genuine contest of wits between the two characters, with its own clear and compelling logic, Lind relies for narrative effect on the grotesque humor of the dialogue and what soon appears to be savagery for its own sake. As a result, the message of the story becomes muddy. The reader is left unsure of the significance inherent in the narrator's finally awakened will to live, while—despite momentary defeat—the murderous immorality of the cannibal appears to triumph.

SOURCES FOR FURTHER STUDY

Hammel, Andrea, Silke Hassler, and Edward Timms, eds. *Writing After Hitler: The Work of Jakov Lind*. Cardiff: University of Wales Press, 2001.

Lind, Jakov. *Counting My Steps: An Autobiography*. New York: Macmillan, 1969.

_____. *Numbers: A Further Autobiography*. London: Jonathan Cape, 1972.

Sicher, Efraim, ed. *Holocaust Novelists*. Vol. 299 in *Dictionary of Literary Biography*. Detroit: Gale Research, 2004.

—*Sidney Rosenfeld*

The Last of the Just

Author: André Schwarz-Bart (1928-2006)
First published: *Le Dernier des Justes*, 1959 (English translation, 1960)
Genre: Novel
Subgenres: Bildungsroman; Magical Realism

This novel contrasts light and shadow, interpenetration of dream and reality, and violence and rescue to convey a vision of a world of ambiguity and anguish. The author's message is clear: Jewish suffering through the ages is the responsibility of a Christianity that turns the cross upside down, wielding it as a sword against innocent victims.

Principal characters:
 The narrator, who presents himself as a friend of Ernie
 Ernie Levy, one of the thirty-six Just Men
 Mordecai Levy, Ernie's grandfather
 Mother Judith, Ernie's grandmother
 Golda Engelbaum, Ernie's fiancé

Overview

Although the bulk of *The Last of the Just* deals with Ernie Levy, it begins with a brief episodic history of his family from 1185 to 1792, for tradition held that God had granted the Levy family, in each generation, one Lamed-Vovnik—a member of the Lamed Vov, the thirty-six Just Men who absorb the world's suffering: "If just one of them were lacking, the sufferings of mankind would poison even the souls of the newborn, and humanity would suffocate with a single cry."

Through the centuries, the Levys wandered and suffered as did all the Jews. A Levy finally settles in Zemyock, a small and isolated Polish town. When, soon after World War I, the town is captured by White Guard Cossacks, the refugee Levys find a place in Stillenstadt, Germany. The patriarch, Mordecai, and his wife, Mother Judith, are supported by their son Benjamin's tailor shop. Then, the almost unreal, idyllic charm of Stillenstadt is shattered by Nazi violence. Benjamin's second son, Ernie, experiences this tragedy with particular intensity; after concluding that he is a Lamed-Vovnik, he attempts suicide.

The Levys become refugees again, managing to find a niche in Paris. While Ernie enlists in the army, the Vichy government rounds up Jews; the Levy family, except for Ernie, is interned and then sent to their deaths. For a time, Ernie sinks into—indeed wallows in—a deliberately unhuman life focused on food and lust, but when a sympathetic Christian refers to his "Jewish eyes," he once again becomes capable of feeling. The twenty-year-old Ernie returns to the Jews left in Paris and falls in love with Golda Engelbaum. When she is taken to the internment camp at Drancy, he follows her. He rides with her and a group of frightened children in the boxcar to Auschwitz. Having comforted and calmed them, as the door of the gas chamber closes, "he knew that he could do nothing more for anyone in the world...."

Although the novel focuses on Ernie, several other characters are also developed in detail. Ernie's grandfather, Mordecai, is large and tough as well as traditionally learned and pious; when Nazis come to burn Torah scrolls, Mordecai charges at them, swinging an iron bar. He is an archetype, the Patriarch, as Judith is the archetype of Mother. Lesser characters, such as Benjamin Levy, are finely crafted, their essential personalities explicated in their idiosyncratic approaches to life. Even Golda, whose late appearance in the novel gives her only scant space, is a fully developed character; the swift and mutual love between her and Ernie has no aspect of literary contrivance. Myriad other minor characters are etched with a sure hand in taut and beautiful prose.

From his birth, Ernie is distinctive: Second to his older brother in size and courage as well as age, smaller even than his younger brother, he has flashes of insight into others' souls, a magical concept of the world. Preoccupied with his destiny as a Lamed-Vovnik, he fantasizes about protecting all the Jews; only after his family's deportation does he attempt to escape his role by means of a Rabelaisian but despairing lifestyle. His return to humanity and the Jews of Paris signals a return to life and love and the working out of his destiny as a Just Man.

André Schwarz-Bart uses various distancing devices to detach the reader from an immediate emotional identification with the characters. The narrator himself speaks with a detached and often ironic tone. Frequently he refers to or apparently quotes from historical records and witnesses. Interspersed with vague chronological references are specific names, places, and dates. The calm and objective narrative is broken only by flashes of irony, but the detachment begins to thin as the narrator approaches the twentieth century. The Levy Just Men become more and more fully developed characters to whom the reader responds, and the novelistic detail intensifies.

Zemyock, where the Levys had originally come to rest, is in almost magical isolation from the brutal realities of the world. Its atmosphere is to be re-created by the author, from time to time, in each of the later places inhabited by the Levys, from Berlin to Auschwitz. This vision is projected often for Stillenstadt, "Quiet City," where Ernie grows up. The pervasive charm of the town provides the magical background for Ernie's discovery of himself as a Lamed-Vovnik and for his attempted suicide as well. Later, in Paris, the charm of a spring day in a park is set against the certainty of the deaths of Ernie and Golda, just as the internment camp rises amid the suburban tranquillity of Drancy. The final reality of Auschwitz seems itself unreal, with an orchestra playing on the route the prisoners take to the gas chambers. Ernie's tears of blood seem merely an acceptable response.

The narrator or a child is usually the medium by which these Magical Realist episodes are described. Stillness, the contrasts of light and shadow, the interpenetration of dream and reality, violence and rescue, all produce not only a narrative but also, and more incisively, a vision of a world of ambiguity and anguish. Schwarz-Bart's prose is never bitter, but his thesis is clear: Jewish suffering through the ages is the responsibility of a Christianity that turns the cross upside down, wielding it as a sword against innocent victims.

Although the thrust of the novel is clear, the author's stance is sometimes ambiguous. Ernie is the last Just Man, yet he dies in Auschwitz. Earlier, there have been ironic comments, such as Mother Judith's "What a great God is ours, . . . and how oddly he runs the world!" There has also been Benjamin Levy's cry, "If God did not exist . . . where does all the suffering go?" In addition, the novel concludes with an anguished prayer interspersed with the names of concentration camps: "And praised. Auschwitz. Be. Maidanek. The Lord. Treblinka. And praised. Buchenwald. Be. . . ." The last word, however, is less ambiguous:

> Yes, at times one's heart could break in sorrow. But often too, preferably in the evening, I can't help thinking that Ernie Levy, dead six million times, is still alive somewhere, I don't know where. . . . Yesterday, as I stood in the street trembling in despair, rooted to the spot, a drop of pity fell from above upon my face. But there was no breeze in the air, no cloud in the sky. . . . There was only a presence.

It is probable that the self-educated Schwarz-Bart was influenced in the 1950's by the work of Jorge Luis Borges, and it is possible also that during that same period Gabriel García Márquez was influenced either by Schwarz-Bart or by similar literary tendencies, which have characterized much modern Latin American literature as well as its European counterpart.

Upon its publication, *The Last of the Just*, while provoking a teapot tempest of criticism, garnered the prestigious Prix Goncourt and major critical acclaim. Thereafter, it fell from notice. It was viewed as outside the French literary mainstream; as Holocaust literature, it was frequently considered in critical categories other than the literary.

Schwarz-Bart later published, with his wife, two novels following *The Last of the Just*: *Un Plat de porc aux bananes vertes* (1967; a plate of pork with green bananas) and *La Mulatresse Solitude* (1972; *A Woman Named Solitude*, 1973), each with a black woman as protagonist. These works bridge the centuries of Jewish agony and the Holocaust, and the centuries of black enslavement, with an explication and a perception of humanity's sufferings. *The Last of the Just* stands not merely as the first of a trilogy, however, but as a major work on its own merits, a work of French literature, of Jewish and Holocaust literature, and of modern Magical Realism.

SOURCES FOR FURTHER STUDY

Kirkup, James. "Obituaries: André Schwarz-Bart, Author of *The Last of the Just*." *Independent*, October 5, 2006, p. 41.

Lazarus, Joyce Block. *Strangers and Sojourners: Jewish Identity in Contemporary Francophone Fiction*. New York: Peter Lang, 1999.

Menton, Seymour. "*The Last of the Just*: Between Borges and García Márquez." *World Literature Today* 59 (Fall, 1985): 517-524.

Popkin, Henry. "Around a Prize-Winner, a Paris Literary Storm." *The New York Times Book Review*, December 20, 1959, p. 1.

Raider, Mark A. "Questioning the Meaning of Martyrdom: A Classic Novel of the Holocaust Returns to Print." *Forward* 104 (June 2, 2000): 11.

Scharfman, Ronnie. "Significantly Other: Simone and André Schwarz-Bart." In *Significant Others: Creativity and Intimate Partnership*, edited by Whitney Chadwick and Isabelle de Courtivron. London: Thames and Hudson, 1993.

—Marsha Kass Marks

Lest Innocent Blood Be Shed
The Story of the Village of Le Chambon, and How Goodness Happened There

AUTHOR: Philip P. Hallie (1922-1994)
FIRST PUBLISHED: 1979
GENRE: Nonfiction
SUBGENRES: Ethics; history; philosophy

In one of the most important books published on Holocaust rescuers and altruism, Hallie relates in intimate detail the lives and actions of the people of a village in southern France who, despite horrific peril, saved more than twenty-five hundred Jews from the Holocaust.

PRINCIPAL PERSONAGES:
  André Trocmé, the pastor of Le Chambon
  Magda Trocmé, André Trocmé's wife
  Édouard Theis, the assistant pastor of Le Chambon

OVERVIEW

As a youthful victim of violent anti-Semitism and as a soldier ordered to kill in World War II, Wesleyan University philosophy professor Philip P. Hallie was inexorably drawn to an inspiring true story of positive ethics in which great human goodness triumphed over evil nonviolently. Hallie's deeply moving and uplifting book *Lest Innocent Blood Be Shed*, appropriately subtitled *The Story of the Village of Le Chambon, and How Goodness Happened There*, documents the too-seldom-recognized human capacity for nobility, conscience, and generous goodness even under the most horrific conditions—specifically, the human-created evil of the Holocaust.

In 1940, the Nazis conquered France and divided it into two zones: the north, which was ruled by the Nazis, and the south (Vichy), which was ruled by Nazi collaborator Marshal Philippe Pétain. Le Chambon-sur-Lignon was a small village in southern France, its population of about twenty-seven hundred made up mostly of Huguenots, Protestants who had been persecuted by the Catholics dating back to the sixteenth century.

Perhaps their own anguished persecution primed the Chambonnais to shelter and save the latest victims of undeserved hate: Jews.

To illustrate the dynamic of goodness in Le Chambon, Hallie begins with the frightening night of February 13, 1943, when two Vichy police arrived at the home of the Reverend André Trocmé, the conscience and "soul" of Le Chambon, who had inspired his parishioners to resist Nazi evil, not with guns but with the "weapons of the spirit." Trocmé was out visiting the leaders of his Bible study group, and when his wife, Magda—the steadfast, intelligent, hardworking "heart" of Le Chambon—heard the knock, she quickly hid the Jews her family was sheltering and invited the policemen in to wait. André returned for dinner, and Magda invited the policemen to join them. (When asked later how she could feed men who had come to arrest, even kill, her husband, she replied, "What are you talking about? It was dinnertime. We were all hungry; the food was ready.") After dinner, many parishioners came by to give gifts to Pastor Trocmé before the police took him away; they surrounded the policemen's car, singing the Lutheran hymn "A Mighty Fortress Is Our God."

Next the car picked up Édouard Theis, assistant pastor of Le Chambon and administrator of the school that Trocmé and Theis had founded in 1938, the Collège Lycée International Cévenol. Hallie describes Theis as the "rock" of Le Chambon; his ferocious belief in the dignity and equality of all people matched Trocmé's. Third to be arrested was Roger Darcissac, administrator of Le Chambon's public school and a staunch ally of Trocmé and Theis. These embodiments of goodness and grace, after having their noses measured to determine their "Jewishness," were placed in a concentration camp near Limoges. The other prisoners resisted the three men at first but soon joined them in Bible study and prayer.

One month later, Trocmé, Theis, and Darcissac were summoned to see the camp director, who demanded that they sign loyalty oaths to Pétain. Darcissac had already signed such an oath as a condition of his employment and was released, but the other two refused to commit themselves to an immoral government that was ordering Jewish deportation. They had their noses remeasured and were remanded back to the camp. The next day, Trocmé and Theis were mysteriously set free while all remaining inmates were sent to their deaths in Poland. Trocmé returned home to continue to lead his village in goodness.

What was the genesis of this dynamic, moral leader, self-described as "a violent man conquered by God"? Born in northeastern France, André Trocmé learned about the preciousness and fragility of life at ten years old, when his mother died in a tragic car accident. As a student at Union Theological Seminary in New York City, he met Italian student Magda Grilli in

1925. "I shall be a Protestant pastor . . . and live a life of poverty," he told her in his marriage proposal. They married, moved to France, and started a family.

In Le Chambon in 1938, Trocmé and fellow pacifist Édouard Theis organized the Collège Lycée International Cévenol, and both of their wives became teachers at the school. By the late 1930's, increasing numbers of refugees were fleeing Adolf Hitler's hate and some found Le Chambon, where Trocmé gave powerful sermons on the irreplaceable value of all human life and the necessity of resisting evil nonviolently. Above the entrance to his church was emblazoned the admonition "Love One Another." Those who simply stand by in the face of overwhelming evil, Trocmé believed, are "the most dangerous people in the world."

In 1941, the Nazi deportation of Jews to death camps was accelerated. In resistance, Trocmé, Theis, and Darcissac began what Hallie terms an "intimate, unglamorous kitchen struggle" to assert conscience over blind obedience. Their organized nonviolent resistance started with refusal to salute the flag; they then refused to sign loyalty oaths to the state, and, in 1941, they refused to ring the church bell to "celebrate" one year of Pétain's power.

Le Chambon's communitywide undertaking to save Jews had humble beginnings but quickly grew. Magda Trocmé, who said, "I do not hunt to find people to help. But I never close my door," answered a knock one night to face a terrified German Jew who was in danger and sought refuge in Le Chambon. "Naturally, come in, come in," was Magda's reply. As more and more refugees arrived, countless Le Chambon townspeople and rural farmers provided safe shelter. False identity papers and ration cards, essential for the protection of Jews, appeared anonymously. Soon phone calls mysteriously came to the Trocmés, providing accurate warnings of imminent Nazi roundups. Hallie reports that one Jewish refugee was stunned when a Le Chambon woman gathered her family to announce, "Look! We have in our house a representative of the chosen people."

During two summer afternoons in 1942, some twenty-eight thousand Jews in Paris were rounded up and deported to Auschwitz; none of the more than four thousand children among them survived. By late fall of 1942, the Nazis were sending buses to Le Chambon to arrest all Jews. Trocmé's network of local young people spread the word and quickly effected, in his words, "the disappearance of the Jews" into the thick woods surrounding the town. Although the police scoured countless homes and farms, no Jews were ever betrayed.

As the war dragged on, the Nazis fought even more desperately, using murder and intimidation to eliminate all Jews and their protectors, while the Chambonnais fought even harder with faith and steadfast determination, the "weapons of the spirit," to save every Jew in their charge. Often threatened with arrest, Trocmé moved from home to home to conceal his whereabouts, barely escaping capture—but he never relented.

Trocmé's beloved cousin Daniel was deported to and murdered in the Majdanek death camp near Lublin, Poland, because the Nazis assumed that anyone who spoke sympathetically of the Jews must be one. Until the very end of the war, the Chambonnais sheltered Jews and shepherded some to Switzerland. In addition to the more than twenty-five hundred Jews saved by the Chambonnais, Hallie concludes, the inspiration of the townspeople's actions "saved" him too.

The residents of Le Chambon saw no difference between Jews and non-Jews. Just as theologian Martin Buber taught in his 1923 book *Ich und Du* (*I and Thou*, 1937), they didn't relate to others coldly and condescendingly as "I" and "It," but rather with warm respect and appreciation for "I" and "Thou." When a local prefect came to search for Jews hiding in Le Chambon, Trocmé asserted, "We do not know what a Jew is. We know only men."

Critical reception for Hallie's beautiful testimony to the powerful "contagion of caring" was uniformly enthusiastic. By 1979, when *Lest Innocent Blood Be Shed* was published, virtually entire libraries had been published about what Hallie terms the "glamour of wartime events," the evil perpetrated by Hitler and his henchmen. Very little, however, had been written about the "unglamorous" bright light of human goodness in the midst of the darkness. After the publication of Hallie's vital, passionate, life-giving study on Le Chambon, however, other superlative books about courage, rescue, and altruism during the Holocaust appeared.

One small incident that took place thirty years after World War II ended encapsulates the quintessence of Le Chambon. Hallie and Édouard Theis were leaving a church together in Le Chambon when Hallie witnessed many parishioners as well as Theis putting large monetary contributions into the church's donation box. When Hallie asked whom the money would help, Theis replied, "Oh, I don't know. They're people."

SOURCES FOR FURTHER STUDY

DeSaix, Deborah Durland, and Karen Gray Ruelle. *Hidden on the Mountain: Stories of Children Sheltered from the Nazis in Le Chambon*. New York: Holiday House, 2007.

Draper, Allison Stark. *Pastor André Trocmé: Spiritual Leader of the French Village Le Chambon*. New York: Rosen, 2001.

Fogelman, Eva. *Conscience and Courage: Rescuers of Jews During the Holocaust*. New York: Anchor Books, 1994.

Gilbert, Martin. *The Righteous: The Unsung Heroes of the Holocaust*. New York: Henry Holt, 2003.

Rittner, Carol, and Sondra Myers, eds. *The Courage to Care: Rescuers of Jews During the Holocaust*. New York: New York University Press, 1986.

—*Howard A. Kerner*

LETTERS AND PAPERS FROM PRISON

AUTHOR: Dietrich Bonhoeffer (1906-1945)
FIRST PUBLISHED: *Widerstand und Ergebung: Briefe und Aufzeichnungen aus der Haft*, 1951 (English translation, 1953)
GENRES: Nonfiction; poetry
SUBGENRES: Letters; lyric poetry; meditation

This collection of poems, papers, and letters to friends and relatives preserves some of Bonhoeffer's thoughts during the period when he was imprisoned and awaiting death at the hands of the Nazis.

OVERVIEW

The son of a psychiatrist teaching at Berlin University, Dietrich Bonhoeffer decided early to study theology. He served as pastor, lecturer, and theology professor in Spain, America, and England as well as Germany. Bonhoeffer became an outspoken critic of the Nazi government and an active member of the resistance movement. In 1943, he was arrested and imprisoned by the Gestapo and two years later was hanged. His other important works include *Schöpfung und Fall* (1933; *Creation and Fall*, 1959), *Nachfolge* (1937; *The Cost of Discipleship*, 1948), *Gemeinsames Leben* (1939; *Life Together*, 1954), and *Ethik* (1943; *Ethics*, 1955).

Letters and Papers from Prison is not specifically focused on the Holocaust, and the book is not intended to present a systematic set of ideas; rather, it posits questions and suggestive answers, or suggestive lines along which one may look for answers. As Bonhoeffer himself says, "I am led on more by an instinctive feeling for the questions which are bound to crop up rather than by any conclusions I have reached already." However, one gets the feeling when reading this material that there was a book brewing in his mind. Just as one may think of Bonhoeffer's previous work as a book on the theme of Christ as Lord of the Church, one could think of *Letters and Papers from Prison* as a work dealing with the theme of Christ as Lord of the world—for it is Christ and the world in the twentieth century and how one can be a disciple of Christ that seem to have been occupying Bonhoeffer's mind. One of Bonhoeffer's questions raised here, for exam-

Dietrich Bonhoeffer. (Deutche Presse Agentur/Archive Photos)

ple, and one that would greatly influence later theology, is "How do we speak . . . in secular fashion of God?"

It is the secularization of the world in the twentieth century that seems to preoccupy Bonhoeffer. He sees the world with its science and technology as having "come of age," and the world and human beings as having become autonomous. We do not need God as the answer to problems as we once did. This he takes to be a fact with which theology must deal, but he also does not take it to be a bad one. When humanity can resolve its problems itself, to force human beings to rely on God is merely to force them back into adolescence. In the light of this, he calls for a "religionless Christianity," one that does not rest on some a priori religious need for God. "The time when men could be told everything by means of words, whether theological or pious," he tells us, "is over and so is the time of inwardness and conscience, which is to say the time of religion as such."

A religionless Christianity stands in contrast to a Christianity that maintains that humanity has problems that only religion can answer. Of religion, Bonhoeffer writes:

> Religious people speak of God when human perception is (often just from laziness) at an end, or human resources fail: it is always a deus ex machina they call to their aid, either for the so called solving of insoluble problems or as

support in human failure—always, that is to say, helping our human weakness or on the borders of human existence.

This is precisely the role for God that Bonhoeffer takes humanity's "coming-of-age" to have rejected. It is the kind of situation, also, that we find reflected in Paul Tillich's method of correlation, which maintains that human reason raises questions that it cannot answer and that these questions find their answer in Christianity. This is to base Christianity on a false religious premise. In reference to Tillich's attempt, Bonhoeffer remarks that Tillich "sought to understand the world better than it understood itself, but it felt entirely *mis*understood and rejected the imputation." If the disciples of Christ are to be messengers, as was called for in Bonhoeffer's previous work, then they must know how to be messengers to humanity "come of age"; otherwise, Christ cannot fulfill his role as Lord of the world.

In positing a "religionless Christianity" in a secular age, Bonhoeffer essentially shifts responsibility from an external, dogmatic godhead to an internal God, resident within the human soul and requiring religious institutions that work in the world. Two things that Bonhoeffer thinks the Church must take seriously if it is to speak to humanity "come of age" are, first, that

> God is teaching us that we must live as men who can get along very well without him.... God is weak and powerless in the world, that is exactly the way, the only way, in which he can help us. Matthew 8:17 makes it crystal-clear that it is not by his omnipotence that Christ helps us, but by his weakness and suffering.... This must be the starting point for our "worldly" interpretations.

The second thing the Church must take seriously is its place in the world: The Christian Church must see itself as belonging to the world, but as powerless in the world, like its Christ, and existing for humanity: The Church "must take part in the social life of the world, not lording over men, but helping and serving them."

SOURCES FOR FURTHER STUDY

Bethge, Renate, and Christian Gremmeis, eds. *Dietrich Bonhoeffer: A Life in Pictures*. Translated by Brian McNeil. Minneapolis: Fortress Press, 2006.
Godsey, John D. *The Theology of Dietrich Bonhoeffer*. Philadelphia: Westminster Press, 1960.

Haynes, Stephen R. *The Bonhoeffer Legacy: Post-Holocaust Perspectives*. Minneapolis: Fortress Press, 2006.

———. *The Bonhoeffer Phenomenon: Portraits of a Protestant Saint*. Minneapolis: Fortress Press, 2004.

Kelly, Geffrey B., and F. Burton Nelson. *The Cost of Moral Leadership: The Spirituality of Dietrich Bonhoeffer*. Grand Rapids, Mich.: Wm. B. Eerdmans, 2003.

Marsh, Charles. *Reclaiming Dietrich Bonhoeffer: The Promise of His Theology*. New York: Oxford University Press, 1994.

Matthews, John W. *Anxious Souls Will Ask: The Christ-Centered Spirituality of Dietrich Bonhoeffer*. Grand Rapids, Mich.: Wm. B. Eerdmans, 2005.

Nickson, Ann L. *Bonhoeffer on Freedom: Courageously Grasping Reality*. Burlington, Vt.: Ashgate, 2002.

Plant, Stephen. *Bonhoeffer*. New York: Continuum, 2004.

Roberts, J. Deotis. *Bonhoeffer and King: Speaking Truth to Power*. Louisville, Ky.: Westminster John Knox Press, 2005.

—Bowman L. Clarke